TEAMWORK IN THE AUTOMOBILE INDUSTRY

Teamwork in the Automobile Industry

Radical Change or Passing Fashion?

Edited by Jean-Pierre Durand, Paul Stewart and Juan José Castillo

From the International GERPISA Programme 'Emergence of New Industrial Models'

338.476 29222
TEA

© Jean-Pierre Durand, Paul Stewart and Juan José Castillo 1999

The authors have asserted their right to be identified as the authors of this work in accordance with the Copyright, Designs and Patents Act 1988.

First published 1999 by
MACMILLAN PRESS LTD
Houndmills, Basingstoke, Hampshire RG21 6XS
and London
Companies and representatives throughout the world

ISBN 0–333–74482–9

A catalogue record for this book is available from the British Library.

This book is printed on paper suitable for recycling and made from fully managed and sustained forest sources.

10   9   8   7   6   5   4   3   2   1
08 07 06 05 04 03 02 01 00 99

Printed in Great Britain by
Antony Rowe Ltd
Chippenham, Wiltshire

Contents

v

Foreword (*GERPISA*)

GERPISA (Groupe d'Etudes et de Recherches Permanent sur l'Industrie et les Salariés de l'Automobile: Permanent Group for the Study of the Automobile Industry and its Employees) was formed in 1981 as a multidisciplinary group of researchers from economics, management, history and sociology with interests in the automobile industry. The network was initially directed by Michel Freyssenet and Patrick Fridenson at the Ecole des Hautes Etudes en Sciences Sociales (School for Advanced Social Science Studies) in Paris.

In the early 1990s, discussions within the Group came to focus on debates about the emergence of 'new industrial models'. The influential book *The Machine that Changed the World*, by J.P. Womack, T.D. Jones and D. Roos (directors of the International Motor Vehicle Program, IMVP, at the Massachusetts Institute of Technology) argued that a new industrial model had been born in Japan. This model, which the authors called 'lean production', was said to be universally superior and transferable to other countries. It was set to become the industrial model for the twenty-first century, just as 'mass production' had been for the twentieth century.

The leaders of GERPISA therefore decided to invite colleagues from many different countries to participate in an international programme, The Emergence of New Industrial Models, which would seek a response to questions about the nature and dynamics of industrial models. GERPISA did not seek to imitate the centrally directed and costly research structures of the IMVP. Instead it launched on open network of international co-operative research, based upon common interests and the free exchange of ideas, focused on debates and discussions at a series of international meetings and seminars.

Almost two hundred researchers from twenty countries participated in the programme, to varying degrees. Four working groups were formed: trajectories of automobile producers, transplantation and hybridisation of industrial models, variety and flexibility of production, and teamwork and employment relations. The most active researchers in these groups became their moderators and the editors of the resulting books. Along with a representative of the French automobile producers, Jean-Claude Monnet, they formed the programme's steering group. The scientific directors of the programme, Robert Boyer and Michel Freyssenet, were responsible for the overall co-ordination and leadership of the scientific debate. An annual meeting was held to present the results, to clarify theory and methodology, and to discuss successive theoretical analyses. The University of Evry and the Ministry for National Education and Research provided GERPISA with support for a secretary and two research staff, making it possible to establish a secretariat. These two institutions, along with the European Union (DGXII, Human Capital and Mobility Programme), the Committee of French Automobile Producers, PSA, Renault and France Télécom provided the financial and material support necessary to organise the meetings and international colloquia, and to co-ordinate the research.

At the end of the programme the participants reached the shared conclusion that both theoretically and in practice there have been, there remain today, and there will probably be tomorrow, several successful industrial models. The reasoning behind this conclusion is presented and discussed in the four collective books produced by the four working groups, which represent different elements of the integrated project.

Two of the books are being published by Oxford University Press. *One Best Way? Trajectories and Industrial Models of the World's Automobile Producers*, edited by Michel Freyssenet, Andrew Mair, Koichi Shimizu and Giuseppe Volpato, analyses the trajectories of fifteen automobile producers since the 1960s and reveals the variety of solutions adopted and possible conditions of success. *Between Imitation and Innovation: The Transfer and Hybridization of Productive Models in the International Automobile Industry*, edited by Robert Boyer, Elsie Charron, Ulrich Jürgens and Steven Tolliday, analyses more than a dozen subsidiaries of Japanese, American and European manufacturers in nearly ten different countries. It reveals the particular historical conditions in which transplantation succeeds and shows in particular how the creation of a subsidiary most often gives rise to hybridisation and sometimes to a new industrial model as a result of the constraints and opportunities offered by the host region. Also under consideration for publication is *Coping with Variety: Product Variety and Production Organization in the World Automobile Industry*, edited by Yannick Lung, Jean-Jacques Chanaron, Takahiro Fujimoto and Daniel Raff, which defines, dates and compares the evolution of product variety and analyses how firms have adopted different ways of effectively managing this variety in production, design and relations with suppliers and distributors. The present book, *Teamwork in the Automobile Industry: Radical Change or Passing Fashion?*, edited by Jean-Pierre Durand, Paul Stewart and Juan José Castillo reveals the wide diversity of practices, objectives and outcomes hidden by the general adoption of teamwork, through case studies of more than twenty automobile factories.

Each book has its own particular focus, but all explain the plurality of industrial models. The thesis of convergence towards a single model is based on the idea that success comes from combining the methods which appear to give the best results, assuming that the environment is largely common to all firms. But reality suggests otherwise. Successful techniques are so only under certain economic and social conditions. Although growing liberalisation of international trade and economic deregulation in many countries may have led to a convergence in competitive conditions, other factors are creating fresh sources of differentiation in both demand and cost structures. Indeed industrial models emerge from these partly unintended processes which result in coherence between strategies, organisational forms and practices, and the fit between these and the economic and social environment. It is the process of achieving internal coherence and external fit which makes companies successful, because it enables them to reduce the uncertainties in work and markets in the time and place in which they operate. Yet their very success often modifies the environment and the conditions which made their models viable. At this point, a new era commences in which firms must seek out new forms of coherence. Manufacturers in a common environment cannot simply copy the most successful company, since by definition the latter has a competitive advantage in having developed the appropriate strategy and model earlier than its rivals. On the contrary, the other producers must try to find a strategy which permits them to compete effectively yet avoid direct confrontation. Accordingly, not only is there no global model, but there is also no national industrial model which firms are obliged to adopt. There are, instead, a limited number of possible models in a given historical period.

While the members of GERPISA, and especially the members of its steering committee, reached agreement on these conclusions, they did not reach agreement on precisely how to characterise the various models. Time and resources did not permit full development of the debates, and, therefore the contributors to the four books have adopted their own characterisations of industrial models, leaving the door open to further theoretical work in this area. The scientific directors of the programme, Robert Boyer and Michel Freyssenet, have, nevertheless, developed an analysis of the industrial models which have been used in the twentieth century automobile industry, based on the research undertaken during the programme and their own work, in an effort to create an appropriate theory. This will appear in a further book, *The World that Changed the Machine*, which follows the origin, development, diffusion and crisis of industrial models, and offers an explanation based on the evolution of markets and work in different contexts.

The results that GERPISA present in these books are the fruit of the patient and co-ordinated work of their fifty or so authors, as well as of the various contributions made by all the participants in the programme. Other material published by the programme includes over a hundred issues of the GERPISA newsletter, *La Lettre du GERPISA*; the publication of articles in the *Actes du GERPISA*; and the work-in-progress papers presented to the annual meetings. Many people have contributed to this large-scale international co-operative project and we thank them all. We would also like to thank the representatives of the French Automobile Manufacturers, particularly Annie Beretti of PSA, Frédéric Decoster and Jean-Claude Monnet of Renault, and Béatrice de Castelnau and Christian Mory of the Committee of French Automobile Producers, who were not content merely to follow the GERPISA programme on behalf of their companies or institution, but actively participated in the network's theoretical development. The programme would never have been successfully completed without the liaison, documentation and editorial activities and the organisation of annual meetings undertaken by the members of the GERPISA secretariat, Carole Assellaou, Kémal Bécirspahic dit Bécir and Nicolas Hatzfeld, under the direction of Michel Freyssenet, the interpretation of Jacqueline Colombat's team, the translations of Teresa Hayter, Sybil Hyacinth Mair, Jennifer Merchant, Eunice Nyhan and Mark Teeuwen, and the organisation of working group meetings at Lower Slaughter by Andrew Mair, Bordeaux by Yannick Lung, Venice by Giuseppe Volpato, Berlin by Ulrich Jürgens, Lyon by Jean-Jacques Chanaron, Paris by Robert Boyer and Elsie Charron, and Madrid by Juan José Castillo. We also wish to thank Sarah Gape of Cardiff Business

School for her secretarial assistance. The publication of these books bears witness to their contributions.

The steering committee of the GERPISA programme 'Emergence of New Industrial Models' is made up as follows:

Robert Boyer (CEPREMAP-CNRS-EHESS, Paris), Juan José Castillo (Complutense University, Madrid), Jean-Jacques Chanaron (CNRS, Lyon), Elsie Charron (CNRS, Paris), Jean-Pierre Durand (University of Evry), Michel Freyssenet (CNRS, Paris), Patrick Fridenson (EHESS, Paris), Takahiro Fujimoto (University of Tokyo), Ulrich Jürgens (WZB, Berlin), Yannick Lung (University of Bordeaux IV), Andrew Mair (Birkbeck College, University of London), Jean-Claude Monnet (Research Department, Renault), Daniel Raff (University of Pennsylvania), Koichi Shimizu (University of Okayama), Paul Stewart (University of Cardiff, Wales), Steven Tolliday (University of Leeds) and Giuseppe Volpato (Ca' Foscari University, Venice).

Participants in the GERPISA Programme 'The Emergence of New Industrial Models':

Argentina: Martha Roldán (FLACSO University, Buenos Aires) and Miguel Zanabria (Ministry of Industry, Buenos Aires).
Australia: Greg Bamber (Griffith University, Brisbane), Russel Lansbury (University of Sidney).
Belgium: Michel Albertijn (Tempera, Antwerp), Leen Baisier (Stichting Technologie Vlaanderen, Brussels), Rik Huys (University of Leuven), Geert Van Hootegem (University of Leuven), Johan Van Buylen (European Centre for Work and Society, Brussels) and André Vandorpe (Stichting Technologie Vlaanderen, Brussels).
Brazil: Ricardo Alves de Carvalho (Minas Gerais Federal University, Belo Horizonte), Nadya Araujo Vastro (São Lazaro Federal University), Jussara Cruz de Brito (CESTEH, Rio de Janeiro), Edna Castro (Federal University, Belem), Afonso Fleury (University of São Paulo), Robero Marx (University of São Paulo), Mario Sergio Salerno (University of São Paulo), Rosa Maria Sales de Melo Soares (IPEA, Brasilia) and Mauro Zilbovicius (University of São Paulo).
Canada: Daniel Drache (York University).
Colombia: Elba Cánfora de Zalamea (National University, Bogotá) and Anita Weiss de Belalcázar (National University, Bogotá).
France: Délila Allam (University of Paris I), Annie Amar (IREPD, Grenoble), Michel Aribart (Ministry of Industry), Etienne de Banville

(CNRS, Saint-Etienne), François Beaujeu (University of Paris IX), Kémal Bécirspahic dit Bécir (University of Evry), Marie-Claude Bélis-Bergouignan (University of Bordeaux IV), Muriel Bellivier (University of Marne-la-Vallée), Annie Beretti (PSA Peugeot–Citroën), Géraldine de Bonnafos (France Télécom, Paris), Gérard Bordenave (University of Bordeaux IV), Robert Boyer (CEPREMAP, Paris), Christophe Carrincazeaux (University of Bordeaux IV), Béatrice de Castelnau (CCFA, Paris), Sylvie Célérier (University of Evry), Jean-Jacques Chanaron (CNRS, Lyon), Elsie Charron (CNRS, Paris), Bertrand Ciavaldini (PSA Peugeot-Citroën), Yves Cohen (CRH, Paris), Guy Cornette (University of Evry), Emmanuel Couvreur (Renault), Isabel da Costa (CEE, Paris), Frédéric Decoster (Renault), Gabriel Dupuy (CNRS, Paris), Jean-Pierre Durand (University of Evry), Joyce Durand-Sebag (University of Evry), Béatrice Faguet-Picq (INTEC, Evry), Simone Feitler (Renault), Michel Freyssenet (CNRS, Paris), Patrick Fridenson (EHESS, Paris), João Furtado (University of Paris XIII), Christophe Gallet (University of Lyon II), Annie Garanto (University of Paris X), Gilles Garel (CRG, Paris), Patrick Gianfaldoni (University of Provence), Armelle Gorgeu (CEE, Paris), Nathalie Greenan (INSEE, Paris), Françoise Guelle (IAO-MRASH, Lyon), Dominique Guellec (OCDE, Paris), Cândido Guerra Ferreira (University of Paris XIII), Christian Guibert (France Télécom, Paris), Armand Hatchuel (Ecole des Mines, Paris), Nicolas Hatzfeld (University of Evry), Helena Sumiko Hirata (CNRS, Paris), Jean-Paul Hubert (University of Paris XIII), Marie-Noëlle Hume (University of Evry), Hee-Young Hwang (University of Paris X), Didier Idjadi (University of Paris XIII), Bruno Jetin (University of Rouen), Bernard Jullien (University of Bordeaux IV), Alex Kesseler (CRG, Paris), Gerson Koch (University of Lille), Alain Kopff (University of Paris), Daniel Labbé (Renault), Anne Labit (University of Rouen), Lydie Laigle (LATTS, Paris), Pascal Larbaoui (University of Paris XIII), Marc Lautier (University of Paris), Jean-Bernard Layan (University of Bordeaux IV), Nathalie Lazaric (University of Compiègne), Yveline Lecler (IAO-MRASH, Lyon), Danièle Linhart (CNRS, Paris), Jean-Louis Loubet (University of Evry), Yannick Lung (University of Bordeaux IV), Jean-Loup Madre (INRETS, Paris), Olivier Maréchau (Rectorat de Créteil), Claire Martin (Renault), René Mathieu (CEE, Paris), Alain Michel (EHESS, Paris), Christophe Midler (CRG, Paris), Jean-Claude Monnet (Renault), Christian Mory (CCFA, Paris), Aimée Moutet (University of Paris X), Jean-Philippe Neuville (CSO, Paris), Jean-

Pierre Orfeuil (INRETS, Paris), Alfredo Pena-Vega (Paris), Monique Peyrière (University of Evry), Jean-Marc Pointet (University of Paris XIII), Emmanuel Quenson (GIP Mutations industrielles, Paris), Jean-Philippe Rennard (Paris), Luiz Rothier Bautzer (University of Paris IX), Patrick Rozenblatt (University of Paris X), Frédérique Sachwald (IFRI, Paris), Laurence Saglietto (University of Nice), Jean Sauvy (Paris), Benoît Schlumberger (University of Paris IX), Klas Soderquist (ESC, Grenoble), Jean-Laude Thenard (GIP Mutations industrielles, Paris) and Benoît Weil (Ecole des Mines, Paris).

Germany: Peter Auer (WZB, Berlin), Bob Hancké (WZB, Berlin), Jörg Hofmann (IG Metall, Stuttgart), Peter Jansen (WZB, Berlin), Ulrich Jürgens (WZB, Berlin), Martin Kuhlmann (University of Göttingen), Steffen Lehndorff (Institut Arbeit und Technik, Gelsenkirchen), Roland Springer (Daimler-Benz, Stuttgart) and Frank Wehrmann (Volkswagen, Wolfsburg).

Italy: Giovanni Balcet (University of Turin), Arnaldo Camuffo (Ca'Foscari University, Venice), Aldo Enrietti (University of Turin), Massimo Follis (University of Turin), Stefano Micelli (Ca'Foscari University, Venice) and Giuseppe Volpato (Ca'Foscari University, Venice).

Japan: Tetsuo Abo (University of Tokyo), Hisao Arai (University of Shiga), Takahiro Fujimoto (University of Tokyo, Masanori Hanada (Kumamoto Gakuen University), Masayoshi Ikeda (Chuo University, Tokyo), Yasuo Inoue (Nagoya University), Osamu Koyama (Sapporo University), Kazuhiro Mishina (JAIST Institute, Tokyo), Yoichiro Nakagawa (Chuo University, Tokyo), Hikari Nohara (Hiroshima University), Masami Nomura (Tohoku, University of Sendai), Ichiro Saga (Kumamoto Gakuen University), Shoichiro Sei (Kanto-Gakuen University), Koichi Shimizu (Okayama University) and Koichi Shimokawa (Hosei University, Tokyo).

Korea: Myeong-Kee Chung (Han Nam University, Taejon) and Hyun-Joong Jun (Seoul University).

Mexico: Jorge Carrillo (Frontera Norte College, Tijuana), Patricia Garcia Gutierrez (Autonomous University of Mexico), Sergio Fernando Herrera Lima (Autonomous University of Mexico) and Yolanda Montiel (CIESAS, Mexico).

Netherlands: Ben Dankbaar (Catholic University of Nijmegen), Frank Den Hond (Free University, Amsterdam), Winfried Ruigrok (Erasmus University, Rotterdam) and Rob Van Tulder (Erasmus University, Rotterdam).

Portugal: Paulo Alves (University of Lisbon), Antonio Brandão Moniz

(University Uni-Nova, Lisbon), Ilona Kovàcs (University of Lisbon), Maria Leonor Pires (University of Lisbon), Marinùs Pires de Lima (University of Lisbon), Pedro Pires de Lima (University of Lisbon) and Mario Vale (University of Lisbon).

Spain: Ricardo Alaez (University of País Vasco, Bilbao), Javier Bilbao (University of País Vasco, Bilbao), Vicente Camino (University of País Vasco, Bilbao), Juan José Castillo (Complutense University, Madrid), Juan Carlos Longas (Public University of Navarra), Javier Mendez (Complutense University, Madrid) and Manuel Rapun (Public University of Navarra).

Sweden: Christian Berggren (Institutet för Arbetslivsforskning, Stockholm), Per Olav Bergström (Metallförbundet, Stockholm), Anders Boglind (Volvo Car Corporation), Göran Brulin (Institutet for Arbetslivsforskning, Stockholm), Kajsa Ellegård (Göteborg University), Tomas Engström (Chalmers University of Technology, Göteborg), Henrik Glimstedt (Göteborg University), Nils Kinch (Uppsala University), Lars Medbo (Chalmers University of Technology, Göteborg), Tommy Nilsson (Arbetslivsinstitutet, Stockholm), Lennart Nilsson (Göteborg University) and Åke Sandberg (Arbetslivsinstitutet, Stockholm).

Switzerland: Ronny Bianchi (Bellinzona).

Turkey: Lale Duruiz (University of Marmara) and Nurhan Yentürk (Istanbul Technical University).

United Kingdom: Philip Garrahan (University of Northumbria), John Humphrey (University of Sussex, Brighton), Arnoud Lagendijk (University of Newcastle), Andrew Mair (University of London), Mari Sako (London School of Economics), Elizabeth Bortolaia Silva (University of Leeds), Paul Stewart (University of Wales, Cardiff), Joseph Tidd (Imperial College, London) and Steven Tolliday (University of Leeds).

USA: Paul Adler (University of Southern California), Steve Babson (Labor Studies, Detroit), Bruce Belzowski (University of Michigan), Richard Florida (Harvard University), Michael Flynn (University of Michigan), Susan Helper (Case Western Reserve University, Cleveland), Harry Katz (Cornell University), Ruth Milkman (University of California, Los Angeles), Frits Pil (Pittsburgh University), Daniel Raff (Pennsylvania University), Saul Rubinstein (New Brunswick University) and Harley Shaiken (University of California, Los Angeles).

All other information concerning GERPISA activities can be obtained by contacting GERPISA International Network, Université

d'Evry-Val d'Essonne, 4 Boulevard François Mitterand, 91025 Evry cedex, France.
Phone: 33(1)69477023; Fax: 33(1)69477007.
E-mail: contact@gerpisa.univ-evry.fr. web page http//www.gerpisa.
univ-evry.fr

Contributors

Paul Adler is a Professor in the Department of Management and Organization, Marshall School of Business, University of Southern California, USA

Michel Albertijn established the independent research bureau Tempera in Antwerp, Belgium

Steve Babson is Labour Program Specialist at the Labour Studies Center, Wayne State University, USA

Leen Baisier works for the Social Economic Council of Flanders/Flemish Foundation for Technology Assessment, Belgium

Göran Brulin is Associate Professor at the School of Business at the University of Stockholm and a Researcher at the National Institute for Working Life, Stockholm, Sweden

Arnaldo Camuffo is Associate Professor of Organizational Behaviour at the Ca'Foscari University of Venice, Italy

Guy Cornette is an Assistant Professor at the University of Paris, France

Michel Freyssenet is a Sociologist and Research Director at the National Scientific Research Centre (CNRS), Paris, France

Detlef Gerst is a Researcher at the Soziologisches Forschungsinstitut (SOFI) at Göttingen University, Germany

Masonori Hanada is Assistant Professor of Economics at the University Kamamoto Gakuen, Japan

Thomas Hardwig is a Researcher at the Soziologisches Forschungsinstitut (SOFI) at Göttingen University, Germany

Nicolas Hatzfeld is Researcher and Lecturer at the University of Evry, France

Rik Huys is Senior Research Associate at the Higher Institute of Labour Studies at the Katholieke Universiteit Leuven, Belgium

Martin Kuhlmann is a Researcher at the Soziologisches Forschungs-institut (SOFI) at Göttingen University, Germany

Anne Labit has a doctorate in Social History from the University of Rouen having spent five years in Germany in different research organisations

Andrew Mair is a Lecturer in Management at Birkbeck College, London University, Great Britain

Roberto Marx is a Lecturer at the Production Engineering De-partment at the University of São Paulo, Brazil

Javier Mendez is based at the Universidad Madrid, Spain

Stefano Micelli is a Researcher at the Ca' Forscari University of Venice, Italy

Tommy Nilsson is an Associate Professor at the University of Stock-holm and a Researcher at the National Institute for Working Life, Stockholm, Sweden

Hikari Nohara is Professor of Political Science at the Graduate School for International Development and Cooperation, Hiroshima University, Japan

Ichiro Saga is based at University Kumamoto Gakuen, Japan

Mario Sergio Salerno is Associate Professor at the Product Engin-eering Department at the University of São Paulo, Brazil

Michael Schumann is Professor of Sociology and President of Soziologisches Forschungsinstitut (SOFI) at Göttingen University, Germany

Johan van Buylen is an expert of the Socialist Metal Workers Trade Union – ABVV, based in Brussels, Belgium

Geert van Hootegem is Project Manager at the Higher Institute of Labour Studies at the Katholieke Universiteit, Leuven, Belgium and a Part-time Lecturer at the Nijmegen Business School, Katholicke Universiteit Nijemen, the Netherlands

Jean-Pierre Durand is Professor of Sociology and Chair of the Centre de Recerches Pierre Naville at the University of Paris–Evry. He is the co-author of *After Fordism* (1997) with Robert Boyer, and is a member of the International Steering Committee of GERPISA

Paul Stewart is a Research Fellow in the Sociology of Work and Employment at the University of Wales, Cardiff. He is co-author of *The Nissan Enigma* (1992), with Phil Garrahan. He is published widely in the Sociology of Work and the Labour Process and is a member of the International Steering Committee of GERPISA

Juan José Castillo is Professor of Sociology of Work at the University Complutense Madrid. He is co-director and editor of the Journal of Sciologia del Trabajo. He is President of the Research Committee 30 'Sociology of Work', International Sociological Association. He has written widely in the areas of the Sociology of Work and Employment. He is a member of the International Steering Committee of GERPISA

INTRODUCTION
The Diversity of Employee Relationships

Jean-Pierre Durand

(Translated by Teresa Hayter)

The automobile industry, in the United States and then in Europe, was one of the first sectors affected by the current phase of crisis in capital accumulation which began at the end of the 1970s. In successive waves, in North America (1979–82) and in European countries (France: 1981–85, Germany: 1988–91, Italy: 1989–91) markets collapsed and then returned to their usual levels. At the same time, new Japanese competitors entered first North American and then European markets with products of superior quality at lower costs. These lower costs were partly the result of the favourable exchange rate of the yen. They were also the result of Japanese superiority in manufacturing methods, and the fact that their cars were easier to assemble, when the Japanese assemblers established themselves in North America and Europe to overcome economic or customs barriers in the target countries.

In response to the cyclical crises of the automobile industry and to the new competitive realities, the American and European assemblers adopted a number of tactics. These were both macro-economic (acceleration or reinforcement of the internationalisation of their activities, development of financial activities and/or industrial diversification, etc.) and micro-economic (lowering of the break-even point of their factories, integration of design and manufacturing activities, reorganisation of their relationships with suppliers, increased contracting out of activities – from 30–40% previously to 60–70% currently, a substantial reduction of manufacturing costs and improvement in the quality of vehicles). The MIT book, *The Machine that Changed the World* [1], was in some respects a 'manual' for these transformations, based on the concept of lean production and transforming the latter into a new 'one best way'.

1

In fact this book, and the Japanese contexts examined by a multitude of specialist missions, were adopted by the majority of producers as guiding principles for the reorganisation of production in general and manufacturing in particular. But the implementation of this single model came up against the historical realities which characterise markets, producers, the role of the state, the skills structure of employees. The result is a great diversity in the forms of adaptation and the new rules which have been introduced to face the uncertainties of the market. It was on the basis of a recognition of this diversity that GERPISA [2] built its international programme of research (1992–96) on the emergence of new industrial models. These industrial models are based both on a macroeconomic approach, which encompasses the products market (with state policies on taxation, incomes, international trade, etc.) and the labour market (skills, professional relationships), and a microsocial approach which includes the organisation of work (the division of labour, hierarchical relationships), the evolution of the products themselves (innovations) and the technical and organisational production processes (including supervision of procedures and relationships between firms).

Among the sub-systems which constitute and define the different industrial models, this book intends to study especially, but not exclusively, the subject of teamwork, a symbolic element of the 'Japanese model', and its socio-organisational environment (the employee relationship as we define it below) in its recent transformations. The concept of teamwork was systematised when the Japanese transplants and Japanese–US joint ventures (NUMMI, CAMI) were set up in North America. The question then arose of the transfer of Japanese forms of organisation in a completely different social context: strong militant trade union traditions, low skills levels, high wages unrelated to work results, etc. A succession of adjustments, after trial and error, made these transfers possible. The Big Three, soon followed by their sisters on other continents, were inspired by and copied these transformations.

The attempt by North American and European producers to imitate and transfer the new model did not take place in virgin territory either. The ensuing hybridisation was the product of the historic trajectories of the producers, the socio-professional structures of the labour force, the state of trade unionism and the social and legal system for the protection of employees. The still provisional result is a multiplicity of situations which can be ascribed to the same organisational principle or which may appear very similar, but which have very different significance in terms of the involvement of employees and their autonomy at work.

This diversity of situations is what will concern us here and what we shall seek to bring together and organise in broad categories, models and types. The following chapters compare the contexts in more than twenty production facilities, mainly final assembly plants, of the major world producers of cars. As everybody knows, the automobile industry has the ability to show the way or ways in which work and professional relationships can be reorganised to benefit the whole of manufacturing industry and the service sector: banks, insurance companies, but also large-scale distribution and the fast food sector.

After a detailed presentation on the topic of employee relations, this Introduction will examine the nature of the changes that are taking place. We shall then look at the history of teamwork, the diversity of its origins and the reasons for its generalisation. It will then be possible to produce a table comparing the state of employee relations at the different production facilities (see Table 1 in the Conclusion to this book, 'The state of employee relations at different automobile manufacturers'). In the Conclusion we shall then group them into five broad categories or models, distributed across all the continents.

The employee relationship, a relevant theme

The question of the employee relationship must be clearly distinguished from the theme of wage relationship or employment relationship popularised by the French Regulation School, which is based on macro-economic analysis. The employee relationship, on the other hand, is a micro-social or more precisely a micro-sociological issue, which is nevertheless affected by its social and economic environment: the state of the labour market, trade unionism, employment legislation and the role of the state.

Unlike other approaches, we shall not focus on a single element characterising work (skills, the organisation of work and the nature of professional relationships). Instead we shall endeavour to look at the whole range of dimensions which emerge from work as it now exists. The need is to put the immediate act of work into context, or rather to attach to the social, economic and historic environment of the work process all the importance which it should never have ceased to have. Thus the topic employee relationship includes within itself concerns which normally arise from several decision-making centres within the company, in particular from the human resources department, from factory management, from the engineering department, and also from the trade unions, all of which operate on very different, even contradictory, principles.

This desire to integrate sub-topics in the employee relationship does not merely arise from academic preoccupations. It is at the heart of the strategies of enterprises, whose results largely depend on the convergence and integration of the operating principles of the different constituent parts, based, where possible, on social consensus.

The question of the employee relationship brings together the following four, closely linked, sub-topics, which are summarised below:

- *Work organisation*, in the sense of the establishment of relationships between shopfloor operators with certain technical means at their disposal, and the relationships with the various categories of employees who work alongside the operators (engaged in the functions of supply, preparation, scheduling and maintenance, i.e. all the extra-productive functions which require indirect work and are essential to the manufacturing process itself). This is the terrain of the many debates on the division of labour and on co-operation, around, for example, the questions of skills and autonomy at work.

- Teamwork, in the current meaning of the word, is thus only one of the possibilities for the organisation of operators among themselves. It will nevertheless be at the heart of the debate, first because of the polysemic nature of the term, linked to the history of collective working, and second because of the diversity of concrete situations, which raise the issues of educational qualifications, skills levels, satisfaction and involvement in work. Another concern is the nature of the relationship between the work team, on the one hand, and the surrounding extra-productive functions, on the other.

- *Hierarchical relationships* with local management around the carrying out of tasks. Supervisory roles have evolved considerably as a result of the creation of the function of team leader (whether nominated or elected) and the appropriation by the work team of certain tasks which were previously the responsibility of supervisors or foremen. The number of levels in the hierarchy has sometimes been reduced, often with the creation, to compensate, of deputies jobs. An evolution towards fewer disciplinary and technical functions, in exchange for more substantial administrative and motivational tasks, seems to be the general tendency.

- *Payments systems* in the broad sense of the term, i.e. including the make-up of wages and bonuses (with the procedures for annual increases), the procedures and possibilities for promotion (on the basis for example of individual evaluations), employment guarantees – without forgetting the socio-economic context determined by the surrounding wages and unemployment levels, compared with those in the company in question.

  The payments system, and in particular the possibilities for promotion and for a career, is one of the essential methods for involving employees which may be supplemented by other more symbolic reward systems (respect, gratitude, delegation of responsibilities).

- *Trade union attitudes* in the face of the reorganisation of work (especially teamwork), the changes in payment systems and the reductions in the workforce. These attitudes depend on the unions' representativeness, their combativity, their strength and sometimes their divisions (internal conflicts or competition between trade unions). In the majority of the cases studied, the trade unions had to accept management's proposals for the reorganisation of work; the employment situation was so unfavourable to them that they accepted the new organisational principles (lean production, teamwork) and payments systems; negotiations then took place around methods of implementation and certain adjustments to these principles. Thus in certain factories there were debates on the methods of designating team leaders (and sometimes their functions) and the new payments systems based on individual merit. On the other hand, the powerful tendency, in Europe, towards the decentralisation of wage negotiations from the national level of the sector towards the level of the firm, or even the unit, was not really debated between the employees' trade union organisations and the employers' organisations, but rather imposed by the latter.

The employee relationship, with its four components (work organisation, hierarchical relationships, payments systems, trade unions), constitutes a system whose coherence has as its objective, at equal technical levels, continuous increases in work efficiency, through the involvement, commitment and 'motivation' of employees (see Figure 1).

The use of the concept employee relationship means that we assume that the four main components of this relationship achieve coherence so as to increase the efficiency of work, which in turn is itself reinforced, from the point of view of the employers, by maximum employee involvement, adequate skills levels and minimum labour costs. However this coherence is not immediate. On the contrary, it is the objective to be achieved in the factory (or in the office), while the main protagonists act according to different, and even divergent, logics. The personnel department seeks to reduce labour costs, in opposition to the trade unions, while local management seeks to increase its numbers in order to avoid any local tension. Finding and organising coherence between these components, at an always provisional point of balance, is a long process during which the different logics confront one another without any of the actors seeing clearly the goal to be attained, because it is never really defined. The Fordist employee relationship could be said to be an impressive example of this coherence. Never explicitly sought, it functioned on a long-term basis because it effectively integrated contradictions and conflicts; any disagreement at work (or in general any demand) was characteristically resolved through wage increases.

Today – and following essentially the crisis in capital accumulation of the late 1970s – the Fordist solution to macro-economic regulation is no longer in operation and the components of the employee relationship are as a result modified. The labour market has been transformed (pressure of unemployment on employees) and trade unions have been weakened, while the new Japanese competitors propose a new form of work organisation (teamwork) and different payments methods (meritocratic system). The problematic which underpins the use of the concept of employee relationship could therefore be set out as follows: how can long-term coherence in the four components of the employee relationship (work organisation, hierarchical relationships, payments systems, trade unions) be constructed while respecting the double constraint of the products market and the labour market?

The hypothesis is thus that the producer who achieves the greatest work efficiency on the basis of the establishment of coherence

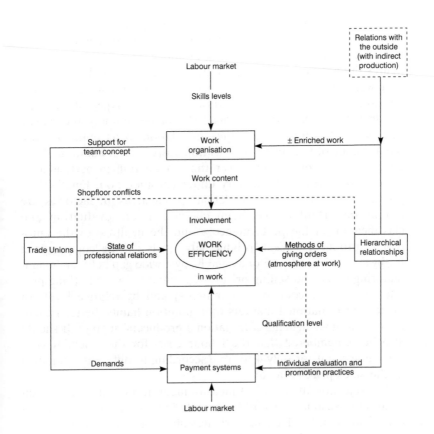

Figure 1 *The coherence of the employee relationship.*

between the four components of the employee relationship is the one that will achieve the best overall results. This hypothesis warrants some comments.

Work efficiency in several factories can only be compared at equal activity rates (for example, and if possible at full capacity) and equal levels of automation. This immediately brings up the question of the methods of measuring work efficiency. It might be expected that a book such as this would produce comparative figures on the factories studied, as MIT's IMVP programme does. We have deliberately rejected such an approach, since it is unsatisfactory on several counts. The figures produced by MIT in 1989 showed that Toyota's Japanese workers were 2, 3 or even 4 times more productive

than workers in American and European companies. If these figures
had any meaning, several non-Japanese producers should by now
have disappeared. If they have not disappeared, this is because the
figures did not faithfully reflect reality [3]. The methods of calculation were inadequate; in particular the statistics were not fully
adjusted to take into account variations in the types of vehicles,
the degree of integration, the vehicles' manufacturability, the activity
rate of the factory (for example, in relation to its optimal rate),
the accuracy of the stated rectification costs, etc. In addition, these
elements vary considerably over time in relation in particular to
the activity rates of the factory under consideration. Finally, it is
probable that the figures on labour productivity in factories are
not as important as has been claimed in the evaluation and
classification of the performance – and the health – of the automobile producers. Weak productivity levels can be compensated
for by simplicity and ease of assembly, by a wide gap between 'manufacturing costs' and selling prices, by economies of scale (long production runs or common components) and by relative levels of
protection in national markets (consumption habits, better match-
ing of consumer demand with national producers' supply). It should
also be remembered that the labour costs for the assembly of a
vehicle account for only 4 to 6% (according to different estimates)
of the sales price of a car!

The rejection of statistical measurement at all costs is a difficult
position to sustain in a world dominated by the religion of numerical calculation. We have nevertheless abandoned the use of figures
on productivity, given that they are extremely rough as a basis for
comparing different firms [4] and also 'ideological', since they are
invariably used to show shopfloor employees that they are behind
or that they will soon be caught up. In other words, what interested us in this international comparative approach was how change
occurred and the processes involved in the implementation of goals
common to all the producers – more work efficiency – to improve
both the quality of the products and the profitability of the firms.
This means also that our approach is more qualitative. It proposes
to analyse the process of establishing coherence in the components
of the employee relationship, rather than its results; in this sense
we are acting as sociologists rather than as economists. In the same
way, and without posing the question explicitly, we examine why
there was this search for an increase in work efficiency. Was it a
question of the survival of the firm and therefore the preservation

of jobs for some and profits for others? Was it a question of sharing the gains from productivity, equitably or otherwise, between employees on the one hand and shareholders on the other? Or is it possible to imagine some possibility of reducing working time on the hardest jobs, or even of reducing the pace of work (or at least ceasing to increase it)? Such questions, too often rejected by researchers, belong to our theme of the 'employee relationship' since the answers have a direct influence – together of course with other factors such as the state of the labour market and the quality of hierarchical relationships – on workers' involvement, and hence also on the efficiency of work.

What are the new models of employee relations?

The Fordist employee relationship, which reached its maturity in the last decade of the thirty years of prosperity which followed the Second World War, was based on a substantial coherence in the four components of the employee relationship. The labour market offered the automobile sector a workforce with few skills which was then employed on monotonous and repetitive tasks in assembly, tightly controlled by a somewhat authoritarian management. The products, of average or even mediocre quality, found buyers in constantly expanding markets. It followed that in order to keep production running, any wage demand was rapidly met, to the benefit, it could be said, of all concerned. The fact that the (macroeconomic) wage relationship made the contradiction between capital and labour 'functional', by means of the virtuous circle of wage increases/demand growth/development of production (and capital accumulation/wage increases) was the basis of the success of Fordist employee relations within the firm.

When markets stagnated – with the transition from new products markets to replacement markets – the virtuous circle became a vicious circle which led to the difficulties we now know: lowering of the break-even point of factories, considerable reductions in the workforce and accumulated losses for the shareholders. It was also the moment for new competitors to enter the market when their products seemed better adapted (price and quality) to the new conditions. After the success of these new (Japanese) competitors, the traditional American and European producers tried to imitate their methods.

The idea was that lean production would be the solution to the problems posed by the difficulties of the American and European automobile producers. For a long time the debate turned around the possibility that the Fordist model of employee relations could be replaced by one unique model, that of lean production. Then the debate turned towards the question of the ways in which the implementation of lean production would be affected by national characteristics (Berggren, 1993a; Jürgens *et al.*, 1993) or the business environment (Mueller, 1994), which some have called 'business culture' and others 'firms' trajectories' (Freyssenet *et al.*, 1998), while some producers or factories remained unreceptive to the new concepts. Thus a multiplicity of situations arose, which we shall try to bring together in meaningful groupings, which we have termed types. Each type of employee relationship corresponds to an original way of achieving coherence in the four components of the employee relationship cited above.

While the general question posed by this book relates to the emergence of these different models of employee relations in the productive units of the automobile producers, the central question which permeates each of the following chapters can be stated thus: how is coherence achieved, with the goal of greater work efficiency, between work organisation, hierarchical relationships, the payments system and trade union activity?

Among these four components, we have given most weight to the organisation of work, because of the major effects which the changes resulting from the adoption of teamwork in many factories have had on it. Our particular interest is in the diversity of forms of implementation. We recognise that the new principle of rationalisation of work represented by teamwork is not unique, and that the traditional Fordist team still makes important contributions to productivity. In addition, our reasons for paying particular attention to teamwork are partly that it is tending to become generalised outside the automobile sector, throughout industry and also in services.

Beyond the organisation of work, the chapters are concerned with methods of worker involvement, since these are a first condition (together with the adequacy of skills for given socio-technical requirements) of work efficiency. For workers to be involved, or committed, they need to be satisfied on the following three issues:

- the content of work (work organisation);

- ways in which orders are given and the atmosphere at work (the state of relationships with management);
- the level and methods of remuneration (including in relation to neighbouring firms).

In order to obtain unity and consistency in the chapters and, more importantly, to compare employee relations in the units studied by twenty-seven researchers dispersed in ten countries, we asked them to fill in Table 1 (Researcher's checklist) which is reproduced below. So as to allow for common evaluations of different situations to be reflected in our results, a fifteen-page guide explained the detailed meanings of the items and the ways in which they should be marked from 0 to 10. On the basis of a selection of eight items we were able to construct the models and types of employee relationship which we present in the Conclusion after the field studies, represented graphically by 'radar' images so as to make their interpretation clearer. In the Conclusion the consolidation of these eight selected items is represented in Table 1, 'The state of employee relations at different automobile manufacturers'.

Comments

In Table 1, the first two sections set out the organisation of work based on the principles of teamwork as they have been described in management literature as an ideal, or model. The question of whether the team leader is nominated or elected appears to be one of the differentiating characteristics in the implementation of teamwork, together with job rotation. The third section, on production work, aims essentially to evaluate the degree of workers' real autonomy over issues concerning the pace of work (supervision and self-organisation of their work), the quality of the product and the maintenance of their machines. The question was not only whether the operators practised self-regulation or carried out maintenance on their machines, but also whether they influenced – and to what extent – policies on quality or on maintenance. The length of cycles and the presence or otherwise of buffer-stocks were a way of evaluating both the evolution in working conditions and the degree of pressure imposed by the production line on daily flux in the work schedule. The section on the role of supervision has as its essential aim the evaluation of the degree of local management autonomy in its policies in production and in the

Table 1 *Researcher's checklist*

NAME OF RESEARCHER	DATE
NAME OF PLANT (OR WORK AREA)	ACTIVITIES
CHARACTERISTICS	

Adoption of teams (year started   ):

Proportion of factory in teams E ( ) G ( ):   0 10

Teams constituted by management (0) or by
negotiation (10):   0 10

Internal functioning of a team:

Degree of polyvalency of team members (weak: 0;
strong: 10)   0 10

Degree of actual rotation of production workers
(weak: 0; strong: 10)   0 10

Nomination (0) or election (10) of leader. What is the
leader called?   0 10

Degree to which leaders rotate (none: 0; frequently: 10)   0 10

Absence of hierarchical structure between members and
team leader (absence: 10)   0 10

Production work:

Length of cycles (short: 0; very long: 10)   0 10

Standards imposed by industrial engineering dept (0)
or negotiated with the team (10)   0 10

Quality control only by separate quality dept (0) or
with the participation of production workers (10)   0 10

Maintenance carried out only by an external dept (0)
or undertaken with the team (10)   0 10

Zero buffers production (0) or buffer level
negotiable (10)   0 10

Role of managerial hierarchy:

Repetitive administrative work (0) or ability to plan
with budgetary powers (10)   0 10

Personnel management by a personnel dept (0) or
decentralised autonomy and authority (10)   0 10

Authoritarian command (0) or negotiated
decisions (10)   0 10

Worker involvement:

High local unemployment (0) or situation of full
employment (10)   0 10

Insecurity of work (0) or 'guaranteed' employment in
the company (10)   0 10

Salaries level with local average (0) or significantly
higher (10)   0 10

Salaries according to post occupied (0) or according to
appraisal of results (10)   0 10

Individuals refuse to become involved (0) or are very
much involved in (improving) their work (10)   0 10

Union(s) reject the new way (0) or are completely
involved in it (10)   0 10

Comments:

management of employees. The last item seeks to describe the nature of hierarchical relationships, while evaluating the extent to which negotiations are possible between the operators and their supervisors.

The final section compares the employment and wages situation and the extent of guarantees on job security, in relation to the local context, as a constituent element in workers' involvement. The fourth item ranks payment according to the job, as in the Fordist situation (0), according to the objective results of the work carried out (10), or according to a more subjective evaluation of the behaviour and potentialities of the worker (5). The other rankings correspond of course to intermediate situations. Finally, the last two items define on the one hand the degree of involvement of the workers (based on opinion polls conducted in the workplace) and on the other hand the official position of the trade union or unions in the face of the changes taking place.

This comparative methodology derives additional validity from the fact that nearly all the cases we looked at were final assembly lines, apart from a few exceptions such as the pressings plant at Rover–Swindon (Britain), engine manufacture at Fasa–Renault (Spain) and the body plant at Volkswagen–Hanover (Germany). These exceptions were worth looking at since, in spite of undeniable technical differences (procedures and products), the principles of the transformation of the employee relationship and the introduction of teamwork were as much in evidence as in most of the final assembly plants. As we have said, we are mainly interested in the principles and in the analysis of their effects, rather than in the technical details. As far as the great majority of the assembly lines we studied are concerned, i.e. more than twenty, we encountered great technical homogeneity: short or relatively short cycles from 1 to 2.5 minutes, more or less segmented assembly lines (i.e. with some buffer-stocks between segments), parallel lines for sub-assemblies (doors, dashboards, engine casings) and robotised assembly for some elements (dashboards, windscreens and rear view mirrors, wheels, sometimes seats) [5].

We now return to some aspects of the history of work organisation, and in particular to the confusions and oscillations between the terms teamwork and group work.

History of team and group working

Teamwork, of the type that is tending to become general in auto-mobile factories and firms, originates in Japan. But, as Masanori Hanada likes to remind us, this type of organisation is normal, 'natural' in Japan [6]. It is Westerners who have made it into a particular object by formalising it, in order to transfer and implement it in conditions which are different from those in Japan. The specific role of the concept of lean production, through its diffusion in management circles, was to systematise the differences in order to emphasise the collective character of work in the Japanese team. But this leads to an important observation: work has always possessed a collective character, including in the West (cf. the concept of co-operation in Marx) and the Fordist team did not depart from this social arrangement of individualities (Martinez Lucio and Stewart, 1997).

As we have already indicated, the notion of a team, of team working or of a work team is thus largely polysemous: is one speaking of the traditional Fordist team or the modern team born of the reorganisation of work on the basis of the 'Japanese model' and the 'teamwork' which came out of it? In the face of this possible confusion, we use the concept of teamwork to speak of the current forms of reorganisation of the employee relationship, so as to make a clear distinction between these and the earlier Fordist teams. Obviously the situation is not as simple as this, first because the 'Japanese model' is itself largely Fordist through the systematic adoption of line production (Wood, 1989; Boyer and Durand, 1996) and second because teamwork takes over from traditional Fordist teams (in the United States, France, Great Britain, Italy), while this same traditional organisation frequently resists the introduction of teamwork. Where does one end and the other begin?

The differences between the two forms of work organisation are to be found at several levels. In the Fordist firm, the skills levels of operators are low, indeed very low, and workers specialise on one particular job (cf. the 60 to 110 specialisms of US non-skilled workers, written into the UAW/Big Three agreements); only relief workers are multi-skilled; the career prospects of the workers without recognised skills are extremely poor. Japanese workers, on the other hand, have a much higher general level of education and they acquire multi-skilling through systematic rotation of jobs in the team, within and between departments; for those who submit to strict standards of behaviour, career prospects are open (up to the equivalent of production engineer for the best and the most motivated) [7].

In both situations, the tasks carried out by the workers are pre-scribed with work standards and operating procedures imposed by the engineering department or by a technical service near the work area (Japan). In the Fordist system, the standard times established by the engineering department change little, in particular because of worker resistance. At Toyota, the aim of Kaizen is to reduce drastically these standard times: supervisory staff, supported by technical staff specialising in this activity, are central to the reduc-tion of standard times (on the basis of which they are themselves evaluated). This reduction in standard times and the technical ad-justments which accompany it are achieved as near as possible to the immediate work situation.

The overall effect of these structural differences is that super-visors in Western firms have a mainly disciplinary role in the im-mediate monitoring and management of employees (which goes down to the level of foremen and setters who, while having a technical function, also have a management and disciplinary role). In Toyota, the function of supervisors is essentially technical (monitoring pro-duction, supplies, kaizen, various adjustments, quality) with econ-omic objectives (cost reduction) while their only social function is in the evaluation of subordinates. This means, for example, that the cleanliness of the job station, or the so-called '5 S', is easily secured. The group leaders, while having a role of social support (welcome of new recruits, their training and the monitoring of job rotation), have basically a technical role: filling in, help for em-ployees who hold up the line, running technical meetings, etc. Respect for order is integral to the meritocratic system. Potential deviants are kept in order or discouraged by their peers (see below) and/or by the potential loss of promotion prospects.

In summary, we have two situations characterised by the work team but in which the contents, the meaning of work and the or-ganisation of work differ. Table 2 analyses these differences – **in our conclusion to the book we have consolidated these into just three models (Fordist/Japanese-lean production/Kalmarian)**. We have added to the first two differentiated models the hybrid model of lean production. This model was systematised by the MIT re-searchers and implemented outside Japan, first in the Japanese transplants in the USA (and in Britain), but especially in the ma-jority of car companies which experienced institutional forms of

Table 2 *The four canonical models of work organisation*

	Traditional Fordist team	Teamwork: Toyota–Japan	Teamwork outside Japan	Semi-autonomous workgroups: Sweden and Germany in the 1970s
Nature of tasks	• Prescribed tasks and compulsory operational methods	• Prescribed tasks and compulsory operational methods (a small amount of internal autonomy)	• Prescribed tasks and compulsory operational methods (a small amount of internal autonomy)	• Work is freely organised within the group
	• Timings based on time & motion method with little modification; goals of productivity increase are absent or few	• Timings must be continuously reduced. Kaizen: minor role for the operators and major role for supervisors and technical staff in attaining the new objectives	• Reduction of timings. Kaizen carried out by management; the goals are contractualised (but not negotiated)	• The standard timings can be negotiated within certain limits. Production takes place on the basis of more or less negotiated goals
	• The Engineering Department is centralised and clearly identified; it is the basis for organising the shopfloor	• The engineering function is dispersed throughout the shopfloor and offices	• The Engineering Department is still centralised but with a breaking down of barriers between the functions Research/ Engineering/ Manufacturing (increase in exchanges between them)	• The Engineering Department is centralised but without barriers between it and the shopfloor

• Unskilled operators and relief by 'multi-skilled' workers	• All workers are multi-skilled as a result of their high educational level and job rotation	• The majority of workers are multi-skilled (in the team) in a fairly narrow range of activities	• The workers are in general multi-skilled (through job rotation; multi-skilling is paid for). Substantial professional training
Role of supervisors • Their role is primarily disciplinary (the foremen and setters have technical roles and the latter also have a disciplinary role): • no motivation system • respect for discipline • no local goals	• Their role is not disciplinary but fundamentally technical: monitoring of production, Kaizen. They also carry out individual evaluation: • motivation through meritocracy • importance of peer role (support, training, absenteeism)	• Their role is primarily 'administrative' with inadequate time available to devote to workers (Just-in-Time imposes discipline): • motivation through meritocracy • interest in work through changing its image (diversification of tasks, quality, approval, planning, without genuine responsibilities • role of peers (absenses, co-operation)	• The role is 'administrative' and directed towards the workers and their motivation: • motivation through interest in the work and attractiveness of the jobs • the spokesperson of the group (group leader) and supervisors expected to build a 'good environment' at work
Interpretation • System emphasising discipline	• System emphasising techniques (no emergent disciplinary questions)	• System focused on economic goals	• System concentrating on the quality of life at work

resistance (derived from the general organisation of the company, its methods of setting wages together with the skills levels of the workers) or worker and trade union resistance.

We understand canonical model in the sense of an idealised system (on the lines of the Weberian ideal-type) which has never existed, but which is constructed on the basis of strong characteristics which combine together to provide systematic coherence. Of course these 'models', since they are canonical, function both as systems combining their components and as models to copy in order to achieve the coherence necessary for work efficiency. While the traditional Fordist team and Japanese teamwork break with each other in many respects, the exported version of teamwork constitutes the adaptation of Japanese teamwork to Western conditions (labour markets, labour legislation and strong trade unionism). It is therefore already a hybrid model or a semi-model – that is, it has lost some of its canonical power relative to its Japanese matrix – but in our view it does constitute a model since the combination of components which it advocates leads to the quest for a new type of coherence. Finally, it gives rise to new hybrid applications which in each case take account of national and local circumstances. Thus the importation of lean production brings about not only a new or different form of work organisation, but above all new rules for securing work. The latter are accompanied sometimes by changes in the workforce (raising of skills levels and setting aside of workers whose training/bringing up to required levels is considered too onerous) and especially by the will to transform the conditions in which work takes place: attempts to weaken trade unions (by force, bypassing them or by integrating them), setting up systems for evaluating operators (with, for example, the individualisation of wages), supervised development of competition between workers (contained in the evaluation system itself; see Boyer and Durand, 1996) and the reinforcement of job insecurity [8].

This picture of canonical models would be incomplete without the 'Swedish model' and in particular the system of group work or semi-autonomous group work which was created in Sweden in the late 1970s (at Electrolux, Saab and Volvo in particular) and then spread into Germany, while it had an influence on certain companies in France (Renault) and in Italy (Fiat). Its principles represented a fundamental break with the preceding canonical models since it proposed attaining its economic objectives (more or less negotiated with trade union organisations) through the transformation of work: self-organisation, enlargement of the autonomy of individuals and groups, and improvement in the quality of life at work. An improvement in productivity was to be obtained through deepening the collective character of work and through methods of fixing goals which commit the actors themselves, all of which are psycho-sociological dimensions which define group working (Larson and LaFasto, 1989). Group work was also the chosen method for making assembly line work, which is normally repetitive and monotonous, more attractive. This was the means used by Volvo on two occasions, when automobile demand was increasing and when young people were turning away from assembly plants. The Kalmar and Uddevalla plants opened respectively in 1974 and 1989, with organisational paradigms which broke with the past, in order to attract young people of both sexes (Durand, 1994). This is why we have included Kalmar as a 'canonical model' since, while maintaining the Fordist principle of the moving line (unlike Uddevalla), this factory put forward real alternatives in work organisation (Berggren, 1993b; Durand, 1994) through the organisational autonomy of the groups, better industrial democracy, rewards for multi-skilling and the election of group 'spokespeople'.

Although this canonical model is tending to lose ground in the face of the offensives of lean production, both in Sweden and in Germany, researchers in these countries continue to refer to it as though it were dominant. This is because we are in the midst of a real confusion in vocabulary, which mixes up, knowingly or otherwise, group working and teamwork. Superficially the two concepts resemble each other, at least in their stated purposes: reinforcement of collective work, development of autonomy in the team or the group and increases in skills. But it seems to us essential to differentiate between them, given the extent to which their real goals, the logic of their operation and the daily realities of working conditions under them diverge, as manifested both in the projects themselves and in the results of our fieldwork.

The situation is complicated by the fact that the promoters of lean production use the concepts and vocabulary of the supporters of group work to dress up teamwork and to make it more acceptable to workers and their union organisations [9]. In Germany, IG Metall was obliged to accept lean production in a balance-of-power situation which made it impossible to reject it. In accepting it, the company hoped also to have an effect on its implementation, through modifying it and using it as a lever to further the principles of group work (especially in work autonomy) developed in certain manufacturing sectors which used mainly skilled employees (Roth, 1994; Murakami, 1995; see also Chapter 16). This represents a particular type of hybridisation which integrates – at least at the level of stated aims – divergent or opposed principles in work organisation. This makes fieldwork and the interpretation of facts more arduous, but also more rewarding. Our hypothesis is that teamwork responds better to the economic preoccupations which dominate during a cycle of accumulation crisis in capitalism (when the supply of labour is much greater than the demand for it), and that it therefore wins. It is the most fertile form of organisation, even if it sometimes takes on the forms of group work in order to gain acceptance. We shall return to some of these forms of hybridisation at the end of this introduction.

The coherence between Just-in-Time and teamwork

Just-in-Time systems have become generalised in the automobile industry to such an extent that there are now synchronised flows for a number of parts or sub-assemblies. Thus each sub-assembly is dedicated to a particular body shell and their 'marriage' is intended to take place at a particular moment and only at that moment. If there is a fault, the vehicle cannot be assembled and it is removed from the line. In general terms, Just-in-Time systems (i.e. where an absence of buffer-stocks makes synchronisation necessary) induce vulnerability in production, compared with the traditional (Fordist) assembly line systems with buffer-stocks. Teamwork is one of the most effective ways of organising work to meet the socio-technical requirements of Just-in-Time. But it cannot be too often repeated that, while it is one of the most effective ways, there are others, less spectacular because they are compatible with the traditional Fordist system of working in teams. These are to be found in France for example, in many units of Peugeot SA, and they have for a long time been dominant at Volvo–Ghent or at Volvo–Torslanda. Ford–Dearborn ranked high in the 1995 Harbor Report classification while continuing to use traditional Fordist organisational methods, before it eventually adopted the team concept.

Nevertheless, in meeting the requirements of Just-in-Time, teamwork has some advantages. According to Frank Mueller, it has economic, social and cultural dimensions – see Figure 2.

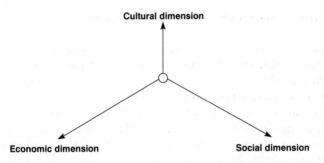

- Make people identify with company
- Achieve a common outlook
- More solidarity between exployees
- Climate of trust
- Commitment
- Management and labour share goals
- Improvement in absenteeism and labour turnover

Cultural dimension

Economic dimension

- Removing demarcations
- Flexible working practices
- Higher capital productivity
- Better quality
- More local responsibility
- More decentralised decision-making
- Inspection and maintenance become part of operator job
- Support given to new and flexible technology

Social dimension

- Work more satisfying
- Higher earnings
- Less isolation
- Opportunities to acquire more skills
- Less physical strain
- Better ergonomic arrangements
- Longer job cycles
- Reduced machine pacing
- Better health and safety

Figure 2 *The three dimensions of teamwork.*

This presentation, from a management point of view, underlines the importance of the team concept not only in resolving technical issues, through a form of work organisation better adapted to the requirements of Just-in-Time, but in stimulating workers, who benefit from better working conditions while sharing the goals of management. But as the author writes: 'Our own interviews suggest a stronger emphasis on the productivity dimension, with job enrichment having a complementary role at best' (Mueller, 1994, p. 390). This is hardly surprising since lean production and its accompanying teamwork clearly have an economic priority of cost reduction [10]. In fact, the strength of lean production lies in its ability to ally reduction in labour costs and the satisfaction of the requirements of Just-in-Time and its vulnerability. This alliance is achieved through instruments such as collective responsibility, socialisation of knowledge and know-how, greater interchangeability between workers, peer pressure, continuous increases in the pace of work and emergence of the ambivalent position of team leader, all of which derive from a concern to increase the productivity of work. We shall examine each of these in turn.

Collective responsibility and continuous flow

Whereas previously Fordist teams were a juxtaposition of individuals responsible only for their own tasks and whose mistakes were rectified at the end of their particular section of work, today the team is collectively responsible for the quality of its work – that is, for the quality of the product – which it must carry out without interrupting the flow of production. Hence the encouragement of practices such as mutual help between workstations, and more generally the role of the team leader, who helps the worker in temporary difficulties while making sure of the quality of the product which leaves the team's area of responsibility. In most factories, it is expressly stated that any worker can stop the assembly line by pulling an emergency cord – which is the proof of each individual's autonomy. In fact, in most cases, pulling the cord once means calling for the help of the team leader. It is only the latter who can pull it twice to stop the line in cases of absolute necessity; the team leader must then give an account of why the stoppage was necessary.

To meet its objectives, the team must be 'welded together'. Its success depends on its cohesion, in spite of a drastic reduction in numbers compared with the Fordist team (in particular the elimination of relief workers, the end of 'double stations' where a worker assembled one out of two cars because of the difficulties involved, etc.). Hence the importance of the collective quality of teamwork, with an insistence by management on comparisons with sporting teams; there is an attempt to promote the notion of team by choosing attractive examples (sports team, surgical team, management team, etc.). But above all the whole team is directed towards a single goal (Parker and Slaughter, 1988; Larson and LaFasto, 1989): quality is to be achieved at the pace set by the conveyor belt. The team has a variable geometry: the work team is expected to meet the challenge of achieving the quality and productivity objectives set for it, and the company or the plant is expected to compete with other producers. This represents both the search for social integration common to any management and the ideological function of the notion of team, which is supposed to bind together in one entity shareholders, management and employees.

Socialisation of know-how, co-operation and reduction in labour costs

At the level of the work process, on assembly lines, teamwork promotes the development of multi-skilling, in the sense that each employee is capable of doing all the jobs in the team, and perhaps beyond it. The main results of job rotation and multi-skilling are that the knowledge and know-how of each employee are made public and shared, in order to keep up the pace of work. Previously private, this know-how constituted an individual means of protection for the workers which enabled them to devise some free time for themselves (a few extra minutes, not counted in the official tables of the engineering department) and which gave them a small degree of autonomy in the organisation of their work or their job.

Today, multi-skilling and job rotation have made this know-how public and transparent so that it is appropriated by engineering departments, which integrate it into their calculations of timings and scales. This analysis makes it easier to understand why many employees – especially the most experienced – resist job rotation and the multi-skilling which is linked to it. For them this is the best way of defending their know-how and preventing it from being made public, shared and incorporated into the schedules and training programmes. Finally, because of the large numbers of audits which monitor conformity to the production schedules, employees' autonomy in organising their jobs is considerably reduced. Teamwork means that workers carry out each operation in practically the same way; this standardisation of work is, according to engineering departments, the condition for quality and the regular flow of production (meeting the requirements of the line). We can see that Taylor is not far away; Taylor, as we know, merely organised scientifically the complex co-operation which Marx described. Thus, whether through engineering departments or through the operation of kaizen (continuous improvement), this socialisation of know-how intensifies co-operation between workers. The latter transforms individual work capacities into a collective worker whose efficiency is greater than the sum of individual abilities. Moreover this effect of co-operation is not paid for, as Marx suggests (*Das Kapital,* Volume 1, Chapter 13).

Multi-skilling, with the standardisation of work which accompanies it, allows complete interchangeability between workers and rapid changes between jobs, even transfer to another team, if necessary. This is a profound change, especially in the United States where unskilled workers were allocated between 60 to 110 different classifications (Parker and Slaughter, 1988). Interchangeability of course makes it easier to eliminate relief workers and means a significant economy in labour power. On assembly lines engaged in direct work, reserves of relief workers are considerably reduced since the team leader takes over the jobs of absentee workers. In the areas where the work is mainly indirect, especially in process monitoring (body shops, paint shops, tool-making), the workers who are present do the jobs of absentee workers, whose replacement is no longer even considered.

Coercion through the pace of work and peer pressure

The regular flow of production requires cohesion within the group. It is therefore essential that workers have comparable levels of efficiency; otherwise the best will do the jobs of the least efficient, which is acceptable during a period of socialisation and apprenticeship but not thereafter. Thus within the group a sort of average work standard is created, based on the work requirement derived from the pace of the line itself and from the numbers of employees assigned by management to a particular section of the line. This average work standard, constituted through this double form of coercion, is imposed on the group. Its members are expected to ensure that it is respected and that the work is not affected by the failure of any member of the group to carry out a part of it. Hence the pressure of peers on the operator who is too often absent, too slow or who lacks good will; this group self-discipline prevents any deviance much more effectively than a supervisor would be able to.

Peer pressure of this type characterises teamwork in the places where it has been most successfully implemented, in Japanese factories, in the Japanese transplants in the United States and in Britain, at NUMMI and at Saturn. This is 'management-by-stress', the term used by Parker and Slaughter (1988) to describe the way in which pressure is exercised on the pace of work. Henry Ford used the pace of the line as a means of overcoming the problem of porosity in the working day (Garrahan and Stewart, 1992). The Just-in-Time system has the ability to increase the pressure on employees 'naturally': each fault is immediately discovered since it makes assembly impossible further down the line, or causes the line to stop. Just-in-Time thus creates a real transparency in the actions and behaviour of each employee in the collective work of the team, thus increasing peer pressure on the individual actor. There is thus a real dialectic of the individual and the collective: the cohesion of the group, promoted through a system of challenges and goals and encouraged by the leadership of the team leader, puts pressure on the individual to respect prescribed standards (of behaviour and work). This means that the real autonomy of the worker within the group is reduced. Organisational transparency is supplemented by very rigorous prescription of the operations to be carried out, in cycles whose length is continually being reduced [11], with the number of workers similarly declining. Scrupulous respect of the standard, on the basis of the coercion imposed by Just-in-Time which exposes any imperfection, is the daily condition of existence of team-work, one of the foundations of lean production.

Reduction in management layers and functions of the team leader

By regulating the pace of work, Just-in-Time incorporates the disciplinary role which was previously played by supervisors in the Fordist team. Thus, from the point of view of the management of workers, the Just-in-Time principle is much superior to the traditional intervention of supervisors monitoring and controlling workers' activity. The relationship between workers and supervisors was always subject to argument and conflict because of human imperfections and subjectivity. The Just-in-Time principle appears neutral, independent of social relations, 'natural' and often integrated by the operators themselves. This 'naturalisation' of work and production relations is much more effective than the previous system. Finally, it permits a shortening of the management chain, thus reducing the number of indirect production jobs.

While one management layer is suppressed thanks to the virtues of Just-in-Time, teamwork introduces a new function, that of team leader who, as the name indicates, inspires and leads the team.

With some exceptions (Renault, Fiat), team leaders have no management power and are not part of the management chain. They are shopfloor operators whose technical abilities have been recognised (in particular on the basis of a table showing the evolution of each member of the group towards a greater degree of multi-skilling) and human qualities (communications skills, ability to inspire and lead their peers). They possess a dual role which supervisors, because they were managers, lacked, precisely because their position as managers made it difficult or impossible for the operators to express themselves freely.

Thus the role of team leader forms part of the same logic of rationalisation of unpredictable social relationships. Team leaders organise both horizontal communication within the group and vertical communication with management (hence the designation 'spokesperson' adopted for team leaders in Northern Europe). Because they are the pivot between these two systems of communication, they help them to communicate with each other (Durand-Sebag, 1992). So the position of team leader brings together two functions which were previously heterogeneous, exclusive, even antagonistic, those of horizontal communication and those of the management prerogative. Each person derives some advantages from this situation, from the operator who no longer has permanent direct contacts with supervisory staff, to managers who re-establish communications with operators and the heart of the production process, and the team leaders themselves whose dedication to carrying out their contradictory functions is enhanced by their knowledge that they have been chosen for possible promotion. There remains the question of the costs for the team leaders themselves, placed in a contradictory situation, with all the consequences in nervous tension and stress which may follow (hence the frequent resignations of team leaders in certain work areas). The category of team leader is a category with ill-defined roles, that is to say roles which are multiple, centrifugal and heterogeneous and which are difficult to hold together. Not only is the position ambivalent, but its legitimacy is questionable. The latter depends largely on the methods for designating team leaders, and especially on who designates them. Thus, although the team leader's role is defined in broad outline, the way in which it is carried out depends to a great extent on the origins of its legitimacy. If team leaders are nominated by management (without any rotation of leaders) and if in addition they receive a bonus, they obtain their legitimacy from management and have to win acceptance from their peers. If they are elected by their peers, they must continually prove their loyalty towards management without losing the confidence of their peers. Moreover, if they are the candidate of the trade union, the likely confusion over their status makes the function impossible to fulfil (hence, for example, the frequency of resignations at Saturn or at least the non-renewal of team leaders' mandates). Where trade unions are strong (in Sweden, Germany and older factories in the United States), they confront management to ensure that they are the source of the team leaders' legitimacy, hoping thus to promote their point of view and to defend workers' interests more successfully. But there is no indication that in most cases the 'double bind' which characterises the position of team leader does not work out to the advantage of management, simply by defusing potential crises which would have blown up in traditional situations.

In all of these cases, the function of team leader disperses throughout the team the tasks arising from the technical requirements imposed by Just-in-Time, and it secures external communication while maintaining a strong internal social cohesion. It contributes to softening the constraints and reducing awareness of the rigid discipline associated with Just-in-Time, through obtaining if need be employees' consent to this discipline. Thus it is one of the cornerstones of teamwork. Teamwork, in turn, both satisfies the intrinsic requirements of Just-in-Time and, in a social context which is quite restrictive, makes discipline at work appear neutral, a product merely of technical necessities 'naturalised' by Just-in-Time. In this way, it is an inherent part of the new employee relationship and the new conditions for employee involvement.

Teamwork and forced involvement

To return to the diagram representing the coherence of the employee relationship (Figure 1), it will be recalled that the four components of the model (work organisation, hierarchical relationships, payments system and nature of trade unionism) converge towards one result: involvement in work, which is the condition for its efficacy.

According to the canonical models of employee relations presented above, the main sources of involvement in work differ profoundly. In the Fordist model, involvement is essentially based on wages (Linhart and Linhart, 1985), that is demands are primarily wage demands, while any disagreement on the question of hours, poor conditions, health and safety is negotiated in exchange for a substantial bonus. In the Kalmar model, or group work, involvement is achieved more through the attractiveness of jobs and an improvement in working conditions. This model, which appeared in the 1960s and 1970s, was supported by some senior management and some states, under the New Factory programmes in Sweden and the humanisation of work programmes in Germany. It also spread in the United States at the end of the 1970s with the Quality of Work Life (QWL) programmes of General Motors and Employee Involvement (EI) at Ford. Today, most of these programmes have been overtaken by the diffusion of Japanese methods of workforce management associated with lean production. But their significance, linked to the durability of the spirit of group work, continues to influence the methods deployed to secure work involvement; in a sense the models confront one another, with the group work model resisting lean production to some small extent. In the same way, lean production has to adapt to the resistance of the Fordist model, with trade unions, where they are still strong, giving priority to wage demands or at least resisting Japanisation practices.

The question then is what is unique about employee involvement in lean production, and especially employee relations in its progenitors, the big Japanese exporting companies. The answer is that it is a meritocratic system (the satei system), under which the best employees are rewarded through advancement and promotion. This system prevailed from the period after the Second World War until the crisis of the early 1990s. It is being transformed essentially as a result of the weakening of demand for labour in Japan in relation to its available supply.

As its name indicates, the meritocratic system in large companies is based on an individual evaluation of employees – in this case of shopfloor workers – by the manager immediately above them. The evaluation is then validated by the next manager up the hierarchy, before being sent to the personnel office. This procedure includes an evaluation of the objective results of the work provided, but above all it is an evaluation of the behaviour and attitudes of the employees and in particular of their conformity with the standards expected of them; this is what we call the subjective dimension of the evaluation. Some limitation on the competition between employees is instituted through a system of percentages to which the evaluators must adhere: 5 % of very good and 5% of bad subjects, 20% fairly good or bad, and the rest around the average.

The results of the evaluation have a direct influence on wages and bonuses, which can be the equivalent of 4 to 6 months' wage. But above all it is on the basis of these evaluations that workers can or cannot become team leaders and supervisors. In the period of industrial expansion in Japan a large number of workers could hope for such promotion or could choose the less prestigious path of technical advancement; today this is hardly possible any longer because of the limited supply of jobs. Those who receive less positive evaluations may themselves decide to leave the big company, knowing they are not wanted there.

But remaining in a big company and pursuing a career in it has many advantages (under the system of 'corporate welfare'). Direct wages are 15 to 20% higher than those in smaller companies. Welfare, including pensions, jobs for life, subsidised loans and the social status conferred by belonging to these keiretsu are some reasons for conforming to the standards expected in the large company, if one is to stay in it. These standards imply involvement, putting oneself at the service of one's company through the acceptance of constraints (intensive pace of work and long hours for the workers, transfers throughout Japan or abroad for skilled employees) in order to deserve to remain in it. In other words, employees who have chosen to make a career in a big company have no choice in other respects; they must conform to the expectations of management and must involve themselves in their work. This is why we designate as forced involvement the method of involving employees used in the big Japanese exporting companies (Boyer and Durand, 1996; Durand and Durand-Sebag, 1996).

Although this system of forced involvement does not properly speaking belong to the lean production model, since its MIT promoters had little interest in sociological questions, its rapid expansion in the West and in most of the automobile producers is nevertheless striking. Not only have evaluations, including those of workers, become generalised, but they are more and more concerned with the subjective state of employees. Employees must therefore adopt behaviour in conformity with the norms, which also means in conformity with the requirements of Just-in-Time. The essential difference with the preceding period is that conformity to the norm is not rewarded as it was previously (by a wage increase) or as it could be (by a reduction in working time, or by a symbolic reward through more respect being given to those operating it): conformity to the norm takes place without counterpart, except that of keeping one's job. Thus, the threat of job losses in Europe or the United States fulfils the same function as the desire to remain in the big company in Japan in order to receive the benefits of its 'corporate welfare'. In both cases, the concept of forced involvement defines the nature of employees' commitment to work. Employees follow the behavioural norm because they have no choice.

In the West, the long lasting crisis in employment is an important factor in workers' involvement. This is why we have included items on the situation of employment in our table of comparative analysis of factories. (Table 1 in the Conclusion). At the same time, the concept of forced employee involvement does not refer to physical coercion or to any new totalitarianism. On the one hand it should be compared to previous methods of involvement, through wages or through improvements in working conditions; and on the other hand it relates to a social form of coercion, that is to a situation or to an order of things in which, if one wants to attain one's socially determined objectives (to stay in a big company or not to lose one's job), then one is forced to submit to the norm, in this case to carry out a prescribed task [12]. In other words, acceptance of this social coercion does not prevent employees from opening up creative spaces in the chinks in the behavioural norms attached to it, and these permit new social games. In this sense the theses of Burawoy (1979) on the social games accompanying work and exploitation to make them more acceptable remain relevant (Durand and Stewart, 1998). Of course the chinks have become smaller with the generalisation of Just-in-Time!

Individual evaluation and the nature of what is being evaluated also constitute an essential criterion for the definition of the employee relationship. Some trade unions forcefully reject evaluation, while others accept it if it covers only the objective results of the work provided. Other trade unions accommodate it because they are unable to oppose it. Some producers, especially US producers, do not dare even to talk about it, given the solid tradition of payment by job classification and the strength of the UAW's opposition to these evaluation practices.

The management of work through forced involvement is tending to spread as a result of the generalisation of the pressures of underemployment and unemployment on workers. In a number of companies, trade unions are resisting the implementation of this system of forced involvement. Other companies do not need individual evaluation to motivate their employees, since neo-Fordist precepts of discipline continue to be dominant. Situations are diverse, not only as far as methods of involvement are concerned, but also in the organisation of work itself. Following the exploration of the empirical diversity in the following chapters, our aim in the Conclusion will be to evaluate the extent of organisational variety and the dominant tendencies in employee relations in the international automotive industry.

End-notes

[1]   Womack, J.P., Jones T.D. and Roos D., *The Machine that Changed the World*. New York: Rawson, 1990.

[2]   Groupe d'Etudes et de Recherches Permanent sur l'Industrie et les Salariés de l'Automobile. See the brief presentation of the common conclusions of this research programme.

[3]   See Freyssenet M., Mair A. Shimizu K. and Volpato G. (1998) *One Best Way? Trajectories and Industrial Models of the World's Automobile Producers, 1970–2000*. Oxford University Press.

[4]   Even comparisons of the same factory over time pose problems because of the rapid evolution of procedures and products, and above all the heterogeneity of technical and organisational changes.

[5]   This technical homogeneity, in which the principle of moving assembly lines, often operated under the pressures of Just-in-Time, was dominant, led us not to include in our models of employee relations the case of Volvo–Uddevalla, since there is no assembly line in this plant. We nevertheless included Volvo–Kalmar as an extreme case, since it retains the assembly line as an organising principle in production and the employee relationship.

[6]   Which for us does not mean – far from it – agreement with the 'groupist' thesis which maintains that the Japanese can live only in groups. For a refutation of this thesis see Durand and Durand-Sebag 1996).

[7]   The 'crisis' of the early 1990s means that it is necessary to speak of these promotions in the past tense. But this changes nothing in the history of the transfer of the model.

[8]   The fact of the existence of unemployment in the West thus plays, through the threats which it imposes on each employee, the same

role as the fears of leaving the big Japanese company (with the social status and the high direct and indirect income which it offers its employees – the famous corporate welfare system) play in securing conformity to social norms of subjection.

[9] It is moreover one of the essential tasks of the researcher not to take at their face value the fabulous and bewitching declarations of managers when they describe their plans for the implementation of teamwork (in particular, company or factory agreements). The researcher should instead be concerned with results after several years of implementation and interpret them, above all, in relation to the declared objectives. It sometimes happens that because of the closeness of links, or even their subordinate nature (the researcher may also be a consultant for the company or hope to become one), this interpretative work is not carried out with the necessary objectivity.

[10] A critical account of teamwork in the United States appears in Parker and Slaughter (1988) and at Nissan UK in Garrahan and Stewart (1992).

[11] The cycles range from 1 to 2 minutes, but the objective of all engineering departments is to reach the cycle times of Toyota which are around 1 minute.

[12] This forced involvement also means that a number of people employed in the company (workers, engineers, but also staff) pretend – under coercion – to feel involved, since they do not believe in the values which underpin their activity.

References and Bibliography

Abo T. (ed.) (1994) Hybrid factory. In *The Japanese Production System in the United States*. Oxford University Press.

Adler P.S. (1993) The new 'learning bureaucracy': New United Motors Manufacturing, Inc. In Staw B. and Cummings L. (eds.), *Research in Organisational Behaviour*. Greenwich CT, JAI Press.

Adler P.S. and Cole, R.E. (1994) Designed for learning: a tale of two auto plants. *Sloan Management Review*, Vol. 34, No, 3, Fall.

Adler P.S., Goldoftas B. and Levine D.I., (1995) *Ergonomics, Employee Involvement and the Toyota Production System: A Case Study of NUMMI's 1993 Model Introduction*. School of Business Administration, University Southern California, May.

Babson S. (ed.) (1995) *Lean Work, Power and Exploitation in the Global Industry*. Detroit MI: Wayne State University Press.

Berggren C. (1993a) Lean production. The end of history?. *Work, Employment and Society*, Vol. 7, No. 2, June.

Berggren C. (1993b) *The Volvo Experience. Alternatives to Lean Production in the Swedish Auto Industry*. London: Macmillan.

Berggren C. (1994) Nummi vs Uddevalla. *Sloan Management Review*, Vol. 34, No. 4, Winter.

Boyer R. and Durand J.-P. (1996) *After Fordism*. London: Macmillan.

Burawoy M. (1979) *Manufacturing Consent. Changes in the Labour Process under Monopoly Capitalism*, Chicago IL: The University of Chicago Press.

Cusamano M.A. (1985) *The Japanese Automobile Industry: Technology and Management at Nissan and Toyota*. Cambridge MA: Harvard University Press.

Durand J.-P. (ed.) (1994) *La fin du modele suedois*. Paris: Syros.

Durand J.-P. and Durand-Sebag J. (1996) The hidden face of the Japanese system. *Japanese Studies*. Melbourne: Monash University.

Durand J.-P. and Stewart P. (1998) Manufacturing dissent? 'Burawoy in a Franco-Japanese workshop'. *Work Employment & Society*, Vol. 12, No. 1, March.

Durand-Sebag J. (1992) *Un siècle de rationalisation taylorienna: sociologie du travail, représentations et subjectivité*. Université de Paris VIII.

Elger T. and Smith C. (1994) *Global Japanisation?* London: Routledge.

Freyssenet M., Mair A., Shimizu K. and Volpato G. (eds.) (1998) *One Best Way? Trajectories and Industrial Models of the World's Automobile Producers*. Oxford University Press.

Garrahan P. and Stewart P. (1992) *The Nissan Enigma. Flexibility at Work in a Local Economy*. London: Mansell.

Jürgens U., Malsch T. and Dohse K. (1993) *Breaking from Taylorism. Changing Forms of Work in the Automobile Industry*. Cambridge University Press.

Kenney M. and Florida R. (1993) *Beyond Mass Production: The Japanese System and its Transfer to the US*. Oxford University Press.

Larson C.E. and LaFasto F.M.J. (1989) *Team Work. What Must Go Right/ What Can Go Wrong*. London: Sage.

Linhart R. and Linhart D. (1985) *La participation des salariés: les termes d'un consensus*. In Bachet D. (ed.), *Décider et agir au travail*. Paris: CESTA.

Mair A. (1993) *Honda's Global–Local Corporation*. London: Macmillan.

Martinez Lucio M. and Stewart P. (1997) The paradox of contemporary labour process theory: the rediscovery of labour and the disappearance of collectivism. *Capital and Class*, No. 62, Summer, 49–77.

Morris J., Munday M. and Wilkinson B. (1993) *Working for the Japanese*. London: The Athlone Press.

Mueller F. (1994) Teams between hierarchy and commitment: change strategies and the 'internal environment'. *Journal of Management Studies*, Vol. 3, No. 3, May.

Murakami T. (1995) Introducing teams working in a motor industry case study from Germany. *Industrial Relations Journal*, Vol. 26, No. 4.

Normann R. (1984) *Service Management. Strategy and Leadership in Service Business*. Chichester (UK), Wiley.

Ohno T. (1989) *L'esprit Toyota*. Paris: Masson.

Oliver N. and Slaughter J. (1992) *Japanisation of British Industry*, 2nd edn. London: Blackwell.

Parker M. and Slaughter J. (1988) *Choosing Sides: Unions and the Team Concept*. A Labour Notes Book. Boston MA, South End Press.

Roth S. (1992) *Japanisation or Going Our Own Way?* Düsseldorf: IG Metall.

Roth S. (1994) IG Metall: computer sur ses propres forces. A propos de la production au plus juste dans l'industrie automobile allemande. In Durand J.-P. (ed.), *Le syndicalisme au futur*. Paris: Syros.

Rubinstein S., Bennet M. and Kochan T.A. (1993) The Saturn partnership: co-management and the reinvention of the local union. In Kaufman B. and Kleiner M. (eds.), *Employee Representation: Alternatives and Future Directions*. Madison NY: Industrial Relations Research Association.

Shimizu K. (1995) Kaïzen et gestion du travail chez Toyota Motor et Toyota Motor Kyushu: un problème dans la trajectoire de Toyota. *Actes du GERPISA*, No. 8. Université d'Evry.

Sturdy A., Knights D. and Willmott H. (eds.) (1992) *Skill and Consent. Contemporary Studies in the Labour Process*. London: Routledge.

Thompson P. and Wallace T. (1995) Teamworking: lean machine or dream machine? *13th International Labour Process Conference*, Blackpool, 5–7 April.

Womack J.P., Jones T.D. and Roos D. (1990) *The Machine that Changed the World*. New York: Rawson.

Wood S. (ed.) (1989) *The Transformation of Work?* London: Unwin Hyman.

SECTION ONE

JAPAN – TOUCHSTONE OF CHANGE?

CHAPTER 1
The Historic Reversal of the Division of Labour? The Second Stage of the Toyota Production System

Hikari Nohara

Overview of current changes in Japanese automotive firms

Since the end of 1980s there have been very distinctive changes at Japanese automotive firms characterised by flatter organisational hierarchies and increased flexibility (functional and temporal). With regard to the remuneration system, it has become much more meritocratic in contrast to the traditional seniority-based wage system, which is now being reconsidered by many firms. In terms of the so-called lifetime employment system, a variety of different contracts have been introduced, and we are increasingly finding different types of temporal employee. In addition, many workers are now being encouraged or forced to change their jobs by the companies. Finally, at the plant level, the situation is being radically reformed with significant changes to organisational culture and practice. In this paper our concern is to focus specifically on these ongoing reforms at shopfloor level.

In Japan the bulge of eighteen year olds has now peaked and the country is on the long road towards an ageing population. As a consequence, Japanese auto firms cannot avoid the problem of a shortage of younger workers and this will hamper company flexibility as regards employment policy for a considerable period into the next century. Moreover, this problem is reinforced by a number of difficulties, notably antipathy shown by young workers for assembly-line work, the high personnel turnover at plants, the assemblers' policy of non-hiring of foreign workers, and foreign pressure to reduce annual working time per worker.

As a consequence of the new social environment in which the industry operates, various kinds of improvements have been introduced in new plants. These include changes to the design of the assembly line, the work environment, working conditions, ergonomics, the nature of the automation process and work organisation generally. All auto firms emphasise automation together with a positive plant environment from an employees's standpoint. However, it is possible to observe differences among the key firms, notably Toyota and Honda, who are what might be described as work oriented (or at least automation-cost-saving oriented) in contrast to Nissan, Mazda and Mitsubishi, who might be described as automation oriented. In addition, only Toyota officially emphasises the reorganisation of work (described below) for the purpose of attracting workers to the assembly line. So far, other firms in the sector have not been especially conscious of this issue. However, even Toyota's managers and supervisors are not always fully aware of this reorganisation, except when it impinges upon the responsibilities of those managers and engineers directly concerned. We can also find a diversity of reforms at every facility, depending upon plant age (for instance, Toyota Kyusyu and Toyota Motomachi are examples of new plants), car class (executive or compact, for example, Mazda Hofu and Honda Suzuka) and whether its production volume is large or small (for example, Toyota Kyusyu and Honda Suzuka).

In the following section we shall focus on the reform of the shopfloor at Toyota's plants, because here experimentation is significantly original and can be contrasted with such work taking place among Western manufacturers. The other important reason for doing so is that Toyota's work reorganisation has been the most systematic and self-conscious in contrast with other Japanese auto firms.

Reforms at some new workplaces – Toyota (Tahara and Kyushu plants); the place of Tahara and Kyusyu in the history of workplace reforms

As a response to the new interest in the social environment, Japanese auto firms have tried to create new production facilities which are seen to respond to the impetus for physically and environmentally friendly manufacturing processes. In Toyota's case, through running the Tahara facility, especially number 4 assembly plant, they reached a new plant concept which then formed the basis for their newest plant at Kyushu. Through the experience at Kyusyu, the new plant concept and its various constituent elements became much more sophisticated and generalised in terms of production systems. Some of these elements were subsequently transferred to the company's older plants, such as Motomachi and Tutumi, as well as to a number of overseas facilities such as Toyota Motor Manufacturing Inc., Kentucky, USA. Tahara number 4 assembly plant makes the luxury class LEXUS, producing around 400 vehicles per day (457 workers per 2 shifts, in October, 1994). Kyushu's assembly plant makes a more popular model, the so-called MARK 2 and CHASER. In total around 600 vehicles per day roll off the line (765 workers per 2 shifts, in September, 1994) (Shimizu, 1995, p. 68). Now let us take a look at the concrete reforms.

Line layout

The layout of the assembly line has changed. In both plants, short and divided main lines, buffers between lines, sub-assemblies, and a speed-adjustable truck on a conveyer have been introduced. At Toyota Kyushu, one main line which is divided into eleven lines each staffed by a group which consists of 15–20 members, has responsibility for all operations within each corresponding line. At Toyota Tahara's number 4 assembly plant, a line is divided into 12 component parts.

Why is Toyota changing the main assembly lines in this manner? There are two reasons for these changes. The first is because Toyota want to highlight problems which have arisen as a result of technical difficulties in production. The second is that Toyota are seeking to develop an employee-centred production monitoring process so that it becomes clear at specific points in production which group is responsible for which operation, including process and product quality. As a result of the mini-parallel lines, production can continue without halting the overall process. Consequently, each group now feels that it can stop the line much more easily than was the case previously because the impact of a stoppage on one of these short lines means they are under less pressure. In effect we are witnessing a *de facto* increase in shopfloor autonomy. In addition, line lengths, including those for sub-assembly lines, have been decreased because in sub-assembly each module is much smaller than a vehicle body, so that the distance between each component on the sub-assembly line can be reduced. Between lines there are a number of buffers. For example, at Toyota Kyushu the buffer amounts to only 3 or 4 vehicles. The idea now is that the correct inventory level is not necessarily the 'zero inventory', the fabled goal of the lean production school. In this regard we have to pay attention to two points. First, even under the traditional Toyota Production System it may well be that the term 'non-stock production system' (Shingo, 1987, p. 530) is not really an accurate way to characterise Toyota's inventory philosophy. They have, of course, aimed to reduce the amount of inventory, but they have not necessarily pursued a non-stock policy *per se*. In practice, Toyota consider the proper inventory level to depend upon the circumstances even if, somewhat paradoxically, the principle of the drive for non-inventory must always lie behind actually existing inventory levels. Taiichi Ohno's category of 'standard inventory (Hyoujyun Temoti)' (Ohno, 1978, pp. 42–44) seems to imply this. Second, once inventory levels have been balanced accordingly, this will allow the practice of Just-in-Time to operate. Tasks on the main line are transferred on to sub-assembly lines whenever possible and, in consequence, the main line becomes shorter, the intention of this being to ensure that hold-ups at one sub-assembly line station will not spread to the line as a whole.

In many cases the sub-assembly process coincides with modularisation, although there are two means by which modules are completed. In the first instance, one group completes a module, while in the second instance assembly operations are distributed over a number of groups. In the case of the latter, each individual's job consists of many fragmented operations from different modules. At Toyota, the former approach is now preferred. On the conveyer, there are speed and height-adjustable trucks which are separated from each other, and the floor of each is wider than a vehicle which is ergonomically preferable for the employees. This truck has several advantages for line operators. Being separated from each other, these assembly operations avoid the impact of line stoppage on other trucks. As a result of operating on a wider floor base, employees are able to work together on a vehicle without actually walking very far, actually less than is conventionally required in other companies' assembly line configurations. This wider floor also allows the vehicle to be placed across a line on the floor such that operations can be carried out on the front and the rear of a vehicle.

Work environment and working conditions

The working environment has become less noisy, cleaner, more colourful and brighter. Until quite recently, Honda notwithstanding, all Japanese auto firms have operated a full night shift system. In this system, for instance, employees might work from eight to five on the day shift during the week, if overtime is not ordered by the supervisors, while the next week work would be from, say, nine in the evening till six the next morning. Although this shift pattern is repeated on a two-week basis, it is very unpopular and it is likely that Toyota will abolish it. Underpinning this change in management thinking is the fact that shift work has been considerably reduced as a result of the recession, and employees are now being encouraged to take their paid leave.

Ergonomic situation

The aim here basically is to reduce and eliminate wherever possible physically difficult, dangerous and dirty work. Let us take a look at a few examples. As noted previously, Toyota have introduced a speed and height-adjustable truck on to the conveyer which facilitates 'easier' work on the vehicle. The second example is that of the automation of heavy assembly work such as tyre, seat or petrol tank assembly. The third example of ergonomic improvement is that of the automation of difficult assembly tasks, such as the assembly of air conditioning units. The fourth one is known as the 'semi-automation of upward assembly tasks' where, for example, a bolt is partially inserted by an operative and then the rest of the task is completed by a machine. Previously an employee would have had to complete the task from a position where his or her posture would have been under stress. A fifth example is that of the device for reducing the distance that an employee has to walk: a small cart is attached to the line, moving in synchrony with it. The final example refers to the tendency to externalise tasks 'Opun Sagyoka' (Shi, 1994, p. 172) on the line. Thus, for example, where an employee has to continually bend to fix internal trim components, the physical stress imposed is relieved where the individual can sit in a small seat that pivots in and out of the vehicle and that moves in time with the line. This is known as the 'comfortable seat' (Rakuraku).

However, not everything has been transformed and priority still needs to be given to many other arduous tasks in the plants. In this regard Toyota have developed what they term the Toyota Verification of Assembly Line (TVAL) process. This is a numerical evaluation system for the assessment of work load (Imayoshi *et al.*, 1993) whereby each job receives a score according to how onerous it is. As a consequence of this, Toyota are able to decide on priorities for job automation. One interesting point to note here is that some managers see this as allowing for increased communication between employees and the manufacturing and systems designers who have to improve the design of job tasks.

The nature of automation

It is not uncommon now to find automation in many difficult areas of employment, but at Toyota this has been achieved in a distinctive way through what the company refers to as 'semi-automation', or the 'coexistence of man and machine'. During the so-called 'bubble economy' (from the end of the 1980s to the beginning of the 1990s) Toyota had extensive financial reserves but their problem arose (and Toyota did not experience this alone) as a result of a shortage of young workers. As a consequence of this, full automation was introduced in several areas at Tahara including those for engine and chassis modules. However, following these experiments, preference has now been given to semi-automation, as can be seen for instance at the Kyusyu plant. There were several reasons why this path was chosen, none of which arose from technical problems. The need to reduce costs was obviously not unimportant – automated facilities are highly expensive – but space is also a significant feature in the evaluation of the efficacy of any technical improvements. Automating the difficult, heavy and ergonomically inefficient tasks allows individuals to retain a degree of control over the delicate or fine operations, which is also a less expensive strategy besides encouraging further elements of employee-centred job redesign. The latter is important as it clearly fits in with Toyota's principle of the 'co-existence of man with the machine', which has as its guiding tradition the watchwords that it is necessary to 'improve operations first, improve equipment second'. Let us take a look at several examples of this. On the shopfloor at Tahara, a heavy instrument panel is carried by a machine approximately to the position where it should be installed, then the worker fixes it at the right position by bolting it on to the vehicle. At Kyusyu, by contrast, an engine and chassis module is assembled by workers with the support of the machine throughout the module assembly process.

Reforms and the balance of power

Who takes the lead in the introduction of such distinctive improvements? Under the pressure of the push towards a new social environment as indicated at the very beginning of this chapter, the top management provides the general direction for management as a whole to ensure that the workplace becomes more attractive for young workers. The middle management and assistant managers (top rank supervisors) have been making concrete plans for improvements, supported by first line supervisors, which are based upon the general orientation for improvements. In this context we can say that it is bottom-up decision-making and the role of the union in the improvement of final decisions that is critical. The place for the deliberation by union and management occurs in the so-called 'joint committee for improvements'. However, all concrete ideas come from middle management and nothing is enforced by the union. Middle management can enforce line stoppages at its discretion and thus we might say that some degree of autonomy is given to employees in this category. In this respect all other aspects regarding the structure of the managerial hierarchy have not been changed.

What changes have been made with regard to the terms of employee involvement? It is too early to make a final judgement on this but the ratio of turnover of new hires has been radically reduced. So far, reforms appear to have gone down well among employees. According to the 'morale survey' conducted by Toyota in 1991, 21.6% of workers felt satisfied at work on assembly line 4, but the percentage rose to 38.3 in 1993. As a result of their more satisfactory circumstances, employees are more involved or integrated into the firm's overall aims.

Among these developments, improvements to the working environment is the most obvious one from an outsider's point of view, which of course is critical in terms of the company's propaganda. Ergonomic improvements are not immediately transparent to outsiders but these are nonetheless the most important for employees, given the tough nature of assembly line work. Moreover, when we take a longer view, the introduction of work reorganisation should be seen as the most important change on the shopfloor. The really interesting aspect of these improvements is that they may lead to the interruption of the Taylorist division between the conception and execution of work in the long term. Furthermore, they may also arrest the increasing development of the division of labour, which has been regarded as the primary principle for the increase of productivity since Adam Smith's *Wealth of Nations*. The implications of all of this for the concept of lean production are obviously very significant, given its supposed origins in Toyota's assembly plants. Now let us take a closer look at the reorganisation of work.

Reorganisation of work – Problems in the traditional Toyota system and the introduction of the concept known as 'autonomous complete process'

Given present technology and cost conditions, the upper limit of automation on assembly work may be between 20% and 30%, with the other 70–80 % of activity depending upon employees' physical exertion. Because of this, the development of 'meaningful' work has to be realised in assembly work itself.

In this regard the main emphasis so far has been on the importance of line balancing so as to overcome the problems inherent in the old Toyota system. Previously, what happened was that work was divided into as many segments as was feasible. Following this, each element of the production process was fragmented as much as conceivably possible, so that each worker's job consisted of just fragments of work where these fragments had no contextual relations with one another. Consequently, and understandably, each worker could not identify with what he or she was doing. In this case it is difficult to remember, improve upon, and concentrate on the job in hand, not to mention the difficulties inherent in developing one's competence. The intention now however is that the innovations in work organisation will change all of this.

With the introduction of the concept of the 'autonomous complete process', the basic ideas are as follows. Firstly, they achieve the sub-assembly of as many parts as possible and then the parts are put together in a module within a group or team. Each unit consists of many single parts, such as a bolt, a gear, a plate, and so on, each of which cannot be further subdivided. Secondly, each piece will now be assembled in a way which makes work contextually more meaningful for each employee.

Figure 1 shows a rear power seat (electrically moving seat) assembly. This assembly process comprises four elemental tasks: (1) assembly of a seat frame; (2) linking a seat to a wire harness; (3) assembly of a seat cushion with a seat frame; and (4) linking a connector to a seat heater. When all these four tasks have been completed, the function of the rear power seat is finalised. The bottom part of Figure 1 illustrates, by comparison, the traditional mode for seat assembly. Here, the upper part highlights the layout of the assembly lines of a rear power seat.

We can now focus on the lower part. In this area the height of a rectangle (from zero to the horizontal line) represents the cycle time. Each complete rectangle identifies each individual's job, and a rectangle with slant lines shows some elemental task that is relevant to rear power seat assembly operations. The left section indicates the traditional mode of assembling seats. Specifically, the slant lines indicating person A refer to the conveyance of parts from storage. The slant lines representing person B refer to his/ her fastening of four bolts and this task is also separated from 1. Thus even the so-called elemental task 1 is divided between two people (A and B). The slant lines representing person C is tied to elemental task 2. Those for persons D or E relate to elemental tasks 3 and 4 respectively. The new assembly process as can be seen in the right-hand side in Figure 1, offers a compelling contrast to the previous process.

Key points regarding the 'autonomous complete process'

In what ways can we say that the new way of assembling is so distinct from the traditional one? This is specifically related to the following key points. Because of the recognition of the functionally meaningful context in which all new tasks must be carried out, an organisational relationship is now established between each person's physically serial tasks. In addition, all relevant tasks are integrated into the same shopfloor area in such a way that the performance of each unit can easily be inspected. It is as a result of this that we are able to argue that the meaningful context of

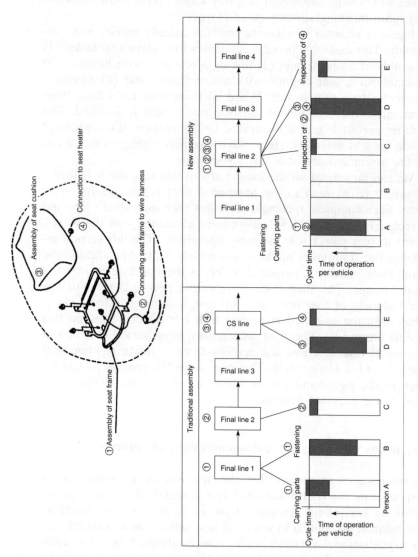

Figure 1 *Assembly of rear power seat.*

both the production and labour processes have been recovered. This recovery of the functionally meaningful context has a special implication. In this recovery, priority is given to a group or a team, but not necessarily to each individual. Of course, although Toyota wish to allow each individual to achieve 'meaningful' work, they argue that to a large degree the fragmentation of tasks is unavoidable in the pursuit of efficiency. While the company may wish to move beyond the group limitations (15–20 people) to the principle of 'meaningful' work for each individual, this is unlikely to come to pass because it would challenge the goal of efficiency and hence productivity. The next question which arises is how Toyota considers that this productivity might be eroded? Unfortunately in this regard it has to be stressed that the criteria remain unclear. However, employee motivation is, according to Toyota, dependent not only upon recognising the contextually specific nature of each job, but also on the obviously crucial issue of one's understanding of the overall operation and function of the vehicle. Toyota understand employee commitment as dependent upon what it refers to as the so-called 'seven tools of motivation'.

The 'seven tools of employee motivation'

These seven tools consist of the interlinking and consequent synergy of the following points of principle. Employees are motivated, according to Toyota when: (1) they develop a broad understanding of each concrete task; (2) they develop an understanding as to how important an individual's fragmented work is in terms of the function of the vehicle; (3) autonomy on the shopfloor increases; (4) they feel that their skill (competence) is developing; (5) to a certain extent, they feel the recovery of contextually meaningful work; (6) operations become less difficult; (7) they feel their work and effort are properly evaluated by supervisors and co-workers. To what extent can it be said that Toyota have pursued this agenda? In terms of tool (6), radical change has occurred. Tools (1) and (2) have been consciously emphasised and systematically introduced into the training programme. As a result of the introduction of shorter divided lines and modularisation, tool (3) has increased. As far as tool (4) is concerned, the new skill training programme 'Gino Yosei Seido' (skill formation programme) has started, although there is insufficient space here to elaborate on it. Nevertheless, this is not the same as job enrichment of monotonous routine assembly line activities but what it does suggest is that workers are becoming increasingly adept at performing a range of simplified tasks. In this regard we can argue that a degree of job enlargement has occurred. The reform of monotonous routine activity is the subject of tool (5). We can argue that tool (5) is taken seriously for the first time in the history of post-war Toyota, because of their power with regard to labour on the shopfloor. In the absence of an autonomous labour movement on the shopfloor, this allows Toyota to effectively develop their own agenda for work organisation and, crucially, labour relations.

The second stage of work standardisation

As a result of the introduction of the concept of the 'autonomous complete process', the new criteria for the development of standardised work are being sought. According to Toyota, thus far line balancing has been seen in terms of its function as a form of waste checking where unnecessary time can be reduced in each task. Yet it is obvious that in each plant this will vary according to history and with little reference to the question of the role of each task in the overall assembly process. In other words, formerly there was no degree of task and line balancing, which could be seen to have made much sense from an employee's overall understanding of the work process.

However, the intention is that this will now change as a result of Toyota's principle of functional contextualisation. Work tasks and activities, it has now been decided, will be sub-classified into two categories: one refers to the vehicle function while the other refers to line sequencing for assembly tasks. As far as vehicle functions are concerned, it is important to note that assembly of the car includes three activities: these comprise trim, upholstery and safety component activities. Altogether 300 basic patterns of assembly are identified and classified, and it is intended that the shift to further standardisation will simplify this assembly process even more.

The really significant impact of this continuing standardisation of performance and function at the point of assembly is that a higher degree of quality can, in theory, be achieved. The other surprising change is that there has been a radical reduction in the amount of on-the-job training because of the impact of making each worker's job more contextually significant. Contextualising jobs has meant that workers can recall much more easily their various activities from the previous day. It has also become much easier for supervisors to understand what their subordinates are doing and thus to decide more rationally where supervision should be focused. As a consequence of this, it is presumed that important and positive developments will occur which can be of benefit to both company and the employees. First, because quality inspection is easier throughout Toyota, all of the work will be more easily understood. Secondly, and associated with this, is the fact that because the intention is that all work throughout Toyota will be standardised, this will allow for the possibility that different manufacturing sites will be able to respond to the same requirement for product and process improvements. In other words, standardisation and quality improvements allow for a particular synergy to develop. It almost goes without saying then that productivity too would benefit from these changes. On the other hand, we have to consider the possibility that this great new approach might pose problems for employees in the future. As we pointed out above, workers will be more integrated into management's goals than is presently the case. However, once they gain experience of this new so-called 'contextually meaningful' workplace, it will be difficult to return to the old forms of work fragmentation where there was little scope for employee initiative and certainly not from the standpoint of organising their own work.

Fordism, the traditional Toyota Production System and the new Toyota Production System: some thematic contrasts

There are many accounts of the Toyota production system which reduce it to single aspects of the production process. Thus, for example, some authors speak of Toyota in terms of the Kanban, Just-in-Time or Kaizen processes, but this misses the point entirely. The Kanban and Just-in-Time systems are just single phases of this wider process, so that they cannot act as descriptions or even synonyms for Toyotaism *per se*. The concept of lean production provides possibly the best (and certainly most influential) example of this misconception. Perhaps it might help if we begin by making sense of the Toyota Production System in terms of what we might call the 'means and aims' nexus (Figure 2). We can see the latter

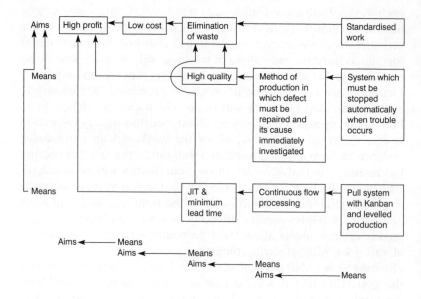

Figure 2   *Overall structure of Toyota Production System: the nexus of means and aims.*

as comprising three elements. The first one refers to work standardisation. The second concerns the scope which employees have for interrupting work when problems occur as a result of either mechanical or human difficulties. The third refers to the pull or Kanban process.

However, there are other significant points of comparison to be made between the Toyota Production System (TPS), the Fordist Production System (FPS) and the new TPS in respect of employee work practices. Let us introduce this by drawing upon the conventional ideal type of FPS – mass production, the hegemonic form of assembly work in the automotive sector in the twentieth century. This is usually understood in terms of an employee experience which is over-determined by monotonous, standardised and simplified work activities. By contrast, although the TPS does comprise the latter, two significant and additional characteristics can be said to distinguish the TPS from the FPS. The TPS also encourages employees to respond individually to fluctuations in production, vehicle mix and line irregularities. The third distinctive feature of the new TPS is that kaizen allows workers to develop task and general knowledge competencies normally provided only to supervisory and maintenance grade staff. The significance of these features is that employees develop competencies to engage in the overall production environment, which in turn provides an impetus for each individual to push for changes on a regular basis.

The important principle therefore concerning the *new* Toyota Production System is that these three dimensions of employee activity remain intact – but with an important proviso. This is that the first element, standardised work, has been changed. This is due to the transformation which, as pointed out previously, allows standardisation to develop in context. Thus, standardised work tasks remain but these cease to act as an impediment to work and task development. Standardisation is a means for ensuring that changes are properly codified, assimilated and made conventional.

Toyota's 'autonomous complete process' and Uddevalla's 'reflective production'

Ironically, what we may be witnessing is the convergence of the Toyota and Uddevalla work processes – the best of both systems brought together to promote the 'autonomous' development of distinctive individual activities in the context of the assembly line. The team at Uddevalla depended upon employees developing an all-round knowledge of the work process but arguably at a lower level of productivity. Reflective production was derived from an assessment of the cognitive basis of human learning and the assembly line was seen to be antithetical to this. However, Toyota have begun to weld together the Uddevalla lessons with their own employee development principles. Specifically, employees will now be able to benefit from the key insight from Sweden which is that process developments and improvements accrue in accordance with one's wider (and deeper) understanding of the overall process. It is true that Toyota does not envisage anything like the end of the assembly line, because this is seen to be the most efficient and practical way to ensure optimum capacity utilisation of human and technical resources. Nonetheless, Toyota's argument is that it is still possible – indeed desirable – to harness the positive aspects of assembly line work to the needs of human beings in the system, and it is to this end that the company are introducing their idea of the so-called 'autonomous complete process'. This is geared to ensuring that employees can gain existing information and knowledge in a context where they will be able to extend this both for their own and the company's benefit. While the technical division of labour in this environment is unlikely to be halted, employees' increasing responsibility for a wider range of tasks will ensure that their knowledge is not detrimentally affected as a consequence. However, while individuals may feel more receptive to this and enjoy some of the benefits of the new TPS, the real improvements are likely to be felt at the level of the team and it is in respect of this difference between group as opposed to individual benefits that the major distinction between the TPS and the Uddevalla system resides.

Conclusion: labour productivity and work systems

The deeper question at the heart of the debate about the efficacy of the new TPS and its relation to other systems of work organisation is that of work humanisation. The assumption is often that there must be a contradiction between the humanisation of work and firm or sector productivity. The central problem however is that while the Uddevalla way can be readily recommended from the standpoint of the humanisation of work, its relative *economic* inefficiencies question its long-term efficacy, especially today as a result of the hegemony of the lean production analysis. In this regard the Uddevalla way has no chance of succeeding. However, the example from Toyota suggests that under the influence of a different hegemonic assembly philosophy, the ideal behind the Uddevalla way is not inherently antithetical to contemporary production values which still retain standardisation, task fragmentation and assembly line technologies.

References

Imayoshi K. *et al.* (1993) *Kumitate sagyo futan no teiryo hyoka ho (TVAL) no kaihatu*. Toyota company document.

Ohno T. (1978) *Toyota seisan housiki.* Tokyo: Daiyamondo sya.

Shi S. (1994) *Toyota seisan hoshiki no aratana tyosen (1).* In Eiji O. (ed.), *Toyota seisan housiki no kenkyu.* Tokyo: Nihon keizai shinbun sya.

Shimizu K. (1995) Humanization of work at Toyota Motor Co. (11). *Okayama Economic Review*, Vol. 27, No. 2.

Shingo S. (1987) *Non sutokku seisan houshiki heno tenkai.* Tokyo: Nihon noritu kyokai.

CHAPTER 2
Nissan: Recent Evolution of Industrial Relations and Work Organisation

Ichiro Saga and Masanori Hanada
(Translated by Mark Teeuwen)

Until the early 1970s, Nissan and Toyota were known as the two great car manufacturers in Japan. Even today, Nissan continues to occupy a prominent position in car manufacturing as the fifth largest producer. However, in the early 1980s, the company gradually lost its competitive edge, and the gap between Nissan and Toyota broadened. Nissan's share of the Japanese internal market dropped to less than 20% (Hanada, 1998). As a major cause for this development, one could point out the fact that industrial relations within Nissan, when compared with Toyota, brought a certain rigidity to company management and work organisation. The management's awareness of this fact, and a sense of crisis among the workforce, finally led to the expulsion of the company's union leaders in 1986. Since then, industrial relations at the company, the mechanism for deciding wages and the organisation of labour have all been subjected to reform. This chapter will examine the characteristics of wage labour relations at Nissan in the light of these historical developments.

The first main section of this chapter will look at the characteristics of industrial relations at Nissan, as they emerged through this historical process. This is necessary in order to identify the social factors that have placed restrictions on the organisation of work within the company. In the second main section, we will examine the mode of labour on the shopfloor from the viewpoint of layered organisation, team work, time management and involvement of the workers. In the final main section, we will conduct a short case study of the Nissan inspection office.

The formation and characteristics of industrial relations at Nissan

During the period immediately after the Second World War, the labour movement conducted integrated struggles straddling whole branches of industry, while at the same time being based on unions that were organised on company level. As the heated labour disputes that spread throughout the nation in the late 1940s and early 1950s ended in defeat, such integrated struggles declined, and the labour movement came to be the domain of unions that were specific to and integrated into single companies. The events of this period were of decisive importance to the history of the post-war Japanese labour movement. Car manufacturing was no exception, and in the history of industrial relations at Nissan, these events form the starting point for developments after the war. One can roughly divide the post-war history of industrial relations at Nissan into three periods, separated by the emergence of the Nissan union, occasioned by the defeat in the so-called 'Great Nissan Dispute' of 1953, and by the collapse in 1986 of what was known as the 'Shioji order' within the Nissan union.

Industrial relations under the leadership of a strongly organised left-wing union (from the end of the Second World War in 1945 to the Great Nissan Dispute in 1953)

The Japanese automobile industry of the late 1940s and early 1950s had its own national industrial union, known as the 'All Japan Automobile Industry Labour Union' (hence AJAILU). The union that was active within Nissan was a branch of this national union. The AJAILU placed great weight on integrated industrial conflict, bundling the unions at Nissan, Toyota and Isuzu, and aimed at establishing a horizontal union that crossed company boundaries both in name and reality.

Among the unions of the automobile industry, Nissan's was most markedly left-wing. The Nissan branch of the AJAILU held the right of decision concerning all matters relating to the struggle of 'the masses' on the shopfloor, such as production, labour conditions, wage allowances and overtime. It is fair to state that the Nissan union was practically autonomous on the level of the shopfloor (Kumagai and Saga, 1983).

However, in the early 1950s the AJAILU faced a serious problem. At this time, the post-war recovery of the Japanese industry began to gather steam, and a large number of companies embarked on drastic personnel cuts and rationalisation. Both Nissan and Toyota experienced great labour conflicts at this time. The development and outcome of these conflicts deeply influenced the future development of both of these companies.

At Toyota, a conflict that took place in 1950 ended in defeat for the union. However, the union itself was not destroyed, and under the leadership of the company an order based on 'trust' between labour and management was soon established. At the labour elections of 1954, the faction that advocated co-operation between labour and management won absolute control over the union, thus contributing greatly to the breakdown of the AJAILU. In 1956, a policy stating that section managers (*kacho*) must be non-union members was implemented, and 1962 saw the signing of the 'Declaration of Co-operation between Labour and Management', a document in praise of mutual trust. During this phase of its development, the Toyota union was completely integrated into the company, and a structure was put in place that made it possible to arrive at an efficient management of the company through the active participation of the union.

At Nissan, however, the Great Dispute of 1953 passed through the phases of heated internal strife within the union, disintegration of the union, and the formation of a second, right-wing union (the present Nissan union), before ending in victory for the latter. In this context, it is noteworthy that the Nissan management proved unable to solve this dispute on its own because of its weakening following the dismantling of the *zaibatsu*. The conflict was brought to a conclusion only by the initiative of the second union, which, while being linked to the company, was nevertheless relatively autonomous. Thus, the industrial relations that resulted after the end of the Great Dispute were not, as in the case of Toyota, a system of co-operation under the leadership of the company. Rather, they were the result of concessions made to the union by a company that had proved unable to control its own workforce without it. This led to the development of a two-tier system of union and management.

A two-tier system of company and union industrial relations (from the defeat in the Great Dispute of 1953 to the collapse of the so-called 'Shioji order' within the Nissan union in 1986)

The Nissan union, which had started as the company's second union, co-operated actively with the management in its effort to raise production and pursue rationalisation, but at the same time also intervened in matters that were in fact the domain of the management: promotions, transpositions of essential personnel, overtime work and even management policy. In particular, the union imposed its own logic on the management of personnel, favouring those with a history of involvement in the union and those with high positions in its own ranks – and the management proved willing to make concessions (Yamamoto, 1981). In fact, the company could hardly do otherwise: in this period of expansion and increase in the workforce it was unable to gain a grasp on all company employees. In this way, a powerful union faction took form within Nissan's management system. In the process of the merger with Prince Automobiles in 1966, the union, and in particular its chairman Ichiro Shioji, wielded great power in smoothing the merger and integrating the new employees by breaking the left-wing Prince union and absorbing its members. Again, the company was indebted to its union and to its chairman, Shioji. In this manner, a symbiotic two-tier system came into existence, consisting of the management on the one hand, and on the other a union that was co-operative but at the same time relatively autonomous.

This type of industrial relations is radically different from the Western model, in which the interests of the management and the workforce are balanced against the background of actions by union members. First of all, the Nissan union formed an authoritative block that greatly limited the free expression of opinion by its general members [1]. General members were excluded from the actual running of the union. Secondly, the union intervened in and controlled management functions not through group negotiations, but behind closed doors in the management board room. There were no express rules for the contents or efficacy of union controls, and the provision of information to the general union members was extremely limited.

As a result, the workers at Nissan were not only controlled by the company, as employees, but also by the union, as union members [2]. This control was termed the 'Shioji order'.

*The establishment of industrial relations under the leadership of the
company, and the restructuring of labour organisation (1986 to the
present)*

In the late 1970s, the decline in results at Nissan became obvious,
and the company began to put more pressure on its union. The
necessity to secure consent from the union, co-operative though it
was, in all matters concerning work organisation, personnel, overtime and even management policy was regarded as an impediment
to Nissan's flexibility as a company. In the 1980s, especially, the
fall in competitiveness, symbolised by a rapid drop in market share,
caused the management to feel a sense of crisis. The two-tier system of company and union rendered the company bureaucratic,
caused sectionalism between various sections within the company,
and hampered the development of a flexible system of production
that would be able to react to market trends and diversification of
demand.

Faced with this situation, the company embarked on a media
campaign that branded the union, and in particular its chairman
Shioji, as the root of all its problems, while at the same time setting up a company faction within the union, consisting primarily of
office workers and technical staff. At the union conference of 1986,
the company succeeded in changing the leadership of the union by
pressuring Shioji, who at the time was becoming a big name in the
Japanese labour movement, into retirement. Making good use of
this opportunity, the company radically revised the industrial relations that had been typical of Nissan up to that time. The voice of
the union was greatly muted, and co-operative industrial relations
under the leadership of the company were established. Since 1987,
Nissan has embarked on radical reforms not only of its labour
management, but also of its production, research and development,
and its sales. After it succeeded in overhauling its industrial relations in 1986, Nissan has been engaged in an attempt to construe a
coherent organisational structure that is able to cope with the crisis that the company has been facing (Hanada, 1998).

Nissan's organisational lay-out of labour and labour management

Next, we will examine the organisational lay-out of labour that has
come about as a result of the historical development of industrial
relations described above. In order to discuss wage labour rela-

tions and team work, which form the theme of this book, it will be necessary to consider labour management at Nissan as a whole.

Organisation of the workplace

Staff structure

The organisational structure at Nissan is centralised, layered and pyramidal. The smallest units, called 'teams' (*kumi*), consist of ten to twenty workers. A number of teams form a sub-section (*kakari*), and a number of sub-sections form a section (*ka*). Teams are units of operational organisation, and at the same time function as the basic units for small-scale group activities such as QC and TPM (which will be discussed below). They are places to which workers feel a sense of belonging. Every layer of the organisation has its manager in charge (*cho*): the foreman (*kocho*) leads the team, the sub-section manager (*kakaricho*) the sub-section, and the section manager (*kacho*) the section. This staff structure is basically the same for skilled blue-collar workers and for administrative and technical white-collar workers, with only minor variations in terminology. The staff structure for skilled workers, which has not changed since the war, can be sketched as follows:

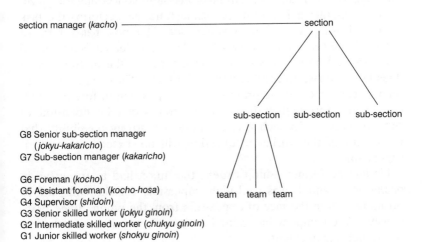

section manager (*kacho*) ——————————————— section

G8 Senior sub-section manager (*jokyu-kakaricho*)
G7 Sub-section manager (*kakaricho*)

sub-section   sub-section   sub-section

G6 Foreman (*kocho*)
G5 Assistant foreman (*kocho-hosa*)
G4 Supervisor (*shidoin*)
G3 Senior skilled worker (*jokyu ginoin*)
G2 Intermediate skilled worker (*chukyu ginoin*)
G1 Junior skilled worker (*shokyu ginoin*)

team   team   team

Of the functions mentioned above, G1 to G4 are performed by general skilled workers; the higher ranks involve work of greater complexity and require expert skills. We will return to this point below, when discussing assessment standards.

Foreman and supervisor

In this layered organisational structure, the foreman and the supervisor [3] play a crucial role. The foreman (G6) is the direct overseer of the team. He is expected to have mastered all the jobs from assistant foreman (G5) down, and it is his task to 'plan and carry out the tasks of production and the rearing of subordinates with good managerial sense'. As a rule, the foreman does not enter the production line. In most cases, the foreman is the face of the management in the workplace, and at the same time performs functions in the union, or has experience of doing so. Thus the foreman has both a managerial role, and the role of representative for the workers in the workplace. During periods in which the union and the company were in conflict, foremen tended to get caught up between these two sides of their position, but now that the union has lost its influence, such dilemmas have ceased to occur.

The official task of the assistant foreman (G5) is to represent the foreman as his proxy, and he functions as an extension of the foreman. The assistant foreman takes decisions concerning the placement of operational staff; at the same time, he performs the task of team leader as the team's supervisor. This post has a term of office of one year, and is renewable. The team leader is appointed from above; the workers do not have a say in the matter, and it does not give rise to conflict within the team. Those with excellent records can expect to be promoted to the position of foreman, but, conversely, foremen with low assessments can be demoted to supervisor (G4). In such a case, there is a strong possibility that the career of the worker in question will not exceed the rank of supervisor.

Under the former 'Shioji order', the union had a strong say in promotions, and it was well-nigh impossible for the company to promote staff in the face of opposition from the union. Since 1986, however, the company has gained exclusive control over matters of personnel management.

Staff ranks and assessment standards

A hierarchical structure such as the above requires the various positions that constitute it to be well defined. Such a structure will not be able to function smoothly unless clear standards are set with regard to promotion, and adequate professional training is guaranteed. Although job classifications in the West are unified throughout entire sectors of industry and are subject to group negotiations, in Japan they are a matter for the management of individual companies. In the case of Nissan, the various ranks are linked with standards for work assessment, which define the contents of the corresponding jobs. Table 1 shows the qualifications required for the jobs of the different ranks of skilled workers (workers who are directly involved in operations).

Two eye-catching characteristics of these job qualifications are the high degree of abstractness of job definitions, and the fact that 'managerial ability' is emphasised more strongly with every step up the ladder. For example, repetitive operations are demanded only of intermediate and junior skilled workers (G2 and G1). Senior skilled workers (G3) are demanded not only to carry out independent tasks, but also to provide guidance to subordinates on a daily basis. In the job description of supervisors (G4), who are general operational workers, we find not only the tasks of senior skilled workers (G3), but also tasks that assist the foreman, such as giving advice to the foreman as the leader of a small group of workers concerning the operational placement and training of these workers. In the case of assistant foremen (G5), it is clearly stated that they must conduct business as the foreman's proxy. The main task of assistant foremen is to assist the foreman in organising operations, training subordinates and offering new ideas.

The foreman concentrates almost exclusively on managerial matters; he enters the production line only in exceptional cases when there is an acute shortage of hands. His functions are making sure that production objectives are achieved, training subordinates, carrying out on-the-job management, and maintaining and raising standards of quality, costs and delivery.

These facts are deeply related to Nissan's approach to skills. 'Skill' is taken not to denote simply the technical ability to carry out certain operations, but rather as the enhancement of the ability to perform certain operations by mastering all the various tasks at a workplace. It refers to the ability to quickly analyse and respond

Table 1

G6 Foreman	(in addition to the functions of G5) Following directions from the division manager (*bucho*), the section manager and the sub-section manager, the foreman: 1. makes sure that production objectives are achieved, and subordinates are given adequate training; 2. conducts business as the sub-section manager's proxy; 3. carries out on-the-job management (*genba kanri*) to those ends; 4. makes arrangements to maintain and raise standards of QCD (quality, costs, and delivery).
H6 Highly specialised skilled worker	Using his broad knowledge and skills concerning automobiles, which are clearly highly distinct from the knowledge and skills of G5, the highly specialised skilled worker assists technical staff, and undertakes initiatives in order to improve the quality of skilled worker automobile prototypes. The highly specialised skilled worker is based in the sub-section or section.
G5 Assistant foreman	(in addition to the functions of G4) The assistant foreman conducts business as the foreman's proxy. In particular, he: 1. makes decisions concerning operational placement, considering the state of production and the training of subordinates, and gives advice to the foreman concerning the training of subordinates and the 'C&J' ('Challenge and *Jissen* [Practice]') programme; 2. in the absence of the foreman, he deals with the business of the team and the sub-section, carries out improvements, and reports to superiors.
G4 Supervisor	(in addition to the functions of G3) The supervisor: 1. gives advice to the foreman as the leader of a small group of workers concerning the operational placement and training of these workers; 2. in case of problems, assesses the extent and the degree of the consequences, analyses the causes, and takes countermeasures.
G3 Senior skilled worker	A senior skilled worker: 1. possesses a sound knowledge of all operations of the team, and while engaging in these operations, provides guidance to subordinates on a daily basis; 2. undertakes initiatives for improvement (*kaizen*) by giving advice to the foreman, or by producing simple tools; 3. promotes activity plans as the leader of a small group.

Table 1 *continued*

G2 Intermediate skilled worker	An intermediate skilled worker is placed under the control of the sub-section intermediate manager and the foreman. He possesses extended knowledge about operational skilled worker procedures, names and kinds of operational objects, and the equipment, machinery and tools used. He carries out relatively complex, repetitive operations.
G1 Junior skilled worker	A junior skilled worker is placed under the control of the sub-section manager and junior foreman. He possesses general knowledge about operational procedures, namely skilled worker procedures of operational objects, and the equipment, machinery and tools used. He carries out general repetitive operations.

to accidents and mishaps, and to take or propose measures to prevent reoccurrence. This development of skills includes not only the ability to carry out multiple tasks, as is often said in the West, but also includes abilities that defy precise technical definition. Moreover, enhancement of skills taken in this sense also includes the ability to co-operate with fellow-workers and the ability to manage subordinates – a fact that must be seen in relation to the practice that skills enhancement takes place at the team level. Thus one could describe skills as something that cannot be viewed separately from the organisational structure of labour, and that is regulated socially in the workplace. The abstract job definitions of the various ranks at Nissan are an eloquent expression of that fact.

The difference between this approach and Taylorism, which has been dominant in car manufacturing in the West, is in the vagueness of the division between planning and execution – a division that is at the root of Taylorism. Workers who are directly involved in labour are responsible for a great amount of managerial work. Moreover, even though individual operations are standardised and detailed, this does not mean that they are the only tasks that workers are asked to carry out. Below, we will look deeper into this matter from the viewpoint of team work.

Team work in the workplace

Flexible job contents

What is indicated in the 'work assessment standards' is in fact not a classification of work, but a classification of people. In other words, these standards lay down the abilities that workers must have in order to function in the various ranks. Therefore, these standards cannot be expected to detail the contents of actual operations. These operations are, after all, changeable, and people move around the company. We will explain this matter in more detail. Although there are differences between workplaces, it is normal practice to rotate operations within teams. Team members may swap operations halfway through the day, or on a day-by-day basis. Thus, although detailed standard instructions are drawn up for each individual operation, it is expected of the workers that they master a fair number of different operations. We must distinguish between the practice of standardising operations in detail, and that of keeping people permanently in these standardised operations. At Nissan, workers are trained on a daily basis to be flexible and to perform a variety of operations. The standardisation of operations and the development of a wide range of skills in workers are combined into one system. After the 1980s, standardisation has been pursued even more strongly, mainly as a way to cut costs. Standardisation of operations means at the same time formalisation of operations. This has become crucial because of the increase of the transfer of labour within the company, which is necessary in order to react to the growing number of car types and to fluctuations in demand and supply. The basis for this kind of skills development lies in the workplace, and in its organisational unit, the team.

Flexibility of internal transfers

The standardisation of operations and the development of a wide range of skills in workers are conditions for the realisation of flexibility in production. If one is to deal with fluctuations in demand and supply by keeping stocks at a minimum level, production capacity has to be variable. It is to that end that workers are moved around the company at frequent intervals. The most common practice is short-term transfer of workers, mostly within the same section, under the title of 'assistance' (*oen*). The period of time for such a transfer ranges from several hours to a month. Often, transfers for 'assistance' are occasioned both by fluctuations in the volume of production within the section, and by reasons of personnel management, such as absence, dispatch of operators for production tests, or leave for occupational training. Fluctuations in the volume of production are dealt with by means of assistance between different sections or factories. This practice is subject to conventions between labour and the management, and is carried out with the understanding that in principle, assistance should lead to the enhancement of the skills of the worker involved. The maximum term for transfers for 'assistance' is two years.

Dispatch to other companies is called 'transfer' (*shukko*). Recently, the most common type of this kind of transfer has been the dispatch of workers from the manufacturing sector to sales outlets. Again, Nissan uses this kind of internal transfer to deal with fluctuations in production volumes: workers are transferred to production units of popular car types, and when faced with a general fall in production, production workers are transferred to the sales sector. Because of the fact that the decline of sales and marketing is seen as an important factor in Nissan's recent loss of competitiveness, transfers to the company's sales sector have been very common. Such transfers offer a way of combining the retainment of employment and the strengthening of sales, and since the latter half of the 1980s, they have affected some 2000 to 3000 workers. In the case of a transfer of this type, the transferred worker is accepted by a new team, and will be integrated into the workplace of which this team is a unit.

As is the case with 'assistance', this second type of internal transfer is generally subject to conventions between labour and management. In the period up to 1986, when the 'Shioji order' was in place, internal transfers were a recurring point on the agenda for the monthly labour–management meetings. The union had a strong say, and the management did not have a free hand in deciding transfers. This was a crucial point of difference between Nissan and Toyota. However, after the change of union leadership, the union lost its power to influence transfers, and it was after this that internal transfers of labour became a flexible and much-used tool for the company.

The raising of productivity and standard time management

Even though flexibility of production at Nissan is attained by improving organisational flexibility, as described above, this does not mean that this is done at the expense of productivity. The strength of Japanese-style production methods lies in the fact that they realise productivity and flexibility at the same time. This does not preclude the laying down of standard operations and standard operation times, as is typical of Taylorism. Rather, it should be understood that if one takes the internal transfer of workers as a premise, the standardisation of individual operations is the very key to the realisation of flexibility at Nissan. It is on the basis of this understanding that standard operations are defined in detail and standard operation times are set. As at Toyota, the stopwatch is very much alive at Nissan.

The fundamental method for time management employed at Nissan is based on the concept of so-called 'work factors'. Rather than measuring the time spent on a task as a whole, each operation is analysed into the detailed basic actions necessary for its accomplishment, and an amount of time is set for each of these actions. Using this method, the time needed for one operation is calculated in promilles. The time calculated in this manner is called the 'net time', and is not identical with the standard time. The standard time is the sum of the net time plus a margin rate:

$$\text{standard time} = \text{net time} \ (1 + \text{margin rate})$$

Thus, if the production facilities remain unchanged, time can be saved on the operational level by reducing either the net time or the margin rate. The net time is a theoretical entity, and a certain margin is necessary when conducting operations in practice. The margin rate comprises two different rates: the fatigue of the operators (the margin rate of operators) and the adjustment of tools (the margin rate of the production line, dependent on production facilities and machinery). The margin rate of operators is not so much the time in which operators can take it easy, as the time operators need for dealing with accidents and problems. Accordingly, this margin rate depends on the type of labour organisation and the social relations between labour and management on the workfloor. Both of these margin rates are the subject of industrial negotiations. During the period in which the union was led by Shioji, margin rates were set at a relatively high level in order to allow union commissioners to engage in union activities during working hours. After 1987, margin rates have come to be set under the leadership of the company, and at those workplaces that we have been able to observe, the margin rate of operators has remained stable at 15%, but the margin rate of the production line has been reduced from 5% in 1984 to 0.5% at present. In reply to the shortage of labour in industry that hit Japan in the late 1980s, the general trend has been to improve labour conditions; Nissan has been no exception to this rule, and this circumstance has set limits to the direct method of saving time through major reduction of the margin rate of operators.

Workers' participation and involvement

Above we have discussed organisational techniques for the enhancement of productivity. At Nissan, as at most Japanese companies, the strengthening of workers' involvement with the company has been emphasised in this respect. In this context, we will now take a closer look at the so-called 'P3 Movement', a movement aiming to improve productivity that was conducted during the 1980s, as well as at developments after that. However, before going into this movement itself, we must give some attention to the type of industrial negotiations at Nissan, as conducted at the all-important Management Board (*keiei kyogikai*). This is necessary in order to gain an understanding of the way in which the P3 Movement has been conducted from above, first, when the union was strong and deeply committed, by the combined forces of the union and the company, and later, after chairman Shioji had left and the influence of the union had been curbed, under the leadership of the company alone.

The Management Board

At Nissan there are two frameworks formally involved with industrial relations: first, 'group negotiations' (*shudan kosho*), where negotiations over wages and related matters are conducted, and second, the 'Management Board', which aims to enhance mutual understanding concerning matters such as production conditions and management problems, and to enable the company to be run in a smooth manner through co-operation. The Management Board has been instituted as a means to deal with possible problems inherent in the hierarchical structure of Nissan's organisation, by bringing together the central, factory and workplace levels of the company. Its fundamental principle is that it provides an opportunity for the management to explain its policies to the union; for the union to give its opinion; and for both to exchange opinions. The Management Board does not offer a framework for negotiations or the signing of agreements. Both its legal status and its status according to the company statute render this impossible. However, under chairman Shioji, the reality of the situation was that without the consent of the union at the Management Board it was impossible for the company to embark on trials unilaterally. Moreover, the contents of the discussions at the Management Board were not limited to matters of welfare and labour environment, but also covered managerial matters such as production planning, personnel problems and management policy. Thus, the Management Board occupied an extremely important position in the industrial relations at Nissan.

The P3 Movement and its failure

In the 1970s Nissan proposed various productivity-enhancing policies, especially for dealing with the problems caused by the first oil shock. As, subsequently, the gap between Nissan and its rival Toyota began to widen, the company announced a plan in 1976 to improve productivity by 30% within three years. This aim was to be achieved by rationalising production without increasing the workforce. In reaction to this, the labour union objected that immoderate rationalisation will lead to a deterioration of work conditions and proposed to embark on a productivity-enhancing movement called the 'P3 Movement'. 'P3' stands for 'Participation, Productivity and Progress'. After the matter was discussed in the Central Management Board, this proposal was accepted, and committees for the conducting of the P3 Movement were set up by both labour and the management. In return for its co-operation in the movement for enhancing productivity, the union gained the authority to regulate work environment and labour conditions on different levels in the company.

What actually occurred in the workplace was the activation and development of so-called QC circles, which had been set up since 1966, and which concentrated on spiritual and motivational matters, as well as the system for the making of suggestions (*teian*) by workers, which had formally been in place since the 1950s. These activities were promoted not only through the organisational mechanisms of the company, but also through the union – which was, at least formally, independent of the company. In other words, they were carried out under the combined pressure of the two organisational pillars of the company. The relation between the union and the company was symbiotic: first, as stated above, the union controlled not only the workplace but extended its influence into matters of personnel management, and second, management policies could be enforced only with the co-operation of the union. Seen from the standpoint of the workers in the workplace, this P3 Movement was a mobilisation movement laid upon them from above, but not least because the union acted as a brake on the intensification of labour, the movement did achieve some results.

However, after the late 1970s the decline in Nissan's competitiveness as compared with Toyota became more and more glaring. The management laid the responsibility for this with the union, and began to try to curb its influence. In the early 1980s, the conflict between the management and the union – or, to put it differently, between company director Ishihara and union chairman Shioji – escalated sharply, and in the years 1981 and 1982 the union resisted by organising repeated production line stops under the pretence of accidents [4]. The union was especially opposed to the company's foreign expansion strategy of the early 1980s, notably the opening of factories in, for example, the United Kingdom, and for a period of time the Management Board ceased to function. In the autumn of 1982, the union decided to halt the P3 Movement. Thus the combined management–labour movement for productivity enhancement came to a stop. At the same time, this also meant the end of the union's intervention in management matters through the Management Board. The intention of the company camp, led by director Ishihara, was to reshape the Management Board from a place for strained discussions, into a place for the mere offering of information. This meant at the same time that the company had to take over the task of improving workers' ambition and morale.

The movement for 'involvement of all workers' under the leadership of the company

In order to improve workers' involvement with their work, the company considered that the union itself had to change. This led to the dramatic downfall of chairman Shioji in 1986. After this, the movement to improve workers' involvement developed into nothing more than a means to raise productivity under the leadership of the company. It was implemented with some force, in combination with other means of labour management. Especially, much attention was given to the reform of the wage system and to the assessment system in place at the company. We will touch upon these points in the following sub-section.

Special attention must be given to the facts that after 1987, every section appointed a sub-section manager responsible for training; that so-called 'T-GK' (Total *Genba Kanri*) was implemented; and that under this system a programme called 'TPM' (Total Productive Maintenance) was started, attendance at which is compulsive for all employees.

T-GK is a system of target management at the level of the workplace, in which employees of the foreman or sub-section manager class draw up detailed management and activities plans for their workplace, and monitor progress against this plan. Targets for quality improvement, cost price reduction and safety are expressed in numbers, and progress towards these targets is monitored on a monthly basis. Under this system, special attention must be given to raising the managerial abilities of foremen and sub-section managers.

The TPM programme conducted under this system is described by the company as a programme to improve company results and produce a workplace that gives workers a sense of purpose, by removing completely any waste of facilities, and by pursuing the limits of efficiency of these facilities. Productive maintenance is a technique for managing technical facilities focusing on maintenance, originally developed in the United States. When it was introduced to Japan, the division between maintenance sections and manufacturing sections was blurred, and productive maintenance took the form of small group activities attended by all employees. Moreover, the activities of the so-called QC circles were continued in parallel with the TPM programme [5]. These QC circles are in principle (though not in practice) informal activities independent of the company management. Their aim is to improve operations with an eye on quality, and at the same time to raise workers' involvement with their work. In contrast, the TPM programme is integrated into the staff ranking system, and aims to raise productivity and improve quality by improving workers' skills in handling the machinery and facilities at the workplace, and by reducing waste of facilities to a minimum. Such a policy is indispensable if one is to continue to raise productivity in a period of slow growth, while at the same time introducing further automation. Thus the raising of workers' ambition and morale is rooted firmly in the company organisation. It takes a concrete form, combined with the development of skills and the improvement of managing work conditions, and it is pursued on the level of the workplace.

For these reasons, a revision of the assessment system and the wage system were indispensable.

The wage system

The basic framework for deciding wages at Nissan was established in the 1950s, and although the wage system experienced some adjustments, the old system was still in place in 1986. The change in the union leadership in this year enabled the company to revise the wage system fundamentally.

First of all, we will point out some characteristics of the mechanism for deciding wages at Nissan. First, wages are set during the industrial group negotiations that take place on a yearly basis in the spring (*shunto*). In car manufacturing, the various companies conduct these negotiations simultaneously, but this does not mean that negotiations or agreements cover the entire industry; wages are invariably set within each separate company. Secondly, negotiations deal with the general wage increase rate only, and do not touch upon wage increases for individual employees. This is because individual wage increases are decided on the basis of performance assessments. In this sense, wages have become increasingly linked to individual ability. Thirdly, wage levels do not necessarily correspond to a worker's job or his classification within the company. This is because, owing to frequent internal transfers (as discussed above), it is not possible to fix wages for individual jobs. Fourthly, wages are based on the premise of long-term employment at the company, and they are expected to allow workers to maintain their living standards throughout their career. This expectation is expressed by the age-linked portion of the wage, which amounts to 25% of the total, by the yearly regular wage rise, and by the family allowance which is based on the number of family members. Finally, wages have a built-in incentive in order to enhance involvement with production and work within the company. Moreover, this is implemented in such a way that it relates to the long term. The age-linked wage system, which is generally regarded as typical of Japan's wage structure, is far from automatic. The differences in wages that result from each individual performance assessment may be small, but when regarded from the perspective of a long-term career, wage differences accumulate to become significant. Moreover, low performance affects the yearly bonus, which amounts to the wages of five months, as well as the allowance paid on retirement, which amounts to the wages of thirty to forty months. Thus workers at Nissan are subject to long-term wage incentives.

The above covers no more than the general principles of the setting of wages. The practical process of deciding wages is, of course, greatly affected by the characteristics of industrial relations at the company.

The meaning of the revision of the wage system in 1987

Until 1986, the deciding of wages was the task of the wage specialists of the union and the management, and individual workers had no access to information about the grounds on which their wages were set. Up to three-quarters of wages consisted of 'special allowances'. These special allowances were based on the company's function assessment system. Of course, as Nissan is a large company employing some fifty thousand workers, wages were not set arbitrarily. However, general workers had no way of knowing the rules that governed the setting of wages (Saga, 1984). The end of the 'Shioji order' within the union brought great changes to this situation.

Under the new wage system, new wage components have been introduced: the 'job wage', which reflects the ranking level of the job carried out by the employee, the 'performance wage', based on the annual assessment of the employee's results, and the 'age wage', supplying living expenses corresponding to the employee's age. Moreover, a 'job assessment system' has been put in place, under which the abilities of individual employees are assessed, and jobs are ranked to different levels. The resulting new wage system is made up of the following components:

1. Collective fixed component 30% 'basic wage', 'qualifications allowance'
2. Job-based component 40% 'job wage', 'performance wage', 'operations allowances'

3. Living expenses component 30% 'age wage', 'family allowance' [6]

The company explains that this new system is in fact a reformulation of norms for the calculation of 'special allowances' laid down in the past by the personnel section, and states that the rates of the various components have not changed significantly (Nissan, 1987).

What now was the objective of this revision? First of all, the new wage system enables wages to reflect ability in a manner that renders it possible to make the organisational structure of labour more flexible. This is expressed most clearly in the 'job-based component' (Kamii, 1994). In fact, this component has been enlarged to 50% in an adjustment of the wage system published in 1994, reducing the collective fixed component, which is based on seniority in the company, to 20%. Wages are increasingly individualised on the basis of ability, reflecting performance in the workplace, and a meritocratic personnel management has become easier to pursue under the new system. This point becomes even more clear when we consider it in relation to the integrated manufacturing and sales system, based on a computer network, which has been developed by Nissan during the early 1990s. The change in work contents, occasioned by the increased automation of local plants such as those in Kyushu and Iwaki, has necessitated a system of setting wages based on ability to execute jobs.

In this context, one may further point out that the life wage curve (the wage profile) has been changed under the new system. When compared with Toyota, the wage curve of the average worker at Nissan was favourable for those in relatively long-term employment, and topped at 55 to 60 years. In the new system, however, reflecting the shortage of young workers in manufacturing, the wage levels for 30 to 35 year-olds have been raised, and the peak has been reduced to 50 to 55 year-olds. The 'basic wage' no longer rises after 55.

Moreover, taking advantage of the revision of the wage system, and reflecting the drop in company results, the company plans to make savings on wages. Allowances for late-night labour and for work on holidays have been reduced, the allowance for those who commute by car has been cut back to petrol bills only, and car-users are charged for using the company parking space.

The problem of the transparency of the wage system

Another important change that has been brought about by the revision of the wage system is the fact that workers have for the first time been given some insight into the mechanisms for deciding wages, which before completely lacked transparency. This change carries two meanings. The first pertains to the industrial relations peculiar to Nissan, and the second to the company's incentive mechanism.

Nissan's employment statute states only that 'wages are set in monthly amounts', and is silent about the factors that govern the setting of wages (All Nissan Motor Workers' Union, 1987). During the period in which the labour union had considerable influence, this meant that the union intervened in the setting of wages (or, at least, was thought to do so) in order to guarantee fairness as against the norms of the union – without informing the union members of any details. If one considers that the union was in a symbiotic relationship with the company, and that it performed an important role in the integration of workers into the company and in labour management, this state of affairs may be regarded as a necessity. However, after the downfall of chairman Shioji, labour management became the exclusive domain of the company management. Under these changed circumstances, it was necessary to clarify the rules of the new system of ability-based wages with an inherent incentive mechanism, in order to convince workers and strengthen their involvement. The clarification of incentive rules and their acceptance by the workers was one of the objectives of the company in reviewing the wage system.

Nevertheless, it is obvious that it would be impossible to make the entire wage system transparent if one considers the flexibility of job contents of individual workers. It would be impractical to draw up an exhaustive list of strict standards for ability assessment, because this would render job contents and their scope inflexible. In other words, one could say that the system of various incentive wages as seen in Taylorist labour organisation is incompatible with flexibility of functions. For example, it should be pointed out that Nissan's job assessment system is not merely an assessment of the past job results of individuals. The company states that this job assessment is an assessment of a worker's spirit of seeking new challenges in order to achieve higher targets and to make full use of his abilities. In short, it assesses not only an individual's past results, but also his latent abilities and possibilities for the future. However, such an assessment is extremely difficult to implement in practice, and it is hard to imagine how it could be carried out on the basis of objective standards.

In other words, the assessment standards do not contain a mechanism that guarantees fairness in the setting of wages; rather, the assessment system can be characterised as a system of mutual assessment. Initially, direct assessments are made by the worker's foreman. Subsequently, these assessments are discussed at the section board of foremen. The results are then scrutinised at a board which includes sub-section managers and section managers. This assessment system was not new in itself; what is new is that on the occasion of the adjustment of the wage system in 1994, the system was explained to employees. It is important to consider the fact that general workers can expect to rise to the positions of foreman or sub-section manager through the internal system of promotions, as well as the fact that with regard to such internal promotions great weight is given to the ability to give guidance to subordinates and to managerial ability in the team. It would seem reasonable to state that there is some guarantee of fairness in the sense that the receiver of a wage can be given new incentives only if he can be convinced of its fairness (Nakanishi and Inaba, 1994).

A case study: the case of the inspection office

An overview of the workplace

The main task of this workplace is the inspection and adjustment of tyres, steering wheels, brakes, driving, exhaust fumes (carbon monoxide) and so forth of finished cars.

The company management has consistently stressed that quality is achieved not by inspection, but by the operations of the production process, and orders for quality checks to be carried out at different stages of the production. In addition to these checks, the inspection office carries out a final inspection and adjustment of finished cars. Although this workplace has been repeatedly reduced and reintegrated, it cannot be abolished altogether. Not only is a final inspection indispensable, it is actually required by law, and is partially carried out in commission of the Ministry of Transportation. At present, employees of this section number about three hundred. There are four sub-section managers and thirteen foremen.

Within this office, the testers team is a small team of some ten members. It comprises one foreman and two supervisors (team leaders). The task of the testers team is to inspect cars on the basis of different set tables of inspection standards, and to record the readings of different meters on inspection cards. Operations are rotated on a daily basis. The operators of the testers team master all operations carried out at their workplace. This is said to take two years, during which a new operation is learned every few months.

Teamwork

All operations carried out at this workplace are done by teamwork. The supervisor decides the daily rotation of jobs. The role of workers within the team is not limited to just the carrying out of operations. They are also assigned tasks which are not directly related to production, such as fire prevention, the switching on and off of lights, and cleaning. The assignment of tasks is decided in consultation by the foreman and the two supervisors. The aims of this practice are to heighten workers' awareness that they are participating in the everyday running of the workplace, and to provide opportunities to raise the job ranks of individual workers.

Interviews we conducted with the members of this team suggest that teamwork is seen as a matter of course. However, it would seem that Nissan has begun to reappreciate the importance of teamwork after its expansion abroad. In other workplaces, workers could be seen wearing a formerly unknown badge reading 'team leader'.

Involvement

In addition to older types of small group activity, such as the QC circles, programmes to stimulate workers' involvement include the sharing of necessary chores, TPM (discussed previously) and C&J ('Challenge and *Jissen* [Practice]').

TPM started at this workplace in 1995. In that year, the team made an effort to win the TPM Award, which is a company competition. Meetings were held outside work time, an hour a month, on the initiative of the supervisors. The themes that the team took up were *kaizen* (improvement of labour conditions and operational procedures) and cleaning, but at the time of our investigation no concrete proposals had as yet been formulated. The supervisors themselves could be heard complaining that 'we don't want to increase the workload'.

C&J was taken up in 1993. The idea behind this programme is that individual workers set their own targets and discuss their progress towards them with the foreman on an annual basis. However, the foreman is always busy, and the regular meetings necessary for C&J tend to be put off for indefinite periods of time. A C&J-type system of target management has been in place for some time for employees at the foreman level, but it has recently been widened to all employees, including general operators.

The system of making 'suggestions' (as discussed previously) used to be quite popular, but has become less so in recent years. This is also true at the inspection office. The reasons are twofold: first, the submitting of suggestions by individuals is no longer enforced as it was before, and more importance has come to be attached to QC proposals; second, it has become difficult to win remuneration for individual suggestions. The company has made its standards for the acceptance of suggestions more strict, and has ceased to display the numbers of target suggestions made.

In general, the workers at the inspection office display a rather passive attitude towards these activities for stimulating involvement. Since the P3 Movement, a wide variety of such activities has been introduced, and it would seem that the latest initiatives in this field have lost their freshness and novelty in the eyes of the workers.

Recent changes in job contents

After 1987, a *Manual of Standard Operations* was drawn up at the inspection office, and operational styles were changed. Before that time, there was only a simple booklet known as the *Instruction Manual*. Workers were expected to grasp the outlines of operations by looking at this manual, and then go on to master them by copying the operational methods of their colleagues. Since the *Manual of Standard Operations* has been drawn up, however, workers carry out operations following fixed procedures, as laid down in the new manual. Operations have been standardised and fixed in this way. Operators regard this change as the loss of the old element of craftsmanship in their work. As reasons for this development, they mention that the standards of inspection machinery have risen, that the quality of finished cars arriving at the inspection office has improved, and that problems have become less common.

At the same time, operators regard these new work conditions as an intensification of labour. Indeed, the operation time of workers ('tact time') has been reduced from two minutes to one minute and thirty seconds, and it is no longer possible to take time off for a cigarette. Moreover, preparations for new operations are done outside work time. Unpaid overtime has increased, and work routinely continues into the midday break or after work time for fifteen or thirty minutes. In view of these conditions, operators have taken to dismissing T-GK (Total *Genba Kanri*) as '*Totemo Genba wa Kurushii*' ('the workplace is sheer hell').

From these observations, we can draw the conclusion that various measures taken by Nissan during the latter half of the 1980s have failed to achieve its aims on the level of the shopfloor. Strategies for countering the fall in competitiveness in the 1980s have been drastic, even if we limit ourselves to the field of wage labour relations; but these strategies have been lacking in coherence and contain contradictions. These contradictions would seem to be due to the following of a policy that has limited itself to shifting the problem to the labour sector, in order to achieve the short-term aim of regaining market share fast.

Conclusion

In this chapter, we have pointed out that labour organisation at Nissan is closely related to the industrial relations peculiar to the company. Moreover, we have made it clear that teamwork, which is the main theme of this volume, is deeply integrated in the organisation of production and labour not only at Nissan but at other Japanese companies as well. In this sense, Japan has progressed along a road different from Taylorism. In the 1970s, methods based on social techniques such as Sweden's 'semi-autonomous groups' have been studied in Japan, but they have not taken root. The main reason for this has been the fact that these methods are incompatible with the economy of scale through production of many types in great volumes, as pursued by Japanese makers. It would appear to be clear that labour organisation at Nissan and other Japanese makers is quite distinct from its Western-European counterpart.

At Nissan, industrial relations peculiar to Nissan functioned in co-ordination with labour organisation at least until the late 1970s, thus rendering company growth possible. However, this system ceased to function in the 1980s. Industrial relations at Nissan, characterised by forceful intervention of a labour union that is co-operative but relatively autonomous, ceased to be the propelling force behind company growth, and developed into a factor that rendered labour organisation inflexible. Faced with this reality, the company set out to reform its industrial relations and to review its wage system and personnel assessment system, and took measures to heighten workers' involvement with the company. The picture emerged of a management that has been liberated from its dependence on the union, and has embarked on a variety of new experiments. Even so, it is as yet far from clear whether these experiments have produced the desired results, and whether they are viable in the long term. It is highly questionable whether the management has been able to arrive at a 'Nissan model' which presents a co-ordinated way of integrating industrial relations, labour organisation and company strategy into one consistent whole. The integration through a manufacturing and sales information network, as actively pursued by Nissan in the 1990s (Hanada, 1998), and the resulting restructuring of labour organisation are still in the early stages.

As a further condition for this 'Nissan system' to be viable (in addition to consistency), one must bring up the question of whether workers at the company will continue to accept the reforms at Nissan in the long term. Not only at Nissan but throughout the country, labour organisation on meritocratic principles is beginning to have an impact as a means to integrate the goodwill of workers in the company. This is what foreign observers have interpreted as a 'spirit of service to the company', or as 'loyalty to the company'. The system of internal promotion, which is founded on the premise of long-term employment and has no reference to the world outside the company (Kurita, 1994), was important during the period of company growth, as a means to share the fruits of that growth. However, in a period in which growth stagnates, or the company actually shrinks, the meritocratic principle becomes a principle for removing workers who fail to fulfil the requirements of the company. This means that incentive mechanisms founded on the active ambitions of workers change into mechanisms enforced by the ambitions of the company.

At present, there is a strong possibility that this is exactly the direction that Nissan's wage system, which assesses individuals' work efforts, and its policy for organising labour and raising productivity, based on this wage system, will take. If that is the case, considering that there is little expectation of renewed growth on the scale experienced in the 1970s, there is no guarantee that workers at Nissan will continue to accept this development. After going through recent reforms, there is increasing pressure on Nissan to ensure the goodwill of its workers, and to present to them the direction that the company will take in the future in a way that carries their consent.

End-notes

[1]   In union elections there were no counter-candidates, and polling scores routinely varied between 98 and 99%. Moreover, activists who were critical of the mainstream of the union were expelled, and it was not unusual for the union to proceed to demand dismissal on the basis of the union agreement.

[2]   At Nissan, as at nearly all large Japanese companies, union membership is obligatory for all employees. With the exception of some in managerial positions, and of the members of a minority left-wing union, all workers are organised in the Nissan union.

[3]   Being a 'supervisor' is a task given to operators, and is not always necessarily a staff rank. At workplaces with a greater number of workers per team, workers with the rank of supervisor (G4) perform the function of leading the team, while the assistant foreman (G5) concentrates on supervision.

[4]   In all but a very few cases, these acts of resistance were carried out on orders from the central office of the union, without consultation of union members, or even sufficient explanation.

[5]   The main activity of QC circles is drawing up concrete suggestions around a set theme and target in small groups. These groups may consist of all workers in one workplace, or larger workplaces may be divided into two or three different groups. However, because there was a tendency for the making of suggestions to be regarded as an aim in itself, leading to a disregard for the practicality of suggestions, Nissan decided to change the remuneration norms for suggestions, and to take only those into consideration that could be proved to be efficient. The same applies for suggestions submitted by indi-

viduals. As a result, the number of suggestions submitted after the 1980s is said to have declined rapidly.

[6] The 'basic wage' (*honkyu*) is set at the time of hiring and subsequently raised on a regular annual basis, taking into account the employee's performance assessment. The 'qualifications allowance' (*shikaku teate*) is said to reflect the employee's rank within the company, independent of his post; but in practice, it appears to be based almost entirely on seniority. The 'job wage' (*shigoto-kyu*) is set on the basis of a table of job ranks with corresponding sums of money. The 'performance wage' (*seiseki-kyu*) is set on the basis of an assessment by the employee's direct superior, and does not accumulate. 'Operations allowances' (*sagyo teate*) include allowances for dangerous work and for night shifts. The 'age wage' (*nenrei-kyu*) is set according to a table which links the employee's age with a fixed sum of money. The 'family allowance' (*kazoku teate*) is based on the number of the employee's dependants. Dependants include wife, children and parents.

References

All Nissan Motor Workers' Union (1987) *Kiyaku, Kitei, Rôdô Kyôyaku* (Settlements and Joint Agreements). Internal document.

Hanada M. (1994) Modalités de la fixation des salaires au Japon et en France: Etude du bulletin de paye de Nissan et Peugeot. *Japon in Extenso*, No. 31, April.

Hanada M (1998) Nissan: restructuring to regain competitiveness. In Freysennet M. *et al.*, *One Best Way? Trajectories and Industrial Models of the World's Automobile Producers*. Oxford University Press.

Kamii Y. (1994) *Rôdô Kumiai no Shokuba Kisei* (The Influence of the Enterprise Union at the Shopfloor Level). Tokyo University Press.

Kumagai T. and Saga I. (1983) *Nissan Sôgi 1953* (Labour Problems at Nissan in 1953). Tokyo: Gogatsusha.

Kurita K. (1994) *Nihon no Rôdô Shakai* (The World of Labour in Japan), Tokyo University Press.

Nakanishi Y. and Inaba S. (1994) *Nissan Jidosha no Kyûyo Meisaisho* (Nissan Bulletin on Wages), Discussion Paper 94-J-10. Faculty of Economics, Tokyo University.

Nissan (1987) *Nissan News*, Section Formation du DRH.

Saga I. (1984) *Kigyo to Rodokumiai: Nissan Roshi Kankei Ron* (The Factory and the Trade Union: A Study of Professional Relations at Nissan), Tokyo: Tabata Shoten.

Yamamoto K. (1981) *Jidôsha Sangyô no Rôshi Kankei* (Industrial Relations in the Automobile Industry). Tokyo University Press.

SECTION TWO

THE AMERICAN RESPONSE – DIFFERENT PATHS, DIFFERENT GOALS?

CHAPTER 3
Saturn: Re-engineering the New Industrial Relations

Guy Cornette

The historical background: Japanese competition

When, in January 1985, the Saturn project was launched, it was done with all the hype and publicity that such a huge venture deserved. Estimated at the time at $5 billion (later to be scaled down to $3.5 billion), it was the largest private enterprise ever started in the United States and probably in the world. In that grey and cold morning of January 1985 in Detroit, when Roger Smith broke the news and announced the launching of the Saturn project, it was supposed to be the ray of sunshine that would warm up the spirits of General Motors, be the promise of a new Spring that would see the giant rise from the ashes.

As a matter of fact the GM situation at the time was extremely preoccupying, as was the situation of the whole automobile industry in the United States. After the two oil shocks of 1973 and 1979, the Japanese invasion – as it came to be described – was a reality. The Japanese car manufacturers had taken hold on American soil: their market share which was non-existent in 1960, had taken off to 6% in 1971 and rocketed up to reach the 23% mark in 1981. Toyota, Nissan, Honda and the rest had managed to corner nearly a quarter of the aggregate American market. Moreover, in the small car segment, they had about half of the market.

The *Voluntary Export Restraints* – disguised quotas – signed in 1981 were supposed to limit the number of Japanese imports on the American market at a level of 1.6 million cars, i.e. around 20% of the market. The figure was raised to 1.8 million units in 1985. If the MITI and the Japanese car manufacturers had ultimately accepted these quotas, they nevertheless found them profoundly unfair in the context of a free-trade economy. The Japanese carmakers were not long before finding a way of by-passing those restraints. Honda was the first manufacturer to build the first transplant in Marysville (Ohio) in 1982, and was soon to be followed by Nissan in Smyrna (Tennessee) in 1983, and Toyota later on in 1988 in Georgetown (Kentucky). The production of these units was not to be counted in the quota figures. This enabled the Japanese manufacturers to import categories of cars other than the small cars assembled in the transplants and thus to successfully attack other more profitable segments of the market (medium sized, luxury and sports-utility vehicles). Other smaller Japanese car manufacturers and one Korean set up plants in North America with a yearly production capacity of 2,270,000 cars by 1990 (Table 1). The fact that all of these plants (with the exception of Japanese–American joint ventures) were non-union also sent a warning signal to the UAW. Union jobs (and fees) were lost in America and were not compensated in quantity or quality by the hirings made in the transplants.

In the mid-1980s, the giants of Detroit were on their knees, not really knowing where the next blow would be. Researchers and analysts had drawn up a bleak picture of the situation. Whatever their comparisons they were never in favour of the US manufacturers. The first comparisons to be conducted were on the cars themselves. In that domain, even if the small Japanese cars were compared with traditional American cars (larger, roomier, more comfortable) the results were largely in favour of the former. The general public was very impressed by the fit and finish, the reliability, the price of the cars and the after-sales service offered by the dealers. Even Detroit car people admitted, though reluctantly, that the Japanese in some fields were as good as and often better than their American counterparts (Table 2), and some writers did not hesitate to write it with enthusiasm and a touch of lyrism:

The Accord looked exquisite even to the most unpractised eye. Its painted surface shimmered like a miniature Rolls-Royce. The minimal chrome brightwork trim fit perfectly; the bodypanels appeared to have been aligned by a surgeon's scalpel. The interior upholstery and vinyl trim had the look and functional elegance normally associated with expensive European cars and executive jet aircraft. The instruments had black, high-tech faces and sharp-edged, sans-serif letters and numerals. The switches and controls worked with the precision of a fine automatic pistol. There was no evidence of old Detroit styling-tricks – phoney

Table 1 *Transplants in North America*

Company	Site	Capacity by 1990	Start-up year	Unionised plant
Diamond Star**	Bloomington, Illinois	240 000	1988	yes
Subaru/Isuzu	Lafayette, Indiana	120 000	1990	no
Honda	Marysville, Ohio	460 000	1982	no
Honda	Allinston, Ontario*	80 000	1988	no
Hyundai	Bromont, Quebec*	120 000	1989	no
Auto Alliance****	Flat Rock, Michigan	260 000	1987	yes
Nissan	Smyrna, Tennessee	240 000	1983	no
NUMMI***	Fremont, California	260 000	1985	yes
Suzuki	Ingersol, Ontario*	200 000	1989	no
Toyota	Cambridge, Ontario*	50 000	1988	no
Toyota	Georgetown, Kentucky	240 000	1988	no
		2 270 000		

* = Canada; ** = Mitsubishi/Chrysler; *** = Toyota/GM; **** = Mazda/Ford.
Source: *Auto in Michigan Newsletter*, May 1988.

Table 2 *US and Japanese passenger car comparisons*

	Higher quality	About same	Lower quality
Fit and finish	1%	14%	85%
Basic structural integrity of body and chassis	42%	45%	13%
Engine and drivetrain integrity and durability	22%	29%	49%
Maintenance requirements	22%	42%	35%
Corrosion resistance	61%	32%	7%
Ride and comfort	58%	34%	8%
Styling	36%	40%	24%
Handling	21%	46%	33%

Survey conducted among 250 managers of the US automobile industry in 1986.
The University of Michigan Transportation Research Institute Research Review, March–April 1987, p. 11.

chrome bezels, fake burled walnut instrument facia, logotypes inspired by resorts on the French Riviera [1].

The cars were understandably the first things people tried to compare but, given the results, they tried to find the reasons for the Japanese success. They compared US factories and Japanese factories, and there again the results they obtained were appalling. The lean system of production as applied by Toyota was a clear winner in comparison with the traditional American fordist system and its variables or adaptations. A survey conducted by James P. Woomack and his team [2] on the performance difference between US and Japanese production sites produced results which came as a shock, not only to American car industry managers who were more or less prepared for it, but also to the general public who could not understand how their country could have fallen so low in comparison with the losers of the Pacific War in 1945. The management of the Big Three had accepted the idea that they had much to learn from the Japanese, but the average American citizen was confronted with the painful experience of admitting that there were fields of excellence where the United States was no longer the number one nation. The company that would dare change such a hierarchy would immediately benefit from general public sympathy and no doubt could capitalise on that feeling to transform offers into sales.

Last but not least, an analysis of the management system, the structure, the organisation and the evolution of American automobile companies and their workers led one to think that, if they did not want to go under, they would have to drastically adapt to the new ballgame. If it was to have any chance of surviving, the American automobile industry would have to get rid of:

- the *blue-collar blues* characterised by a lack of commitment and a lack of attachment to the companies;
- the practically non-existent training given by companies;
- the rigidity and unadaptability of middle management;
- the continual dualism and opposition between white and blue collar workers;
- the priority given to finance people over 'car guys' for promotion to top jobs;
- the short-sightedness of some strategies, exclusively dictated by the omnipresent *bottom-line policy* imposed by Wall Street.

The general picture was very bleak and the future did not look bright at all. One of the main sectors of the economy was in shambles. The morale among people throughout the sector was very low. Nobody knew exactly what to do and the very few who had ideas in confronting the size of the undertaking did not dare express them. The managers were characterised by John McTague, a Ford vice-president, as: 'a bunch of Neanderthals. They were in trouble, they were way behind the technological curve ... these guys were a bunch of losers. The US auto industry was the kind of place you didn't want to be' [3]. Obviously, the house was burning and some-one had to decide to go out and buy a fire tender! The options as to which fire tender to buy were few!

First there was the solution of a massive recourse to automation. Between 1980 and 1985, the Hamtramck plant, for example, became one of the most heavily automated General Motors' plants. As Roger Smith put it: "every time the cost of wages goes up a dollar, one thousand robots begin to look economical" [4]. But the introduction of new technologies is not that easy to implement and many still had the apocalyptic visions of: 'the maniac robots ... whose tasks it was to install windshields, but instead were misdirected by computer command to drop them; the unsupervised paint robots that spray everything in sight except the cars; and the robots that systematically installed body parts on the wrong cars' [5]. The analysis was to be made *ex post* by Bob Stempel, Roger Smith's heir: "we couldn't run it (the Hamtramck plant) because our people didn't understand what we were asking them to do. We literally had to stop the assembly line to get the reading and maths skills up" [6].

The second option was to go into partnerships with the Japanese instead of confronting them head on. NUMMI (New United Motor Manufacturing Inc.), a GM/Toyota joint venture, was created to try and get, without too many risks, quick and easy access to the Japanese methods of management and production systems that were the key to the $2,578 difference in the production cost of a small car in the United States and in Japan. That strategy was used by the two other big manufacturers: Ford with Mazda at Auto Alliance and Chrysler with Mitsubishi at Diamond Star. Though satisfactory at many levels, these alliances were never given their full development potential and remained limited efforts on special projects in a single location.

General Motors reaction: Saturn

General Motors must be credited with the idea of trying a third solution to get significant change under way. The giant of Detroit was the one with the courage to try and invent a new system to design, manufacture and market an all-American car that could successfully compete with the Japanese compacts in terms of quality, reliability and price. Surprisingly enough, the UAW was invited to be a joint partner in the venture, an invitation the union did not refuse, thus starting a new, not to say revolutionary, process in establishing new social relations within the company to serve a very interesting purpose: Saturn Corporation.

Saturn organisation

From what we have seen above, and given the terrible situation of the automobile industry in the early 1980s, the chosen approach was to do something completely new. Though totally different from traditional methods, the view was that it should not imply taking too many risks. The solution was to capitalise on the best industrial practices copied from all sorts of successful companies throughout the world. The now mythical 99 group that had to select the best manufacturing, business and selling practices and to transfer them to Saturn Corporation came up with two basic recommendations as far as the organisation of production was concerned. First, they recommended that the whole system be based upon teamwork and second that the hierarchy should be flattened so as to bring the decision-making down to the level of the team as often as possible. As Skip LeFauve, the President of Saturn Corporation, puts it:

> Saturn is almost without management layers. It's almost concentric circles, starting with the workplace and going from there. The workplace is the focus, and the team that's there to produce the product is supported by all the other people in the organization [7].

The work unit

The basic unit in the Saturn organisation is the *work unit*. It represents a group of 10 to 15 members in charge of a sequence of work. This in itself is not particulary new but the real innovation is that the team is regarded as a small business unit in its own right. The work unit:

- runs its own budget;
- plans its operations and assigns jobs among the members;
- decides on job rotatation and at what rhythm;
- determines the frequency of meetings within the team or with other teams;
- organises holidays, days-off and absenteeism;
- manages the 5% of working time dedicated to training either by enrolling on ready-made programmes or by requiring specific training programmes where necessary;
- recruits new members on the basis of skills but also on the capacity of the applicant to get on well with the existing members;
- manages supplies;
- performs minor maintenance or crisis-interventions;
- controls quality.

The main purpose of the 99 group was to completely redesign the way work was conducted on the shopfloor and the way decisions were made. They came to the conclusion that Saturn would have to put people first if it were to succeed, and the only way to do that was to empower the people in the workshop. The whole organisation is based on that principle.

Above the work unit

If one considers the work unit as the basic unit of the structure, there are four levels in the hierarchical structure. Above the work unit is the Work Unit Module (Figure 1) which groups several work units represented by their elected team leaders. Above the work unit module is the Business Team Unit where the representatives (both management and UAW) of several work unit modules sit (Figure 2). There are three Business Units: Body Systems (stamping, body fabrication, injection moulding, painting), Powertrain (fast foam casting, machining and assembly of engines and transmissions) and Vehicle Systems (vehicle interior, chassis, hardware trim, exterior panels and assembly)

The same system applies to the upper level, the Manufacturing Action Council (Figure 3), where management and UAW representatives of the different Business Unit Teams sit. The Technical

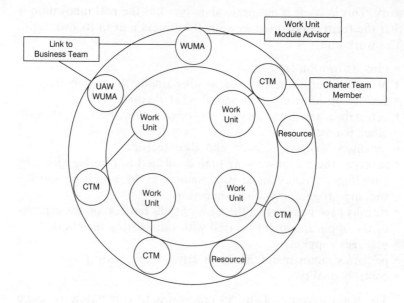

Figure 1   *Work Unit Module.*

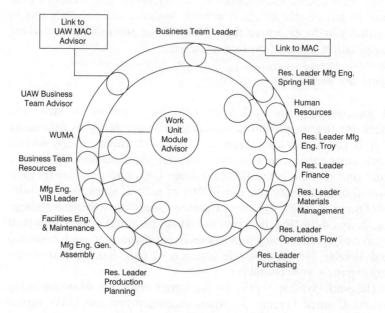

Figure 2   *Business Unit Team.*

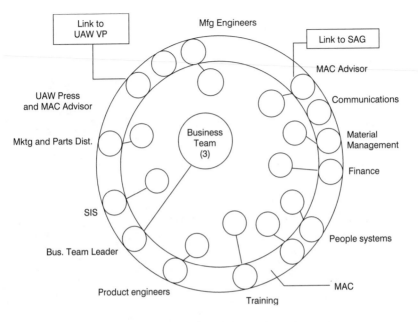

Figure 3 *Manufacturing Action Council.*

Development Action Council and the Customer Action Council are at the same level as the Manufacturing Action Council. The Manufacturing Action Council takes all the decisions with regard to manufacturing for the whole plant, the Technical Development Action Council is in charge of all the technical aspects of the car and the Customer Action Council works on the marketing of the car.

The Manufacturing Action Council, the Technical Development Action Council and the Customer Action Council form the Strategic Action Group in charge of defining the new products of the company and is in fact in charge of guiding Saturn Corporation into the future (Figure 4).

The presence of a UAW representative at each level of the structure clearly shows the desire to implicate employees: it is the guarantee that, at each level, the voice and the advice of the base will be heard and taken into account.

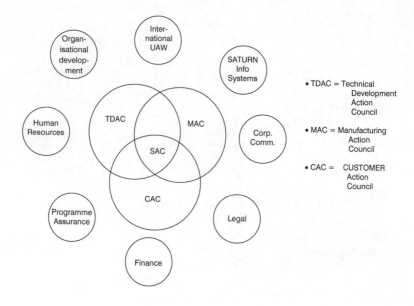

Figure 4   *Strategic Action Group.*

Consensus decision-making

To empower the work unit and the production workers, the principle of *consensus decision-making* has been retained. It stipulates that all key stakeholders in a decision participate in the decision process and are given all the information they need to make up their minds on any particular point. From there a decision is taken if, and only if, it obtains more than 70% of the votes. Those not in favour of the project are given the opportunity to come up with a realistic, workable proposition that can achieve greater support. When a decision is taken, even with only a 70% backing, 100% of the people are expected to commit themselves to implementing the decision.

Of course, this system is part of the every day life at the level of the work unit. If we refer to the above list of the work unit prerogatives, we can see that people can effectively act on decisions that really affect them. The UAW representation in each unit, module, team or council has, thanks to the consensus decision-making process, given the workers a say, for example, in the selection of the advertising agency in charge of the Saturn budget, in the selection and hiring of some executives, in the determination of the salaries of others, and in the selection of the dealers who have the very important mission of selling the product.

Work organisation at Saturn

The organisation of work on the shopfloor, the assignment of tasks, is done by the team, here again on a consensual basis. Depending on the sequence of work performed by the team, the number of people in the team, their skills, strengths and weaknesses, the organisation of work will be different from one team to another. The rotation of jobs and the assignment of non-production tasks can differ but basically will be based on the same idea: the people will organise themselves within their units without reporting to management for approval. The team can also suggest how to redesign its sequence of work and even how to reshape the team itself – to increase or reduce its size. There are examples of teams that suggested ways of doing the same amount of work with fewer people through a reorganisation of production or the use of new tools.

Each time that decisions affect a group of teams, the question is debated and voted along the same lines in the Work Unit Module; if the question affects several work unit modules it goes to the Business Unit Module.

In that context, the role and input of management changes completely. Middle and senior managers become resource people who can be tapped for information and advice. They are but one, as opposed to *the* element in the discussion. Financial and/or production managers, engineers and so on will be called in for their expertise, suggestions and advice on a specific idea which the team might want to implement.

At each level, the UAW representative can make sure his voice and the voice of the workers he represents will be heard. The fact that this union representative is chosen by his fellow workers, rather than being appointed by management, is a form of guarantee that the contribution from the workers will be taken into account.

A new type of industrial relations

The organisation of the Saturn Corporation and the type of structure chosen is a complete departure from traditional organisational types and structures in the automobile industry. The historical context described above called for such drastic changes. The workers accepted them for one basic reason: they realised that the old ways no longer worked and that their survival as workers and the survival of their industry depended on their ability to invent new ways and methods.

The union for itself accepted it because its leaders were tired of losing jobs and members, and hence union dues and representation. Wherever those jobs went, to delocalised or non-union plants, each job lost caused heartbreak for union leaders. Other ways had to be tried if the union wanted to survive to stand for worker rights.

Those unemployed former GM workers, who had been deceived by the traditional system, which had used and then abused them by depriving them of their jobs and their pride, were very sensitive to the philosophy developed for Saturn Corporation by the 99 group:

> We believe that all people want to be involved in the decisions that affect them, care about their jobs, take pride in themselves and in their contributions and want to share in the success of their effort. By creating an atmosphere of mutual trust and respect, recognizing and utilizing individual expertise and knowledge in innovative ways, providing the technologies and education for each individual, we will enjoy a successful relationship and a sense of belonging to an integrated business system capable of achieving our common goals which insures security for our people and success for our business and communities.

Those same unemployed people could not refuse an offer based on *guaranteed jobs for life*, or permanent job security as the UAW puts it. Living on employment benefits, in a region that had been devastated by the slump in an industry that had lost so many jobs and seemed ready to lose even more, the hope of getting back to work, the hope of a meaningful future where plans could be made, where children could be raised, where the best was to come, that hope alone was sufficient to attract them to Spring Hill (Tennessee), the chosen location for the Saturn plant. No one would ever be laid off at Saturn except in case of an 'unforeseen or catastrophic event', and even then the union would have to concur with management before a situation could be called 'catastrophic'.

The fact that Saturn workers would see 20% of their salary pegged to performance objectives, product quality and Saturn profits did not turn applicants away. The basic salary at Saturn would represent 80% of competitive rates at other UAW-represented domestic plants in the automobile industry.

The promise that there would be no 'second-class citizen' at Saturn was, in contrast, an important factor in attracting workers to the plant. The workers would all be called Saturn members and all status symbols, privileges and perks would be abolished. In accordance with this principle, all workers at Saturn, whatever their classification, are paid salaries, a privilege traditionally reserved for management.

The classifications are much fewer than in any traditional automobile plant. There is one basic classification for production (operating technician) and from three to five for basic skilled trades classification.

The UAW and Saturn

As we have seen, the UAW was a key element in the development of the Saturn concept. A majority of the 99 group were from the union. In the early 1980s, the UAW was trying to define a new strategy. After the golden years of the boom period from after the Second World War until the 1970s, when the automobile worker had secured for himself the best salaries and the best fringe benefits of the working class through a strategy of 'we grieve, they grant', a powerful union and dramatic market growth, the slump of the late 1970s demanded drastic changes. From a strategy of opposition, the union was turning to a strategy of co-operation.

This strategy breaks away from the traditional union doctrine and explores new grounds that are different from, if not opposed to, the customs that had prevailed in American union–management relations since the New Deal of the 1930s. The collective bargaining system becomes obsolete from this point of view and gives way to a partnership based on mutual respect and cooperation.

The Japanese example seemed to prove, in a different context and with a different background and environment, that co-operating with management was not necessarily making a pact with the devil and that a form of worker co-operation could be envisaged.

It is clear that the new road chosen by the union and management was paved with good intentions on both sides. If the union had no clear idea or strategy for the future, neither did management. After all sorts of attempts, such as extensive automation, diversification into non-automobile sectors of activity, difficult new marketing techniques and financial gadgetry, management of the Big Three had decided to get back to basics, trying to manufacture good, reliable, affordable cars. To do that, management could not do without the workers, their union or their know-how and experience.

The negotiation and the signing of a specific contract at Saturn was a key element for both parties. It meant a lot for the union: the job-for-life reference, fewer job classifications, teamwork and the consensus decision-making process – all so different from traditional practices – deserved special treatment. For management, the unrestricted involvement of the UAW on co-operative lines was also worth a special contract, particularly as it could help control labour costs and improve productivity.

There were very few critics of the new social relations that were being created in the mid-1980s at Saturn. Some hardliners on both sides could be heard but the general feeling – tainted here and there with some form of scepticism – was that all this was worth a try.

Many things started changing after 1992 with the recovery of the American automobile industry. The job loss was halted, market share was gradually regained from the Japanese automakers and sales went up, as did profits. Top management of both the Big Three and the union did not need more than that to return to their old ways. For GM, Ford and Chrysler it was a strategy based on a bottom-line policy aiming at quick profits to comfort Wall Street (between 1992 and 1994, the Chrysler share went up by 411%, the Ford share by 163% and the GM share by 122%). For the Union it was a confrontation policy, a return to collective negotiation and to more power in national representation and decision-making, as opposed to company or even plant level representation and empowerment.

As every automaker and every plant was starting to rehire on-the-dole workers to meet the new demand, the rules of the game changed. The union was able to demand more, and management was prepared to grant more but basically along the old lines, i.e in terms of wages. Job security, better working conditions and a new organisation of work were not relevant issues on that type of agenda. The recovery provided an opportunity for the union to obtain financial dividends for what it considered had been a decade of unilateral efforts on their part: "contracts were reopened, unpopular decisions were made by our union; our members had to make sacrifices for the consequence of problems not primarily created by them" [8], and of making the automakers pay for their support of NAFTA – the trading agreement which the UAW had opposed.

The situation at Saturn was also influenced by that change. When the time came to increase production and to introduce new platforms and new models in the product line, the question of a second unit (*Saturn Module 2*) led to conflict between the UAW International and the UAW Local 1853. The central union wanted the new module to come under the GM contract and at the time demanded a renegotiation of the Saturn contract along the lines of the wider GM contract. The local union wanted it to be under the Saturn contract terms. Management was indecisive on this issue and needed to maintain good relationships with the national representation and the local representation, but it was also eager to use the production capacity available in other sites which would require less investment.

Michael Bennett, the local UAW representative, firmly supports the Saturn contract and is still backed by a majority of the Saturn members but his margin for manoeuvre is narrow. The 10-hour working day and the compacted week (four working days and three days off) that were part of the deal have turned sour as overtime has changed into five 10-hour working days on rotating shifts which draw on the physical and mental health of the workers, jeopardising their family lives and leisure activities. The adoption of permanent shifts would mean a return to a traditional seniority rule (workers with more seniority get first shot at day shifts, leaving other workers with less desirable shifts) which would be against the *Saturn spirit* of 'no second-class citizen' and difficult to implement as many workers have the same seniority at Saturn. A vote on that point on 3 December 1994 left the UAW International with egg on its face as the result was 3,472 votes to keep things as they were, with 2,310 votes for change. Shift-alternating was kept, so as to spread the burden and benefits of each shift.

It is clear that Saturn is still popular with the people that work there. The image of Saturn in America is very positive, which is hardly surprising considering the reality: employment-for-life

guarantee and the opportunity of getting a job back in the automobile industry after months or years of unemployment. The *1995
UAW Annual Member to Member Report* shows that 73% of the
5,900 Saturn workers interviewed are satisfied or somewhat satisfied with Saturn and the way work is organised there. The main
issues were: benefits (68%), compensation (36%), representation/
decision-making (35%), partnership structure and decision-making
(21%), shift scenarios (18%), attendance programme (14%), running the business (14%), and manpower (12%) [9].

Two sides to the coin

If the general picture of Saturn is rather favourable in terms of
marketing results (consumer satisfaction indexes, sales, image of
the company), and if it has interesting features in terms of industrial relations (job-for-life, teamwork, union involvement), it also
has some bleak spots and over the years the bright colours have
given way to darker tones and blurred images.

The Saturn contract is a typical local contract which the International Union feels is dangerous. First of all, local contract concessions in general have not saved jobs, although they have often
provided the opportunity for GM to pit locals against one another
in a jobs bid – 'whipsawing' – (Norwood, Ohio vs. Van Nuys, California, at the end of the 1980s). In addition, they have allowed for
a reduction of job-classifications so as to impose more flexibility
and tasks on individuals (the basic notion of working smarter and
not harder has turned sour). It has also been the opportunity for
outsourcing cheaper supplies to non-unionised companies. Union
leaders who were against teamwork and labour–management co-
operation in the past have now become more vocal. United and
organised, they have been campaigning under the 'New Directions'
banner. The current President of the UAW, Steve Yokich, has always shown reluctance towards the implementation of such
programmes, and has often expressed extreme reservation about
the Saturn contract.

The notion of co-management has been a recurrent question for
the union. Backing away from a strategy of, 'management plans
and controls, workers execute and union defends workers' rights',
Local 1853 at Saturn has taken up management responsibilities. If
we can consider that being involved in the decision-making pro-

cess does have some positive points, nevertheless many Saturn workers still seem to regret that strategy. First of all, union officials have been obliged to take decisions on issues that basically are drawn up by top management at GM, and/or have to act to please the finance people preoccupied by bottom-line results. In 1992, some union officials at Saturn opposed a strike called by their union colleagues at a stamping plant in Ohio. Moreover, Saturn even at full capacity has been unable to meet the demand from customers. Further sales were lost as a result of the stoppage of production because of a shortage of parts during the dispute, but the astonishing feature of this was that Saturn Local 1853 did not hesitate to demand parts from the striking plant. The Local's leaders argued that workers should be allowed to cross the picket line and go to work for Saturn's parts supplier. Union solidarity suffered a terrible blow in that instance. More dangerous than the blow itself was the feeling that union people could oppose other union people.

The decision to create a larger Saturn has also been a cause of opposition between Local 1853 and the International Union. Local 1853 had long been very vocal in being given the chance to increase the capacity of Saturn to cater for another segment of the market and to accompany loyal customers upmarket. GM has decided to build a larger Saturn (known as 'Innovate') based on an Opel Vectra platform. Local 1853 wants this new model to be assembled in Spring Hill but the International Union has bargained with GM to have it built in a Wilmington (Delaware) plant threatened with closure, in order to retain employment under a GM as opposed to a Saturn style contract. In exchange, GM has been allowed to outsource parts – mainly from Mexico and non-UAW plants. If this type of decision shows a lack of consensus within the UAW, it demonstrates even more that GM's commitment to co-management and joint decision making is somewhat limited. Local 1853 input seems to be welcome for the day-to-day running of the operation, but strategical decisions still rest with GM's Board of Directors and are based on bottom-line financial policies.

Co-management has also led Local 1853 into decisions that can be called into question as far as the well-being and the protection of the workers' interests are concerned. Among them is the approval of 10-hour shifts over 4 days. If it is clear that this is a way of making the most of equipment, we can nevertheless wonder if it does not put too much emotional and physical stress on workers.

The air-conditioning of the plant and the rather good ergonomic working conditions cannot offset the weight of 10 hours' work per day. Moreover, in such a context the only solution for overtime is to add a fifth working day, bringing the working week to 50 hours! Though precise figures are impossible to get on the subject, it seems that workplace injuries are more frequent than in comparable plants and not surprisingly happen at the end of the shift.

The acceptance of teamwork and the organisation around the Work Unit, which is a correlate of union–management 'jointness', has also brought about some problems. Teamwork implied the rotation of tasks among the team members, admittedly a good solution to unite the team, to lessen the work load (some jobs being harder than others), and to prevent boredom and repetition. However, the question arises as to the fate of the injured worker who cannot rotate team tasks and who likewise cannot physically perform every job. Reports [10] tend to prove that disabled workers are being discriminated against, not only by management but also by the union and sometimes by other team members on the basis that they cannot rotate on all the jobs and so are not full members of the team. The company, with the support of the local union, applies a rule that if an individual cannot perform every single team task, then the individual cannot be assigned a position with the team. The consequence is that the disabled worker is placed on disability leave and sees his/her pay drop by 40% after 60 days.

Last but not least, because it is the core of the co-operative system, co-management creates some element of a union elite wherein a lot of power is concentrated in the hands of a few top leaders. These union officials – some are elected, others are not – spend much time working with management at the level of the MAC or SAC on key issues where they lose sight of the rank and file. They forget or ignore the basic preoccupations of the workers and become unable to correctly analyse and address issues regarding members' rights. The union's philosophy at Saturn is not to represent workers but rather 'to balance the needs of the business with the needs of the people'.

Saturn: a transferable model?

When he announced the creation of Saturn Corporation on 8 January 1985, Roger Smith made no secret of the fact that he thought Saturn would be a learning laboratory for GM. He said: "we expect that what we learn at Saturn will spread throughout General Motors, improving the efficiency and the competitiveness of every plant we operate and every product we build". *This idea was formalised in the Saturn's Memorandum of Agreement:* "SATURN MISSION: market vehicles developed and manufactured in the United States that are world leaders in quality, cost, customer satisfaction through the integration of people, technology and business systems and *to transfer knowledge, technology and experience throughout General Motors*".

The verb 'to saturnize' and the noun 'saturnization' have been coined by the U.S media to describe the transformation of a company or a process along the Saturn line. Capitalising on the media coverage given to Saturn and on the success of the car (one of the very best consumer satisfaction indexes, best sales figure per dealership, best dealership-satisfaction index, excellent conquest rate over Japaneses models), the company has created an 'Outside Services'. This service is acting as a consulting and training service for other private companies or public services recruiting along the following lines:

> The learnings from our development of social and technical systems is applicable to your business too. The drive for quality, globalization, learning new ways of doing and being is tough. That's why we can help. We've been there, and we came out winners.

In April 1993, only nine months after the creation of this service, more than 100 companies had followed the training programmes and 400 more applied for the rest of the year. Around 75% of the applications were directed to courses concerning the social system implemented at Saturn and 25% on the new technologies. Clearly, industrial relations as applied at Saturn (teamwork, union implication, consensus decision-making) were the focus of outside interest.

The fact that teamwork and labour–management co-operation are still limited experiences in the automobile industry proves that mentalities and strategies are hard to change. Though 'workers' participation and partnership between workers and management' is the priority from among 15 recommendations recently made by the Dunlop commission on the future of industrial relations in the United States, these are often implemented only when the future of the company is very bleak (that is to say, in the worst possible conditions) and organised by and around very strong and convincing personalities, whether in management or union.

The International UAW is conscious that things change, and people and trade unions have to change. One of the leaders of UAW Local 1853 argued in front of the UAW–GM council at Cincinnati, Ohio, in 1995 that: "what good jobs are left, we have! In order to keep these good jobs, we need to change as individuals and as a Union. UAW Local 1853 wanted to set the example of living up to this mission to exemplify collectively the type of behaviour we need to exhibit in order to accomplish this mission" [11].

It seems that other companies, in addition to General Motors, want to learn from Saturn. Roger Smith and Donald Ephlin are no longer heads of GM and the GM/UAW respectively, and the conditions that ensured their commitment to Saturn have changed too. As such, their successors have no reason to tread the same path. Saturn will probably never be given the opportunity to design, assemble and sell a complete line of cars appealing to different segments of the market. The stagnation within one market would probably fatally damage the company (Saturn) in the long run and undoubtedly eclipse all the experiments that were conducted there: new industrial relations, new work organisation, new production or selling techniques. Following such a failure, the UAW might find sufficient reason to distrust management, and with it, any further co-operation.

More generally, the UAW's challenge at the dawn of a new millennium is to walk a very thin line: strong and fighting, it might frighten management into delocalisation to countries with lower labour costs (as is the case at the moment with a general movement towards Mexico). On the other hand, if it is too open to new industrial relations and an easy willingness to 'co-manage', it cannot defend its members and will have to accept some arm-wrenching situations in the name of more 'profitability and productivity' – management's mantra in the decade of economic globalisation.

End-notes

[1]   Yates, B., *The Decline and Fall of the American Automobile Industry*. New York: First Vintage Books, 1984, pp. 38–39.

[2]   Womack, J. *et al.*, *The Machine that Changed the World*. Cambridge MA: MIT Press, 1990.

[3]   McWhither, W., Back on the fast track, *Time*, 13 December 1993, p. 43.

[4]   Fisher, A., GM's unlikely revolution, *Fortune*, 19 March 1984, p. 82.

[5]   Keller, M., *Collision*. New York: Doubleday, 1993, p. 170.

[6]   Taylor, A., On the record, *Fortune*, 9 March 1992, p. 60.

[7]   Hamilton, K., Richard LeFauve, the president of Saturn Corporation discusses the process of launching the first Saturn car, *Automotive News*, 6 June 1988, p. E16.

[8]   Frame, P., Yokich: UAW helps, not hinders Big 3 to compete, *Automotive News*, 17 January 1994, p. 20.

[9]   *1995 UAW Member to Member Report*.

[10]   Disposable workers, *The Disability News*, July 1996, p. 2.

[11]   *1995 UAW Member to Member Report*, pp. 1–2.

Bibliography

Altshuler A., Anderson M., Jones D., Roos D. and Womack J. (1986) *The Future Of the Automobile*. Cambridge MA: MIT Press.

Dyer D. (1987) *Changing Alliances*. Boston MA: Harvard Business School Press.

Hammer M. and Champy J. (1993) *Reengineering the Corporation*. London: Nicholas Brealey Publishing.

Iacocca L. (1986) *Iacocca: An Autobiography*, New York: Bantam (paperback edition).

Katz H. (1985) *Shifting Gears*. Cambridge MA: MIT Press.

Keller M. (1993) *Collision*. New York: Currency Doubleday.

Matthews J. (1989) *Age of Democracy, the Politics of Post-Fordism*. Oxford University Press.

Singleton C. (1992) Auto industry jobs in the 1980s: a decade of transition, *Monthly Labour Review*, February.

Sloan P. (1963) *My Years with General Motors*. New York: Doubleday.

Sobel R. (1984) *Car Wars*. New York: Truman Talley Books.

Unterweger P. (1994) The auto parts industry restructures: workers under pressure, *International Metalworkers' Federation Conference*, Madrid, 28 February–2 March 1994.

Unterweger P. (1994) Work organization: Taylorism, lean production and union alternatives, *Notes for International Metalworkers' Federation Seminar*, Bratislava, 21 September 1994.

Womack J. *et al.*, (1990) *The Machine that Changed the World*. Cambridge MA: MIT Press.

Wright P. (1979) *On A Clear Day You Can See General Motors*. New York: Avon.

Yates B. (1984) *The Decline and Fall of the American Automobile Industry*. New York: Vintage.

CHAPTER 4
A Factory which remains Fordist: The Ford Dearborn Assembly Plant

Steve Babson and Jean-Pierre Durand
(with Paul Stewart)

Our primary focus is to produce a world class quality vehicle at a competitive price with a skilled and trained workforce that participates in decisions that affect them and their families and fosters pride in their contributions to the overall success of the organisation (Non-traditional Operating Agreement – Ford Motor Company–UAW, 1995)

The factory analysed here is located in the River Rouge district of Dearborn, Michigan, the historical centre of the Ford Motor Company. The Dearborn Assembly Plant (DAP) is one of the dozen major factories that Ford built in the 1920s at the Rouge complex, which still includes blast furnaces, steel mills and plants building everything from engines, to stampings, to glass. The history, the power and the vertical integration of the Ford Motor Company are omnipresent in this part of Dearborn, a suburb of Detroit.

At the beginning of the 1980s, the assembly plant employed 4,600 hourly workers and 550 salaried managers, engineers, and other 'white collar' employees. Today, the factory only employs 1,800 hourly workers and 200 salaried employees, producing about 150,000 Mustangs per year. The sales position of the Ford Mustang is slowly eroding, as a result of the high cost of insuring it against theft and especially because of the competition from 4 × 4 leisure vehicles.

The factory buildings are very old, with the original two-storey assembly hall dating from 1918. A few workshops still have wooden floors, and the assembly line retains the traditional pits for work underneath the vehicles. Just-in-Time is not the usual practice and large quantities of buffer-stocks and reserve parts clutter the buildings; space is certainly not a problem, since the level of production on this site has diminished. In addition, buffer-stocks beside the assembly line are more voluminous than in most other automobile plants.

The outdated state of the buildings does not prevent the introduction of the most modern type of procedures in certain productive sectors. Newly installed robots predominate in welding operations, and sophisticated automation is used, for example, to position and install engines. On the secondary assembly line for instruments panels, the change from screwing to clipping has halved the number of workers. The installation of instrument panels into the body shells remains manual with the help of a manipulator, but since the cycle time is too long in relation to the normal cycle of 1'30", the assembly of the instrument panels is carried out by two mini teams of two people.

This mixing of technologies creates a certain number of problems. Since there is little integration between production sectors, there is a great deal of handling, in particular in the body shop. The handling techniques and the assembly of certain parts are not always ergonomic; for example, the preparation of back axles takes place on machinery dating from 1932. As in a number of factories, the conveyor carries only the car bodies and the workers must perform their tasks as they walk. Finally, the conveyors are noisy, producing a heavy background noise which workers counter by wearing individual radio headphones.

In these characteristic surroundings of the old US automobile industry, Ford management has tried, from the beginning of the 1980s, to transform work in order to increase its productivity. As we shall see, in spite of fairly sophisticated control systems and operational methods, this attempt produced only modest results at DAP. More far-reaching transformations in work organisation were agreed to only in 1995 with the negotiation of a new collective bargaining agreement between Ford's Dearborn management and UAW Local 600. Since the team-based production system mandated by this new agreement has yet to be fully implemented, it is too early to evaluate its impact on work and workers at the DAP. We can, however, raise questions about the characteristics of this new system and why its implementation has been repeatedly postponed.

The employee involvement programme in DAP

At the time of the automobile crisis of 1979–83, with Ford and especially Chrysler on the verge of bankruptcy, it became clear that the UAW could not ask for wage increases from employers who were losing money. The employers, in turn, insisted that there was an urgent need to improve the productivity of the industry in general and workers in particular. While GM expanded its previously negotiated programme for improving the *Quality of Work Life* (QWL), Ford and the UAW set in train, from 1979 onwards, an *Employee Involvement* programme (EI) that would also solicit worker suggestions for improving the production process. The early 1980s were thus marked by a kind of general bargaining process: the union would commit its members to increasing the productivity of work in exchange for job security with the Big Three and some of their unionised suppliers.

Don Ephlin, then Vice-President of the UAW, was the main proponent of this way of thinking inside the union, believing that it was the only way to secure the survival of the US automobile industry and of the UAW itself; hence the acceptance of the GM/Toyota joint venture (NUMMI) and support for the Saturn project (see Chapter 3 and 5). The idea, shared by Don Ephlin and the top management of the Big Three, was to bring about a convergence of the efforts of management and workers by developing communication and trust between the two parties. According to management, it was not a question of working harder or of increasing the pace of work, but of eliminating waste in materials and in people's time. In exchange, while workers accepted smaller wage increases, all but the least senior among them were assured of retaining some form of employment and/or income.

In this difficult situation, the senior management of the Big Three and the international leadership of the UAW [1] were in agreement on the transformation of employee relations in a non-zero-sum game: both parties were to make gains, the former through increasing productivity and quality, the latter through obtaining employment and income protections. But although the top leadership of both parties could reach agreement on the Employee Involvement programme at Ford, the attempt to put it into practice faced considerable opposition in the factories, where long-standing animosities made many workers and lower rank managers wary of the new initiative. When Ford management wanted to bring the latter together to involve them in its new policy, very few volunteered to take up the challenge. Many of them just wanted to wait and see, or indeed were openly hostile to the EI programme.

The Dearborn Assembly Plant's Joint EI Steering Committee was set up in October 1980 to put the programme into practice in the factory. This committee brought together seven representatives of management (including the deputy director of the factory) and six union representatives (including the President and Vice-President of the local union). The Joint Steering Committee co-ordinated the efforts of seven Action Groups, also joint, corresponding to the seven main areas of the factory: body shop, chassis, pre-delivery, trim, paint shop, materials handling, and maintenance. In each of these areas, joint 'facilitators' chosen by management and the union organised quality circle meetings for workers and supervisors to discuss process improvements; participation by workers was voluntary, and their time away from the job was compensated.

The goals assigned to the EI programme at Dearborn Assembly were 'the improvement, on the one hand, of the Quality of Work life, attitudes, working relationships and communications for all employees and, on the other hand, of Product Quality' [2]. The means for improving product quality were as follows:

- Ensuring that all employees understand the basic concept of EI and the fact that EI is a 'way of life' and an active operating principle in DAP.
- Maximising employee participation through development of new avenues for participation: *elimination of apprehension that limits full participation/commitment; provision of greater recognition of employees who are participating*; and *implementation of a schedule that allows for EI meeting during regular working hours.*
- Improving communications between all employees, thus reducing the need for discipline and the need for employees to use subterfuge in their daily working lives.
- Continuing to expand the *EI Newsletter*, closed circuit TV network, and other in-plant means of communications to include plant-wide participation.
- Developing a sense of pride at working in Dearborn Assembly Plant and projecting this pride and the fact that EI is working at DAP to the outside world.

Together, these means of improving product quality and the factory's competitiveness were the local manifestation of the 'Mission, Values and Guiding Principles' which Ford published at the end of 1983 and whose essential elements were the three 'P's – People, Products and Profits. At least in theory, the priority given to people took precedence over the concerns about markets and products. The charter proclaiming Ford's new principles therefore took the following form:

> How we accomplish our mission is as important as the mission itself. Fundamental to success for the Company are these three basic values:
>
> *People*: Our people are the source of our strength. They provide our corporate intelligence and determine our reputation and vitality. Involvement and teamwork are our core human values.
>
> *Products*: Our products are the end result of our efforts and they should be the best in serving customers worldwide. As our products are viewed, so are we viewed.
>
> *Profits*: Profits are the ultimate measure of how efficiently we provide customers with the best products for their needs. Profits are required to survive and grow.

For many UAW members, and particularly for the militant core among them, these managerial initiatives appeared to be a means of controlling them better and enlisting them into the company's goal of maximising profits. Many complained that the entire programme seemed to be a means for undermining collective bargaining: rather than negotiate with the union over working conditions and methods, management could go directly to workers and grant them improvements through EI that they had previously refused to grant in bargaining. The message appeared to be that EI could deliver more tangible results than the union. In order to confront this resistance and to gain the allegiance of UAW members, the Dearborn management explained in its 1988 draft EI program what Employee Involvement is not:

- EI is not a passing fad.
- EI is not a replacement for collective bargaining.
- EI is not a substitute for the grievance procedure.
- EI is not the answer to all the plant problems, although it has great potential for improving employee satisfaction and organisational effectiveness.
- EI may not be the same in all locations or even in different departments at the same location.

- EI is not a productivity gimmick, although increased job satisfaction and employee contributions may result in better products.
- EI does not represent a threat to the union's power or the Company's authority.
- EI is not just for one group – it can benefit employees, the Union, management and customers.

Despite these reassurances, the majority of DAP workers remained sceptical about EI, and the programme suffered accordingly. Initially, there was a modest amount of enthusiasm for a programme that paid workers to sit in conference rooms and discuss problems. Many workers appreciated the fact that their early suggestions for installation of better lighting, more drinking fountains and other improvements produced positive results. But over time, an increasing proportion of suggestions from EI groups was rejected by management, often because of budgetary concerns, but also because some engineers resented the intervention of non-professionals.

Complaints by workers that 'foremen run the groups' became more common. At its peak in the mid-1980s, the EI programme enlisted the voluntary participation of only 25% of the workforce, and participation dropped dramatically after 1987. In general, workers were suspicious of techniques which dispossessed them, without counterpart, of their knowledge and know-how. Many foremen and engineers, on the other hand, saw in the possible increase in workers' autonomy an attack on their prerogatives and the slow disappearance of their socio-organisational functions. Faced with the EI programme and the new role accorded to workers, a number of foremen saw this as the end of their authority, since all were now able to express themselves and make their point of view heard through the appropriate channels.

In fact, many UAW workers and foremen preferred to keep to the traditional relationships, which are well tried and in which each party (the workers, the trade union, the foremen) has a role well known to everyone, which there is no danger of overstepping. But, at the beginning of the 1990s, a new management initiative was introduced to upset the balance of social relationships and work organisation in the factory: this was the arrival of the *team concept*.

The vicissitudes of teamwork in a traditional factory

The idea of radical transformation and modernisation of employee relations derives from at least three sources: the multiplication of Japanese transplants in the United States; publication of the MIT book on 'lean production'; and intensified global competition, which promotes among Big Three managers a crisis mentality and ever more dramatic efforts at self-renewal.

Dearborn Assembly nearly succumbed to this crisis mentality in the early 1980s, when Ford's upper management decided it would discontinue the ageing Mustang model and close the DAP, its oldest assembly plant. But to the surprise of many, the Mustang continued to sell at a healthy pace of roughly 200,000 a year, and closure of DAP was repeatedly postponed. The recession of 1990, however, finally brought matters to a head. As sales dropped sharply, management began to close the plant for periodic inventory adjustments, with twenty-two week-long shutdowns in 1991 alone. At the same time, however, Ford's upper management had decided that the intense loyalty of Mustang buyers, many of them expressing public opposition to Ford's plans to discontinue the model, warranted investment in a new version of the ageing 'muscle' car. Ford authorised $700 million to design and retool a new Mustang, the 'SN95', but management made no commitment to build it at DAP.

In 1991, management announced that unless UAW Local 600 was willing to renegotiate the local collective bargaining agreement for the DAP, the company would move the SN95 to another location. Upper management also made it clear that such an agreement would have to incorporate work teams and other elements of 'lean production'. This kind of management ultimatum was not an unusual tactic in the Big Three. The practice of 'whipsawing', in which UAW Locals are forced to compete against each other for future work by bidding downwards on their local working conditions, had become endemic at General Motors, where falling sales had produced huge amounts of excess capacity and repeated rounds of plant closings. Ford had not overbuilt its capacity in the mid-1980s, as GM had, and so this dynamic was less common in the assembly sector of the number two automotive manufacturer. But after years of living on 'death row', with continual speculation on when – not whether – Ford would close the plant, UAW leaders and members had little reason to believe that management was bluffing. With the threatened plant-closure hanging over them, union leaders signed a 'Modern Operating Concepts' agreement in November 1991, that committed them to team production, job rotation and pay-for-knowledge. The document was barely six pages long, and lacked any enabling language for actually installing such a new work system. But the 'MOC', as it was called, pledged the union to fulfil this preliminary commitment by negotiating the details later. In return, management announced it would commit the $700 million investment in the SN95 to Dearborn Assembly.

As the company began to 'gut' the old plant in 1992 and install the new machinery, bargaining on the actual 'Modern Operating Agreement', or 'MOA', proceeded slowly. Neither party, as it turned out, was in a hurry. The union was understandably apprehensive about a new form of work organisation forced upon it by ultimatum. The local plant managers responsible for bargaining the details of the MOA were also uncomfortable with the prospects of a new work system that promised, according to the MOA, to create what Ford describes as 'natural work groups' with elected team leaders. According to the MOA these 'natural work groups' can: 'foster cooperation, increase work force versatility by affording employees opportunities for job rotation, provide the consensus problem resolution where applicable and appropriate, and contribute to the overall objective of producing a best-in-class quality vehicle. A natural work group will consist of one or more 'teams', each having a team leader elected by team members from a list of candidates who meet mutually agreeable criteria'. (Modern Operating Agreement, 1995)

If EI, even with its voluntary nature and its low participation, was seen by many supervisors and engineers as undermining their authority, then the MOA was all the more of a threat – teams were mandatory for the entire production workforce, and their 'empowerment' would permanently transform supervisory practice in ways that EI's off-line meetings could never match. Upper management had bought into the abstract idea of work teams and had pushed the MOC agenda at Dearborn, but many of the local managers at the bargaining table lacked the same commitment to the new approach, and were uncertain how to proceed.

By the late summer of 1993, it was evident that production of the new Mustang would begin without an MOA and without a significant transformation in work organisation. Bargaining continued, but the pressing demands of actually building the new car absorbed

the energies of managers and workers alike, and the fact that production was being organised around the old collective bargaining
agreement reinforced the inertia and resistance to the 'distractions'
of the MOC. Launching both a new model and a new work
organisation was beyond the capacity, and perhaps the will, of both
the local union and the local management.

The MOA, it was decided, would have to follow the launch of
the new car, but the company's continued commitment to team-
based production was underlined by a large-scale gathering at
Detroit's major convention centre, Cobo Hall, in September – just
one month before the new model began production. The three-day
orientation brought 2,000 hourly and salaried DAP employees into
four giant ballrooms, all linked by sizable telescreens so the audience could hear speakers from the company, the union and the
federal government (including Secretary of Labour – Reich) com-
mend the virtues of team-based production. Workers got a taste of
the promised participatory nature of the new system as they were
divided into groups of ten employees and led through discussion
exercises in which they 'brainstormed' and posted long lists of
workplace problems and the solutions they might implement under
the anticipated MOA.

The next month, production of the new Mustang began with
widespread media coverage of the model's resurrection and the
new lease on life it had won for Dearborn Assembly. Few in the
media were aware, however, of the announcement which followed
several weeks later, indicating that bargaining over the MOA had
been suspended. The two sides had reached an impasse over a
number of issues, including job rotation, pay-for-knowledge and
election of team leaders. Ironically, the union wanted to retain these
features of the MOC, while upper management (as we shall see
below) was no longer so enthusiastic for the principles it had initially proposed. For the next two years, bargaining remained dead-
locked, while the plant worked at full capacity on two ten-hour
shifts a day, with weekend overtime, producing cars under the old
agreement. Whatever enthusiasm had been generated for the MOA
at the Cobo Hall meetings gradually faded until the very term 'MOA'
became a bitter reminder of unkept promises. When the company
and the union finally reached a compromise agreement in late 1995,
it was recast as a 'Non-Traditional Operating Agreement'. Even with
this unassuming title, when the union first conducted a vote among
DAP members on whether to accept its terms, the 'NTOA' was

defeated. In a subsequent vote, a majority narrowly ratified the NTOA, but implementation of its terms was postponed as the DAP struggled with a sudden downturn in sales and frequent shutdowns to clear inventory. When the plant was operating, considerable energy during 1996 was focused on training the workforce for compliance with ISO 9000 standards. As a result, the first two work teams did not begin training until November of 1996, and these two pilot teams were not installed on the shopfloor until early 1997. This tiny beachhead was all there was to show for the six years of bargaining that had followed the initial MOC.

Producing 'new' cars with 'old' work systems

In early 1997, not only did teamwork not exist in the Dearborn Assembly Plant, but multi-skilling was at a low level and job classifications were still narrowly defined. There was virtually no job rotation and, as yet, no training programme to widen workers' skills.

The original MOC of 1991 specified that production workers would be assigned to 'natural work groups' and made no mention of retaining job classifications, implying that (as is the case at NUMMI and other lean production plants) these would be abandoned or dramatically reduced. Under the NTOA – negotiated in 1995 but still not implemented in early 1997 – job classifications will be retained, but in reduced numbers. For example, in the trim department there will be five job classifications under the NTOA: team leader, team technician/repair, team technician/utility, team technician/inspector and team associate. Each production area (body, paint, trim, chassis and quality control) will have the same team structure, with 15 additional classifications plant-wide for such specialised jobs as material handling, motor repair and 'dingers' (skilled metal finishers). While still numerous, job classifications in the NTOA are far less specialised than the older system of job demarcations still in use. Until the NTOA is finally implemented, the new Mustang is being built with a job classification system which, in the trim department, has traditionally included over a dozen narrowly defined specialisations – one for 'Glass Setter', another for 'Headliner', another for 'Trim Panels', and so on, as well as the numerically predominant 'Assembly' positions. Pay rates between these positions vary by only a few cents an hour, but job content and work intensity can be significantly different. Overall, the DAP entered 1997 with 65 production classifications. Within the predominant classifications ('Assembly' in the trim department or 'Metal Finisher' in body) there is a wider task variety and some *ad hoc* movement of personnel, but the number of specialised classifications limits such movement and senior workers strongly oppose it. Many of them have used their seniority rights under the traditional agreement to 'bid' for jobs they prefer or find easier, and some do not look forward to the wider latitude for flexible deployment of labour under the anticipated NTOA.

Currently, few things are negotiable with management or with the engineering department as far as the organisation and content of work are concerned. The latter have been inherited and can barely be modified, especially as the relative size of buffer-stocks allows adjustment to all situations. Nor is there much quality self-regulation by workers. In the mid-1980s, the company did install 'stop buttons' along the line and urged workers to stop production if quality problems needed to be addressed. But, in practice, workers who use the stop buttons feel they are victimised by production-conscious supervisors, and the system is widely regarded as a failure. As recently as June 1995, the UAW Plant President for DAP commented in the union newspaper that the: "Quality Stop-Button Program has been nothing short of a laughable joke, in that most of you [members] are petrified where it concerns pulling the stop cord for quality related defects".

Maintenance is carried out by a department separate from the manufacturing process and gives rise to several confrontations and arguments between production workers and skilled trades. These confrontations arise above all from the fear of skilled workers that many of the tasks for which they are now responsible will be carried out by production workers, a fear based on explicit language in both the 1991 MOC and the still-to-be implemented NTOA that production workers will, indeed, be responsible for 'minor' and 'preventative' maintenance. This intention is quite explicit in the agreement: thus, "The parties have agreed to implement the 'team concept' for non-skilled employees utilising an Ability Rate Progression System which recognises broader job knowledge, employee versatility, and expanded job content, including minor maintenance, housekeeping ... seek and repair, 'team concept' process participation, and other similar functions. These matters will be addressed in more detail ... as the parties jointly become more familiar with the expanded job content ... associated with the 'modern operating

concepts'." (MOA, 1995, p. 3). Skilled workers see these encroach-
ments as yet another threat to their traditional craft jurisdictions,
which are already under pressure from new technology and the
growing use of outside contractors to service the machinery. Competition between production workers and skilled trades for the 'low-
end' maintenance work is exacerbated by the fact that, unlike other
UAW locals which include skilled and production workers under
the same collective bargaining agreement, at the Rouge, skilled
workers are members of separate units with separate bargaining
agreements – one for the maintenance trades and another for tool
and die workers. This means that at each factory in the Rouge
complex, including DAP, the 'Maintenance Unit' of Local 600 jeal-
ously guards the prerogatives of the trades. In fact, their opposition to the MOA was a contributing factor in slowing negotiations.

For their part, foremen have also resisted negotiation and implementation of the MOA/NTOA. While the latter document promises to 'empower' production workers, foremen feel they already
have little autonomy or power to share. As the NTOA states: "Central
to this 'team approach' is the empowerment of each team and
employee with greater operational responsibility and authority and,
dependent on the situation, the use of directive, participative and
empowered management styles" (NTOA, 19 October 1995). They
have neither budgetary autonomy nor autonomy in the administration of wages, which are contractually fixed. Moreover, the traditional collective bargaining agreement still in effect at the DAP
specifically forbids foremen from doing the work of UAW members; the same contract puts additional limits on their ability to
move people from one task to another or to assign overtime work.
The foreman's main function is to ensure that production takes
place, supervising both the men and the material conditions for
the correct carrying out of the work. Beyond this, much of their
energy is absorbed in continual low-level conflict with the union,
as foremen seek to circumvent contractual limitations on their
unilateral action, and the union files formal grievances protesting
the foreman's violation of the contract.

Working conditions are harder than they were previously (as a
result of reductions in the workforce greater than the reduction in
production) but less hard than in many places where teamwork
exists. The work continues to be repetitive and monotonous, with
little interest, on machinery which is not very practical and is not
ergonomic. The workers accept these conditions not only as a re-

sult of the pressures of unemployment in the area, but primarily because wages in the US automobile industry are well above the average ($19.5 an hour in 1996, plus fringe benefits). The size of the wage is thus the main source of motivation and commitment among the workforce.

This accounts for the institutional importance of the trade union, which is there to protect workers against over-drastic wage cuts [3] and to maintain employment in the unionised plants. It is then possible to understand the safeguarding and determined defence by the workers and their unions of certain principles and institutions, such as multiple classification systems, seniority transfer rights, work standards and grievance procedures. The latter act both as an immediate means of defence for the workers and as tools which justify the existence and power of the trade union in the relationship between workers and their employers.

For example, changing the sequence and 'mix' of various models on the assembly line has a direct impact on work intensity, often increasing it as option-loaded models are added to the sequence and workers are pressured to adjust their efforts upwards; consequently, the collective bargaining agreement has carried over from 1949 to today regulations governing 'Adverse Model Mix' that obligate management to slow the line or increase manning when the model mix shifts. Even when these provisions are routinely ignored by management, they still protect workers who passively resist the upward ratcheting of the work pace. Union committeemen will sometimes tell their members to continue working at a 'normal' pace, leaving some portion of their work unfinished as it moves down the line. If management attempts to discipline these workers, the union has the contractual right to file a grievance on their behalf and take it to a neutral 'umpire' (mutually agreed to by management and the union) who referees unresolved disputes. Though these arbitrators vary in their interpretation of the collective bargaining agreement, most would find that the contract's explicit 'Adverse Model Mix' language puts the onus on the managers who failed to abide by its stipulations, not the workers who continued at a normal pace. Consequently, rather than entangle themselves in this quasi-legal wrangling, managers will instead try to bluff unwary workers and invoke 'emergency' measures, or cut a deal with union representatives by making concessions in some other area.

In other words, the will of trade unionists to preserve institutionalised mechanisms in the worker/employer relationship is not the product of a commonly denounced archaism, but constitutes a UAW and workers' safeguard against precipitate changes which damage their interests. This vigilance was also highlighted in the correspondence between the UAW and Ford during the negotiations over the NTOA. While in a general sense the radical positions of the UAW have been blunted, this is on the one hand the result of compromises unfavourable to workers (where these institutional mechanisms have disappeared), and on the other the result of the growing use of outsourcing: Big Three management are considerably reducing their in-house activities in favour of suppliers and they give preference to non-unionised companies. However, some local unions actively resist these developments, as is evident in the many recent strikes by GM locals over job losses and under-staffing. In the same way the question of sourcing from unionised suppliers occupied a large part of the UAW/Big Three discussions at the time of the negotiations on the 1996 Agreements, together with the question of maintaining employment.

Towards teamwork in the Dearborn plant?

> We believe that world-class quality and productivity is achievable only with the full and active participation of our workforce. We want to empower our employees where ever possible with greater defined operational responsibility and authority.... We envision the team *not* as 'independent' but rather as highly '*inter*dependent' with other teams and line supervision. We expect the significant increase in quality focused vertical and horizontal communication to drive continuous improvement. (Ford Dearborn Study Group, undated)

Until early 1997, employee relations at the Dearborn Assembly Plant remained somewhat traditional, that is to say Fordist. With the signing of the NTOA in 1995 and its anticipated implementation in 1997, it appears DAP may be taking the final step towards installing work teams. These will not, however, be the same kinds of teams that the MOC originally called for.

With the MOC, both labour and management agreed that team leaders would be elected, though little was said about such details as who would vote, who could be a candidate, how long their term would be, or if they could be removed. As bargaining proceeded, it became evident that management no longer favoured the wide-open selection process implied in the MOC. Eventually, management indicated they wanted to appoint the team leaders, with the union participating in the selection. Union negotiators, however, were determined to retain some form of election, since otherwise the team leader would become – or in any case, would appear to be – a mere assistant to the foreman; indeed, a 'junior' foreman in the eyes of many. A majority of union negotiators believed that membership resentment over such a top-down selection process would jeopardise the anticipated MOA, and (no small consideration for elected leaders) produce a backlash that might thus jeopardise their chances for reelection. Management, on the other hand, were concerned that election would elevate the more popular workers at the expense of the more qualified; they expressed doubts about the relevance of such 'democratic' procedures in a factory context, and probably worried that elected team leaders would behave like stewards.

The final compromise under the NTOA borrowed from both sides of the debate. Team leaders under the NTOA will be elected by their team, but only candidates who are deemed qualified for the position will be allowed to seek it. A joint committee (UAW and management) will evaluate each candidate against a negotiated list of criteria, including previous training, attendance record, seniority and competence in team tasks; points will be assigned according to a scale, and all candidates with more than 70 points can stand for election. The team leader will be completely independent of the union structure, and will be paid a premium of 28 cents an hour (the union wanted 50) for co-ordinating the work of the team, keeping records, scheduling vacation and overtime, troubleshooting problems and filling in for people called away from the line. The NTOA expressly states that the team leader is 'not responsible for employee discipline nor for authorizing hours of pay'. Their term is 18 months, though team leaders can be removed if members petition the Joint Committee and the offending team leader does not respond to coaching – for example, in extreme cases where removal is sought: "If a minimum of 75% of the team members indicate ... that [a problem concerning the team leader] is unresolved, within ten days, the team leader will be reassigned..." (NTOA, 'Team Leader Election/Removal Procedure').

Job rotation and Pay-for-Knowledge were also focal points of disagreement in bargaining for the MOA, and both were dropped in the NTOA. Here again, the union became the more determined champion of the principles contained in the MOC, while management largely reversed field and eventually favoured more conservative positions. This unexpected reversal stemmed from the context in which the two sides bargained. Union leaders had discovered that a sceptical membership could be won over to the necessity of bargaining the MOA, not only because it would save their jobs at Dearborn Assembly, but also because the promised job rotation and the anticipated Pay-for-Knowledge bonus would increase their wages. This was deemed to be an important selling point for securing the necessary ratification vote from the membership. The two were linked because Pay-for-Knowledge was meaningless if there was not a routine system of job rotation that permitted workers to learn new jobs and thereby increase their pay. Upper management had initially favoured this approach at a time (1990–91) when 'flexibility' and 'polyvalency' were taken as absolutes; subsequently, as management learned from experience in a variety of Ford locations, the issue became more problematic. Local plant managers were often sceptical about sustaining quality and productivity when workers continually moved through a variety of jobs, becoming only average in all of them. Furthermore, moving people through the plant would require massive amounts of training, since each movement brought workers to a new team that required training in not just one job, but half a dozen. Pay-for-Knowledge was deemed to be an expensive and ineffective motivator for sustained improvement, since most workers would soon top-out at the highest grade.

Under the NTOA, there will be no Pay-for Knowledge system and only limited job rotation, most of it within the 'team associate' classification that covers direct-labour tasks. The union abandoned its position largely because, with the industry trend moving away from Pay-for-Knowledge, continued defence of this position seemed futile, and because many senior UAW members, as indicated earlier, are less enthusiastic about rotation.

The company, for its part, wanted 'flexibility' in the deployment of labour, but only up to a point. Its primary goal with the NTOA appears to be the reduction of indirect labour, as many tasks previously located in off-line support departments – maintenance, inspection, repair, co-ordination – become the shared responsibility of team members. If the teams function 'as advertised', they may also be able to quickly rectify problems at their source, rather than simply sending defective work down the line; if the teams fail to match these expectations, it will probably come as no surprise to the many sceptics in the plant who saw the 'stop button' programme installed with the same high hopes and the same disappointing results. For these sceptics, many of whom voted against the NTOA, the worst case scenario is that management wants to use the team structure to 'harness' workers more tightly to management's agenda, using teams to foster a form of peer pressure that results in self-induced speed up. Union negotiators have expressed similar fears, and did manage to include some protections against this outcome in the NTOA: for example, retaining procedures for election and recall of team leaders, and specifying that team leaders were not to be used for absentee coverage.

All sides can agree that Dearborn Assembly is now on the verge of uncharted territory as the long anticipated team structure is about to be installed – at the very moment when declining sales are generating new rumours that the ageing plant is once again slated for the dustbin of history.

Conclusion

The Dearborn Assembly Plant is one example of the general situation in US automobile manufacture. Far from the transplants and the joint ventures, a large proportion of US vehicles are constructed in plants which retain significant elements of traditional Fordist practice. Ironically, Dearborn Assembly, Ford's oldest and least 'modern' of plants, has for years retained a reputation for being one of Ford's most profitable: in the 1980s, DAP was building a popular rear-wheel drive car that sustained full utilisation of the factory, using tooling that had long ago been fully depreciated, to assemble components that had long ago been 'de-bugged' for easy assembly. Only the Wixom (Michigan) plant, building the luxury Lincoln automobile, was said to be more profitable. When the recession of 1990 and the gradual shift towards 4 × 4s and trucks finally deflated Mustang sales, the company and the union began the painfully slow process of 'modernising' DAP. The results have been a disappointment for both parties. While they could initially agree on the abstract principles of team-based production, when it came to negotiating the particulars – the 'nitty-gritty', as Americans say of everyday details – they discovered that these matters were far more contentious than anticipated. Six years after the start of negotiations, there was still no team-based production at DAP. In the meantime, the plant has been building the new Mustang with old work methods, and initially doing so with considerable success as sales ballooned. Yet once again, with sales slumping, the future of DAP is in doubt, and so too is its long anticipated team-production system.

It seems safe to conclude that however much the advocates and critics of lean production may argue the merits of new work organisation, it apparently has far less impact on the viability of a plant than the fundamental question of what kind of vehicle the factory is building, for what kind of market, and with what kind of prospects for fully utilising plant capacity.

End-notes

[1]   The international leadership of the Detroit UAW represents auto workers in the United States; the Canadian Auto Workers, once a region of the UAW, broke away from the parent union and became a separate organisation in the 1980s. The UAW has only a single Canadian local, but retains the title 'International'. It is organised internally into separate departments for each of the Big Three companies, and additional departments for industry groups and suppliers.

[2]   *Guidelines and Procedures for Employee Involvement Groups,* Dearborn Assembly Plant, 6 December 1988 (draft). Hereafter references are to the 1995 goals.

[3]   Even though the workers' hourly wages have declined by more than 20% in real terms since the beginning of the 1980s, they remain well above the average. In addition there are fringe benefits, compensation for loss of employment, early retirement in cases of redundancy, and pensions which are much higher than those offered in other sectors.

Bibliography

Ford–UAW (1991) *Modern Operating Agreement.* Dearborn Michigan, November.

Ford–UAW (1985–95) *Correspondence between Ford and the UAW with respect to implementation of the Modern Operating and the Non Traditional Operating Agreement.*

Ford–UAW (1995) *Non Traditional Operating Agreement.* Dearborn Michigan, October.

Guidelines and Procedures for Employee Involvement Groups. Dearborn Assembly Plant, 6 December 1988 (draft).

CHAPTER 5
Teams at NUMMI
Paul S. Adler

Introduction

This paper analyses the team-based organisation of work at one auto plant in order to gain insight into the antecedents and consequences of this increasingly common form of organisation. My investigation is framed by two puzzling findings, one concerning the prevalence of teamwork in the US economy as a whole, and the other concerning its prevalence in the auto industry. Close analysis of the latter will help clarify the former.

To resolve these two puzzles, I analyse the context and content of teamwork at NUMMI, a joint venture of Toyota and GM whose day-to-day operations are under Toyota control. NUMMI has from its inception adopted the Toyota team-based model of work organisation and a broad set of supporting policies and practices. By locating teams in the broader context of NUMMI's employment relationship as a whole, I will highlight some of the NUMMI teams' key features, their promise and limitations, and their wider significance.

Two puzzles

This study is framed by two puzzling findings. The first is the astonishing speed of diffusion of the team form of work organisation in the US economy. A survey of the *Fortune* 1000 largest US firms (Lawler *et al.*, 1995) found that in 1987, 28% of the employees in the sample were in firms that used 'self-managed workteams' for at least some employees; by 1995 that 28% ratio had grown to 68%. In 1978, only 6% of employees were in firms that used such teams for between 20% and 40% of their employees; by 1995 that 6% ratio had grown to 15%. These 1995 levels may seem high, but they are broadly consistent with Osterman's (1994) survey which finds that 32% of manufacturing plants use teams for over 50% of their core workforce (i.e. the largest group of non-managerial employees involved in producing the establishment's main products).

According to standard contingency theory (Cummings, 1982), whether teams are technically appropriate forms of organisation depends primarily on the degree of task interdependence. If this interdependence warrants a team structure, the choice between 'traditional work groups' and more autonomous 'self-regulating work groups' depends on the degree of uncertainty in the core tasks. The dramatic increase documented by Lawler *et al.* (1995) constitutes a puzzle because, while many observers would agree that the overall state of the business and technological environment is becoming less stable and that some new technologies facilitate or demand teamwork, it is difficult to believe that in the US economy as a whole there has been such a substantial, rapid and widespread shift in the level of task uncertainty or interdependence as to warrant such a substantial, rapid and widespread shift toward self-managed work teams.

The second puzzling finding concerns the contrast between the prevalence of teams in US Big Three auto plants and Japanese transplants. MacDuffie and Pil (1998) report that the percentage of workers organised in work teams among the US Big Three auto assembly plants is very low – 6% in 1993. This result is not surprising to contingency theorists. High-volume auto assembly evidences only modest degrees of task interdependence and task uncertainty, so it is hardly surprising that auto assembly plants rely on 'traditional' job designs, where tasks are grouped into functionally independent individual jobs – rather than groups – and are governed by high levels of external control – rather than by internalised employee self-control. There is nevertheless a puzzle here, since Japanese auto transplants have made production teams, albeit in the form of rather traditional work groups, the basis of their organisational model: in the same survey, MacDuffie and Pil find that in 1993 76% of the transplants' workers operated in teams, up from 71% in 1989. The puzzle only deepens when we note that contrary to the trend in the broader economy, the frequency of teams in MacDuffie and Pil's matched sample of Big Three plants had actually fallen to 6% in 1993 from 10% in 1989. (Note, however, that the difference between the two years may not be statistically significant given the sample size and the fact that union hostility to some 'team concept' programmes may make some management respondents hesitate to use the term 'teams' to describe their work organisation.)

The great difference in teamwork design frequencies between Big Three and transplant assembly plants is a puzzle for contingency theory since tasks in Big Three plants and transplants are essentially identical: producing comparable and high volumes of similarly and only modestly differentiated products using similar equipment. Moreover, using a very different work design, the transplants have in general outperformed their Big Three counterparts in both efficiency and quality. In the sample covered by MacDuffie and Pil in 1993, transplant assembly operations averaged 18.2 hours per car vs. 20 in the Big Three, and 56 defects per 100 vehicles vs. 61. Yet even while a broad spectrum of US industry was adopting teamwork, the Big Three made no move toward this higher-performing organisational design, and may have even moved further away from it.

An analysis of teams at one auto assembly plant, the NUMMI facility in Northern California, provides some insight in the advantages and limitations of teams, and can thus help elucidate these two puzzles. My discussion will first identify the contribution of teams to auto assembly production effectiveness; this will then allow us to develop some hypotheses concerning the causes of the adoption of teamwork in other sectors of industry.

A framework for analysis

In order to understand teamwork at NUMMI, this paper uses a heuristic framework developed by the GERPISA 'Employment relations' group (co-ordinated by Jean-Pierre Durand). This framework highlights four key dimensions: the internal organisation of the production team, the production process within which the team operates, the nature of the managerial hierarchy, and the modes of worker involvement (see the Box).

The following section sketches the history of NUMMI. I then characterise NUMMI under each of the framework headings in turn. To put this discussion of NUMMI in context, I compare this plant with the patterns prevailing in (a) Toyota's Japanese plants, (b) American auto plants and (c) American industry in general.

THE EMPLOYMENT RELATION
1. Internal team organisation:
   • division of labour
   • job assignments
   • Team Leader role
2. Production process:
   • work cycles
   • methods and standards
   • quality control
3. Managerial hierarchy:
   • planning authority
   • personnel management
   • leadership process
4. Worker involvement:
   • involvement mechanisms
   • union role
   • employment security
   • wage determination

My characterisation of NUMMI comes primarily from my field research conducted between 1989 and 1994 at NUMMI (various aspects have been reported in Adler, 1993, 1995, 1996; Adler and Cole, 1993, 1994; and Adler *et al.*, 1995). Grønning (1992) provides a valuable source of similarities and differences between NUMMI and Toyota operations in Japan.

To characterise the policies and practices found in the broader spectrum of American industry, I rely on several recent surveys. Starting with the most general, Lawler *et al.* (1995) surveyed *Fortune* 1000 companies in 1987, 1990 and 1993. Osterman (1994) surveyed a national sample of manufacturing and non-manufacturing establishments in 1992. MacDuffie and Pil (1998) have developed an extensive data set on auto assembly plants in 1989 and 1993.

A brief overview of NUMMI

The NUMMI plant opened in 1984. It was created as a joint venture between Toyota Motor Corporation (TMC) and General Motors

(GM). Its mission was to produce small cars for sale by both partners. TMC agreed to invest $100 million, supply the cars' designs, and manage the factory, while GM would provide the building and market half the cars. Each partner was a half-owner of the new company.

The company took over the GM–Fremont plant that had been closed in 1982. Unexcused absenteeism at GM–Fremont had often run over 20%. Quality levels and productivity had been both far below the GM norm, which itself was falling ever further behind the world-class standard then being set in Japan. Labour relations were, in the words of the Bargaining Committee chair, 'war'.

It was politically impossible for the plant to reopen without UAW involvement. So although TMC was initially reluctant to work with the UAW, they agreed to recognise the union and to give priority to rehiring the laid-off workers. The selection process was done jointly by the union and management. Notwithstanding the three full days of selection, interviews and tests, few workers who went through the selection process were rejected. The entire union hierarchy was rehired, and of the 2,200 workers hired by late 1985, over 95% of the assembly workers and 75% of the skilled trades workers were former GM–Fremont employees.

The initial 1985 collective bargaining contract embodied a very different role for the union than in the Big Three plants. The introduction stated that the union and management: 'are committed to building and maintaining the most innovative and harmonious labor–management relation in America'. Some innovative features of the plant's human resource policies, including the commitment to the team concept of production organisation, supported this commitment.

By 1986, with largely the same workforce and comparable equipment, NUMMI had achieved productivity levels almost twice those of GM–Fremont in its best years, 40% better than the average Big Three assembly plant, and very close to its TMC sister plant in Takaoka. It was also producing the highest quality levels in the industry. In 1989, TMC announced that it would invest another $350 million to expand the plant and begin production of pick-up trucks. This led to the hiring of an additional 700 workers – selected from an applicant pool of 9,000 – bringing total employment up to 3,700. By 1995, employment had risen to 4,200.

Through the early 1990s, the plant continued to excel in quality and productivity. In 1995, J.D. Power and Associates ranked the

Prizm the best built car in North America, the Corolla was number two in the small car segment, and the Toyota HiLux was the best compact pick-up truck built in North America.

A number of indices suggest that worker satisfaction and commitment were also high. Researchers who asked NUMMI workers whether they would switch jobs if there were a Big Three plant across the street received responses that were uniformly negative. According to a biannual Team Member survey at the plant, the number of workers who said they were 'satisfied with [their] job and environment' increased progressively from 65% in 1985 to 90% in 1991 and 1993. The absence rate (excluding only scheduled vacations) remained around 3%, compared with an average of nearly 9% at the Big Three plants in that period, and personnel turnover remained under 6%. Participation in the suggestion programme climbed steadily over the period and had remained over 90% since 1991.

The employment relation at NUMMI

Internal team organisation

Teams were a key component of the Toyota Production System implemented at NUMMI. Workers were organised in production teams of five to seven workers under a Team Leader, and four or five teams comprised a group under the first level of management, the Group Leader. While the focus of this paper is on production teams, we should also note that NUMMI workers were also involved in off-line teams, in the form of quality circles (called Problem Solving Circles at NUMMI) and temporary project teams such as the new model introduction Pilot Teams. While PSCs brought workers from the same work area together, project teams often drew workers into cross-functional and sometimes inter-plant collaborative efforts.

Workers were encouraged to master all the jobs in their production team. NUMMI put great value on workers' multifunctionality. In management's view, multifunctionality allowed for greater flexibility in operations, broadened workers' understanding of the production process and thus strengthened their ability to contribute improvement ideas. In this approach, NUMMI followed TMC's example. At Toyota, there was only one production worker classification and one skilled trades classification, and the division of labour between the two was rather fluid, with production workers performing simple preventative maintenance activities and skilled workers sometimes assigned to help out production activities. By contrast, in the Big Three US auto plants there were often over 80 production worker classifications and over 18 skilled trades classifications, and the division of labour was typically rigid. NUMMI had only three Team Member classifications: production, tool-and-die, and general maintenance; within each category, the division of labour was fluid, but there was little overlap of activities between categories.

In order to create multifunctional workers, NUMMI trained workers for the different jobs within their team. Workers were also encouraged to broaden their skills by moving from one group to another and one area of the plant to another over a period of years; but, unlike TMC, NUMMI did not have any specific plans governing such skill broadening. Traditional American unionised plants rarely allowed rotation, if only because of the extensively differentiated job classifications. Job changes in US unionised plants were typically determined on a seniority basis, and only rarely did unionised companies encourage, let alone plan, such development. When workers did change jobs, it was at their own discretion and usually for personal reasons such as easier work or more convenient hours (Brown and Reich, 1995).

NUMMI had more intra-day, within-team rotation than its sister TMC plant. The aims of rotation were to encourage multifunctionality, to alleviate boredom and to reduce ergonomic strain. Intra-day rotation was only within each production team. The frequency with which teams rotated had, until recently, been left to the discretion of the teams themselves. This, however, led to a gradual decline in the proportion of teams rotating. Some workers continued working with minor injuries and as a result found it hard to rotate into all the team positions. In other cases, workers managed to hold on to easier jobs, sometimes benefiting from a widely shared norm that older or higher seniority workers should have easier jobs. After a spike in injuries brought two 'serious' Cal-OSHA citations in 1994, rotation was made company policy (Adler *et al.*, 1995).

The work team was led by a Team Leader who was an hourly worker and a UAW member. Team Leaders were paid a premium of $0.60 per hour. The Team Leader filled in for absent workers, trained new workers, assisted workers having difficulty in their jobs, recorded attendance, assigned work when the line stopped, assisted team members in minor maintenance and housekeeping, assessed new team members, led kaizen efforts, facilitated PSCs and organised social events outside the plant. Team Leaders were supposed to work on the line some 40% of the time, filling in for absent or temporarily reassigned workers.

Team Leader openings were posted. People wanting promotion to Team Leader underwent 20 hours of pre-selection training in their own time, and selection was based on their performance in these classes and in their current jobs. In NUMMI's early years, there were persistent complaints of favouritism in management's selection of Team Leaders; as a result, the union and management negotiated a more formal process in which the evaluation and final selection are conducted by a joint union/management committee. In this new process, seniority was only used as a tie breaker. At TMC, by contrast, promotions were based primarily on supervisors' confidential assessment of the worker's ability and attitude (Grønning, 1992, pp. 177ff.).

Unlike some US organisations using self-directed teams, and unlike some socio-technically inspired European approaches to teams, Team Leaders at NUMMI were not selected by the Team Members as 'team representatives'; their role was seen as primarily technical – more like a 'lead hand'. In this, NUMMI followed Toyota's lead, privileging depth of technical expertise over the social and political aspects of team operations. Union leaders concurred with this approach, since from their point of view, union co-ordinators and committee people constituted a sufficient mechanism for interest representation.

Production process

The 'team concept' was seen by NUMMI and Toyota managers as one component of the Toyota Production System (TPS). However, all the components of TPS were closely interconnected, weaving together both its various technical features and its technical and social dimensions.

The first component of TPS was the kanban system. NUMMI did not use a computerised scheduling system. Instead, signs ('kanban') were passed to the upstream department whenever a pallet or dolly needed to be replaced. When no kanban arrived, the upstream department stopped production because no inventory was allowed to build up. Behind this innocuous-sounding innovation lay a fundamental shift in management methods, away from the reliance on work-in-progress inventory as a way to buffer tasks from upstream variability, towards a tightly-coupled system in which problems at any point in the process trigger a halt in production and a burst of problem-solving efforts (Schonberger, 1982).

The implications of kanban for workers were considerable. First, since small perturbations stopped the whole line, they occasioned considerable pressure and stress. Second, since up- and down-stream operations were so tightly coupled, the system eliminated any control by the worker or the team over the pace of work. Kanban was at the polar opposite of the system used at Volvo's Kalmar plant, where buffer inventory was a key mechanism for assuring the autonomy of the production teams (Gyllenhammar, 1977).

The second element of NUMMI's production system was the effort to assure as stable as possible a production schedule ('heijunka'). In the typical Big Three auto assembly plant, schedules were constantly changing, while at NUMMI, the schedule was stabilised over several months. The logic of the NUMMI approach was that changing production levels meant inevitably that inventory levels would be higher, quality could not be assured and improvement efforts would be stymied. A corollary of level schedules was 'mixed model' production: if, for example, the month's schedule called for 75% of model A and 25% of model B, instead of producing model A for three weeks (or three days) and model B for one week (or one day), NUMMI would alternate three jobs of model A followed by one of model B throughout each day.

From the workers' point of view, production levelling had three important consequences. First, it reduced the stress associated with schedule changes in a taut production system: in a Just-in-Time inventory management system, any changes create a lot of stress as workers scramble to re-establish equilibrium. Second, production levelling minimised the risk of temporary lay-off by reducing the risk that part of the workforce would be temporarily underemployed. Third, the mixed model scheduling approach meant that it was harder for workers to establish 'traction' in the sequence of work gestures: mixed model schedules kept workers alert, and, to put it more negatively, increased workers' cognitive load (on traction, see Baldamus, 1951).

The third element of TPS was 'kaizen' – continuous improvement. All NUMMI workers were given training in problem-solving for continuous improvement efforts. Kaizen created important challenges for workers, who were constantly pushed to reduce work times and increase quality. Kaizen happened both through bottom-up worker-initiated mechanisms, such as the suggestion programme and Problem Solving Circles (see below), and through top-down, management-initiated changes driven by supervisors and engineers. NUMMI management believed that the bottom-up process was important for three reasons: the resulting performance gains, the educational benefits that accrued when workers formulated suggestions and estimated their value, and the positive impact of such involvement activities on workers' morale and on their awareness of a zone of common interests with management.

Visual control, the fourth element of TPS, was a set of techniques designed to signal abnormal conditions as rapidly and automatically as possible. Kanban was one form of visual control, signalling the need to replenish inventory. Another key element of visual control at NUMMI was the 'andon' board lights that signalled quality problems on the line. Workers pulled a 'line stop' cord (or pushed a button) when they encountered a quality problem, thus ensuring that it received immediate attention. The commitment to quality implied by this willingness to sacrifice production was appreciated by workers at NUMMI. But under production pressures, Group Leaders would sometimes immediately re-pull the cord to keep the line going and thus postpone efforts to resolve the underlying problems.

Some researchers have seen in visual control a reincarnation of Bentham's Panopticon design for prisons (Sewell and Wilkinson, 1992); but the parallel fails since an essential component of the Panopticon was the invisibility of the warden to the prisoners, whereas at NUMMI, the action and inaction of both workers and managers were immediately visible to all. This symmetrical visibility – when associated with the substantial power of the union – meant that visual control served technical and productive purposes more than social control and political purposes.

The final element of TPS was 'standardised work'. Whereas in the Big Three plants, Industrial Engineers would develop prescribed methods from engineering handbooks, at NUMMI, team leaders and team members were taught the techniques of work analysis – including stopwatch use – and used them to assess alternative work methods. The most effective methods were codified in charts hung beside each workstation. There is little doubt that as a result of standardised work analyses and the constant kaizen process, workers at NUMMI worked harder than they did at GM–Fremont. Standard task times at GM–Fremont were set to occupy the experienced worker approximately 45 seconds out of a hypothetical cycle time of 60 seconds. In practice, 35 seconds was not uncommon. NUMMI's norm was closer to 57 seconds out of 60.

The standardised work process was evaluated positively by most workers but negatively by some. Workers appreciated the superior quality of the resulting methods: methods developed with worker input were more appropriate to the real work tasks than methods derived by engineers from handbooks and imposed unilaterally; and the standardised work process was thus experienced as helpful in performing work and in identifying the source of problems. Standardised work on the assembly line and finer-grained discipline in the supply of parts and tools facilitated traction and alleviated the stress that would have otherwise accompanied the increase in seconds worked per cycle. Many accepted that the competitive survival of NUMMI required an intensification of work relative to the GM–Fremont days. And workers appreciated the political and ethical significance of allowing their participation in defining and refining methods. However, some workers resisted being drawn into what they saw as a technique for speeding up their own work and that of their colleagues.

Several indicators suggest that positive assessments of the overall production system were far more common than negative ones: over 90% of workers participated in the suggestion programme, and 90% of workers expressed themselves satisfied with their work environment in anonymous employee surveys. The conjunction of TPS's intense discipline and workers' high satisfaction and commitment strikes some observers as implausible at face value (Parker and Slaughter, 1988). Others see it as evidence of internalised domination, as 'hegemonic despotism' (Burawoy, 1985). Without denying the significance of ambivalence and fatalism among workers, I find it difficult to dismiss altogether the evidence of workers' commitment. This commitment can, I believe, be attributed to the relatively participative and 'democratic' form of Taylorism as it was implemented at NUMMI, which contrasts strongly with Taylorism's more traditional, autocratic and 'despotic' form (see Adler, 1995).

Managerial hierarchy

The first level of management at NUMMI was the Group Leader. Several features of the Group Leader's role distinguished it from that of the traditional American foreman.

First, in keeping with the strong technical role Toyota accords the managerial hierarchy at all levels, NUMMI's Group Leaders had responsibility for tasks that in the US Big Three plants remained industrial engineering staff responsibilities. This reflected Toyota's commitment to the 'Training Within Industries' methodology developed in the US during the Second World War (Schroeder and Robinson, 1991; Robinson and Schroeder, 1993). In the immediate post-War years, Toyota found itself with the same dearth of engineers as US industry during the War. Toyota was attracted to the solution developed by TWI and formalised in the TWI 'Job Methods' programme: delegate methods engineering and line-balancing tasks to the foreman, and encourage the foreman to perform these tasks in collaboration with experienced workers. The TWI Job Methods programme virtually disappeared in the US after the War (except for pockets of 'work simplification' programmes), but it was embraced by numerous Japanese firms during the Occupation years and continues to exercise enormous influence in Japan. NUMMI inherited the TWI practice, renamed 'standardised work', from the parent company.

Group Leaders were also responsible for some human resource management activities that in many American firms were either ignored or handed off to the Personnel department, in particular, training. At NUMMI, as in all Toyota plants, line managers were responsible for on-the-job training (the Personnel department was responsible for off-the-job training). In this OJT, NUMMI, like TMC, relied on a second component of the TWI programme, 'Job Instruction'. Toyota's use of JI has not been discussed much in the research or practitioner literature, but it was seen by management as an essential ingredient of its success. Most American workers learn how to do their job by working alongside a more experienced worker for a short period, after which they are left to improvise and develop their own methods to deal with the demands of the job. Consistent with Taylorism's commitment to identifying the 'one best way' of doing each job, and consistent with its relatively 'democratic' form of Taylorism, NUMMI combined Job Methods – which allowed experienced workers to codify the most effective gesture-by-gesture sequence for performing the job, along with the 'key points' that explicated the important control items at each step – with Job Instruction – a formalised four-step programme for teaching new workers this sequence of steps and their key points.

Group Leaders also took responsibility for some more traditional, administrative and disciplinary functions. NUMMI's absence policies, for example, were very formalised and rather strict. There was no official distinction between excused and unexcused absences outside annual vacations and other officially sanctioned leaves of absence. After three absences within a 90 day period, the Group Leader submitted a written warning. After three more occurrences within 90 days, the Group Leaders submitted a further warning and the worker had to undergo counselling. Three more occurrences led to a final warning and further counselling. Three more occurrences led to dismissal. Dismissals were reviewed by a joint labour/management review committee. Repeated absences were the single most common reason for dismissal.

Group Leaders shared responsibility for many personnel issues with the Human Resources department. At NUMMI as in TMC, the HR department was a political 'heavyweight', whereas in the political landscape of corresponding American firms, the HR department was a minor player. For example, NUMMI's HR department, like TMC's, was directly involved in placement, appraisal and promotion of all management personnel, whereas in the typical US company, HR is involved in the careers of only 'high-potential' personnel. The HR department even exercised budgetary control over manufacturing headcount.

The leadership process at NUMMI, as exercised by Group Leaders as well as at higher levels, was also rather different from that found in the typical Big Three plant. In visiting US companies, I have been struck by how rarely meetings include more than two contiguous layers of the hierarchy. If middle managers' subordinates are included in meetings with superiors, the middle managers will often express concern that the subordinates may be trying to 'go around' them, or that the superiors might be 'undermining their authority'. By contrast, at NUMMI as at TMC, many meetings included three, four or even more layers, and as a result, there was probably more 'fact-based management' and less covertly political behaviour. For example, after each model change, there was a plant-wide meeting to discuss lessons learned. This meeting was typically attended by the President, the relevant vice-presidents, general managers, assistant general managers, managers and assistant managers. Strong and weak points in the management of the model change were all discussed in this open forum. By contrast with most US firms, this kind of meeting structure was common at NUMMI.

Worker involvement

NUMMI mobilised impressive levels of worker involvement through on-line mechanisms such as the andon cord and standardised work, and through off-line mechanisms such as Problem Solving Circles, other off-line teams, and the suggestion programme. We have already discussed the on-line mechanisms; here we focus on the off-line mechanisms and on the broader context that sustained worker involvement.

NUMMI's Problem Solving Circles were relatively recent, beginning in 1991. Toyota and NUMMI managers thought of QC circles as an advanced practice, requiring deep production knowledge that takes years to acquire; by contrast, American companies often interpret QCs primarily as an employee relations tool (and not surprisingly, the 'mortality rate' of these QC programmes is very high: see Lawler and Mohrman, 1985). NUMMI's PSCs were more truly voluntary than at TMC, although participation was expected of workers hoping for promotion to Team Leader positions. PSCs were structured as standing committees based on work Groups (not Teams, as in TMC). Each PSC selected a problem within its area of control. The company paid for members' lunch, but unlike TMC, NUMMI did not pay overtime for PSC activity. In an average month during 1994, 14% of NUMMI workers participated in the PSC programme. NUMMI managers thought this proportion was too low, and attributed it to a high frequency of overtime during that year (averaging one hour a day).

NUMMI workers were also involved in other off-line project teams, such as the Pilot Team mobilised to prepare for model changeovers. The changeover to the 1993 model-year passenger car, for example, started up in early 1992 with eight members; by August 1992, there was a total of two Group Leaders and 32 Pilot Team members drawn from the ranks of the plant Team Leaders (usually one Team Leader per group). Seven months before the start of production at NUMMI, the Pilot Team travelled to Japan to study how the Takaoka plant was building the vehicle. They worked on the Takaoka assembly line to learn how their counterparts had designed the specific jobs in the part of the line for which they were responsible. They worked with TMC engineers, proposing design changes to facilitate production of the somewhat differentiated American models. When they returned from Japan, the Pilot Team brought with them large binders containing illustrations of individual parts and explanations of how they should be assembled. They then experimented in NUMMI's pilot area, modifying this information to fit the specifics of NUMMI's line, and turning it into detailed draft work instructions for production Team Members. They also worked with plant engineers to design the appropriate equipment for each job.

Such 'off line' teams are increasingly common in US industry, although the specific case of worker involvement in multifunctional model changeover teams is still rare. Some 65% of Lawler's *Fortune* 1000 sample used off-line teams, and in more than half these cases, they covered over 20% of the workforce. Osterman found that 29.7% of manufacturing plants that he surveyed used QCs for over 50% of their core workforce. For the auto sector, MacDuffie and Pil found that in 1993, 90% of workers in Japanese plants participated in some kind of employee involvement group; the comparable figure for Japanese transplants in the US was 14%; and for US manufacturers, the ratio was 20%.

Alongside the PSC system, NUMMI put great emphasis on individual and team suggestions. Like TMC, NUMMI management's primary goal was increasing participation – unlike the focus on a few big suggestions that prevails at most American programmes. By 1994, well over 90% of workers were participating. Like TMC, the suggestion system was run by Group Leaders with very light administrative support – unlike the more typical American pattern where the programme is run by a specialised staff. Moreover, consistent with the goal of encouraging participation, considerable effort was made to explain to workers the nature of the evaluation process and its criteria, and to assure rapid processing of suggestions – on these dimensions too, NUMMI differed from most American firms. MacDuffie and Pil found that whereas Japanese auto manufacturers received on average 48 suggestions per employee per year, with an acceptance rate of 90%, the comparable figures for the Big Three plants were 0.2 suggestions per employee and 34% accepted. NUMMI workers contributed around 8 suggestions per employee and around 80% were implemented.

What were the sources of NUMMI's considerable success in mobilising worker involvement? A number of factors appeared to be operative. First, alongside workers' involvement in production there was a parallel structure that assured workers' involvement in plant governance. NUMMI and UAW Local 2244 put into place an extensive set of joint committees. There were weekly meetings between management and the union Bargaining Committee, weekly safety committee meetings, weekly meetings between section managers and committee people, and quarterly three-day off-site meetings between union and company leaderships. The relations between management and union have been largely co-operative. In recent years, the Administration Caucus had been displaced by the People's Caucus (with the exception of the Local President, who is affiliated with the Administration Caucus). The People's Caucus sought a more assertive role, and criticised the Administration Caucus for 'being in bed with management'. It drew relatively stronger support from the newer, younger workers hired with the start-up of the truck line. Symbolising the Local's new assertiveness, there was a two-hour strike during the contract negotiations in 1994. But, in substance, relations between union and management have remained largely co-operative.

One facet of the union's involvement in governance was through its role in assuring an equitable treatment of worker grievances. NUMMI's 'Problem Resolution Procedure' resembled TMC's in its emphasis on joint problem-solving in the first step, but the three subsequent steps brought it closer to the traditional formalised UAW–Big Three model with external arbitration as the final step. The collective bargaining agreement also differed from standard practice in specifying that there was no recourse to an arbitrator over standardised work or health and safety issues. Instead, in case of unresolved disputes in these matters: "Either party may call upon the UAW Regional Director and W.J. Usery for final resolution of the problem" (1994 Collective Bargaining Agreement, p. 163; Bill Usery is a mediator who was instrumental in forging the initial agreement with the UAW).

A second factor in mobilising worker involvement was the threat of unemployment. Brown and Reich (1989) cite data from the California Employment Development Department indicating that 40% of the displaced GM–Fremont workers were still unemployed at the end of 1983, and that displaced workers who did find other jobs experienced pay-cuts averaging approximately 40%. There were no comparable union-scale jobs to be found in the region then, and none materialised in the intervening years. NUMMI was tied to the national pattern of UAW–Big Three wage rates, and over the intervening years there had been no reduction in the size of the premium separating NUMMI wage levels from those of alternative job opportunities. Workers who could bear the considerable physical and mental demands of work at NUMMI thus had little incentive to leave, and personnel turnover at NUMMI averaged less than 6%. Employment security against the temporary lay-offs, so common in the Big Three, was a third factor buttressing workers' involvement. Employment security was written into NUMMI's collective bargaining agreement:

> New United Motor Manufacturing, Inc. recognises that job security is essential to an employee's well being and acknowledges that it has a responsibility, with the cooperation of the Union, to provide stable employment to its workers. The Union's commitments in Article II of this Agreement are a significant step towards the realisation of stable employment. Hence, the Company agrees that it will not lay off employees unless compelled to do so by severe economic conditions that threaten the long term viability of the Company. The Company will take affirmative measures before laying off any employees, including such measures as the reduction of salaries of its officers and management, assigning previously subcontracted work to bargaining unit employees capable of performing this work, seeking voluntary lay-offs, and other cost saving measures.

NUMMI did not have a Supplemental Unemployment Benefit fund of the kind found at the Big Three (which supplements the meagre unemployment benefits available in the US); so this commitment was very important in assuring workers' income stability. NUMMI lived up to the commitment in 1987–88, when capacity utilisation fell to under 60% but no one was laid off. Workers were put into extra training programmes and were put to work on kaizen projects and facilities maintenance jobs previously contracted out.

Unlike TMC and many 'high-involvement' American plants, NUMMI did not use individual or team performance pay incentives, nor skill-based pay. Management's assessment was that such incentives would undermine the teamwork they sought to encourage. Two exceptions to this philosophy proved the rule. The suggestion system did offer financial rewards based on the savings generated, but the amounts were very modest, with the average suggestion earning its author around $25, and the reward was greater for a suggestion coming from a team than for the same suggestion coming from an individual. NUMMI also had a gainsharing-type programme (PIPS), introduced in 1991, but it paid all workers identical amounts based on the company's quality and productivity improvement. In 1992, each worker received $1600.

The main avenue for pay progression was promotion to Team Leader. All Team Leader positions and about 80% of Group Leader positions were filled from within. A secondary avenue was the skilled trades apprentice programme. The apprentice programme began in July 1987, and the UAW offered a 10 week pre-apprenticeship training programme. Of some 209 workers who applied for the apprentice programme, 43 were finally selected. By 1995, a total of 88 workers had entered the apprenticeship programme and 53 had graduated.

Peer pressure was a final factor explaining NUMMI's success in mobilising worker involvement. Whereas American firms' teams often have 15, 20 or even 25 members, NUMMI followed Toyota's model and kept teams to between four and six members so as to maximise the social interdependence created by work interdependence. Peer pressure has often been presented in a negative light, as a manifestation of internalised domination (see, for example, Barker, 1993), but NUMMI workers' descriptions leave me sceptical that it can be reduced so neatly. To quote one worker:

> Once you start working as a real team, you're not just work acquaintances any more. When you really have confidence in your co-workers, you trust them, you're proud of what you can do together, then you become loyal to them. That's what keeps the absenteeism rate so low here. When I wake up in the morning, I know there's no one out there to replace me if I'm feeling sick or hung-over or whatever. Not like in the old Fremont plant where they had 20% more people than they should have needed just to cover absences. At NUMMI, I know my team needs me. They need my loyalty like I need theirs.

Co-operation is a spontaneous, anthropological fact; it does not cease having this quality merely because its fruits are appropriated or because more complex forms of organisation are erected alongside and on top of it.

The dynamics of diffusion: some hypotheses

To return to the two puzzles framing this paper, why did NUMMI and other transplants use teams so extensively where the Big Three plants did not? My analysis of teamwork at NUMMI and its role in the overall structure of the employment relation suggests three factors. Further research will be needed to assess this argument and whether these factors are equally pertinent at other transplants.

First, as a matter of history, NUMMI used teams because NUMMI was managed along Toyota lines, and teams were a key component of the Toyota production system. In some policy domains (such as benefits), NUMMI adopted American-style policies, and in some other domains (such as grievances), NUMMI hybridised American with Japanese approaches, but in domains that were part of the plant's 'productive core', Toyota's policy was that its overseas' subsidiaries had to conform to the Toyota production system (see Adler, 1996).

Second, NUMMI used teams because managers saw the production task as embodying high levels of interdependence and modest but not insignificant levels of uncertainty. Like TMC, NUMMI's managers saw assembly-line work tasks as embodying considerable interdependence: while the assembly-line technology minimised the interdependence of work tasks within a given cycle, interdependence was high across cycles when workers rotated tasks or models changed; moreover, looking beyond the immediate production task, interdependence was high in the tasks of defining and refining standardised work charts and PSC activity; and finally, management consciously used team structures and extra-work team activities to create social interdependence. Task uncertainty was also significant: whereas managers at the Big Three traditionally assumed that the production task in auto assembly was so routine that workers could be trained in a day or so, NUMMI's managers inherited from the parent company the assumption that workers' tasks embodied a significant level of uncertainty, thus motivating a continued high emphasis on kaizen. NUMMI thereby created (or 'enacted' in the sense of Weick, 1979) a different task environment, one with a higher degree of uncertainty than their Big Three counterparts. Through kaizen, the production task was continually reanalysed to generate an ever-deeper knowledge and ever-more effective technical control. As a result, NUMMI's teams, while far from the 'self-regulating' variety favoured by socio-technical theory proponents, were not entirely under the external control that characterises the 'traditional work group' model. The resulting performance gains legitimated and reinforced these initial assumptions of high task interdependence and modest uncertainty.

Third, the teamwork approach to production was not only symbolically and technically legitimate in the eyes of NUMMI managers because of its association with TPS, but it was also seen as posing few risks to control. While over many decades the Big Three managers consciously sought to individualise jobs in the name of managerial control over the shopfloor, NUMMI operated on the assumption, once again inherited from their parent company's experience, that under the right social conditions, workers' interdependence can be harnessed to productive ends without undermining social or technical control. NUMMI thus created a different sociopolitical environment within the plant, one that attributed great importance to 'mutual gains' for management and labour, and that made such gains seem within reach. This attribution represents a more novel feature of NUMMI's approach, since in Toyota's Japanese plants, social control could rely to a greater extent than was possible in the US on a cultural norm of 'groupism' (Lifson, 1992); at NUMMI, mutual commitment was based on a more calculative, bargaining model. When performance benefits manifested themselves in the form of world-class and continuously improving efficiency and quality levels and in the corresponding benefits to workers – enhanced job security, bonuses and the psychological rewards of 'self-efficacy' (Bandura, 1977) – these benefits reinforced the credibility of the initial mutual-gains assumption.

If these three factors help explain why NUMMI used teamwork, why have the Big Three not followed the example of NUMMI and the other transplants – why have they not adopted teamwork too? This is all the more puzzling when it is recalled that all three of the US manufacturers have North American joint ventures with Japanese companies which use teams and perform very well. Moreover, MacDuffie and Pil's data show that between 1989 and 1993, the US Big Three have made as little change to other dimensions of work organisation as they have in their use of teams. The contrast is striking with European-owned plants in Europe, where change in work organisation has been massive: the ratio of workers in production teams, for example, leapt from 0.4% to 75% between 1989 and 1993.

One possible explanation emerges from MacDuffie and Pil's performance data: while the gap between the Big Three and both the transplants and Japanese plants remains important in both productivity and quality, the Big Three have made large gains and have narrowed these gaps somewhat – and they have done this by making changes to the more technical elements of their production systems but without making substantial change to their work organisation. Pil and MacDuffie (1995) review a number of theories (such as March's theory of competency traps, and Argyris and Schon's theory of organisational learning) that predict that when organisations are able to respond to performance pressures without making radical organisational changes whose implementation is difficult and uncertain, they will take the easier route even if the results are only partially adequate.

This proposed resolution of one puzzle suggests a possible resolution of the other, the rapid diffusion of teamwork across firms in the broader spectrum of industries. Many US firms under pressure from new domestic and foreign competitors have been jolted from their complacent assumption that they have been operating at or close to the production possibilities frontier. They have recognised that their organisations harboured a lot of slack that they now cannot afford, and that they must identify and root out this slack. Data on the differential adoption of new forms of work organisation across industries support the hypothesis that the intensity of domestic and foreign competition is a key driver of work redesign (Osterman, 1994; Lawler *et al.*, 1995, section 17). In some cases, managers' centralising instinct is too strong, and they have adopted heavy-handed, top-down 'business process re-engineering' approaches. The high frequency of failure of this path has rapidly discredited it. In many more cases, however, US managers have acknowledged that slack cannot be identified and remedied without considerably greater employee involvement. Simultaneously, the current ideological climate in the US, the persistent employment insecurity and the declining threat of unions give managers a greater level of assurance that a modest degree of employee self-regulation and more extensive teamwork can be pursued without the risk of losing control. Re-interpreting their organisations' key tasks as embodying higher uncertainty and greater interdependence than they saw in them in the past, managers have thus discovered the virtues of teamwork.

This interpretation is rather different from that implied by theories of cycles of control advanced by Ramsay (1977) and by Barley and Kunda (1992). As opposed to the pendulum swings described by these accounts, my interpretation attributes considerably greater significance to the real productive efficiency of teamwork: insofar as firms are put under competitive pressure, the move toward teamwork appears less like a pendulum swing and more like a step forward along a development path that may be difficult to reverse. The two stories are not entirely incompatible however. It would seem likely that long-term progress along such a development trajectory would indeed be accompanied by cyclical swings around that trajectory. A test of this hypothesis would be provided by a closer analysis of the data on which Ramsay and Barley and Kunda rely, to see whether in the later swings, it was really a matter of returning to an earlier state, or if instead the historical process appeared more like a spiral in which the reappearance of old forms in management discourse and practice was accompanied by significant long-term shifts of focus.

But why has the shift to teamwork in US industry been so sudden? One hypothesis for future research to explore is that while the competitive pressures may have built up gradually over two decades or more, changes in work organisation follow a non-linear process. This non-linearity results from two complementary effects. First, there is the threshold effect: it is only when the symbolic legitimacy of teams in the eyes of American managers reached a critical threshold that they were willing to take on the difficult task of the broad-ranging organisational change required to make teamwork effective (Jenkins, 1994; Lawler *et al.*, 1995). Second, there is the contagion effect: managers are far more likely to find arguments in favour of new forms of work organisation compelling when these arguments are based on examples from firms that they believe are directly comparable to their own, either as peers or as competitors. It is well established in the network theory literature (Burt, 1982) that given threshold and contagion effects, changes in population characteristics are typically rather abrupt.

References

Adler P.S. (1993) The learning bureaucracy: New United Motors Manufacturing, Inc. In Staw B.M. and Cummings L.L. (eds.), *Research in Organizational Behavior*, Vol. 15, pp. 111–194. Greenwich CT: JAI Press.

Adler P.S. (1995) 'Democratic Taylorism': The Toyota Production System at NUMMI. In Babson S. (ed.), *Lean Work: Empowerment and Exploitation in the Global Auto Industry*, pp. 207–219. Detroit MI: Wayne State University Press.

Adler P.S. (1996) 'Hybridization: HRM policies at two Toyota transplants', working paper.

Adler P.S. and Cole R. (1993) Designed for learning: a tale of two auto plants. *Sloan Management Review*, Vol. 34, No. 3, 85–94.

Adler P.S. and Cole R. (1994) Rejoinder. *Sloan Management Review*, Vol. 35, No. 2, 45–49.

Adler P.S., Goldoftas B. and Levine D.I (1995) Ergonomics, Employee Involvement, and the Toyota Production System: A Case Study of NUMMI's 1993 Model Introduction. *Center for Research on Management Working Paper OBIR-64*, University of California, Berkeley Business School.

Baldamus W. (1951) *Efficiency and Effort*. London.

Bandura A. (1977) Self-sufficiency: toward a unifying theory of behavioural change. *Psychology Review*, Vol. 54, 191–215.

Barker J.R. (1993) Tightening the iron cage: concertive control in self-managing teams. *Administrative Science Quarterly*, Vol. 38, 408–437.

Barley S.R., Kunda G. (1992) Design and devotion: surges of rational and normative ideologies of control in managerial discourse. *Administrative Science Quarterly*, Vol. 37, 363–399.

Brown C. and Reich M. (1989) When does cooperation work? A look at NUMMI and GM–Van Nuys. *California Management Review*, Vol. 31, No. 4, 26–37.

Brown C. and Reich M. (1995) 'Employee voice in training and career development', paper presented at the IRRA meetings, Washington DC.

Burawoy M. (1985) *The Politics of Production*. London: Verso.

Burt R.S. (1982) *Toward a Structural Theory of Action*. New York: Academic Press.

Cummings T. (1982) Designing work for productivity and quality of work life. *Outlook*, Vol. 6, 35–39.

Grønning T. (1992) 'Human value and "competitiveness": on the social organization of production at Toyota Motor Company and New United Motor Manufacturing, Inc.'. Diss., Ritsumeikan University Graduate School of Sociology.

Gyllenhammar P.G. (1977) *People at Work*. New York: Addison-Wesley.

Jenkins A. (1994) Teams: from 'ideology' to analysis'. *Organization Studies*, Vol. 15, No. 6, 849–860.

Lawler III. E.E. and Mohrman S.A. (1985) Quality circles after the fad. *Harvard Business Review*, Vol. 85, No. 1, 64–71.

Lawler III. E.E. Mohrman S.A. and Gerald Jr. E.L. (1995) *Creating High Performance Organisations*. San Francisco CA: Jossey-Bass.

Lifson T.B. (1992) Innovation and institutions: notes on the Japanese paradigm. In Adler P.S. (ed.), *Technology and the Future of Work*. New York: Oxford University Press.

MacDuffie J.P. and Pil F.K. (1998) International trends in work organization in the auto industry. In Turner L. and Wever K. (eds.). *The Comparative Political Economy of Industrial Relations*. IRRA [forthcoming].

Osterman P. (1994) How common is workplace transformation and how can we explain who adopts it? *Industrial and Labor Relations Review*, January, 175–188.

Parker M. and Slaughter J. (1988) *Choosing Sides: Unions and the Team Concept*. Boston MA: South End Press.

Pil F.K. and MacDuffie J.P. (1995) *The Determinants of Diffusion of High Performance Work Practices: Forces for Change in the World Auto Industry*. Wharton School, University of Pennsylvania.

Ramsay H. (1977) Cycles of control: worker participation in sociological and historical perspective. *Sociology*, Vol. 11, No. 3, 481–506.

Robinson A.G. and Schroeder D.M. (1993) Training, continuous improvement, and human relations: the U.S. TWI programmes and the Japanese management style. *California Management Review*, Winter, 35– 57.

Schonberger R.J. (1982) *Japanese Manufacturing Techniques*. New York: Free Press.

150   *Teamwork in the Automobile Industry*

Schroeder D.M. and Robinson A.G. (1991) America's most successful export to Japan: continuous improvement programs. *Sloan Management Review* Spring, 67–81.

Sewell G. and Wilkinson B. (1992) Someone to watch over me: surveillance, discipline and the Just-in-Time labour process. *Sociology*, Vol. 26, No. 2, 271–289.

Weick K. (1979) *The Social Psychology of Organizing*, 2nd edn. Reading MA: Addison-Wesley.

CHAPTER 6
Teamwork in General Motors Brazil (GMB): What is Changing in the Organisation of Work?

Roberto Marx and Mario Sergio Salerno

Introduction

Since 1990, the Brazilian automotive industry has been revitalised for a variety of reasons. Already established companies (Ford, GM, VM, Fiat, Scania, Volvo and Mercedes-Benz) and possible new-comers (Renault, Kia, Honda, Toyota, Mercedes-Benz car division) are planning investments in new plants or in brownfield modern-isation owing to a growing demand in the country itself and in the Mercosul market as a whole (which joins Brazil, Uruguay, Para-guay and Argentina in a common market). The reduction of im-port tariffs has made international competition both a reality and a pressure for more competitive products and organisational pro-cesses, giving rise to a very different environment from that which has existed since the 1970s.

Some data can better express this revitalisation process: while in 1990, 914,000 vehicles had been produced, in 1995 this number had grown to 1,700,000 vehicles (Anfavea, 1995) and by 1999 the country will produce about 2,000,000 cars, not to mention the growing number of imported vehicles that have been sold since 1990.

The restructuring processes that have occurred in Brazilian automotive brownfields since then have almost always included a teamwork programme. It should be noted that the main source of ideas and solutions for this restructuring process was the Toyota model (or the 'lean production model'), as in most of the world.

But local conditions and each company's choices in adaptative strategy gave different individual trajectories to those movements.

In this chapter we discuss teamwork experience by analysing the General Motors Brazilian branch (GMB) case; other experience will be briefly discussed in order to provide a broader panorama.

The discussion is focused firstly on the historical background of the plants, followed by the overall transformations in the organisation, the characterisation of the team concept, the role of the unions and the analysis of work content. Finally, we discuss what has changed and what remains as part of the 1970s model regarding the way work is organised. During this discussion it is assumed that the lean production model is a case of limited change, based mainly on employee flexibility of workers and the recognition that workers do have the capacity to improve quality and productivity results by following the general principles of lean production. On the other hand, the semi-autonomous groups model, originating from the Socio-Technical approach (see, for example, Herbst, 1974; Pasmore, 1988; and more recent developments such as Beyerlein and Johnson, 1994) and adopted in some very limited cases in the automobile industry (see, for example, the case of Uddevalla and other Volvo plants developed by Berggren, 1992; and Ellegard *et al.*, 1992), was more accepted for cases like process plants, and can be considered as a reference for deeper changes in work organisation. This is because it is directed to giving workers more autonomy and resources (in knowledge, information), as part of an organisational design that considers this autonomy to be strategic and also more efficient than the classic Fordist model.

Historical perspective

The General Motors Brazilian branch (GMB) has approximately 22,000 employees, 82% of them direct workers (18,040), as at 1995. It has two plants, a larger and older one located in São Caetano do Sul on the outskirts of São Paulo, and a second one in São José dos Campos, 100 km away from the former. The company has been in Brazil since 1925 but only started producing automobiles in 1968.

Since 1991, both plants have begun a strong restructuring movement in the direction of the Japanese concepts of Just-in-Time and Total Quality Control. One of the key aspects of this process was the implementation of a teamwork scheme, which will be our main focus in this paper [1]. Both plants are trying to develop and improve the same main ideas and techniques.

The driving force behind the overall restructuring process was the growing competitive environment that was brought about by the market liberalisation initiatives undertaken by various governments since 1990. One of the main initiatives of GM in trying to respond to this environment was to launch two different models every year.

During this period, the total number of employees was stabilised, but in part this is due to the growing market demand observed in the last three years. The most important increase was observed in the segment of small and cheaper models, subject to tax deductions as a result of the Sectorial Chamber Agreement (see Salerno, 1994) involving unions, government and firms. Labour turnover was expected to be nearly 1% in 1994 (and this can also be considered a result of the Agreement).

The reference case for almost all the managers interviewed was the NUMMI plant, a well-known GM–Toyota joint venture located in Fremont, USA. Another very important case was the Ramos Arispe GM plant in Mexico. It was very clear that, before the implementation phase, the managers only visited and tried to learn and discuss other experiences within the GM group. Today, GMB is considered by the majority of other firms' managers to be a highly successful example of the changed work process and many firms, especially those in the components industry, are trying to learn lessons from its success.

The process of change occurred in both plants in the same way and was sponsored by the GMB chairman, himself a former NUMMI director. In 1995 he used to visit the shopfloor once or twice a week, in an effort to show how important the firm considered personnel, cleanliness and efficiency-related matters. There were some (symbolic) initiatives by means of which the company tried to reduce hierarchical differentiation, for example, the firm reduced the types of restaurant used by its employees from three to two.

One of the main results claimed after this process was an increase in the number of cars produced per hour: from about 20 to 26 (in the São Caetano plant), with the same personnel. In terms of cars produced, the numbers are: 162,012 in 1991 and 233,817 in 1994 (Anfavea, 1994).

The general quality standards in the Brazilian auto industry are increasing significantly. Between 1990 and 1994 the average defects per 100 vehicles measured for all plants decreased by 50% (Sindipecas, 1994). In 1994, GMB was considered the best firm in terms of quality by the same research. GMB has always looked to offer a wide spectrum of different market alternatives. The difference here is that GMB, especially at the São Caetano plant, is responsible for producing parts and assembly for four of its five different models within the same facility. By 1995 the São Caetano plant was responsible for Omega, Vectra, Monza (the old J model, Cavalier in the UK or Ascona in Germany) and Kadett. This fact inevitably led to some idle time and other production problems in a very poorly focused plant in terms of product. Focused plants seems to be the tendency in more modern plants around the world: NUMMI, for example, was producing 60 vehicles per hour (34 for GMB) of only two different models by 1995.

The constitution of teams

The formal definition of teams used by GMB managers is: 'People organised around a set of tasks, with complementary skills, deeply involved with common and clear goals'.

It is possible to say that both plants are wholly organised around teams with approximately ten employees each and one co-ordinator [2] who was selected by the managers at the beginning of the process. By 1994, there were 856 formally implemented teams. The co-ordinator is a normal worker who assumes most of the team's daily organisation activities. Naturally he must know all the tasks performed in his team, must have at least a high school degree and receives a 15% permanent addition to his wage. There is no rotation of co-ordinators at GMB, this is a fixed position. There is also a supervisor for each four or five co-ordinators [3]; supervisors are monthly paid employees responsible for dealing with technical and personnel issues.

Before the implementation of teams, co-ordination activities were performed by leaders (with 10% wage addition) and two other different supervisory levels. One of these levels has now been eliminated. Some of the old supervisors were laid off during this process while others remained as co-ordinators or supervisors. However, the most significant difference was the introduction of the team concept and team organisation dynamics which did not previously exist.

Table 1   *Hierarchical structure at GMB*

Before 1991	After 1991
Worker (BC*)	Worker (BC)
Leader (BC)	Co-ordinator (BC)
Supervisor level 1	Supervisor 1
Supervisor level 2	
Manager	Manager
Director	Director
Chairman	Chairman

(*) BC means blue-collar workers; all others are white collars.
Source: Interviews with GMB managers.

Table 1 summarises what has happened in terms of hierarchical changes since 1991.

The way each team is organised depends on the specific production process, although the overall scheme changes very little in its principal aspects. The main criteria of the team formation were physical proximity and type of machine/process that was being dealt with. Teams were also introduced in the maintenance and quality control departments and they are now collectively responsible for responding to production needs. Before this, each technician was assigned to a specific production area and was not responsible for the requirements of other sections. The initiative was taken to introduce flexibility and productivity via multi-skilling in these two areas.

It can be said that all the main decisions in the design and implementation of the process were taken by the managers, especially by the middle managers directly linked to shopfloor activities. Strong pressures were brought to bear on managers by the company chairman and directors to initiate and foster the introduction of teams. However, the NUMMI and Ramos Arispe plants were always considered (by every manager involved) examples to be followed or adapted and the main source of ideas and new concepts. Almost all middle managers spent at least some days in NUMMI; two of them studied the NUMMI teamwork concept for three weeks before returning and initiating the designing and implementation of teamwork in GMB.

A training programme was set up to support the process. The first phase was a 5-day training period dedicated to all supervisors and managers during a holiday period for the rest of the company. Quality concepts were transmitted to technical and managerial staff in a 30-hour programme. Eighteen thousand workers were trained in an 8-hour training programme. Team co-ordinators received an additional 32-hour training period. The implementation began in the assembly area and was then extended to the rest of the facility. The cycle time in the assembly line is 100 seconds and it did not change with the teamwork scheme. The assembly floor area remains divided by ink marks so as to show each worker the relevant space within in he or she should remain to perform his or her task, just as it was before teamwork was implemented. It is thus a very traditional assembly line design. Each worker can stop the line by activating a kind of Andon: a yellow light means a workplace needs attention and a red light signifies a more serious problem; in this case, the co-ordinator, along with a maintenance technician and the supervisor, can decide to stop the line after checking out the situation. In this area, teamwork meetings are very difficult to organise since the noise level is very high. When it takes place, the team meeting has to move to another area or building; that is why the teams need to meet once or twice a week (we will discuss this point further below).

Each team has a special area where it can develop small group activities such as process improvements. It is located very near the workplace. Each team is also responsible for producing general data and specific indicators of the team's performance: component photos, names of individuals, the team's name, the team's productivity and quality achievements, the range of tasks each is able to perform, and other related information, some of it chosen by the team itself to fit the specific area reserved for this purpose. It is the co-ordinator's responsibility to ensure that all this information is up-to-date and to make it visible for everybody passing near the workplace.

Two of the less developed changes during the restructuring process are related to the job structure and the wage system. Although they are being discussed internally, both remain very much as they were prior to the changes begun in 1991. For blue-collar workers, there are eleven basic wage levels with three steps in each. Each employee has the right automatically to move up one step in a 6 months' fixed period. Passing from one wage level to another depends on individual evaluation conducted by the supervisor and a local manager's final judgement and authorisation.

Work content

The initial effort at the beginning of the process (which took about 2 years) was to improve productivity and quality in production, with a special effort being made to eliminate general waste. Several mechanisms were used to involve workers directly in this process, since this was considered the key aspect to ensure success. The main mechanism considered to be the most important by those managers interviewed was the PMC programme (Portuguese initials for Continuous Improvement Programme): a very well-planned and strict programme that involves a task force of about 8 employees belonging to different departments and/or functions (normally maintenance, general workers, process technicians, team co-ordinator, engineers and supervisors).

Currently, this task force is set up and conducted by a local manager to try to eliminate waste and improve productivity and quality in a specific area. The task force lasts only (and always) 5 days, during which period the group has to define problems, perform tasks and find solutions for the kind of problems cited above. Normally it is the local manager who has the final word on the problem which has to be resolved. The sequence of activities each group has to develop is fixed. For example, on the first day – if required – everyone has to receive training on the PMC rules and operation dynamics; on the second day, the group analyses and selects the problems to be worked on; each day there is a fixed and previously planned activity to be completed. The group also has the responsibility for implementing all approved ideas and preparing a well-documented explanation of its achievements. There are no direct monetary incentives for these activities but every good result will receive some kind of recognition, normally a ceremony in which the chairman praises the efforts, an item in the internal newspaper and so on. During this week, all members have to be dedicated full-time to the PMC project.

Each local manager (around 20 in each plant) has as a goal to organise four PMC programmes per year, two per semester. From the workers' point of view, PMC tends to intensify the work pace. Sometimes the workplace is very different from what it was the previous week when the workers arrive on Monday morning, and some members of the working group are allocated to other areas [4].

From the company's point of view, some positive results, resulting in the main from PMC groups activities (between 1992 and 1994) have been obtained:

- Floor area reduction: 47,000 m^2
- Inventory reduction: equivalent to US$5.4 million
- Productivity measured by pcs/man/hour: 26%
- Throughput reduction: 40% in time.

Another type of activity developed outside the daily activities is the 'suggestion plan', in which one worker or a team proposes a solution for a productivity/quality problem. The main difference from the PMC programme is that the 'suggestion plan' is an informal one. There is no pressure to submit suggestions. However, if a proposal is considered to be a good one and chosen to be implemented by the production process department, the worker or team receives 20% of the first annual earnings. The company encourages the production of suggestions as a team activity, although this is not mandatory. Some managers argue that this initiative inhibits individualism and competitiveness between teams.

Before the implementation of the teamwork concept, the only participatory initiative taken by the company was to set up a suggestion box where individuals (only) could prepare and submit quality and productivity suggestions. A QCC programme (Quality Control Circles) was set up during the 1970s but it did not last, as was the experience of most other automobile assemblers at that time.

The teamwork itself runs on the shopfloor. The work content has changed in only some minor respects. The more significant aspects of the work are designed and being done in the same way as the previous situation: methods and work pace are defined initially based on an externalised approach, as well as the number of workers in each area/team [5]. A traditional assembly line is utilised. Fine adjustments are gradually being made by the co-ordinators, on an empirical basis. When a major balancing problem arises, a group of co-ordinators assisted by a supervisor can develop a project around the case. It can also be the subject of a PMC group. General workers normally do not take part in the balancing studies nor in other simpler time studies. However, instead of being just tasks for managers or supervisors, the intention is to give co-ordinators the responsibility for most of them.

Flexibility of worker allocation to different machines is being obtained both by formal and on-the-job training. Each worker has his capacity to operate different machines and other activities in his team traced on a 'skills map', so that anyone can check what jobs each person can perform. This is also useful as a pre-selector of who could be the next team co-ordinator should this necessity arise. This kind of map is more a conventional job-enrichment (or multi-task activities) aid than a multi-skill environment, although the company is considering the possibility of introducing a 'pay-for-knowledge' payment system based on this scheme.

Team members (including the co-ordinator) have responsibility principally for maintenance, housekeeping, multi-tasking, safety and quality, although the team is not measured against these aspects. The existing indicators (productivity, quality, number of accidents, inventories, set-up and lead-time) are followed through machine, process and plant. There is no strong emphasis on competition between teams.

It is also interesting to note that, until now, this kind of plan did not affect wages. Another important issue is the lack of team autonomy to choose its components: at GMB, this is a manager/supervisor's responsibility. It means workers do not play any role in the process of hiring and firing people, as well as in changes in teamwork composition. With reference to the degree of autonomy to define work content, pace and methods, the managers interviewed were very assertive: 'autonomy still belongs to the firm, everything in this restructuring plan is a company's decision'. To some extent this can be understood as a signal of the union's weakness in GMB plants.

In principle, it is possible for the team to have meetings during working hours, since this is authorised by the local manager. But in many cases, such as the assembly line and press shops, the inter-dependence between machines and processes conducted by the different teams does not allow this kind of autonomy. In most cases, this kind of meeting is planned in advance: once or twice a week, depending on the individual case, teams can discuss for about 20 minutes those issues that they consider important. Some of these meetings are used by the manager to communicate information relevant to all the teams under his co-ordination. The teamwork co-ordinator conducts the majority of these meetings. The local manager or the supervisor decides and plans the duration and the content of these meetings.

It is possible to say that the co-ordinator seems to be gradually assuming some important supervisory daily activities, which could be considered a more decentralised decision-making process. For example, on an *ad hoc* basis, some supervisors delegate to the co-ordinators the right to control and manage absenteeism. In this scheme it seems to be important for the firm to choose the co-ordinators, since they must be the 'voice' of the supervisor/manager in the shopfloor area. Nowadays the co-ordinator is expected to divide his working hours in the following major activities: 50% of productive activities and 50% of others, such as training, conducting meetings etc. The supervisors are still considered to be the real authority on the shopfloor but some of their old prerogatives are being delegated to the co-ordinators, mainly those which are better performed if a closer contact exists between workers and co-ordinator.

Quality methods such as statistical process control are being introduced and workers are being trained to obtain more skills on the subject. Quality inspectors have been removed from the plant. In 1994, the goal was to give each worker an average of 50 hours/year training on aspects such as: how to work in teams, how to participate in local meetings, problem analysis and solutions, and quality techniques. The TPM (Total Productive Maintenance) consists of a training programme together with the intention that there will be a gradual assignment of maintenance activities directly to workers instead of via the traditional maintenance department.

Unions, management and employee roles and involvement

According to Brazilian Trade Union structure, defined by law, the GMB workers are assigned to the São José dos Campos Metalworkers Trade Union in the São José plant, and the São Caetano Metalworkers Trade Union, in the São Caetano plant.

Although these unions have different political and ideological orientations, it is possible to say that they did not participate in the restructuring of GMB, and specifically that they neither bargained nor tried to influence the introduction of teamwork. The situation is different in the Ford, VW and Mercedes plants located in São Bernardo, where the local union (the ABC Metalworkers Trade Union, the strongest Brazilian union) have a policy of bargaining and influencing the restructuring process of the companies. In order to understand union activities and influence in Brazil, it is necessary to discuss some historical and institutional issues regarding trade union structure and evolution.

Trade union structure in Brazil

Brazilian trade union structure and labour legislation are still derived from the Italian Fascist Mussolini's Labour Act. The structure of trade unions is defined by law, and the law is different from the ILO 87th Convention recommendations on the right of free association.

Trade unions in Brazil are structured by branch and by region, e.g. São Caetano Town Metalworkers Trade Union, ABC Region Chemical Workers Trade Union, São José dos Campos Town Metalworkers Trade Union etc. And they are unique: by law, it is forbidden to set up more than one union by branch or region. As a general rule there is no right to set up factory committees or workers' representatives inside the companies in the automobile industry. Only those companies located in São Bernardo (Ford, VW, Mercedes-Benz Trucks and Scania) have specific agreements with the ABC Metalworkers Trade Union to set up factory committees. Companies outside São Bernardo, including Fiat, General Motors and Volvo, have no factory committee facilities.

By law, a compulsory contribution must be made to the union by all individuals. Every worker must pay, whether affiliated or not. Thus many unions have good financial resources but few members; as a general rule, unions have low levels of influence in companies' policies. The unions have the power to sign agreements involving all the workers, whether affiliated or not.

In accordance with the law, a 'Labour Court' with 'normative power' exists: it has the power to impose an agreement on both parties. Collective contracts last one year and if after this period the parties do not agree after the bargaining process, the Labour Court can define a new contract.

The bargaining process is decentralised. By law, only the branch/ regional union has the right to sign agreements, and they must also be signed by all the companies concerned. As a general rule, there is no negotiation on issues such as time standards, work organisation and industrial restructuring. In only a few companies in São Bernardo (Ford, VW, Mercedes-Benz) has the union been successful in bargaining on these issues. In GMB plants, there are no negotiations on work organisation and restructuring.

Perhaps the greatest trade union influence in the automobile industry was obtained in the so-called 'Câmara Setorial da Indústria Automobilística' – Chamber of the Automobile Industry Sector.

The Chamber was set up by the government in the late 1980s, involving government and companies and, in 1991, the ABC Metalworkers Trade Union decided to participate, playing a major role in the constitution of the developments in the sector. The Chamber discusses and tries to negotiate important aspects of the industry.

This has led to a number of important agreements which have impacted upon employee relations. A notable early measure saw a cut in the consumer price by 22% through reducing both tax and profit margins. The employment level was assured during the life of the agreement, and wages were re-adjusted on a monthly basis according to the cost of living. As a result, production rose 11% in 1992, and several other aspects of the industry and work relations were discussed, including import barriers and tariffs, the structure of collective bargaining, quality, productivity, technological innovation, professional education and so on.

A critical agreement was signed on 15 February 1993, reducing taxes once more, raising financial limits (there were restrictions to credit sales), reducing companies' margins, setting up production goals (1,200,000 units in 1993, 1,350,000 in 1994, 1,500,000 in 1995, 2,000,000 in 2000), employment goals (in 1994, 4,000 new jobs in auto companies, 11,000 in the components industry, 5,000 in dealers and the like, 70,000 in other sectors, a total of 91,000) and investment goals (US$10 billion for the auto industry, US$6 billion for the components industry, US$1 billion for the tyre industry, US$3 billion for the foundry and forge industry, raw materials and dealers, a total of US$20 billion up to 2000), and specifying wage increments (monthly re-adjusts by inflation rates + 6.27% real increase/year up to 1995). Depending upon the model, prices were reduced from 9.54% to 10.22%.

However, the Chamber lost almost all its importance when Fernando Henrique Cardoso took office in 1995. The tax policy was maintained and the production goals were surpassed, but stability and growth in employment were not maintained. Nevertheless, one important consequence was that the agreement led the unions back to a broader discussion of industrial policy, which in turn reflected their growing strength inside and outside the plants.

Union influence in GMB plants

It is important to note that the militant Brazilian Metalworkers Trade Union movement was and still is concerned with the ABC

Metalworkers Trade Union (in the towns of São Bernardo, Santo Andre and Diadema [6]), but not in São Caetano, where the main GMB plant is located.

São Caetano Metalworkers Trade Union has a history of 'yellow unionism' and allegations of corruption; the only automobile company in the 'ABC' region without a factory committee is, significantly, the GMB plant. In São Bernardo, the last committee was set up in the Mercedes-Benz plant in 1984. This helps to explain the ease with which teamwork was introduced in GMB–São Caetano (considering company–union relations), and the fear of managers regarding a possible change in trade union practices in São Caetano.

The situation in São Jose is somewhat different. Although formally linked to the CUT, the union board is mainly formed of traditional leftists (Trotskyists and others), and considers bargaining restructuring a mistake ('it is to manage capitalism'). In fact, such a statement mainly hides the weak union organisation inside the companies. Specifically at the GMB São José plant, the union suffered a significant defeat when it tried to occupy the plant some years ago, causing the dismissal of union officials and the breaking of the already weak union organisation inside the plant. Nevertheless, the São José Metalworkers Union is stronger than the São Caetano one, and the hegemony of ABC metalworkers inside the CUT may to some extent change the position at São José. Thus, there is virtually no union influence specifically on the teamwork issue and on work and production organisation in either of the GMB plants analysed in this chapter [7].

Union influence in other Brazilian auto plants

The Fiat case is very similar to the GMB one, but with a much more flexible use of the workforce. Fiat organised a night shift and claimed that this resulted in increased production capacity without investment, and GMB followed the same path. Just-in-Time, outsourcing, total quality control and the like are well developed in the Fiat plant.

Teamwork in the Brazilian Fiat plant is known as 'elementary work unit'. The team is conducted by a supervisor, and can have 30 workers or more. It is mainly concerned with flexible allocation of the workforce according to production needs. The trade union has a very limited influence on Fiat's plans. The relationship between Fiat and the metalworkers union has been historically very conflictual and since the plant's opening, the union has been denouncing Fiat for its anti-union activities [8].

VW has introduced some multi-task activities into its machining shop. The changes were discussed with the union (ABC Metalworkers) and with the factory committee: a formal agreement was signed by both parties regarding these and the outsourcing policy issues. Workers are responsible for production, inspection and set-up, with a wage increase (6.83% on average) to facilitate change. Press shop and body assembly (welding) already have statistical process control (SPC) performed by the workers themselves, and time standards have been adjusted to incorporate the new tasks. But on the final assembly line, workers refused to perform SPC without a change in work pace. The ABC Metalworkers Union is playing a key role in discussions over this and other issues.

Since 1995, VW has changed its strategy in Brazil. The end of Autolatina meant the return of heavy investments to modernise the São Bernardo plant (US$500 million), and two new plants were announced: a truck plant and an engine plant. In principle, the recommended teamwork concept is the 'work unit elementary' scheme which FIAT adopted. However, it is still too early to collect sufficient information to analyse these new plants.

Mercedes-Benz and Scania truck plants in São Bernardo are introducing teamwork, to some extent along the lines of the traditional model (like that of NUMMI, GMB etc.). The Mercedes case is the more interesting, where the ABC Metalworkers Union and the factory committee made their own suggestions with regard to teamwork, an unprecedented initiative in Brazilian terms. The union's proposal was much more advanced than the company's, and Mercedes refused to discuss work autonomy. The company insisted on formalising the notion that every team should have a supervisor appointed by management, and some pilots schemes have been set up in the machining areas and the final assembly lines. In the middle of 1995, Mercedes abruptly halted the negotiation process with the union by firing 1,200 workers. The most interesting bargaining process in the Brazilian automotive industry is currently in a state of hibernation.

So, we can say that, at the time of writing, there is no genuine innovative organisational system in the auto assembly industry in Brazil. In teamwork-related matters, it seems that the companies intend to implement schemes similar to the GMB experience – a NUMMI hybridisation, as we already discussed.

On the other hand, if one takes into account the fact that several other assemblers are announcing plant investment in Brazil – Renault (100,000 cars/year), Mercedes (80,000 small cars/year), Kia Motors (light commercials), Honda (20–30,000 cars/year) and Toyota (20,000 cars/year) – one must wait until the beginning of the next century to analyse both the new forms of teamwork and the influence which the plant unions will have upon them before fully comprehending the configuration of the emergent Brazilian automobile industry.

Conclusions

The conclusions one can draw after analysing the teamwork concept in the Brazilian auto industry must take into account some very important macro-economic and social aspects:

1. There are still no greenfield automotive plants in the country, except for a few producing components. GMB has very old plants in terms of its basic design concepts. The Fiat plant was built in the mid 1970s and is the newest in the country.
2. A long period of protection against foreign competitors, which lasted until 1990, contributed to the lack of investment in new technologies and new forms of production organisation. Since 1994, investments are being made as part of the expansion of old sites and/or a policy of modernisation (as in the cases of GMB, Ford and VW). This seems to he one of the ways in which companies are trying to cope with the growing market demands expected in the years to come.
3. However, there has been some interest in new plant investment, as stated by several multinational companies (those already operating in the country and some other probable newcomers, such as Renault, KIA Motors, Mercedes Benz car division, Honda and Toyota).

Accordingly, we can make the following conclusions:

1. In comparison with NUMMI and other greenfield plants that based their restructuring processes on the Toyota case, GMB can be seen as a 'good student' when the local conditions mentioned above are taken into account. There are some differences, for example where NUMMI has only one wage level for its blue-

collar workers and where team co-ordinators rotate and do not earn any kind of bonus. In the GMB case, it has already been said that the way the company pays its workers did not change from the previous situation, although there is an ongoing discussion about this. There are enough signs to conclude that GMB policy regarding wage structure will follow the Brazilian pattern in the automotive industry: 5 levels and 7 steps instead of the present 11 levels and 3 steps, independently of performance results. In almost all other aspects, GMB has tried to emulate the NUMMI model. When compared with the previous situation (stagnation since the early 1980s) the process can be considered as a success in two ways. Firstly, there has been progress if the results obtained in quality, waste reduction and assembly lead-time improvements are taken into account, even though market share did not increase in the period considered. Secondly, it has been a success in so far as it is a reference model for other Brazilian firms (in their efforts to improve the above indicators), especially for the GMB network of suppliers.

2. The unions' role must be considered as two-fold: firstly, there are basic differences concerning influence and bargaining power among the unions. The ABC Metalworkers Union is the only union that is organised inside the plants (factory committees), and to some extent has the effective power to bargain over industry restructuring. The recent history regarding discussions on factory committees' organisation, time standards, wage structure, automation, employee involvement, outsourcing and multi-task principles and policies may have paved a road to a stronger bargaining position for the union in the present broader restructuring process. Secondly, in the case of GMB (both in the São Caetano do Sul and São José dos Campos plants), it remains to be seen if internal discussions and external pressures will lead the unions to a more aggressive position with reference to teamwork and other practices.

3. Considering the extent of the changes in respect to the autonomy given to workers and other work content aspects, one can say that there is limited progress. Considering autonomy as *the extent to which workers can design, decide about and implement their own work pace, work methods and job allocation*, the GMB case shows that little has changed. The lay-out remained the same, as is the way tasks are allocated to workers: each worker is assigned one task (single or multiple, but a pre-defined task) and,

if necessary, may assist other team colleagues in doing their jobs in order to prevent 'work idleness'.

The task force concept (or small-group activities, called PMC at GMB) was also introduced, but the prevailing situation is that these groups are not integrated into the daily activities, neither do the workers have autonomy to decide about those problems which have to be addressed.

When compared with a traditional Fordist automobile organisation and hierarchical structure (such as that which prevailed until the 1980s), GMB cannot be said to be a typical representative. It is very clear that some work reorganisation movement has taken place in the plant since 1991. There has been a clear tendency to decentralise authority and power to the team co-ordinator, although this is an ongoing process: by the end of 1995 it was the supervisor (and the local managers) who took almost all the daily decisions related to the team activities. In the near future it is possible that one will see the co-ordinator more and more as the local production chief, with some expected benefits, especially in the sense of better co-ordination and communication processes within (and between) teams and with other support groups. In addition, fewer supervisors and possibly fewer managers will be necessary, representing cost-cuts in the medium and long term. Given the high number of GMB platforms cited above, flexibility and better co-ordination processes seem to be very important competitive resources. Implementing this kind of teamwork approach is clearly a high-level decision. But it is also clear that the control and extent of the autonomy that each team will have are limited.

GMB management is very emphatic in defining the limits of workers' autonomy. We can highlight some hypotheses on the reasons for this [9]:

- Hypothesis (1) Autonomy is limited because the GMB team model is an emulation of the NUMMI and Toyota team model, and GMB does not want novelties.
- Hypothesis (2) GMB was concerned about 'losing control' of the programme.
- Hypothesis (3) The lean production model is seen by GMB as the most adequate for the automobile industry; from GMB's point of view, the model has demonstrated its efficacy.
- Hypothesis (4) The lack of social pressure for autonomy and the high wage differentiation among skilled and unskilled workers

would contribute to the limitation of the GMB teamwork model. Neither union nor worker pressure was observed over these issues at GMB. However, some observations can be made in respect to changes observed in the content of direct work.

The company is trying to reorganise the skills needed to perform direct jobs: instead of considering the classic relation of one person to one task, it is changing to something like one person to a group of tasks, which introduces more flexibility in the way work is done. As part of these initiatives, there has been a growing sense of co-operation between members of a team. In future, one can envisage changes in the way wages will be defined. In addition, training is being considered more and more as part of workers' activities. In the past, almost all training was given in a short period when the worker started in the company. Finally, if one takes into account the growth in production levels and in the scope of direct workers' responsibilities, it is possible to say that, in a situation of employment stability, the pressures on each individual have also increased considerably since 1991.

As can be seen, this is a very different approach when compared with the idea of the semi-autonomous work groups that were designed, for example, in the Uddevalla plant in Sweden, or are being adopted in other Brazilian plants outside the auto assembly industry [10]. In this kind of plant, autonomy is something different from the 'self-control' concept that is being used by some auto assemblers. Nevertheless, GMB has to some extent recognised workers' potential and given them better conditions and resources to improve quality and productivity indicators. Moreover, it would seem that, though following somewhat different pathways, other automobile companies are taking the same trajectory as GMB.

This led us to the conclusion that although GMB is thinking in terms of variations around the NUMMI model, deeper changes are being tried in respect of worker autonomy in other industries, with reasonable success. Empirical indications regarding Brazilian automobile plants in which the above results could also be applied to semi-autonomous work groups are not currently available. Investment in new plants which are not operating at the time of writing will, in the future, offer a very rich and extensive field for comparative research in brownfield and greenfield plants in respect of teamwork practices.

End-notes

[1] For other aspects on the GMB restructuring process, see Fleury (1994) on the GMB trajectory since 1929 and Marx (1994) on the relationship between automotive plants and their small and medium suppliers from 1988 to 1994.

[2] The ratio between number of employees and the co-ordinator, 1:10 in GMB, is known as 'the span of control' by GM technical staff.

[3] This is know in GM as 'the span of support'.

[4] In other plants, with stronger unions, PMC-like programmes are a key point, because of workers' claims concerning work intensification.

[5] Procedures are designed by workers using time and motion methods in NUMMI.

[6] Lula, the Workers' Party founder who achieved second place in the last two Brazilian presidential elections, was the leader of the São Bernardo and Diadema Metalworkers Trade Union. A few years ago, there was a merger with the Santo Andre Metalworkers Trade Union, and the creation of the ABC Metalworkers Trade Union: 'A' from Santo Andre, 'B' from São Bernardo. 'C' would have been from São Caetano, but the board of São Caetano Metalworkers Union decided not to join the ABC Union, in spite of the workers' desire for such a merger, as shown by an opinion poll. The ABC Metalworkers Union is linked to CUT (the largest and more active national confederation); and the São Caetano metalworkers Union is linked to Força Sindical, the second national confederation, which is closer to the traditional North American trade union style.

[7] NUMMI and the UAW (United Auto Workers) union signed a formal agreement after negotiations upon wages and production and organisations issues. There is an explicit no-lay-off policy in this agreement. In NUMMI, managers and union officials jointly evaluated applicants for the hourly jobs. The union also influences the managers' selection process.

[8] For instance, it was stated that Fiat was asking unionised workers to cancel their affiliation, otherwise they could be fired.

[9] We would like to thank Mauro Zilbovicius for these comments.

[10] The most interesting examples can be found in the food industry, chemical consumer products (cleaning products, for example) and personal products. There are some highly successful cases,

international benchmarks in organisation and 'empowerment', to employ a fashionable word: one of these plants has no supervisors and for almost all the working hours, the plant is run by blue-collar workers only.

References

Anfavea (1994) *Statistical Yearbook*. São Paulo: Associação Nacional dos Fabricantes de Veículos Automotores.

Anfavea (1995) *Carta da ANFAVEA* 105. São Paulo: Associação Nacional dos Fabricantes de Veículos Automotores.

Berggren C. (1992) *Alternatives to Lean Production: Work Organization in the Swedish Auto Industry*. Cornell WI ILR Press.

Beyerlein M. and Johnson D. (1994) *Advances in Interdisciplinary Studies of Work Teams: Theories of Self Managing Work Teams*. Greenwich CT: JAI Press.

Ellegard K., Engstrom T. and Nilsson L. (1992) *Reforming Industrial Work – Principles and Reality*. Stockholm: Arbetmiliofonden.

Fleury A.C.C. (1994) The trajectory of General Motors in Brazil, paper presented at *The New Industrial Models of Automobile Firms*, GERPISA, Paris.

Herbst P.G. (1994) *Socio-Technical Design: Strategies in Multidisciplinary Research*. London: Tavistock Publications.

Marx R. (1994) The modernization trajectory in small and medium-sized firms in Brazilian automotive industry, paper presented at *The New Industrial Models of Automobile Firms*, GERPISA, Paris.

Pasmore W. (1988) *Designing Effective Organizations: The Socio-Technical Systems Perspective*. New York: Wiley.

Salerno M.S. (1994) The historical trajectory and future perspectives of Autolatina's development in Brazil. *Actes du Gerpisa* (Paris), Vol. 10, 191–236.

Sindipecas (1994) *Estratégia Setorial para a Indústria Automobilística*. São Paulo.

SECTION 3

EUROPE – HESITATIONS AND DIVERSITY

CHAPTER 7
The Effectiveness of Tradition: Peugeot's Sochaux Factory

Jean-Pierre Durand and Nicolas Hatzfeld
(Translated by Sybil H. Mair)

Automobiles Peugeot considers the Sochaux site to be its birth-place. The site had been acquired in 1912, and activities there gradu-ally expanded in tandem with the development of a production system based on principles of rational organisation that were adopted during the First World War. Sochaux remained the sole assembly factory of Automobile Peugeot until 1971, when a new assembly plant was opened at Mulhouse. Poissy, purchased in 1978, was later to be-come the company's third assembly plant. For several decades, then, Peugeot–Sochaux was home to all the major activities involved in automobile production: foundry, forging, mechanical components, stamping, painting and final assembly.

The period following the Second World War represented a new phase in the factory's history: an enormous expansion of produc-tion levels based on the principle of producing a single model: the 203, the 403 and later the 404. From 1965, with the launch of the 204, complementary models were produced, and by 1972 a whole range of five models was made at Sochaux. The size of the workforce increased in tandem, to just over 37,000 in 1977 (to which tem-porary workers must also be added).

The role played by the Sochaux factory was then transformed considerably, both through the formation of the PSA group [1] and through changes in the market. On the one hand, the factory lost some of its activities, which were assigned to other factories in the group (such as forging, engine and gear-box production, body parts stamping for some models) or to suppliers. Its assembly lines now concentrated on upper segments of the range (M2 and S, then M3), with other models only produced at Sochaux as an adjunct (I, then M1) [2]. On the other hand, a major programme of modernisation that had been undertaken following PSA's financial recovery in 1987 was reflected in massive investments to modernise certain activities (stamping, body production, painting, final assembly). Moreover, the workforce was now significantly smaller: by late 1995 there were 19,000 employees, of whom 14,000 worked in production and 5,000 in research and development or production engineering (DETA: Direction des Etudes Techniques Automobiles, and DMI: Direction des Méthodes Automobiles). With a theoretical capacity of 1,800 vehicles per day, Sochaux produced about 1,250 in early 1996.

Although it is now smaller. Peugeot–Sochaux continues to dominate its regional labour market. Indeed the region is home to a wide range of suppliers, some of them long-standing subsidiaries [3], others having recently located in a new industrial zone on the outskirts of Sochaux at Etupes (such as seats, wiring harnesses, plastics). The workforce remains varied: residents of the old towns or the big new developments in the Pays de Montbéliard agglomeration, residents of the towns and countryside of the region, a foreign workforce (primarily Moroccans, Yugoslavs, Turks, Algerians and Portuguese) which, despite the curtailment of recruitment abroad since 1980, still represented 14% of the workforce in 1995. The key characteristic of the personnel at Sochaux is perhaps its age. Virtually no employees were hired between 1980 and 1987, and few have been hired since. The result is a high proportion of older, long-serving workers: in 1994 the average age was 42 years, the average seniority 21 years [4].

Is Peugeot still a different kind of company?

Peugeot remains very discreet about its internal policies – its methods of vehicle design, its human resource management policies, and the reforms that propel the company forward [5]. Besides historians who have access to the company archives, few researchers have studied the company, in stark contrast to Renault, which, as a 'window onto society' under Pierre Dreyfus (1955–1975), became the primary focus of research on the French automobile industry.

This does not mean, however, that Peugeot is inward looking and inattentive to outside developments [6]. Peugeot also practises benchmarking, has sent numerous missions to Japanese and American producers, sometimes over long periods, and today participates in several European research programmes. However, external influences remain moderate and the 'company culture' persists, despite the significant internal changes that have been necessary to maintain international competitiveness.

The central question in this chapter is thus how to interpret the realities of the employment relationship at Peugeot–Sochaux in the context of the models currently produced? The research focuses on one assembly line [7] in each of the two major workshops which make up the Bodywork (Carrosserie) Department [8], Trim (HC: Habillage Caisse) and Car Assembly (MV: Montage Voiture) areas. About 1,260 cars were produced per day at the time of the study, largely M3s, but also M2s (station wagon/estates in particular), Ss (about 50 per day) and M1s.

In the HC area, the body comes out of the paint shop and receives parts such as wiring harnesses, carpets, safety belts, rubber seals, interior plastic parts, the pedal set and some of the hoses. The doors are trimmed separately from the four parallel lines where the bodies themselves are trimmed. On Line 1, the line studied here, only left-hand drive M3s and M1s were made. The models required different cycle times – on average 2.3 minutes for the M3 and 1.8 minutes for the M1 – and an M1 passed by about once every 20 minutes.

The MV area undertakes the final assembly. The four lines begin by assembling the mechanical components (front drive train, rear axle, exhaust, fuel tank, wheels) and then 'marrying' them to the body, prior to various fixing and connecting operations, the assembly of doors, seats and accessories, the filling of liquids and the testing of functions (brakes, electrical connections). The MV line studied only produced M3s (various types), with a cycle time of about 2.6 minutes.

MV receives car bodies and doors from HC, and conveyors supply the front and rear mechanical sub-assemblies as well as the seats. The conveyors as well as the many other parts deliveries are managed centrally. The whole system therefore starts and stops together every two hours (to permit the two ten-minute breaks and the thirty-minute 'snack' break). A further functional link between HC and MV is that each line in one area is linked to a line in the other. However, HC is located in a new building. Thus, the HC line studied is on the first floor of a new building constructed in 1991: natural lighting from the exterior is complemented by intense artificial lighting (neon). MV, on the other hand, still operates in old buildings with a technical structure that has been fixed for decades. To better understand the organisation of work at Peugeot–Sochaux, it is important to take into account both the differences between the two areas and their different histories.

The organisation of assembly work: a brief history

Paradoxically, it is perhaps MV that has the more straightforward social legacy, despite its venerable age, so evident from a technical standpoint (the lines are quite close – less than ten metres between them – which leaves little room or flexibility for supplies at lineside). From the point at which the mechanical components are fixed to the body, which is undertaken by lowering the body shell by means of large 'pincers', the car is fitted with wheels placed on two ground-level conveyor belts. Work is then carried out walking, both alongside and underneath the vehicle in a pit that runs between the two conveyor belts for most of their length. Except for some positions equipped with programmable automated equipment that can often be moved along over several metres, the operator must pick up the tools and components he needs at fixed points, which requires considerable motion: the cycle time is about 2.6 minutes, and the operator follows a path about six metres long (about 1.5 m between each car). Information concerning each group's activities is mainly posted in the foreman's office. The denseness of work on the lines goes hand in hand with dense working relationships. While there are rest and meal areas around the edges of the work area, most operators prefer to take their breaks and snacks near the line in small areas arranged with tables and seats that are squeezed between the stocks of components. The relative lack of light and the patina of time completes the impression of a factory from a bygone age, suggestive of the weight of the factory's social inheritance: new model launches, recompositions of teams and workstations, variations in production, workforce and schedules, the careers of the personnel and social conflicts. This weight is all the more keenly felt since most of the workers are over forty years of age.

The transformation of HC, which was previously a similar environment, is part of a plan for the step-by-step modernisation of the whole 'Centre de Production de Sochaux' (CPS). It was thus designed as one step in the remodelling of the whole 'Carrosserie' department. The goal was to effect a radical transformation by acting on several fronts: simultaneously replacing the product, the process, the buildings and the way that work was organised.

As far as the product was concerned, the aim was to make a successful transition to new quality requirements during the launch of the new 'S' luxury model. The vast and luminous new buildings were constructed on unused land within the Sochaux site, and required the canalisation and diversion of the local river, the Allan. The operation was complex, as revealed by a flood which inundated part of the Centre in 1990. The new investments brought with them more productive and ergonomic processes. The pits have disappeared, although there are still operations carried out beneath the car at the end of the line. The organisation of work was restructured, with the development of teamwork, the broadening of the operator's scope of responsibility, a shortening of the hierarchical line and a greater training effort. The plan for the new area had been prepared after numerous missions to observe factories in Japan and the United States, and was the responsibility of an interdepartmental working group named 'NUMMI': a name symbolising the fascination with an idealised vision of 'Japanese methods' conceived as a system which was characteristic of the late 1980s.

Implementation of the HC project took place in two stages, HC1 and HC2. The first stage, HC1, was more difficult than expected and produced ambivalent results. The personnel involved came from the former HC site (then named HC0), a rather traditional area, as we have seen, and they had their own views. These employees began work in the new area a few at a time, following a strict procedure: the individual selection of operators (entailing the decomposition of teams in HC0), training according to the new principles, each individual's acceptance of these principles formalised by signing of a charter, and adoption of a new identity symbolised by clothing in a distinctive apple-green colour. While the first operators, who had volunteered, accepted this approach, it became increasingly difficult to ensure adhesion as the group grew, with certain aspects of the transfer perceived as a forced uprooting and the final individuals to move considering themselves to be perceived as the 'bad element'. Further, some of the improvements in work organisation that had been planned clashed with the rigidity of the production flow at the level of the company as a whole. Lastly, the participation of the new factory's supervisors in innovative aspects of human resource management was limited. The new norms were soon viewed as dissonant with the previous social inheritance. The first shop steward elections illustrated this, when the CGT union (Confédération Générale du Travail), which was hostile to the new principles, obtained an astonishingly high vote (nearly 60%). When management opened HC2, they placed far more emphasis on continuity. Since then, the gap between the previous situation and the current reality has been bridged, in particular because a number of the innovative principles, such as the greater autonomy of teams in relation to their environment, and indeed teamwork itself, were abandoned. This aborted attempt to transform work remains a black stain on the young memory of HC. Like a mirror, it presents the personnel of the 'old' MV area a somewhat disquieting image of HC and of modernisation more generally.

Maintaining the traditional Fordist group

In both the HC and MV areas, each production line is divided into teams of about thirty workers. Each team has at its head a first-level supervisor (AM1: agent de maîtrise de premier niveau) who is responsible for workers, quality, production processes and so on. The team is subdivided into three groups led by a 'monitor'. The rule is that there is one monitor for each group of about nine assembly workers, one of whom is the group's institutionalised polyvalent worker.

The essential role of the polyvalent operator is that of short-term replacement for other operators, during visits to the doctor, for those leaving early for family-related reasons, or for pre-arranged half or whole day absences. Most long absences are covered by polyvalent operators (called V2 at MV) and by factory-level polyvalent operators known as 'supers'. In fact, most recourse to the polyvalent operator is for numerous but unpredictable short absences [9]: he must be a dynamic worker, often young and full of vitality, who can cover almost all of the thirty positions within the team and not just the eight or nine positions of his group. When he is not assigned to a specific post, which is rare, he walks along the line to assist his colleagues and help them when a problem arises (temporary problem of assembly, upstream work done badly, slippage of work along the line due to problems). Finally, the polyvalent operator trains new arrivals, whether they are young temporary workers or older workers newly transferred to the assembly line [10]. This practical training, which is continued until the activity has been completely mastered, complements training at the Training School situated in the same building but which only lasts a few hours for each position, the aims being to introduce the worker to the range of assembly work, to prepare him to perform his tasks correctly and to sensitise him to the quality of his work by showing him the harmful consequences of poor work on down-stream operations and on the product itself.

The mobility of the polyvalent operator thus responds to con-tinuous shifts in the team's personnel arising from absenteeism (between 4% and 6%, depending on the line) and movements of workers themselves as a result of ongoing adjustments of the labour force to production volumes in and between factory areas. For example, the M3 was launched with the support of temporary workers, but after seven months, at the end of the launch period, the temporary workers left and were replaced by workers from other factory areas. The principal function of the AM1, supported by the monitors, is to assign workers to positions with which the workers are familiar, within 15 minutes of work starting, in order not to 'lose cars', that is, stop the assembly line. For a successful 'start up', the AM1 has to know the male and female members of the team perfectly, know that certain positions cannot be held by certain workers (who are too big or too small. or have medical restrictions, or are not strong enough for the physical tasks, or not nimble enough for a delicate task), including female workers (although not official, there are 'female positions' with shorter cycle times and less difficult tasks). Yet this knowledge of the workers is not enough to ensure a good start-up. Besides the institutional polyvalent operator, other workers too must be polyvalent if adjustments are to be made in the short window of time available. In practice, each team contains former institutional polyvalent operators who have not advanced to the position of monitor yet, and who are capable of readily adapting to a new position if necessary. Furthermore, if there are none of these present, or if they refuse to undertake these further tasks or simply refuse to leave a 'good position', the AM1 can make use of a reserve of workers, often young recruits in whom he is seeking to develop or maintain a certain degree of polyvalency that is more or less linked to possible future promotion. While the polyvalency of the older or newer operators does not always appear on the worker assignment schedule which is posted in the rest area, rapid start-up of work at each post depends upon this widespread but unrecognised polyvalency on the part of a significant number of workers.

While in the past teams were formed and expected to endure over time, this was possible because, in contrast to today's situation, they contained more workers than posts, and production was more regular. For example, there used to be a number of 'double posts' – even 'triple' posts – at which a worker only assembled every second – or third – vehicle because the work was so strenuous, resting while the bodies assembled by his colleagues passed by. The extra workers made it easier to make adjustments within a permanent group. Today, with increasing rationalisation in the calculation of labour force allocation, combined with increased variations in volumes as a function of variations in demand, mobility between factory areas – and sometimes between lines – is far more significant. Hence teams are continuously formed and then broken up, with a volatility that makes the assignment of workers to job positions they are able to cope with increasingly difficult and delicate. Polyvalency is therefore the solution to reduced labour supply in the context of a demanding assembly line. Polyvalency deteriorates if it is not utilised, and since it provides the principal margin for manoeuvre of the AM1 in assigning workers to job positions, he continually encourages it, even though he can only compensate it in part. The quality of an AM1 is in fact evaluated, among other criteria, by his capacity to develop polyvalency voluntarily and informally (i.e. not posting it in the rest areas so that it is not sanctioned and does not become institutionalised). The AM1 certainly needs good human qualities if he is to motivate his workers and increase their competencies but is only permitted to distribute parsimonious rewards.

Indeed the AM1 undertakes these functions and attains these objectives alone, since the monitors who support him (three per team) have no hierarchical role. Their principal administrative role is to verify that all the workers are present at start-up and that the supply of parts is proceeding properly. They work on the assembly line, but do not produce; their main role relates to quality: supervising and supporting workers when they experience difficulties.

According to a document issued by factory management: 'the monitor's mission is to ensure that conditions for obtaining quality are respected, to repair poor quality (curative measures), to eliminate human error, and to encourage improvement (preventative measures)' [11].

The monitor signs the papers that accompany the vehicle, after having visually controlled (what is called a level 2 control) all the operations performed by the group for which he is responsible. The level 1 control is the worker's 'auto-control', which does not allow a car to pass if the task has not been undertaken correctly or remains unfinished (in which case he places an 'X' next to his operation on the accompanying paper so that the monitor can finish the relevant operation). Hence the monitor repairs, but he is also expected to enquire into the cause of problems in order to remedy them upstream (wrong parts supplied, mistakes in upstream assembly and so on), so that they do not recur. In case of major problems which accumulate on the vehicles owing to the constraints of the process sheets (which instruct the workers precisely what to install into each car), the monitor stops the line. This action, which is costly for the company, takes place as infrequently as possible (normally a few minutes per shift) [12]. Of the three monitors in a team, there is often one who replaces the AM1 if he is absent.

The monitor also undertakes 'sequential audits', written reports regarding the process sheets and the quality of work of the assemblers. He also has to periodically supervise the settings of pneumatic screwdrivers, in other words their tightening torques, so that these always correspond to the standards set by the production engineers. Hence the monitor is a key link in the company's quality strategy, because he is responsible for its implementation and for ensuring that the workers observe it. Today the vast majority of workers are conscious of the need to produce high-quality vehicles; when interviewed they emphasise that as clients they would want to buy fault-free cars, or explain that poor quality tarnishes the image of Peugeot, which therefore loses clients, which in turn is detrimental to employment. This does not prevent occasional oversights or involuntary mistakes which are pointed out by downstream areas, or more immediately by the quality inspectors who test a vehicle every two hours on average for each team. Major errors (marked '15 points') are noted, and at HC if there are several of them, the bonus, which is calculated by line, may be reduced. The method of calculating the bonus is in fact linked to several parameters at HC, whereas at MV bonuses are fixed.

The workers attach a certain importance to these level 3 controls, not only because of the bonus but also as a challenge they have failed to meet if their team or group has accumulated the most errors. The results of these controls are posted in the rest areas, but workers do not need to study the tables to know how things stand; word of mouth keeps them informed about the principal defects and their causes. Indeed the information which is posted on team performance – already much less significant here than in other automobile factories in Japan or the rest of Europe – is hardly read, and workers are more interested in the social and cultural activities of the Comité d'Entreprise (Company Council) which are posted at the other end of the rest area.

The quality strategy is also reflected in the activities of quality circles (QCs). A multi-step procedure governs their constitution, functioning and disbanding. Initially envisaged to function for five to seven months on thorny problems, in theory they are made up of workers who have volunteered and are paid overtime since the meetings take place outside normal working hours. In reality, for accounting reasons, management forms quality circles from among the monitors and only occasionally invites the participation of the workers concerned. Knowing that the monitors continue to work when other workers are laid off [13], if the QCs meet on days when workers are laid off it is not necessary to pay overtime. In other words, the QCs play neither their expected technical role (the long periods over which they function, which distances them from urgent issues, does not help), nor their role of social integration and motivation of workers, since they are predominantly formed of monitors and technicians who do not work on the line.

In reality, the rapid resolution of technical problems occurs through *ad hoc* transversal working groups with no institutional base, which include technicians from engineering, design and production along with the relevant AM1s and AM2s. The workers therefore hardly participate at all in the strategy to improve quality; hence, in early 1996, management at Peugeot–Sochaux launched a programme called PCAQ ('Penser Client, Agir Qualité': Think Client, Act Quality), the goal of which was to sensitise workers to their responsibilities regarding the final product. This campaign complemented the AQAP ('Assurance Qualité des Automobiles Peugeot': Automobiles Peugeot's Quality Assurance) and ISO 9000 procedures which had been set up previously, and which aimed to raise the quality of production activities to European norms and norms established by the company that were often even more strict. However, their formalised and restrictive character tended to reduce the scope for initiative on the part of the operators. The dynamics involved here might be questioned, in the sense that the workers receive messages and advice about quality without active involvement in creating a quality strategy.

Workers participate in the improvement of performance more through the suggestion box, which is mainly concerned with productivity (though also safety and quality). Peugeot management has set a target of 12% annual productivity increases. In the assembly areas, this can be attained by improvements in the use of materials and by improved assembly times. Each line has an 'improver' who is responsible for finding sources of improvement. To do this, he analyses and tests suggestions made by workers and often by polyvalent operators and monitors. Sometimes if he perceives an opportunity for improvement, he asks the workers concerned to make the suggestion and helps them to explain it. Once it has been accepted, with the attached bonus distributed to the proposers, these become the 'owners' of the improvement, taking hold of it and actively defending it. Until early 1996, suggestions were remunerated in proportion to the improvements made. Through this suggestion system, modifications to work and work times are more readily accepted since the workers become active agents, which promotes social cohesion.

Hierarchy and social cohesion

The hierarchical line is relatively short: AM1, AM2, 'line chief' (former department head) and area manager, and above him the factory manager who is responsible for the HC area, the MV assembly area and the area that produces the wiring harnesses.

As discussed above, the AM1 is the cornerstone of work quality in his team. He has a great deal of influence over the rate of absenteeism in the team. If he can create a climate of reciprocal confidence and behaves warmly towards his workers, most of them will think twice before being absent, so as not to disrupt his work. Empirical measures reveal that the rate of absenteeism varies by AM1, and that these rates follow them when they are reassigned.

The AM1 has three essential functions: technical, administrative and worker management. Over the years, the technical functions have become less and less important: both monitors and polyvalent operators (particularly with the training of newcomers) have taken up these functions. The technical roles of the AM1 are to ensure that the line is working properly, to supervise the controls carried out by the monitors (over parts supply in particular), and to make sure that the relevant frequent audits take place, regarding quality (he audits the level 2 quality control work of the monitors), rework, tooling and process [14]. He informs the AM2 of these audits if necessary, and the latter is also able to audit the AM1 on the functioning of his team.

The administrative responsibilities of the AM1 are considerably more significant, and occupy most of his time. First, there is the administrative supervision of workers and the team: reporting absences, organising training plans, filling out individual safety training cards, drawing up health and safety signs ('Hygiène Sécurité Personnel') to draw attention to dangerous job positions, encouraging polyvalency and so on. Second, the AM1 is responsible for the management of materials: previous defects which have caused vehicles to be taken off the line for repair, and the supervision of quality (updating of signs or posters, supervision of QCs, assignment of the quality technician to deal with current problems). He is also practically the sole representative of the team to the exterior (daily briefings with the AM2, contact with the 'tracker' [15], components supply, transmission of instructions to the next shift, checking tools with the store, supply of consumables and so on).

Lastly, the AM1 manages the relationships of individuals to each other and to their work. Each time the group starts to work, he has to assign the polyvalent operators (institutionalised or unrecognised) to the vacant posts, as appropriately as possible and as quickly as possible. He also has to examine the clothing of the workers (no tools or belt buckles which might scratch the bodywork), as well as the positions of the protective covers attached to the car wings during assembly. Moreover, he supervises cleaning and the tidying up of tools at the end of the shift. He undertakes a cleanliness audit in his team, which, at HC, can influence the cleanliness bonus (50F per month).

Along with the 'line balancer', he also plans the new 'balances' of the line when there is a change in production volume or car type. The aim is to distribute the various operations between job positions within the theoretical cycle time, taking account of the degree of physical and mental difficulty and of positions acquired within the team. Many posts are occupied by holders who are permanent members of the group, distributed as a function of their height, age and sex [16], medical restrictions (official or otherwise), professional skills or power relationships with the AM1 or monitors. When significant new divisions of labour are called for (reduction from 1,260 to 1,180 cars per day towards the end of our study, with the departure of temporary workers and replacement by workers from other factory areas), negotiations between the AM1, the monitors and the line balancer which respect all the criteria and restrictions may be particularly intensive and long (up to three weeks). In practice, moreover, the line balancer has to take into account the constraints of both shifts.

In undertaking his human resource management function, the AM1 individually interviews each member of his team once every two years (more than two discussions per month on average). The AM1 gives the worker a preparatory four-page questionnaire to fill in, fifteen days prior to the progress interview: description and analysis of the current function, past and future objectives, and so on. Most sheets are not filled in owing to a lack of self-confidence and/or confidence in the hierarchy. The results of the interview are signed by both parties and a copy given to the worker. This includes objectives to be obtained and means of achieving them. During the interview the AM1 raises the subject of the worker's individual evaluation and informs him of his 'potential coefficient'; this is a coefficient that he might hope to achieve at the end of his career. Depending on his current function and his foreseeable development, in other words according to the results of his work and his behaviour over the past year, this potential coefficient may be modified in a minimal way (by giving a +, a − or an =) or more substantially (from one grade to another: 180, 190, 200, 215, 225).

This potential coefficient only gives a rough idea of what the worker may hope to achieve. It can also serve as a shared point of reference that is used effectively and regularly: each AM1 is allocated so many 'progress points' that he distributes according to individual merit (a distribution validated by the AM2). When the sum of the points given over several years approaches a new coefficient scale, the worker is nominated for it if the AM1 or AM2 gives the go-ahead. This range of possible remunerations permits the AM1 to distinguish between and compensate the members of his team with small adjustments even though the salary range is very narrow (assembly workers start with a score of 170, which varies up to 190 or even 200 at retirement). Thus the AM1 can motivate young workers by opening up their chances (a higher potential coefficient) and so accelerate their progress during their initial years at the factory. Conversely, prolonged stagnation is incompatible with a high potential, and the AM1 and AM2 then reduce the 'potential coefficient' in line with the worker's actual situation.

Besides the capabilities described above of maintaining a 'good ambience' and mutual confidence with his team, the qualities of the AM1 encompass the 'savoir-faire' he must possess if he is to distribute parsimonious increases in individual salaries. He cannot side with his team, as can sometimes be seen at other constructors, and argue with management that the rewards he has to share out are inadequate. An AM1 is evaluated through his ability to establish a certain distance with members of his team even as he draws them into his confidence.

The higher level supervisor, the AM2, operates in a similar way, except that he does not have the drawback of being in permanent contact with the assemblers, the technical problems associated with the line or the constraints of cycle times. He supervises the smooth functioning of the operations, follows up quality-related actions and passes information from the top down and from the bottom up; in other words, he supervises. As a former AM1, he possesses these qualities and is dedicated to the company. To organise work on a whole line (four AM1s and a hundred employees) involves arbitrating in the conflicts that can always emerge between workers, suggesting a different spatial arrangement of a work post, harmonising the arrivals and departures of employees on the line, supervising the evaluations made by the AM1, and so on. He also has to know the union officials well (particularly those from the CGT, CFDT and FO) in order, for instance, to discuss problems 'in private' with them before they write down their demands in the special books used for this purpose to be dealt with by the Committee for Health, Safety and Working Conditions. Any such formalisation of demands rigidifies employment relations and is not appreciated by management. The AM2 must be able to foresee any discontent that might crystallise into a movement that makes demands. During national strike actions, he attempts to convince the more militant workers not to leave their work.

Above the AM2, the 'line chief' level is a recent addition, imported from the press shop. Each line chief has full responsibility for one of the trim lines (both shifts plus the adjacent services for his line: line balancer, improver, quality technician, forklift driver). The purpose behind the creation of this new hierarchical grade was the development of forward-looking activities, and particularly quality policies, close to the shopfloor. In practice, the majority of line chiefs find it difficult to move beyond their hierarchical role and do not initiate actions as expected. Indeed some of them are carrying out the same tasks as the AM2, depriving the latter of their legitimacy.

In short, the form taken by the command function has been modified profoundly; the military type of command that prevailed in the 1960s and 1970s, with its barking of orders, has largely disappeared. Members of the hierarchy are more approachable. The existence of the 'individual interview', in particular, contributes to better acquaintanceship and above all to an individualisation of the superior–subordinate relationship, reforming the personnel management methods adopted in the mid 1970s. The AM2s, and especially the AM1s, have to convince, and to bring workers along with them, rather than impose themselves. However, the words 'boss' or 'chief' remain omnipresent for designating the superior, despite management's attempts to discourage their use. The new initiatives on the quality strategy and the accompanying social integration objectives are hardly likely to reduce the fragility of social relations on the assembly line, so monotonous, repetitive and sometimes arduous does the work remain.

A very different form of operator participation

In Carosserie the work remains very physical on three levels:

- the pace of work is very fast: each assembler has to perform several minor operations around one major operation in short cycles (2.3 minutes);
- the various postures (often with the back curved) that are adopted in performing such work lead to lumbago in the lower body while the upper body is subjected to stress, with the risk of traumatic injury;
- certain work posts require the handling of heavy components and sub-assemblies (weighing up to 9.5 kg, for example, in the case of the M3's foot-pedal set).

Working conditions have been considerably improved, particularly at HC in comparison with the old factory. Some operations such as the mounting of windscreens and instrument panels have been automated, thus eliminating the holding of heavy weights at arms' length. The conveyor at HC has been radically transformed through the abandonment of the traditional system in which car bodies sat on trolleys linked together by chains and hooks, themselves sitting on a railway. In the old system, working conditions were very difficult. The workers also had to step over the bumpers of the trolleys which prevented the cars from knocking together. This system has been replaced by a conveyor belt which transports both the worker and the vehicle body, which is placed on a platform, the height of which can be varied according to the work to be done on different segments of the line. The workers therefore work standing still and close to the parts they need, since some of the tools also move along.

And yet perceptions of how arduous the work is in HC2 compared with the old system are ambivalent. Many workers complain of a much faster pace and of being busier than previously. It is true that 'double posts' have been eliminated. In place of very rapid work for two-to-three minutes followed by a rest of similar duration, the assemblers are now permanently occupied (for 85–95% of the cycle time). According to management, the continuous work is compensated for by ergonomic improvements, in particular the disappearance of the obstacles over which workers had to climb.

Each operator has a different perception of the physical work load. Age appears to be the principal determinant, but this factor is mediated by the worker's image of how his current situation fits into his expected career path. By highlighting the worker's expectation, we want to emphasise the fact that the image that each worker constructs of his career is based on what he is told, and on the actual situations that are offered him. In other words, the worker's age is a double determinant of the extent of his participation at work. When he is young, he is physically stronger and can keep up with the fast pace of work. He can also hope for the promotions that are promised as a result of his commitment to the company's objectives. The story changes for those over 37–40 years of age and still working in assembly [17]. Here two attitudes co-exist: one of acceptance, and one of contesting the situation in which they find themselves. The outcome is the existence of three main categories of assemblers which capture the relationships of the majority of workers to their work and to the company. There are individuals who do not fit this classification but closer inspection reveals that they tend to be following their own personal trajectories and so do not undermine it.

The category of young workers comprises workers aged from 23–25 to 37–40, in other words those with less than fifteen years' seniority in the factory. Nowadays they have seldom been recruited without a period as a 'fixed term' (temporary) employee in the company [18]. Definitive employment (with 'contracts of indeterminate duration') may begin after two months or sometimes more than a year of fixed-term employment (depending on the company's needs). Fixed-term employment functions as a trial period during which the supervisor evaluates potential and behaviour. Management believes that the 'professional baccalaureate' [19] is the maximum qualification with which an assembler can be recruited, for fear of having to deal with future aspirations that cannot be satisfied at these jobs. Management prefers to recruit 'professional baccalaureate-level workers' (in other words those who have failed to obtain it) or those at CAP or BEP levels.

These young recruits, who are in good physical condition and often are active in sports, exert themselves on the line without much thought, and for some it becomes a kind of game to perform operations they consider to be easy. They like to change posts and prefer as much variation as possible in the operations they carry out. They like to give complete satisfaction, particularly during their period of fixed-term employment [20]. The majority of them want to become polyvalent (the first step to a better salary) and ultimately to become supervisors. The career path open to them at Peugeot is to move up the hierarchical line to attain salaries much higher than that of assemblers. In practice, the assembly line, with its massive use of living labour, offers no real career prospects. It is seen as a trap from which it is difficult to escape. Once a worker has received good marks, the AM1 tends to refuse transfers to other areas or functions away from the line. The only real possibilities are to become polyvalent operators and monitors, and this therefore appears to be the golden path forward, full of promise and prospects.

A number of workers aged more than 37–40 who have remained assemblers have invested in their work in search of promotions that once seemed possible and were often promised. Yet promotion has not been obtained, principally because it is now impossible, given the reduction of the hierarchical line, the drastic reduction in the number of re-workers due to the integration of quality control in the line, and above all the reduction in the labour force as a whole. The result is that career-end coefficients have stagnated at 190, and exceptionally at 200, even though workers were once given potential coefficients ranging from 215 to 240. For example, former polyvalent operators or off-line re-workers have been assigned to fixed posts. To them the message is clear – there are no further possibilities of promotion – a message which is confirmed by the clear and continuous reduction of their potential coefficient. Some monitors have also been returned to the line and assigned to fixed assembly posts. They may retain their coefficients of 215, but they know that this will now remain their coefficient to the end of their career.

Among these older employees, who account for 60% of workers in both factory areas, those we call the 'disillusioned' accept the conditions in which they find themselves, with no illusions or sense of grievance. They work without complaint and remain committed to the company's objectives of quality, productivity and maintenance of employment. The majority of them vote for the 'reformist' unions and some are, or have been, members of the SIAP-CSL (Syndicat Indépendant d'Automobiles Peugeot, Confédération des Syndicats Libres: Automobiles Peugeot Independent Union: Confederation of Free Unions). In contrast, and much more numerous (see electoral results below) are the older 'radical' workers who feel that they have been duped by a Peugeot management which has not kept its promises on promotions and has not offered them career development. These all vote for the CGT union or for the CFDT (Confédération Française Démocratique du Travail), which at Sochaux is considered to be the 'revolutionary' wing. The extent to which workers are committed to radicalism also depends greatly on their individual trajectories outside the factory.

Until the mid 1980s, workers would leave the assembly line at about 45 years old in order to become re-workers, many more of whom were needed then, or be assigned to off-line posts preparing sub-assemblies. Now all these low added-value sub-assembly posts have been transferred to sub-contractors. Many older workers have therefore tried other strategies to escape from assembly line work, in particular obtaining a medical certificate stating their 'limited abilities'. These may be limited, and temporary, but they justify the reorganisation of a job so that it becomes less strenuous. They may also lead the supervisor to withdraw the worker from the assembly line and assign him to one of the – rare – posts adjacent to production (supplies, sub-assembly, office work). Attempts to adopt such strategies for leaving the line tend to multiply prior to major redistributions of tasks between posts (see above). This reveals both the workers' fear of change and the lassitude and weariness caused by assembly line work. Other more desperate strategies involve shorter or longer absences from work due to illness. This is a riskier strategy since if a 'social plan' [21] is launched, the workers who are most often absent are the first to go. Moreover, all bonuses (monthly, for launch of a new vehicle and so on) are closely linked to absenteeism.

The general fatigue of the older workers, combined with their state of resignation, lead some to wish for more short-term lay-offs, or, for the older workers, the return of the FNE [22] that permitted early retirement at 55 or 56 years old. If they remain on the assembly line at Peugeot it is mainly because they have no other employment opportunities. Consequently, and this is not the least of the paradoxes, the majority of these workers remain firmly attached to the product and its quality. Moreover there is a social life organised around the production lines that gives satisfaction and pleasure, and this makes work more acceptable. Hence the AM1 plays an irreplaceable role in maintaining social cohesion by establishing the rules of the social game within the team, tolerating minor infractions of production norms provided that the team as a whole coheres, and stimulating young recruits to pull the team up. The big question that now faces management is how it will be able to reward the current motivation of young employees while maintaining the productivity levels of older employees and simultaneously not increasing the cost of labour (not yielding to likely future wage demands).

A weak and divided unionism

The role of unions at Peugeot–Sochaux mirrors certain particularities of private sector unionism in France. This is expressed mainly through two elected institutions, the shop stewards and the representatives on the Comité d'Etablissement (Works Council), which is generally informed about the overall direction of the company and directly manages social activities (training, leisure, sports, culture, holidays). The shop stewards inform supervisors of grievances, complaints and demands from the shopfloor and settle local issues with them. Moreover, the unions regularly disseminate tracts concerning major national debates, the company's position and life at the Sochaux factory or a particular area of the factory. Lastly, the unions participate in negotiations with management (wages, 'social plans') at factory level and at company level.

As at most French companies, the unions at Peugeot–Sochaux appear particularly marked by a contrast that seems to characterise representative unionism. For one thing, taking all the union organisations together, the number of members or militants is particularly low, including among the workers. The unions have therefore been affected by the national tendency to disaffection. However, the attachment of the personnel to the presence of unions remain high, as attested by rates of participation in elections, which often approaches 90%. There was a significant example of this attachment during the first elections of shop stewards for the new HC1 area in 1990. The new principles for managing social relations in this area abstracted unionism and presupposed the absence of an oppositional logic. Moreover, worker collectives had been broken up and, with them, the networks of union influence. Yet there were high levels of participation in the elections, and previous channels of influence were redirected towards the unions seen as 'radical' or 'oppositional', principally the CGT.

The union organisations are diverse, and there are six of them: CGT, CFDT, FO, SIAP-CSL, CFTC (Confédération Française des Travailleurs Chrétiens) and CGC (Confédération Générale des Cadres). This number is partly explained by specificities related to categories. Hence, the CGC, which represents middle management, executives, and is also active among the 'ETAM' categories (Employés Techniciens, Agents de Maitrise: salaried employees, technicians and supervisors), was founded on the basis of a dual claim for a specific identity: against company management as a salaried group, and against other company personnel, workers and employees. However, union diversity primarily corresponds to strategic and cultural differences characteristic of French unionism. All the organisations with the exception of the SIAP-CSL are affiliated to central bodies whose national-level representation is legally recognised. Moreover, each strand of unionism can claim a long established participation at Peugeot–Sochaux with a presence stretching back fifty years, and in proportions that have barely changed.

The individual orientations of these unions developed over the course of a particularly turbulent history. The results of a tradition of class struggle, the CGT and FO split in 1948 in a Cold War context, the CGT developing a closer relationship to the Communist Party and the FO opposing this. Christian unionism split in 1964 into two organisations, with the CFDT seeking to be modern and receptive to more combative positions and the more traditional CFTC retaining closer links with religious institutions. Lastly, the SIAP-CSL is a union that supports company management.

An examination of electoral results, company agreements and alliances between unions indicates the power relations between the unions and in their relationships with management. At the level of the Sochaux production centre, the results obtained by the various unions vary little from one election to the other [23]. They indicate two categorical identities, in which the CGT is hegemonic among workers and the CGC among employees, technicians and supervisors. This general polarisation is apparent in the formation of alliances among unions in the management of the Comité d'Etablissement. While the CGT controlled it for many years, it lost this control a decade ago, to a coalition of other unions which at the time included the CFDT. The departure of the CFDT from the coalition led to a new form of power-sharing among the 'reformist' unions, aligned against the 'oppositional' unions.

A contract-based strategy has long been [24] a factor in relationships between management and the unions. It was developed at both company level and at the level of the Sochaux centre. At the latter level management concludes contracts with the unions (twenty-five between 1989 and 1994). It is rare to find a contract signed by all unions, and some are even rejected by all. With the exception of the CGT, which frequently fails to sign, the positions of the unions vary from case to case. Most contracts are concerned with the organisation of elections and the election of shop stewards. Others concern how to organise working time, or other limited aspects of employment relations. Taken as a whole, these contracts present a picture of a management that takes the initiative and unions which adopt varying attitudes.

The outcome of these various factors has been two types of union activity over the decades, separate, but co-existing and perhaps even complementary. One type, represented mainly by the CGT but also by the CFDT, opposes management on the basis of the specificity of the working class, and is supported by more than half the workers despite the low numbers of militants and union members and problems concerning how to implement it. The other favours co-operation with management, within certain limits, and in fact concretises (to varying degrees) the company's own internal cohesion.

This bi-polarisation became even more marked in the period following 1968, during which relations between management and unions assumed a quasi-Manichaean pattern of confrontation or collaboration. It is also linked to features of historical conflicts at Sochaux. Although conflicts are rare they bring a section of the workers face to face with management, often leading to lasting commitments and choices of identity.

In union matters, the Carrosserie plant has two particular features of note. First, in most of MV and HC, on the assembly lines in particular, workers vote for the CGT more than they do elsewhere. Second, in the past this area has often been particularly susceptible to conflict and to the symbolic aspect of the strikes that have taken place at Sochaux.

A neo-Fordism à la française

Endowed with a rich history spanning seventy years, Peugeot's Sochaux factory inherited an inter-war employment relationship characterised by a number of elements: a paternalist tradition (lodgings for workers, shops and sports equipment belonging to the company, financial support for the football team, training schools, and so on), accentuated by the company's hegemony in the region, a discreet but methodical industrial rationality, and a management favouring a Protestant rigour. The years of steady growth shifted these basic leanings towards a more classical Fordism: the rationality of mass production, a giant industrial company, and employment relations combining and sometimes alternating authoritarianism and social compromise. The 1980s, with their cortege of problems, led to a drastic reduction in the workforce, with the corollary of an ageing personnel, a fevered search for productivity and a re-shaping of the employment relationship.

Overall, the employment relationship has remained Fordist, particularly on the assembly lines and despite the modernisation of the conveyors in the HC factory. The domination of the production flow over work activities has been reinforced. Workers have little autonomy and barely participate in activities like line balancing, quality circles, supplies and so on. If they do participate, it is generally through making social adjustments to improve working conditions and production. There is one exception, the widespread participation of workers in trying to increase productivity through suggestions. On the whole, shopfloor management (the AM1 and AM2) is the pivot of the production system and union activism is low, and hence one can speak of neo-Fordism.

As far as employment relationships are concerned, new principles have been adopted during the last twenty years: the individualisation of wages, hierarchical relationships and careers at all levels, without radical reform of the traditional working team and its functioning. Moreover, and not entirely in contradiction with this, a majority of workers claim to support the existence of class-based union representation. This does not prevent employee participation, however. On the contrary, the attachment to and identification of workers with the company appears to be quite high, much higher than the average French company. The theme of quality often serves as a link between the intensity of work, its organisation, company objectives and employment.

Furthermore – although this is not the subject of this chapter – there have been experiments and lasting innovations in other parts of the factory which are rarely if ever discussed at Peugeot. The radical nature of some of these deserves mention: the dressing of the V6 engine of the 'S' model takes place on a ring of automatic guided vehicles, where skilled workers have a cycle time exceeding 90 minutes. The production of the wire harnesses of the 'S' model no longer takes place on the traditional carousel but on a single workbench, with a cycle time of two hours and thirty minutes (700 connections have to be made) and is accomplished by a single skilled worker. These situations emphasise the extent to which traditions are being changed at Peugeot through experimentation, and the extent to which the company possesses strong adaptive capacities. But why change employment relations if those already in place are effective enough? Who knows the costs of taking risks?

End-notes

[1]   PSA Peugeot–Citroën comprises Automobiles Peugeot, Automobiles Citroën and sub-contracting subsidiaries like ECIA (exhaust systems, mechanical parts, etc.).

[2]   To designate the models produced at Sochaux, we have adopted the categories used to segment the European market: hence S is

the upper segment of the market, the Peugeot 605, a luxury vehicle launched in 1990; M2 is the upper middle segment, the 405, a vehicle about to be phased out; M3 is the upper middle segment, the 406, a new vehicle, production of which had just achieved full volume levels at the time of our research; and Ml is the lower middle segment, the 306, a vehicle produced largely at Poissy. Finally, I is the small car segment.

[3]   Hence ECIA, formed in 1987 from several Peugeot group companies, has inherited Aciers and Outillages Peugeot (steel and tooling) and Cycles Peugeot, some of whose factories bore the name Peugeot before the Sochaux plant even existed.

[4]   Thus, for example in 1996 workers under 35 years old accounted for 19% of workers in final assembly. whereas in 1967 they accounted for 54% of all workers at Sochaux.

[5]   The same could be said of Citroën, whose 'Plan Mercure' was only discussed when the employees had to be remotivated in the mid 1980s because the social climate had deteriorated and Citroën had fallen behind Japanese companies (see Sylvie Celerier, 'Le Plan Mercure de la Société des Automobiles Citroën', in *ECOSIP, Gestion industrielle et Mesure économique*, Economica, Paris, 1990; Xavier Mercure, *Citroën, une nouvelle culture d'entreprise*, Les Editions d'Organisation, Paris, 1989; Jean-Pierre Durand, 'Competitiveness of the car industry: the French way', in Paul Stewart, (ed.), *Beyond Japanese Management: The End of Modern Times*, Frank Cass, London, 1996.

[6]   The many agreements with other manufacturers bear witness to this (the association of Peugeot and Renault between 1966 and 1975, the purchase of Citroën in 1975 and Chrysler Europe in 1978, and the current co-operation with Fiat on small commercial vehicles, mini-vans and mechanical components).

[7]   We would like to extend our thanks to the factory management, who supported this research and were interested in obtaining an external view – through an international comparison – of its own factories. The research was always presented to the workers and supervisors as academic research, the results of which were to be made public. All interviews were carried out anonymously. In the HC factory, we undertook in-depth interviews (between 1 and 2.5 hours) with 27 operators mainly from the 'B shift' on Line 1 (a shift that works mornings one week, from 5am to 1pm, and afternoons the next week, from 1pm to 9pm). We also interviewed 5 supervisors and 11 white-collar workers directly or indirectly linked to production. These discussions were complemented by personal observation of assembly line work and adjacent services, and then by a to-and-fro between observation and some discussion with some

privileged interlocutors (supervisors, shop stewards, union repre-sentatives, personnel managers from the factory area and the Sochaux Centre as a whole). On the MV line, one of us worked in a job on the line within a team for four weeks (after a preliminary training course). Outside the team's working hours, we either interviewed or followed certain employees (direct supervisors and eight technicians and white-collar staff working in the factory) who were organising work on the line. At the end of this part of the research, we conducted thorough discussions with 12 operators from the team, enabling us to broaden our knowledge. Systematic collaboration between the two researchers permitted us to exploit the complementarity between methods and sites. Finally, we conducted further complementary visits and obtained any documents we wanted to consult.

[8]   This factory comprises other factory areas, in particular sewing and preparing seats and parts of the car's interior trim, wiring (where half the wire harnesses are made, the other half being made by external suppliers), the area where the front drivetrain is assem-bled from mechanical components, and certain activities to finish, control the quality and protect the vehicles exiting the line.

[9]   Prior to 1990, in the old factory, the polyvalent worker was called a 'dépanneur' (literally, 'replacer'), and he replaced a worker when he went to the toilet, because there could be no pauses, except at the main meal time. However, since this system always caused ar-guments (length of absence, arbitrary decisions on who would be replaced when, and so on), these replacements were eliminated in favour of two ten-minute pauses when the line is halted. These breaks are still, inappropriately, called 'dépannages' (replacement periods).

[10] Since it involves mastery of the work process, acquiring the status of a polyvalent is the obligatory path to becoming a monitor. Monitor status opens the path to becoming a supervisor. The polyvalent operator receives neither a bonus nor an extra salary; he is only assured of acceding more quickly to a higher coefficient.

[11] The hierarchical structure of these activities differs according to team and monitor. However the philosophy at Peugeot is to focus on prevention rather than cure. Hence the mission of the monitor is also expressed as: Prevention → Supervision → Amelioration (Improvement). The acronym in French, 'PSA', gives added significance.

[12] Because of the constraints of the production flow (cycle times of 2.3 minutes) and possible errors in components supply, it may happen that some operations cannot be completed. If the operations that follow, cannot be carried out, they are classed 'TIA' (temporarily impossible to assemble) and the (vehicle) leaves the line at the end of the chain. Otherwise it is declared 'derailed' and downstream

areas are warned so that re-workers can fix it at the end of final assembly.

[13]   Lay-offs have become a solution to adapt production to variations in the volume of demand. Workers stop working and are paid between 65% and 85% of their normal salary by the company, which receives financial support from the public authorities (between 55% and 60% of the payment made).

[14]   The aim is to evaluate whether the demands of the post and the training of the assembler, the tooling, the components to be assembled, instruction notices and so on, are mutually consistent. If this is not the case, a plan of action with a 'pilot' to guide it is organised. A three-page form is used in support of this audit.

[15]   The 'trackers' ('pisteurs') are the forklift truck drivers who belong to the logistics department and supply the assembly lines.

[16]   The percentage of women on the final assembly lines is about 2 to 3%. Slightly more work in sub-assembly areas.

[17]   The average age in the HC factory is 42 years and in the MV factory 43 years. This average age is much less significant than the fact that 60% of assemblers are over 40 years old.

[18]   This means that recruitment by 'family recommendation' (from workers already employed at Peugeot) has discontinued. The disappearance of family patronage indicates a rupture with the culture that was dominant up to the 1960s.

[19]   The 'professional bac' represents eight years of secondary studies, of which four are 'vocational' (in contrast to the traditional bac, which in France refers to general learning at a higher level). Students attending vocational colleges may stop two years before the 'professional bac', that is, after six years of study, and obtain a CAP (Certificat d'Aptitude Professionelle) or a BEP (Brevet d'Enseignement Professionel).

[20]   The regions of Montbéliard–Sochaux and Belfort have experienced high unemployment, and during the mid 1990s Peugeot was one of the only companies to be hiring (besides components suppliers who had just relocated to the adjacent industrial area). Moreover, in practice Peugeot hires for life, in contrast, for instance, to Alsthom at Belfort (which does offer better salaries for those with CAPs or BEPs) or the suppliers.

[21]   The 'social plan' is a procedure (based on a tripartite agreement among management, unions and the state) which organises workforce reductions through early retirement by older workers, financial as-

sistance for immigrants returning to their countries of origin, and the 'reconversion' of employees through training.

[22] Fonds National pour l'Emploi (National Employment Fund). The abridged description of a worker 'leaving on FNF' means that he leaves prior to the usual age of retirement through a social plan and receives between 65% and 80% of salary until the age of 60. In 1994, workers over 56 years and 2 months were eligible to 'leave on FNE'

[23] Among the workers, in 1992 the CGT obtained close to 50%, the CFDT 12% and the others, from the FO to SIAP-CSL, between 15% and 10%. Among employees, technicians and supervisors, the CGC dominated, with more than 55% of the vote; the others, from the CFDT and FO to the SIAP/CSL and the CGT, received 13% to 5% of the vote.

[24] On 10 December 1955, at about the same time as Renault, Peugeot signed the first in a series of social agreements with the unions (except for the CGT).

Bibliography

Boyer R. and Durand J.-P. (1997) *After Fordism*. London: Macmillan.

Burawoy M. (1979) *Manufacturing Consent: Changes in the Labor Process Under Monopoly Capitalism*. Chicago IL: University of Chicago Press.

Corouge C. and Pialoux M. (1982–83) Chronique Peugeot, *Actes de la recherche en sciences sociales*, no. 52–53, 54, 57, 60.

Durand J.-P. (ed.) (1994) *La Fin du Modèle Suédois*. Paris: Syros.

Durand J.-P. (ed.) (1995) *Le Syndicalisme au Futur*. Paris: Syros.

Durand J.-P. and Stewart P. (1998) Manufacturing Dissent? Burawoy in a Franco-Japanese Workshop. *Work, Employment and Society*, Vol. 12, No. 1, 145–159.

Goux J.-P. (1986) *Mémoires de l'enclave*. Paris: Mazarine.

Groux G. and Mouriaux R. (1989) *La CFDT*. Paris: Economica.

Groux G. and Mouriaux R. (1992) *La CGT: Crises et Alternatives*. Paris: Economica.

Guigo D. (1994) *Ethnologie des hommes des usines et des bureaux*. Paris, L'Harmattan.

Hatzfeld N. (1987) Peugeot 1950–1979. In *Pertinence et limite de la notion de rapport salarial dans le cas du secteur automobile*. Gerpisa, rapport Pirttem-Cnrs, 1987, t.l.

Hatzfeld N. (1989) L'Ecole d'Apprentissage Peugeot (1930–1970): une formation d'excellence. *Formation-Emploi*, no. 27–28, Juillet–Décembre.

Hatzfeld N. (1992) Peugeot–Sochaux: de l'entreprise dans la crise à la crise dans l'entreprise. In Mouriaux R., Percheron A., Prost A. and Tartakowski D. (eds.), *Exploration du Mai français*. Paris: L'Harmattan, 1992, t.1.

Jürgens U., Malsch T. and Dohse K. (1993) *Breaking from Taylorism. Changing Forms of Work in the Automobile Industry*. Cambridge University Press.

Linhart, D. (1994) *La Modernisation des Entreprises*. Paris: La Découverte (Collection 'Repères').

Linhart R. (1978) *L'établi*. Paris: Editions de Minuit.

Loubet J.-L. (1990) *Automobiles Peugeot, une réussite industrielle, 1945–1974*. Paris: Economica.

Loubet J.-L. (1995) *Citroën, Peugeot, Renault et les autres. Soixante ans de stratégies*. Paris: Le Monde Editions.

Mispelblom F. (1995) *Au-delà de la Qualité* Paris: Syros.

Morris J., Munday M. and Wilkinson B. (1993) *Working for the Japanese*. London: Athlone Press.

Normann R. (1984) *Service Management: Strategy and Leadership in Service Business*. Chichester: Wiley.

Ohno T. (1988) *Toyota Production System: Beyond Large-Scale Production*. Portland OR: Productivity Press.

Oliver N. and Wilkinson B. (1992) *The Japanization of British Industry*, 2nd edn. London: Blackwell.

Paganelli S. and Jacquin M. (1975) *Peugeot. La dynastie s'accroche*, Paris: Editions sociales.

Parker M. and Slaughter J. (1988) *Choosing Sides: Unions and the Team Concept*. Boston MA: South End Press.

Pialoux M. (1993) In *La Misère du Monde*, sous la direction de Bourdieu P.: 'Le vieil ouvrier et la nouvelle usine, pp. 331, 348; Le désarroi du délégué, pp. 413–432; Permanents et temporaires – avec Stéphane Beaud, pp. 317–329. Paris: Seuil.

Pialoux M. (1996) Stratégies patronales et résistances ouvrières. La 'modernisation' des ateliers de finition aux usines Peugeot de Sochaux (1989–1993). *Actes de la recherche en sciences sociales*, no. 114, septembre.

Pialoux M. and Beaud S. (1993) Ouvriers de Sochaux: l'affaiblissement d'un groupe, hantise de l'exclusion et rêve de formation, *Rapport de recherche pour la MIRE*, avril.

Roth S. (1992) *Japanization or Going Our Own Way?* Dusseldorf: IG Metall.

Sandberg A. (ed.) (1995) *Enriching Production*. Aldershot: Avebury.

Wood S. (ed.) (1989) *The Transformation of Work*. London: Unwin Hyman.

CHAPTER 8
Transformations in the Teamwork at Renault

Michel Freyssenet

Teamwork at Renault has quite a long history and so to understand its form and content it would be appropriate to know what its principal characteristics are. It was first introduced in Renault in the 1970s by a few managers in an attempt to reform work and in particular assembly-line work using the reorganisation which was taking place at Volvo as inspiration. It was not possible to develop it in the manual sectors owing to opposition by certain managers and the fact that it was regarded with a degree of suspicion by the unions. However it reappeared in the automated sectors at the beginning of the 1980s without coming up against any major opposition [1].

In fact, new problems came to light with automation. The form it took on modified the usual norms of work and gave rise to dysfunctions. Different formulas for teamwork were then experimented with, some to accommodate these new work norms and others to overcome the dysfunctions of the automated installations in the way they had been designed.

The reduction in the number of posts that these formulas allowed, along with the necessity to mobilise the personnel to improve results after the 1984 financial slump and changes in alliances between management and unions, led to a consensus among managers on teamwork in the second half of the 1980s. The definition that was then given to it and the fact that it was implemented homogeneously made the more daring formulas that were used at the beginning of the 1980s redundant, both from the point of view of the function of the group leader and relations with maintenance. Although presented as being explicitly inspired from the 'Japanese methods', in fact teamwork at Renault distinguishes itself distinctly as much by its official definition as by its multiple facets (Freyssenet, 1988).

Teamwork to deal with 'the work crisis' at the beginning of the 1970s

At the beginning of the 1970s, two conflicting orientations existed within management at Renault to deal with the work crisis, which manifested itself through often spectacular conflicts, growing absenteeism, high levels of turnover and an increase in the amount of rectification work to be done on vehicles. The first was that of the managing director, Pierre Dreyfus. He felt that it would be impossible to return to what he considered to be a form of neo-artisan work. As far as he was concerned, the only solution was to compensate for the difficulties of assembly-line work by continuing with a policy of increasing workers' purchasing power and especially by reducing working time, thus allowing them to take advantage of social and cultural activities which the industry itself could never bring them, and also by developing in-service training, thereby facilitating professional promotion.

The second orientation aimed at rendering work more enriching by making it more attractive and flexible. Several new forms of work organisation were experimented with by some factory managers: rotation between two or three positions, complete assembly of a mechanism while moving it down the assembly line, lengthening the work cycle by including preparation and rectification, working on 'work islands', etc.; that is to say about fifteen experiments, largely inspired from those at Volvo, with whom Renault had agreements on joint production of mechanical components. Relying on the results of these experiments, a central work group proposed: 'not only to humanise technology, but also to explore new ways of organising the factories and designing equipment and buildings ... [from the point of view of] ... the degree of freedom and of initiative that would be allowed the personnel, the utilisation of its skills, and the possibilities of working in teams'. Several new operations resulted from this: the complete assembly of an engine by a worker at a fixed position, the introduction of four short assembly lines instead of one long one at the new Douai assembly factory, and the generalisation at the Le Mans factory of the assembly of front and rear axles in modules of 3 to 5 workers. These workers took charge of their own organisation, inspected the complete assembly, checked the maintenance of the apparatus, were responsible for quality, carried out rectification work and looked after the cleanliness of the machines and working areas (Coriat, 1978;

Freyssenet, 1979). These experiments in work reform also interested certain production managers who were concerned about the difficulty in dealing with the diversity and the increasing variability in production. Besides being interested from a social point of view, they saw the possibility of adapting the production programme more easily and at a lesser cost. However, despite the results that were achieved, the most radical and novel formula, that of the modules, was the subject of much debate at top levels (Midler, 1980). The work study departments were opposed because it challenged the basic industrial principles of decomposing and recomposing work into elementary operations (additivity) and carrying them out on a line in a sequential way (linearity). The development of teamwork in the manual sectors stopped at that stage.

Nevertheless, the concern to offer unskilled workers the opportunity to progress in the scale of grades right throughout their working lives not only remained but was imposed. In fact, the slump in growth after the petrol crisis and the easing off in hiring at the end of the 1970s made the freeze in professional promotion quite unacceptable.

The company work study departments considered that the best solution for the work crisis was to introduce automation quickly, which in their eyes would allow them to eliminate difficult and repetitive work, and at the same time to develop the functions of running-maintenance in such a way as to make them more attractive and more skilled, to increase the flexibility of the production tools and to raise the quality. And effectively, it is this solution which was finally adopted at the end of the 1970s. Those who were promoting teamwork in Renault had considered extending it to the mechanised and automated sectors very early on. A work group had been set up at the Le Mans factory as early as 1975 to consider the possibility of introducing 'production units' to the manufacturing workshops, which would be autonomous with regard to upstream and downstream, be made up of various different machines and grouped together geographically, where the operators could be responsible in turn for running the machines, adjusting and changing the tools, verifying the quality, and looking after minor breakdowns and maintenance. Teamwork was introduced to and accepted in the automated areas as soon as they were created, which was not the case in the manual sectors. It was accepted, because in the way it developed it did not challenge the principles of additivity and linearity and it could allow problems which appeared with automation to be solved.

The relaunch of teamwork in the automated areas (1979–84)

Automation consisted in integrating in a single line the machines necessary for the manufacture of one part or sub-assembly. Both simple and complex operations were partly or totally automated, leaving the operators to carry out partial or heterogeneous tasks. With regard to more complex tasks, such as repair of breakdowns, it consisted in simplifying them by dividing them up. The machines and production lines were equipped with automatic devices that stopped them in the event of an anomaly, located the incident in equally automatic fashion, and involved 'standard exchange' of the failed component, fuller repairs being postponed to periods outside production.

Three new problems then came to light: how to make these integrated and therefore costly lines function continuously, so as to reduce their number; how to get the new mode of maintenance accepted; and how to divide up tasks, none of which occupied a person full-time. These three problems challenged previous work norms. Production workers previously had daily work quotas to fulfil, which gave them relative freedom to vary the pace of the work. They had tasks which were relatively homogeneous and were easy to classify according to their level of complexity. Maintenance workers could take the time necessary for in-depth diagnosis and repair of machines. So what was now at stake at work in the automated areas, was to ensure that it would be accepted that the machines run continuously, that intermittent tasks at different levels be carried out by the same people, and that breakdowns be repaired rapidly so that production would be disrupted as little as possible. But when this type of automation was put into practice it gave rise to below-average results. The automated machines had been supposed to bring productivity, flexibility and precision but, designed as they were, they caused numerous stoppages in production as well as quality problems in the first half of the 1980s. Several causes lie at the root of this unreliability and the slowness in rectifying it. They include a lack of understanding of the daily production problems on the part of the designers, a desire to pursue technological leaps to make large improvements in a single step, and a mode of calculating the profitability of investments which favoured manpower reductions. These are joined by, a weakness of links between the factories and the central work study department at this period, an opaqueness and needless complexity in the first machines which hindered attempts to make them reliable, and the fact that design technicians and engineers were hired according to their qualifications rather than coming directly from the factory by internal promotion (Freyssenet, 1992).

The organisational solutions found for these problems varied from one factory to another, or even from one work area to another (Freyssenet, 1984; Midler and Charue, 1990). As early as 1982, four forms of teamwork could be observed. These different formula were not mere experiments, but involved whole departments of a factory: machining, welding, stamping, etc. They did not, however, represent the implementation of an official strategy by the company, but rather the fruit of local initiatives by area or department managers. Time would have to pass before senior management and the totality of the management of the company would realise and understand the scope and implications of these new ways of organising work.

The first formula appeared in the Le Mans factory. It consisted of recruiting 'controllers' of automated machine lines among unskilled workers and making access into this new category dependent upon: prior success in psychological–technical tests, a theoretical and practical test following a four-month period of training, an acceptance of certain working conditions (continuous working, three eight-hour shifts, new tasks, team working, etc.), and upon assignment to a specified piece of equipment. This formula aimed at offering unskilled workers a professional classification, in exchange for accepting polyvalent work composed of tasks normally classified at different levels and accepting that the production lines would function continuously.

The second formula, adopted in the robotised welding area at the Douai factory, consisted in offering maintenance workers (professionals and technicians) the possibility of becoming line controllers for a fixed period, and agreeing to certain quality standards and a certain rate of downtime. The reversibility of this choice and the promise of more rapid promotion elicited volunteers. However, under pressure from the production manager to repair breakdowns rapidly in order to achieve production targets and to avoid hold-ups, they were not able to truly exercise their competencies in this function by organising themselves to make full repairs and to seek the fundamental causes of breakdowns in order to eliminate them. A separate maintenance group had to be retained.

The third formula was adopted in the Vilvorde factory in Belgium, also in the robotised welding area. Production workers who carried out unskilled work, but who already possessed technical qualifications, were trained full-time for a year, to enable them to control and repair robotised installations. Organised into groups of five persons, without a leader they were classified as equivalent to 'third level professionals'. It was not planned that maintenance workers would come to their aid.

The last formula was adopted in the welding area at the Flins factory, where maintenance, quality control and industrial engineering had been placed under the authority of the head of department. Each robotised line was controlled by a mixed production–maintenance group, consisting of a technician, a leader, an electrician–mechanic, and three line controllers (former unskilled production workers, classified as 'second level professionals' following their selection and a four-month training period). The division of tasks among them was not rigid, and so the controllers sometimes participated in in-depth breakdown repairs, and even in modifications made by the technician and the electrician–mechanic. This formula was by far the most original, and potentially the most far reaching. It represented a good compromise between, on the one hand, the need to make repairs swiftly, and on the other, not postponing the search for the causes of problems and the activities necessary to make installations more reliable.

Renault discovered the wealth of initiatives that had been adopted in its various factories on the occasion of an initiative launched in 1983 by senior management, which was aimed at mobilising all possible energies in order to deal with the deep financial crisis that had appeared. This initiative was called 'Industrial Restructuring and Social Dynamics' (Mutations Industrielles et Dynamique Sociale: MIDES) and consisted in a wide-ranging debate between managers, trade unions and external experts with the aim of outlining the transformations that the company should carry out. Some new concepts emerged from this debate at the level of the whole company: the basic production units (300 persons), conceived as the basic cell of industrial activity and composed of sub-cells (8–10 persons), the idea of 'the new function of the worker', a structure for the firm which allowed rapid circulation of information, training considered as an investment, and the idea that techniques should meet the aspirations and expectations of the personnel with regard to the content of work, etc. However the internal dynamics triggered off by this collective discussion came to a halt with the financial slump that Renault experienced in 1984 after the resignation of the Managing Director.

The legitimisation, the diffusion and the homogenisation of the different forms of teamwork in the second half of the 1980s

The serious financial crisis in 1984 made senior managers lose faith in their convictions. Many of them left the company, along with middle managers, most taking early retirement, a measure that they had been strongly encouraged to exploit in an effort to enforce the drastic reduction in the workforce that Renault had decided on (Freyssenet, 1998). In this new context, where the company had to draw from its own energy and experience to get out of the crisis, any former opposition was inopportune.

It seemed that teamwork was no longer viewed with suspicion and could be advocated once again by the young managers who had been promoted, taking the place of older ones. It appeared to be a formula which would allow them to both reduce the number of posts and to increase the involvement of the workforce. It allowed the elimination of a number of substitute workers, quality-control staff, rectification workers, 'setters' and foremen, as operators had to be polyvalent and verify the work they carried out themselves. So, it spread again progressively, even in the manual sectors, always on the initiative of the managers of the working areas and of the factory managers.

The manager of personnel and social affairs, who had supported module work in the 1970s without much success, came to consider that, in the end, assembly-line work was unavoidable, for economic reasons, and especially as it had changed in nature owing to the profound modifications it was experiencing. It became much more acceptable in his eyes because of the preparation that took place away from the assembly lines or on the short lines of a certain number of sub-assemblies, also because of the automation of the most tiring operations, and the fact that the workstations were made more ergonomically acceptable. Teamwork got rid of the restricting, parcelised and pure-execution nature of work (Tijou, 1991).

In the automated sectors, the different formulas of teamwork were tending to homogenise. The team of line controllers, former unskilled workers, taking it in turns to undertake the tasks and functions necessary for integrated production lines, became the model in the mechanical components factories. It could do this all the more easily since it revealed itself appropriate to the type of automation adopted. The simplification of tool setting, quality control, problem-spotting and rapid repair allowed these tasks to be entrusted to operators with only a few months' training. In the robotised welding areas, the operating groups formed only of maintenance workers disappeared, to be replaced by groups similar to those which were favoured in machining. The gap between the level of work that had to be done and the competencies of the workers was too wide. The formula of groups composed of former production workers with previous qualifications, and who were trained for a year to operate and maintain equipment, was not sufficient to obviate the need for intervention by maintenance workers. As for the most developed form, that of the mixed production–maintenance groups in the robotised welding areas, it came up against two problems. The first was the reductions in staff which resulted from the work which the teams themselves carried out to make the equipment more reliable. The lack of agreement with management to guarantee jobs provoked a growing reticence on the part of group members to continue their participation in these activities. At the same time, it became more difficult to undertake these activities. The pursuit of automation in the direction of automatic diagnosis for rapid repairs, coupled with the increasing opaqueness of the machines, made it still more difficult for the groups themselves to seek out and analyse the primary causes of incidents. Moreover, the groups were increasingly composed of line controllers who were formerly unskilled workers trained only to operate equipment and repair minor breakdowns.

The adoption of 'Total Quality' by the management from 1987 onwards legitimised and gave an administrative basis to teamwork [2]. It was presented as a method of boosting the trend of improving quality and results, in order to get the operators to support it, and to redefine hierarchical relations and the role of the foremen. Following a period of conflict and tension related to redundancies and reduction in manpower that took place between 1985 and 1987, management simultaneously sought to promote a human resources policy as a strategic choice for the firm. Joint Management–Trade Union groups got together towards the end of 1988. Their work led to negotiations regarding skills, management of working time, organisation of work, training and professional orientation. Several agreements resulted from this discussion: notably an agreement on skills in the automated areas and above all 'The Agreement for Living' (l'Accord' d'vivre) which defined the new principles for contractual relations between the firm and its employees. 'The Agreement for Living' confirmed that Renault wanted to base its success on the competencies of its personnel and the relevance of its organisation. A plan to 'professionalise' production workers would result from it.

The creation and the generalisation of Elementary Work Units, 1991–94

In 1991, Renault decided to generalise teamwork in the form of Elementary Work Units (EWUs). By the end of 1994, its twenty-seven European industrial plants were officially organised in this way, both the production plants and the different services and offices.

Officially, teamwork as conceived by Renault is polyvalent, multifunctional work carried out by a group of 10–20 persons. The unit is defined by the component, mechanism or sub-assembly that it makes up or the service that it renders. It is led by a unit leader, who constitutes the first hierarchical level. It controls and analyses its own production parameters. It enters into buyer–supplier relations with the other teams upon which it depends, upstream and downstream in the production process. What is expected from this form of work organisation is an ability to react to problems, an improvement in the quality of products and the functioning of machines, a greater flexibility of production, a development of competencies, an increased interest in work and, finally, a modification in hierarchical relations.

This definition of teamwork is different from the definitions given by the two other companies that Renault was successively inspired by, that is to say, Volvo and Toyota. And furthermore it encountered difficulties when it was implemented in the middle of the 1990s [3].

So according to this official definition, Unit Leaders have a hierarchical responsibility and do not work on the line themselves. They are not operators among others, as in the Toyota group. Neither are they chosen by the members of the group, as was the case in the Volvo group or in certain automated machining areas at Renault in the 1980s, nor are they rotated with others who fulfil the conditions to assure the functioning of the Unit Leader. Considering what had been done previously in a number of plants, EWUs marked a return to hierarchical management in the functioning of groups.

The unit is defined by size (10 to 20 persons maximum), by a spatial and temporal framework and by a homogeneous activity (a mechanism or a sub-assembly, a service, etc.). The client–supplier relationship with other units defines its perimeters (Decoster and Freyssenet, 1997). These criteria correspond to several preoccupations: a size sufficient to allow movement between stations and substitute workers, a common spatio-temporal framework so that exchange within a unit can happen immediately, and a product unit to allow the group to completely master the production and guarantee good quality. Does the definition given to teamwork correspond with the reality? How does it compare with Volvo and Toyota?

The sizes of the groups at Toyota and Volvo are generally smaller. They have a maximum of about ten people. The product unit is not usual at Toyota, as the classic assembly line prevailed until the beginning of the 1990s, when the lines were divided into sections and buffer-stocks were introduced to relieve the constraints of Just-in-Time (Shimizu, 1995, 1998). From that moment on, an effort was made to make a team coincide with a complete sub-assembly. At Volvo, the product unit exists for off-line production modules. At Renault, despite the official definition, the constitution of EWUs did not entail breaking down the process of manufacturing or assembling, so that each unit could manufacture or assemble a complete product. The EWU was adapted to the existing process and not the contrary. This had many consequences. Boundaries were created between EWUs where they did not always have any real foundation. Unit relations between upstream and downstream were therefore complicated. The units cannot proceed to redivide stations, so as to make the operations that the operators carry out more functional and therefore more intelligible (Ellegard, 1995; Freyssenet, 1995). The division of operations between stations remains the responsibility of the work study department and the foremen, even if the operators are consulted occasionally. This is different from what happens in teams at Toyota, who have to balance out the stations among themselves or with teams upstream or downstream, when the production varies in volume or in variety. At Volvo, the operators who work on a complete product in modules, decide on the order of the operations themselves. They can give them a logic which makes them easy to memorise, despite their variety, something they could not do on an assembly line.

The operators are trained to be polyvalent, which is one of the criteria which affects their career. The function of this polyvalence is to allow workers to be replaced when absent or when there are modifications in production. Teamwork is supposed to facilitate this.

But setting up EWUs on the assembly lines did not entail the redistribution of operations between stations. They still do not have any logical link between them, a link which would be the only way of memorising them more easily and of reducing mistakes or the fear of making mistakes. Because lack of quality has a significant influence on their evaluation, operators consequently try to change workstations as little as possible.

Operators verify their work themselves, as is the case at Volvo and Toyota. If workers notice a problem, they call for someone to intervene and take charge of eliminating the problem. The former is called the Unit's Technical Assistant (UTA). Apart from quality problems, he takes care of equipment, polyvalence training and relations with maintenance. At Volvo the module operator only calls on his team leader, who works on the same line, if he does not succeed in solving the problem. At Toyota, he has the right to stop the line work so that the group can take the time to eliminate the cause of the problem that he has noticed.

Other more peripheral functions (supplies, minor maintenance, etc.) are not really integrated into the assembly EWUs. Because of the short time cycle, the operators are unable to fulfil these functions and leave them to the UTA. On the other hand, at Volvo they fall within the range of module activity (Couvreur and Passard, 1993). The operator takes care of supplies himself and assures preventive maintenance of his equipment. In the machining areas, when machines are automated and operators do not have to load and unload components for each cycle of the machine, they can more easily take responsibility for maintenance tasks, though these are generally limited to cleaning, oiling and minor repairs when machines have stopped themselves automatically. We still see some attempts to create a new concept, that of the exploitant, a worker who fuses maintenance and production tasks. But these remain limited, unofficial and are very strongly resisted. Maintenance at the second (repairing) and third level (diagnosing) remains clearly distinct from production, so much so that that it is sometimes organised into EWUs itself.

In 1995 there were four levels of classification for operators, sanctioned by professional trials: P1, P1 CS, P2 and P3. On the assembly line, it was necessary to know 6 workstations at the first level, 16 stations in the EWU at P1 CS level, and at P2 level, 16 stations within the unit and 10 outside. P3 was reserved for controllers of automated installations who, in fact, had authority over the other operators in the group. These P3 operators relieve the maintenance workers of repetitive maintenance jobs. They can relay their observations to the EWU for maintenance in their common language and can carry out certain interventions when the EWU decides (Hume, to be published). At Volvo in Torslanda, the module operators are classed at the same level, if they assemble the same type of sub-assembly.

The driving force behind the unit is the Unit Leader who presents indicators of results during breaks and has meetings to solve selective problems. A communication area has been fitted up for this. At Volvo in Torslanda, indicators are analysed on a daily basis for a period of six minutes taken out of work time. Every two months, two hours of paid overtime are dedicated to any problems which occur in the module. These meetings take place in a specially fitted-out area. The Unit Leader takes care of relations between upstream and downstream in his sector, according to formal procedures which he activates himself. However client–supplier-type relations are difficult to establish when the unit does not correspond to a complete or easily identifiable sub-assembly. At Volvo, it is the operator concerned who relates with upstream and downstream, according to equally formal procedures. The rectification work is charged to the accounts of whichever workshop is responsible for the fault.

Operators have an appraisal interview on an annual basis, and from time to time when faults reoccur frequently. Appraisal takes place more frequently and systematically at Volvo: there is a weekly audit and a twice-yearly individual interview based on weekly results. At Renault, an annual agreement is signed by the trade unions which gives workers a share in profits which is based on profits for the whole factory. Calculation of the profit share is individualised at Volvo and is based on the weekly quality audit and the volume produced. At Toyota it is included in the salary (which contains quite a significant amount that varies). Salaries at Toyota depend on monthly improvements in standard times for teams, and this is one of the essential elements which explains the involvement of the employees. Toyota was obliged to change its salary system at the beginning of the 1990s as a result of difficulties in recruiting and the fact that workers and foremen refused to increase overtime.

Conclusion

Teamwork at Renault today therefore does not correspond with its official definition or with its successive references, Volvo and Toyota. This is so, first of all because of its history. Far from being a form of work organisation borrowed from the 'Japanese' at the end of the 1980s, it appeared in the manual sectors at the beginning of the 1970s as a means of dealing with the work crisis that Renault and many other European constructors were experiencing at the time. Because it threatened the principles of additivity and of linearity, in its most advanced form, that is to say the production of a complete sub-assembly in a module, it was contested by the work study departments, who managed to prevent it from being generalised in the manual sectors. On the other hand, it was introduced to and accepted in the automated areas which were created at the end of the 1970s. But to make that possible, its content and objectives were changed. Instead of breaking with the principles of additivity and linearity which were now very much part of the architecture and the running of the automated installations, its principal function and reality, in the formula that was introduced, was to ensure that any parts of tasks that were not carried out by the automated machinery would be done quickly by a small group of workers, who would intervene rapidly when problems arose. This would leave maintenance workers and technicians to do more in-depth repair work outside production time. This type of teamwork made it possible to create positions for professional production workers, which opened up new career opportunities for unskilled workers, without it being necessary to have a technical qualification.

Following the financial crisis of 1984, the necessity to reduce the workforce and the workers' increased involvement in the improvement of results, rekindled interest in teamwork in the manual sectors. But this time, far from having the objective of 'breaking up the assembly line', to obtain quality, flexibility, productivity and work satisfaction, as in the experiments at the beginning of the 1970s, the function of teamwork was to obtain quality, polyvalence and productivity, in return for the possibility of becoming a 'professional production worker'. The fact that jobs such as quality control, replacement, cleaning, etc. were kept within the team permitted a reduction in the number of quality controllers, setters, rectification workers and foremen. In the first half of the 1990s, teamwork was brought into general use in all the workshops and services, in the form of Elementary Work Units.

However, the definition that it was given has not been put into practice in every aspect. Thus, the breaking up of the productive process that would have made it possible to attribute one complete product to each EWU, which would then have been really responsible for it, was not systematically carried out. Also, participation of EWU members in the search for and elimination of loss of time and material was not generalised, as it had been at Toyota, owing to a lack of job security and the continuing reductions in manpower. Renault is therefore a long way from the form of teamwork of which Toyota remains the master.

End-notes

[1]   I spoke about teamwork at Renault in a previous text from a more historical point of view: 'The origins of teamwork at Renault', published in Ake Sandberg (ed.), *Enriching Production* (Aldershot UK: Avebury, 1995). In this text, the analysis is centred more on the transformations in its content and objectives. I would like to thank Emmanuel Couvreur, Frédéric Decoster and Jean-Claude Monnet from Renault for their remarks and suggestions. However, I take sole responsibility for the analysis proposed here.

[2]   Quality was officially declared a strategic goal for Renault. The Quality Manager becomes a member of the company's Management Committee. The Renault Quality Institute was created in 1988. Its goal was to train for the tools, techniques and processes of 'Total Quality'. A fact which is more decisive in its repercussions is that the Quality Manager refused to give his agreement to commercialise the R19 when it was being launched, as he considered that the quality was not high enough. This came as quite a shock for the company. It signified that management at all levels would have to change their methods of working.

[3]   This paragraph owes a lot to the comparative survey carried out by Emmanuel Couvreur and Benoit Passard on teamwork at the Renault factory in Sandouville and the Volvo factory in Torslanda, as well as to discussions with Marie-Noelle Hume who in studying the evolution in maintenance at Renault, and to the work of Koichi Shimizu on Toyota. The analysis made here on the differences between the firms cannot be attributed to them.

216   *Teamwork in the Automobile Industry*

References

Coriat B. (1978) La recomposition de la ligne de montage et son enjeu: une nouvelle économie du contrôle du temps. *Sociologie du travail*, No. 2, pp. 19–31.

Couvreur E. and Passard B. (1993) *Comparaison du travail en groupe dans une usine Renault et dans une usine Volvo*. Document Renault (30 pp.).

Decoster F and Freyssenet M. (1997) Automation at Renault: strategy and form. In Shimokawa K., Jurgens U. and Fujimoto T. (eds.), *Transforming Automobile Assembly*. Berlin: Springer-Verlag.

Ellegard K. (1995) The creation of a new production system at the Volvo automobile assembly plant in Uddevalla. In Sandberg A. (ed.), *Enriching Production. Perspective on Volvo's Uddevalla Plant as an Alternative to Lean Production*. Aldershot: Avebury.

Freyssenet M. (1979) *Division du travail et mobilisation quotidienne de la main d'oeuvre. Les cas Renault et Fiat*. Paris: CSU.

Freyssenet M. (1984) La requalification des opérateurs et la forme sociale actuelle d'automatisation. *Sociologie du travail*, No. 4, 422–433.

Freyssenet M. (1992) Processus et formes sociales d'automatisation. Le paradigme sociologique. *Sociologie du travail*, No. 4, 469–496.

Freyssenet M. (1995) La 'production réflexive', une alternative à la 'production de masse' et à la 'production au plus juste'? *Sociologie du travail*, No. 3, 365–388.

Freyssenet M. (1998) Renault, from diversified mass production to innovative flexible production. In Freyssenet M., Mair A., Shimizu, K. and Volpato, G. (eds), *One Best Way? Trajectories and Industrial Models of the World's Automobile Producers*. Oxford University Press.

Midler Ch. (1980) *L'organisation du travail et ses déterminants. Enjeux économiques et organisationnels des réformes de restructuration des touches dans le montage automobile'*. Thèse de 3ème cycle, Paris 1, pp. 24–26.

Midler Ch. and Charue F. (1990) Un processus d'apprentissage à la française: la robotisation des tôleries automobile. *Conference on the Organisation of Work and Technology: Implications for International Competitiveness*, Bruxelles, 31 May–1 June.

Tijou R. (1991) La Chaîne de montage: maillon faible de l'industrie de grande série?' Gérer et comprendre. *Annales des Mines*, Octobre, pp. 79–82.

Shimizu K. (1995) Humanization of the production system and work at Toyota Motor Co and Toyota Motor Kyushu. In Sandberg A. (ed.), *Enriching Production. Perspective on Volvo's Uddevalla Plant as an Alternative to Lean Production*. Aldershot: Avebury.

Shimizu K. (1998) A New Toyotaism? In Freyssenet M., Mair A., Shimizu K. and Volpato G. (eds.), *One Best Way? Trajectories and Industrial Models of the World's Automobile Producers*. Oxford University Press.

CHAPTER 9
Teamwork and New Forms of Work Organisation in Fiat's 'Integrated Factory'

Arnaldo Camuffo and Stefano Micelli

Introduction

The majority of European car makers have recently reacted to market downturn and intense global competition by introducing comprehensive strategic and organisational changes. These consist of new products, new plants or automated equipment, investment in innovative industrial relations and human resource management policies. Fiat too, at the turn of the decade, launched a total quality programme based on the adoption of Japanese management concepts and new human resource policies: the *Fabbrica Integrata* organisational scheme, elaborated and implemented by Fiat during the 1990s, reveals substantial transformations of traditional production systems and work organisation models. In particular, a main feature of the Fabbrica Integrata model is an original form of teamwork – the Elementary Organisational Unit – conceived as the cornerstone of the new factory structure. This chapter aims to shed light on this new form of group work using evidence from fieldwork carried out in two Italian plants.

The main point of this chapter can be summarised as follows: the 'intelligent' application of lean manufacturing (Womack *et al.*, 1990), such as that which can be found at NUMMI, can lead to a beneficial organisational model (a 'learning bureaucracy' (Adler, 1992) in which substantial bottom-up learning takes place thanks to a continuous re-engineering of working methods and organisational processes. However, excessive emphasis on working rules, and exaggerated confidence in the possibility of making the organisation of work in auto assembly plants transparent, objective and 'scientific' (for instance by means of 'management-by-sight' techniques and other lean production-derived mechanisms) could under-estimate the role of hierarchy at the decentralised level. Formal rules and standards, in short, are important managerial tools whose impact must however be considered from a broader and systemic perspective (Crozier and Friedberg, 1977). Their effectiveness largely depends upon managers' ability to use and enforce them in such as way as to avoid producing vicious circles.

Following this tradition in organisation studies, this chapter argues that team leaders or newly designed team leader figures continue to play a crucial hierarchical role, notably in automated contexts, but especially as far as the management of human resources is concerned. In other words, while substitutes for hierarchies (Lawler, 1988) and horizontal co-ordination (Denton, 1991) are usually considered the organisational core of lean or post-lean auto manufacturing, we argue that hierarchy is still crucial, and that HRM activities performed by team leaders are the real drivers of personnel commitment and, eventually, of quality and efficiency.

A flatter, teamwork-based, management-by-sight, decentralised organisation tends to redefine and emphasise the role of hierarchy. This does not mean, as some radical interpretations of lean production seem to propose (Babson, 1992; Williams and Haslam, 1992; Robertson *et al.*, 1993), that the traditional concept of supervision and control has survived Fordism and integrated itself into the new production system; nor does it mean that emerging production systems are pure and simply homogeneous and consistent with Fordism. Multi-skilled workers and self-organised teams represent important solutions to emerging management complexity, but do not completely solve co-ordination problems. As shown in Figure 1, the functions of first-line supervisors are not those of command and control, but of communication, negotiation, empowerment and incentives.

Sketching Fiat's evolutionary pattern: from the Highly Automated Factory to the Fabbrica Integrata

A historical and evolutionary perspective can assist in our understanding of recent developments in Fiat's organisation.

After a widely recognised comeback during the first half of the 1980s, Fiat's situation worsened at the turn of the decade (Camuffo and Volpato, 1994). The emphasis on automation technology and

The team leader role consists in:
- balancing workloads between team members;
- managing information flows and symmetries within the organisational units;
- facilitating systematic training and continuous improvement;
- managing internal and external interfaces (boundary spanning role);
- adjusting the degree of perceived equity of the incentive structure available;
- appraising personnel performances and signalling opportunities for horizontal and vertical mobility as skills are developed and accumulated.

Figure 1 *Key functions of the team leader in the new organisation context.*

the industrial relations characterised by managerial unilateralism and concession bargaining, strengths during the 1980s, became weaknesses as market difficulties increased and international competition became tougher. Fiat also suffered from a somewhat too high degree of vertical integration, an outdated product line, a certain slowness in model renovation, a too heavy reliance on its domestic car market and a marked dependence on low segments.

The emergence of a totally new scenario moved Fiat to launch a five-year programme (Total Quality Programme), articulated in a number of operational projects. The *Fabbrica Integrata* (Integrated Factory) project develops Fiat's new organisational concepts. From an organisational model characterised by technology as the key factor in determining plant productivity and flexibility, Fiat moved to human-centred assumptions. Fiat's emphasis on organisational flexibility, co-ordination and improvement, recognises explicitly that automation and investments on new process technology are no longer to be considered the only drivers of productivity. Organisational variables and human resource policies have become constitutive elements of the firm's competitive performance.

Designed in 1990, the Integrated Factory was first implemented at the Termoli and Cassino plants; a comprehensive implementation of the IF scheme will be achieved only with the setting up of the two new Fiat auto plants in southern Italy – at Pratola Serra, where new cars will be produced, and at Melfi, where Punto production began in the 1996–97 period.

This chapter analyses two different Fiat production plants: the Cassino production line, where the Tipo and Tempra models are produced, and the Melfi plant. Although the two lines are not completely identical and homogeneous, the comparison between them

Table 1 *Hierarchical layers in automobile plants*

	Mean	Median
Japan/Japan	7.9	6.0
Japan/North America	6.5	6.5
US/North America	6.2	6.0
Europe	7.1	6.0
New entrant	6.9	6.5
Australia	5.7	6.0
Fiat Melfi	5	

Source: Plant interviews, and Ittner and MacDuffie, 1994.

is very significant. The Tipo production line represents a good example of how the new organisational model scheme is applied in brownfield settings: the principles of the new work organisation impacted on existing procedures, roles and competencies. Punto production lines, in contrast, were conceived and realised from a totally new perspective: manufacturing process segmentation, training programmes and personnel recruiting policies fitted in with respect to the requirements of the new organisational scheme.

Seeking integration through the Elementary Organisational Unit

The new plant organisation

Fiat plants have been substantially delayered and decentralised. The former sectors are divided into 'Operational Units' (*Unità operative*), by aggregating traditional machine shops. Each Operational Unit is articulated and specialised in two areas: operations and production engineering. Production engineering is a decentralised pool of individuals with a range of technical competencies, working on a variety of operations (see Figures 2 and 3).

The objective is to increase integration. Competitive pressures require a more responsive organisational structure, capable of fast reaction to technological breakdowns and to quality problems, reducing antagonism between the hierarchies within two historically conflicting technical areas: operations and process engineering. The difficulties in attributing precise responsibilities in emergency situations and even in normal routine activities, as well as the cost of

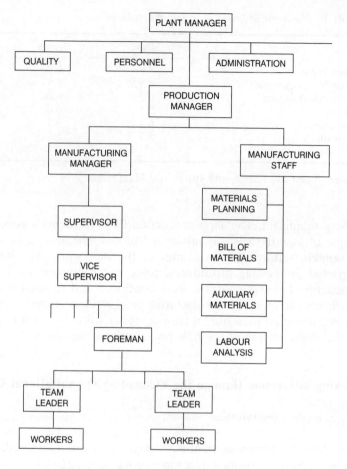

Figure 2 *Traditional plant organisation.*

co-ordinating various professional strands at the plant level, give impetus to the creation of major units whose chiefs are now in charge of production, quality and equipment maintenance.

Through delayering, Fiat has eliminated two hierarchical levels. In Fiat, the delayering process included the so-called *capireparto*, the most traditional foremen figures. This effort toward flatter and more decentralised organisational structures is evident: Fiat's Melfi plant shows a lower-than-average number of hierarchical levels (Table 1). Flatter organisational structures require more horizontal

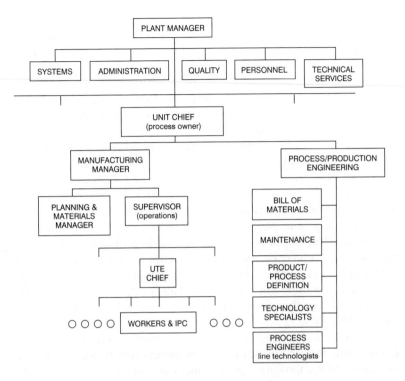

Figure 3 *New plant organisation.*

co-ordination and less vertical supervision. Mutual adjustment (Thompson, 1967; Mintzberg, 1979) is a common means of co-ordination among the UTE's self-regulating units, which interact between each other in a supplier–customer fashion.

Elementary organisational units: the keystone of the new organisational model

The Fiat HRM Department defines a UTE (*Unità Tecnologica Elementare*) as a unit that governs a segment of the process (a technological sub-system), in which such activities as prevention, variance absorption, self-control and continuous improvement are carried on, in order to achieve the firm's goals in terms of quality, productivity/costs and service. The size of Fiat's UTEs varies according to the technological area: while in components and engine manufacturing the average size is 20/30 workers, in body assembly it reaches 40/70 members. Every UTE includes a variety of jobs and skill profiles that are very different from those of the past. Normal workers (blue collar) are assisted (in ratios from 1:10 to 1:30) by highly skilled workers (integrated process operators, integrated process system controllers) whose tasks are quality improvement and personnel training.

The main purposes of these groups are as follows. The first is to solve problems at the lowest possible level: resources and skills are placed so that problems may be solved as and where they occur. The second is to facilitate product and process quality improvement by systematically incorporating the results of organisational learning. Each unit establishes with others, downstream and upstream, a client–supplier relationship: each problem caused by a unit must be solved by its personnel, either through intervention in the unit workplace, or by movement of personnel to other segments of the manufacturing process. Thus each unit is self-regulating and can certify the quality of the activities that it performs (*autocertificazione*) [1].

According to management, organisational structures based on teams allow leaner and smoother manufacturing processes, better job assignments, flexibility enhancement and lower costs. Every unit should be managed and co-ordinated by an information system made up of diagrams consisting of indicators on product and process quality, costs, productivity, workers' skills and maintenance. Most of them are general (so-called institutional indicators), although others are customised and defined according to specific needs. This complex information system (founded on the 'management-by-sight' concept) is composed of sub-systems concerning quality control, manufacturing performance measurement and so on. Each sub-system includes such instruments and indicators as defect ratios, Pareto diagrams, CEDACs, flag systems, labour productivity ratios, radar charts etc. These elements work together to overcome information asymmetries between directing and operating personnel, and to confer transparency to the organisation. Besides *'gestione a vista'* (management by sight), other management techniques, such as statistical process control and TPM, are implemented in order to control microprocesses in all cases.

The UTE chiefs have, at a lower level and scale, the same task as their superiors in charge of the general unit. Their task can be described in terms of internal and external activities. Internal refers to the relationships and resources located within the cell, and external refers to interfaces with other units or organisations. Internally, team leaders manage human and financial resources in order to obtain the results they have negotiated with their superiors. They conduct meetings and group activities so as to make explicit the objectives of the cell, keep control of the main parameters, decide how to exploit the financial budget assigned to limited technical interventions and supervise personnel training. With regard to interfaces with the rest of the plant and externally, it is important to underline the impressive boundary spanning of the UTE leaders' role. They normally interact with other upstream and downstream units to solve production and quality problems, negotiate objectives with superiors, and interact with technology and maintenance specialists to solve important technical breakdowns and changes.

Specialist integration and team leader's span of control: some critical differences between Fiat and other Mediterranean car makers

The organisational scheme implemented by Fiat is similar from many points of view to other restructuring programmes implemented by European car makers. The concepts underlying the general restructuring processes represent a development of the Japanese procedure and are essentially the same in every country. In order to achieve a full comprehension of the Fiat organisational model, we need to highlight and account for two of its critical aspects.

The first concerns the integration of technicians within the elementary unit, especially in automated contexts where technical breakdown and maintenance radically affect the UTE global performance. Two different solutions are equally plausible: the first, implemented for instance in Seat and in Renault plants, is based on a full integration of technicians into a team. Technicians regularly work with operations personnel and hierarchically depend on, the team leader: their specialisation is reduced to take advantage of their integration in daily activities. The second, less radical, links technical personnel to operations in a functional manner, keeping the two professional strands separated in terms of career pattern and incentives. In other words, the technicians are committed to a specific portion of the production process but, in terms of hierarchy, they respond to the production engineering department.

Fiat adopted the second solution: the link between the UTE chiefs and the technology and maintenance specialists remains functional. Technicians intervene within the UTE when necessary. Within the Fiat model, UTE teams (originally called technological teams and composed of the UTE chiefs and the specialists – a maintenance operator, a line technologist, a process/product technologist, a logistic operator and sometimes system controllers) are conceived as *integrators* (Lawrence and Loersch, 1967), organisational devices enhancing horizontal co-ordination, information sharing and organisational learning.

Differences between models should not be over-estimated. In all schemes the rationale is to single out first- and second-level technical activities (re-engineering and maintenance), according to their complexity: first-level operations, which strongly affect economic and qualitative performance of the production line, should be managed by stable teams that develop a deep contextual knowledge of the process. Second-level operations, in contrast, are assigned to specialised groups at unit or higher hierarchical level in order to fully exploit the general and abstract knowledge of the engineers and technicians.

As mentioned before, a second important aspect differentiating Fiat UTEs from other models is the unit chief's span of control. Several car makers, among them Renault and Seat, decided to size teams as small groups, in order to facilitate the UTE chief's role in terms of human resource management. When teams are small, team leaders may be charged with analysing and diagnosing personnel training needs; they can regularly evaluate personnel performance; they also take care of personnel motivation, considering individual specificities and problems; when asked, they may suggest candidates for promotions or rate people for early retirement and lay-offs.

Fiat's UTEs are larger, especially in final-assembly operational units. UTEs' chiefs span of control remains very wide and personnel functions are partially accomplished with the help of IPCs and IPOs: on the whole, HRM activities are more centralised, although each operational unit has a *Repo*, who is in charge of HRM policies co-ordination and the HRM information system, responding hierarchically to the plant HRM manager and functionally to the operational unit chief.

The team leader's role in the new organisational model: commitment building and the reduction in information asymmetry

A specific trait of Fiat' s new organisational model is the emphasis placed on organisation design and human resource policies as new central competitive factors. Fiat has evolved from a stage at which technology was considered the main driver of productivity: the Italian car makers had previously (in the 1970s) experienced new forms of work organisation, not as the result of an achieved awareness of the competitive edge that organisation and HRM can give, but rather as the most appropriate defence against union demands and other social pressures in general. Consequently, new forms of work organisation were not considered as an integrative part of a competitive strategy.

The implementation of the new organisational models based on UTEs represented an important discontinuity in the strategy of the company. From a theoretical point of view, integration is the key word to understand what happened in Fiat; more integration means full commitment to process logic and a reduction of information asymmetries.

The new organisational models can be read as comprehensive attempts to make plant organisation more transparent, to facilitate information exchange and transfer, and to allow the sharing of experiences and knowledge among people. Organisational transparency allows the systematic reduction of the rent and costs associated with information asymmetries, which inevitably produce conflicts. Teams and management-by-sight techniques should, in theory, reduce elusive and opportunistic behaviour, favour social control, and assure the degree of horizontal communication necessary to solve problems as and where they arise.

Managers and scholars have often stressed the importance of techniques and managerial tools in order to activate virtuous circles of organisational learning. The simultaneous diffusion of (often Japanese-derived) management-by-sight instruments in many car makers is evidence of the important role played by the organisational design of non-hierarchical co-ordinating mechanisms. Nevertheless, the analysis of the Fiat case shows that a crucial role in implementing these instruments and activating co-operation throughout the organisation is then played by the newly defined shopfloor management.

Managerial activity is crucial in mobilising competencies and in building commitment among workers through training, communication, performance appraisal, compensation (minor aspects), conflict solution, animation of quality circles and so on.

Management's great expectations

Despite the great emphasis on this new role, it is hard to find a detailed description of what the UTE chief should actually do: it is clear that he has to manage complex and multi-dimensional objectives, that he is supposed to conduct people in order to improve performances, but no specific and synthetic prescriptions are available.

The general definition of the activities of the first-level supervisor derives from two concerns. On the one hand, organisational designers and consultants in charge of defining the new hierarchical line started implementing the reform without precisely knowing its final results. On the other, management refused to provide first-level managers with a list of their functions in order to avoid opportunistic use of rules and procedures: the main objective is to develop a new professional profile capable of autonomous problem-solving. Top management fears strict definitions: traditional forms of codification of organisational knowledge crystallise organisational evolution and lead to defensive personnel routines.

In brownfield settings, traditional shop stewards have to engage in difficult situations: they know their role is no longer what it used to be, without knowing exactly what their job is now. So far as individual competencies are concerned, HR training programmes focused upon relational capabilities and the acquisition of managerial tools; communication efforts were necessary so as to make it clear that the new first-level supervisor required a radically new professional profile. In greenfield settings, the organisational shift did not cause any particular problem; not only did top management have no cultural legacy to cope with, but in addition the technological variables were commensurate with the new factory scheme (see Tables 2 and 3).

Listening and negotiating

Managerial activities at the shopfloor level consist of the continuous negotiation of worker commitment and participation; this effort is essential in order to take full advantage of the potential of

Table 2 *Melfi and Cassino production lines: technological variables*

	Cassino plant Tipo	Melfi plant Punto
Potential production	1800 v/day	1600 v/day
Cycle time	2.6 min	1.6 min
Definitive production sequencing	From assembly	From body welding
Body welding		
Welding points	3083	2200*
Automation ratio (%)	100%	98%
Assembly line		
Variations in assembly line	125	36
Finishing (end of line area)	Yes	No

*Internally welded and not outsourced

Table 3 *Melfi and Cassino production lines: organisational variables*

	Cassino plant Tipo	Melfi plant Punto
Plant personnel	6000	7000
Shifts	3	3
Workers' average age	40 years	26.3 years
Body welding		
Elementary organisational units	7	6
EOU's chief origin	35% Technicians 65% Production	New employees
Average composition of EOU	10/60 people EOU's chief Technological UTE System controller, Workers	
Assembly line		
EOUs	13	17
EOU's chief origin	100% Operations	New employees
Average composition of EOU	25/60 people EOU's chief EOU technician Logistic assistant 1 Maintenance CPI	
Suggestions	Individually paid	Not paid*

*Complex contingent pay scheme related to a weighted average of UTE's and global plant performance.

the available information system, integration mechanisms and co-ordinating devices.

What does a team leader negotiate with his workers? Essentially this consists of two things. First, the acquisition of informal knowledge accumulated (mainly by technicians) through day-to-day activity; second, the commitment of workers to continuous improvement of quality standards and production objectives.

Situational knowledge (Lave, 1988) seems to emerge as essential in the new organisational models. The competencies of graduate engineers in the production engineering department are undoubtedly wider and more flexible than those of technicians included in the elementary organisational units: the theoretical background provides a more general comprehension of the system and how the different production segments work and interact. However, only technicians operating within the UTE develop 'situation specific' knowledge. For example, they acquire particular confidence in dealing with equipment that allows faster and more effective interventions. Looking systematically at machine breakdowns and evaluating equipment limitations in daily activity, technicians gain an important position in solving specific technical problems and can provide unique contributions and suggestions for improving technological efficiency and reliability.

Generic line workers also develop 'situation specific' knowledge. This point, however, has probably been over-estimated by the lean production manufacturing approach: only part of the tacit skills that workers accumulate on the line can be effectively translated in such a way as to produce local process innovation.

Managing relations with technicians is somewhat more problematic. Technicians tend to master technical equipment, preferring to maintain their specialist knowledge rather than contributing to the global performance of the elementary organisational unit. Technician integration inside the UTE depends upon both the technological level of the equipment that the UTE has to deal with and the resources they dispose of for learning. In all the plants considered, UTEs are well established in most automatised units (Body Welding, Painting), while their implementation appears as more difficult in traditional shops (Assembly). Technicians engaged in highly technological UTEs become part of the group because of their contribution to line reliability: their efforts produce both improvements in organisational performance and continuous individual learning. However, individual and organisational learning has a cost:

trial-and-error activity on the job needs time and resources; formal and informal relations, inappropriate technical solutions and the time needed to solve technical breakdowns are all sources of cost for the first-line manager supervisor.

In general, resources dedicated to first-line supervisor activities are a necessary requirement for group creation. Such slack allows a cautious and *ad hoc* manoeuvre of HRM variables at the shopfloor level, which is extremely useful in achieving stronger group integration. For example, training and team meetings 'on the spot' are very important: they allow the unit leader and the technicians to explain interdependencies among different parts of the production system, how a single operation downstream affects the activity of other workers and, from a more general point of view, the logic and costs of the entire system. What is most important is that ordinary production workers are actually part of a group and they can legitimately discuss and negotiate their role inside the organisation.

Brownfields and greenfields

While the training effort realised by Fiat is important, training does not imply co-ordination *per se*. Knowing the interdependencies that link the activities of a factory certainly stimulate a co-operative attitude, but it is hard to believe that workers attention to quality and production is sufficient to determine a co-operative group. What matters is that the team leader has to take into account the needs and will of workers in order to gain their commitment. His role is complex and requires a mix of various competencies and resources that can rarely be found in traditional settings.

The full importance of the team leader profile emerges if traditional settings are compared with innovative ones. At the Cassino plant, the implementation of the *Fabbrica Integrata* has relied, as far as UTEs' leaders are concerned, on former *capisquadra*. In spite of the massive training programmes that they underwent in order to acquire the new required skills, the former team leaders, now UTE chiefs, maintained traditional behaviour and, in some cases, openly resisted change (Cerruti and Rieser, 1992). In other cases, involvement techniques, such as a suggestions system, were misinterpreted.

At the Cassino plant, UTE's chiefs seem reluctant to take up their new responsibilities. An example of such difficulties is making decisions about line stop. Theoretically, UTE chiefs are allowed (and supposed) to stop the production line for quality problems but, in practice, this decision is made one level up, by the operational unit manager. At the Melfi plant, the situation is different. UTE chiefs have been carefully selected and trained; they possess managerial and technical capabilities; they are able and willing to make autonomously important decisions, such as that of stopping the line.

Other European firms currently engaged in analogous restructuring programmes face similar problems. In general, older supervisors resist change and keep acting in a traditional way, not only with their subordinates but also with their hierarchical superiors; they often feel abandoned and cannot cope with new organisational dynamics. While young and well-trained team leaders are able to manage communication and relationships with subordinates, former supervisors encounter several problems in acquiring an effective leadership. Training represents an important tool for upgrading these traditional profiles, but the costs are high. In future, Fiat may consider the possibility of 'exporting' well-trained team leaders and technicians to other plants of the group so as to spread a new management culture.

Economic performances and group creation

The implementation of UTE as the new building block of the organisational structure is the result of a strategic choice that rejects the traditional emphasis on group work as an organisational solution to improve workers' quality of life. The UTE was originally conceived in order to decentralise decision-making on quality and reliability. Social issues were not taken into account: the specific terminology adopted in Fiat is a sign of a break with the past.

Nonetheless, the social dimension of team-building activity today acquires a somewhat unintended relevance. Where team leaders succeeded in listening to and negotiating with their subordinates, improving their units' performance, the degree of perceived equity of the incentive structure increased. In the long term, these punctual exchanges become normal routine, based on the strong feelings of trust shared by all members of the team. In this case, first-line supervisors assume the role of spokesman for their subordinates: a technician in Melfi said 'Our chief is a good one: when there is a meeting he knows how to defend our interests!'. The technician was not just saying that the first-line supervisor is no longer the traditional boss. Rather, he stated that the team is an actual entity that has a holistic and systemic nature.

First-line supervisors seem to become good leaders when they act as an integrative part of the team, rather than as part of the hierarchical chain. UTE chiefs still play a hierarchical role: they manage resources that are fundamental to workers and technicians, and in this sense their effective power has been increased. From this standpoint, teamwork and first-line supervisors' roles in Fiat differ from other versions of lean manufacturing applied, for instance, in North European countries.

Toward a post-Fordist hierarchy?

Fiat successfully started implementing a new organisational model in order to achieve new competitive strength through work organisation and people competencies. The new model adopted many of the typical instruments of lean production to make the organisation more reactive to productivity and quality problems. Although it is difficult to over-estimate the importance of such instruments and techniques, the lower-level role in the hierarchy is still crucial in activating workers' commitment and organisational learning.

The hierarchical function has changed significantly in the last few years. Team leaders are not in charge if line workers effectively execute procedures and routines as specified by engineers and line technologists, rewarding conformity and penalising anomalous behaviour. Their main task is now to build commitment and facilitate organisational learning in order to meet production and quality standards: such an effort requires not only relational capabilities and natural leadership, but also resources and managerial tools. Team leader power is not grounded on traditional bureaucratic authority but on the capacity to negotiate with subordinates, and on information sharing and commitment. Teams then become more than just people working together.

Overall, the organisational schemes implemented by Fiat cannot be considered the simple result of the application of *lean production* techniques to Italian plants; it reveals, on the contrary, original traits that should be considered from an evolutionary perspective. In other words, the specific role played by UTEs appear to be partly related to the historical background of the firm. A hypothesis that is to be considered worthy of further investigation links the importance of team leaders with the tradition of controversial industrial relations at Fiat. The renewed relationship between the single worker and the firm imposed by the implementation of JIT and TQM practices is based on reciprocal trust: only team leaders, continuously facing blue-collar problems, can build such a relationship. From this standpoint, team leaders seem to represent the fundamental connecting link between the workers' needs and the goals of the firms (Nonaka, 1988).

So far as the future is concerned, the terms of the exchange between the firms and their workers will probably evolve, becoming more complex and articulated. The redefinition of hierarchical relationships is probably the first step of a global redesign of employment relationship whose main traits are still evolving and seem difficult to specify. For the time being, team leaders are a fundamental building block in establishing trusteeship and a new cooperative attitude inside traditional and antagonistic factories.

From a more general point of view, Fiat's new organisational model marks a discontinuity with Fordism and with an obsolete conception of hierarchy. However, contrary to the illusions of some scholars, neither lean manufacturing management systems nor flexible automation technology make the factories transparent and self-regulating.

End-note

[1] Despite the fact that these elementary organisational units entail teamwork (although not teamwork in the strict sense proposed by Katzenbach and Smith, 1993), they differ from semi-autonomous groups derived from the socio-technical tradition. These, in turn, were experimented with during the 1970s in many German (e.g. Opel), French (e.g. Renault) and Italian (e.g. Alfa Romeo) companies, under pressure from the unions seeking a new quality of working life. A major difference, for instance, regards team leaders who, at Fiat and Renault, are appointed by managers and not elected by team members.

References

Adler P. (1992) The 'learning bureaucracy': New United Motor Manufacturing, Inc. In Staw B. and Cummings L. (eds.), *Research in Organisational Behaviour*. Greenwich CT: JAI Press.

Babson S. (1992) *Lean or Mean: The MIT Model and Lean Production at Mazda*. Detroit IL: Wayne State University.

Camuffo A. and Volpato G. (1994) 'Labor relations heritage and lean manufacturing at Fiat', paper presented at the *Conference on International Development in Workplace Innovation. Implications for Canadian Competitiveness*, 15–16 June, Toronto (Ontario).

Cerruti G. and Rieser V. (1992) Fiat: aggiornamenti sulla Fabbrica Integrata. *Quaderni di Ricerca Ires*, No. 1.

Crozier M. and Friedberg E. (1977) *L'acteur et le système*. Paris: Le Seuil.

Denton D.K. (1991) *Horizontal Management Beyond Total Customer Satisfaction*, New York: Lexington Books.

Ittner C.D. and MucDuffie J.P. (1994) Exploring the sources of international differences in manufacturing overhead. *IMVP Research Briefing Meeting*, June.

Katzenbach J.R. and Smith D.K. (1993) *The Wisdom of Teams Creating the High Performance Organisations*. Cambridge MA: Harvard Business School Press.

Lave J. (1988) *Cognition in Practice*. Cambridge University Press.

Lawler III E.D. (1988) Substitutes for hierarchies. *Organizational Dynamics*, Summer.

Lawrence P.R. and Loersch J.W. (1967) *Organization and Environment – Managing Differentiation and Integration*. Cambridge MA: Harvard University Press.

Nonaka I. (1988) 'Toward middle-up-down management: accelerating information creation. *Sloan Management Review*, Summer.

Robertson D. *et al.* (1993) Team concept and kaizen: Japanese production management in an unionized Canadian auto plant. *Studies in Political Economy*, Autumn.

Williams K. and Haslam C. (1992) Against lean production. *Economy and Society*, August.

Womack J.P., Jones D.T. and Roos D. (1990) *The Machine that Changed the World*. New York: Rawson.

CHAPTER 10
The Negotiation of Change in the Evolution of the Workplace towards a New Production Model at Vauxhall (General Motors) UK

*Paul Stewart**

Introduction and background: management initiatives and industrial relations

The purpose of this chapter is to draw an assessment of the nature of the changes taking place in Vauxhall Motors, the UK-based automotive assembly operations belonging to General Motors (GM). This has to be set in the context of the debate surrounding the impact of new forms of manufacturing and management initiatives in the automotive sector in general, with a view to delineating the direction *and* the fulcrum of change. In the following account, emphasis will be placed upon new management initiatives and trade union responses to them. With respect to the former, consideration is given to the implementation of new forms of employee participation – understood as teamwork by the overwhelming majority of employees themselves (Stewart and Garrahan, 1995). Whether or not change is tending towards a new industrial model, as some argue, our judgement will have to be based in large measure upon an understanding of the role of the different actors involved, in our case here the trade unions. Ellesmere Port (EP) is of particular interest as an exemplar of the possible way forward for new management practices because of the role played by the trade unions in mediating, and thus – in some instances – redefining management strategies.

* This chapter was written prior to recent changes in working practices agreed between unions and management in Spring, 1998.

236

The current period of social and economic restructuring in general and in the automotive sector in particular raises the question as to the extent and direction of change in the industry. In the general literature on changes in management practices and industrial relations in the UK, some argue (Storey and Bacon, 1993; Kelly, 1996) in terms of the efficacy of 'change–no change'. Researchers in the automotive sector are to be distinguished largely by their assumption that a degree of positive managerial transformation is occurring (Starkey and McKinley, 1989; Jones, 1992; Jürgens *et al.*, 1994). With the exception of Jones, this latter group of researchers recognise the inevitability of some continuity between present and past social arrangements. Nevertheless, there is still a tendency to view new management practices as 'progressive' because of their claimed technical and organisational advances (Jürgens *et al.* at least point to some of the social drawbacks), whereas when unions hold to collective bargaining institutions they are considered traditional, not to say 'retroactive'. However, research both at EP and Vauxhall's other major assembly operation at Luton suggests that this polarity ('progressive management' versus 'unprogressive labour') misconstrues the changing character of managerial initiatives and industrial relations in the UK automotive sector in general and at GM in particular. The rest of this chapter will consider the specific changes and, in some cases, transformations taking place at Ellesmere Port. Because of limitations of space, these remarks will of necessity be somewhat schematic.

From the standpoint of the trade unions, an account and assessment are given of the implementation of the new management practices in the context of the 'V6' Agreement. 'V6' is the code name for the engine plant developed at Ellesmere Port by General Motors, which included investment of £400 million between 1990 and 1994. The engine plant manufactures the V6 engine for GM Europe, including the substantial element of the power train for the Saab 900. The term 'V6' was then given as the title referring to the management–union agreement in 1989 on changes to employee relations and workplace practices (see below). The 'V6' Agreement was so important to management that it became the pre-condition for the £400 million investment programme. The 'V6' allowed for the instigation of teamwork, continuous improvement and a reduction in staffing. In addition, the 'V6', as we shall see, was considered to be the fundamental instrument in the restructuring of industrial relations. In the end, management achieved the introduction of the new workplace institutions (teamwork etc.) but in the context of a strengthened trade union role. Contrary to the injunctions of the lean production school, these outcomes do not appear to be contradictory. In other words, the joint regulation of the workplace, the cornerstone of plant-based industrial relations in the UK auto industry appears – in this case at least – to have been maintained, albeit it, as we shall see, in ways that neither management nor unions expected. In short, the recomposition of the workplace is forcing plant-based union organisation to address issues normally outside the remit of traditional collective bargaining. Research demonstrates the fundamentally significant role played by trade unions in the introduction of new forms of management, highlighting the fact that unions play an important conditioning role on the context and the content of new managerial initiatives.

Ellesmere Port (EP)

The Ellesmere Port (EP) plant was built in 1962, some 37 years after Vauxhall's takeover by General Motors (1925). With the development of the Vauxhall Viva in the late 1960s, the plant shifted from screwdriver status to an integrated assembly facility responsible for engine production, body assembly (Stamping, Body-in-White and Painting) and final assembly (Body and Trim). EP now produces high-value components (specifically transmissions, engines and gear boxes). The employment pattern now looks more secure with 4,500 personnel in 'Body-in-White' (namely, Engine, Body Stamping and Welding, Paintshop) and Final Trim and Chassis (namely 'Marriage line', Sub-assembly of crash pad and dash, Trim).

Owing to the current market situation at time of writing, cycle times are long, with output running at 34 units (Astra and Astra van) per hour. Work standards are set by the Industrial Engineering Department and are in line with the principles governing procedures prior to the 1989 Agreement. Quality control is set by the Quality Department but operatives have to sanction upstream quality. (Employees have a stamping procedure to indicate the site on the line where quality was sanctioned.) Routine maintenance is carried out *in situ* by the team, but diagnostic assessments and 'complex' (e.g. electrical) repair and maintenance are covered by the skilled trades (e.g. electricians).

The general attitude to buffer-levels is negotiated between

unions and management on the Joint Plant Committee (JPC), which is to say that managerial authority is mediated by joint regulation. The JPC is the focal point for decisive issues covering collective bargaining agreements, but each managerial unit in production (section level) has a budget devolved to team level which is responsible for items such as safety glasses, footwear and protective clothing. Other issues associated with production costs are managed centrally, but it is important to note that here, as in all other matters, decisions are negotiated between management and unions. Although management is not specific, it is acknowledged that there is an NUMMI effect here where a degree of emulation of the company's GM–Toyota joint venture in California is taking place on a number of fronts.

Local unemployment in the 'travel to work' area is currently running at 10% and is slightly higher than the national average. The unions have maintained management's 'no compulsory redundancy' pledge and the negotiation of labour attrition in each section has so far been agreed via redeployment. However, it is accepted by both management and unions that any redundancies will be covered by voluntary severance. Salaries are higher than the local average for manufacturing work. There is no appraisal linked to payment, although management did want supervisors to undertake an appraisal system. Appraisal functions to maintain job competence, and possible recruitment to team leader. Improvements to work are confined to process changes as opposed to product changes, but again, these are established via negotiation since they can impact upon work rates and staffing levels. The unions are fully involved in the new management initiatives, and follow the injunction offered by the main union to 'Engage and Change'. This is interpreted variously by different actors, but in essence it represents a commitment on the part of the TGWU (representing the semi and unskilled grades who comprise the majority of the workforce, see below) to take on board the many elements of the new production arrangements which do not diminish employee and union rights, including terms and conditions of the employment contract.

Hopes for the development, not to say the long-term future, of EP were not always so sanguine: 1979 saw a 3-month dispute dubbed the 'We Will Manage' strike after a management circular bearing this famous injunction (Marsden *et al.*, 1985). Following a period of conflict from the mid to late 1970s, Ellesmere Port lost its engine production capacity. However, the mid 1980s also saw new investment in assembly operations with the full production of the

Astra. In 1989, GM went ahead with investment in the 'Eco-Tec V6' which is exported to other GM facilities in Europe. Production is located on the site of the former engine production and assembly facility. In addition, body panels are produced for other European plants, mostly, although not only for Bochum, Germany.

GM's commitment was delivered as a result of a number of significant factors which taken together can be said to support the efficacy of almost £400 million investment [1] in the EP plant: the market context where the UK represents a key European sales area; historically favourable exchange rate; GM historically committed to and cognisant of the UK market; relatively low wage rates for craft workers; industrial relations environment conducive to erosion of workplace rights and collective bargaining; and the impact of Japanese Foreign Direct Investment (JFDI). It is important to note that the raft of government legislation in the 1980s emphasised, *inter alia*, the significance of decentralised bargaining procedures and institutions and that this has dovetailed rather neatly with the history of collective bargaining in Vauxhall. It is this commitment to decentralisation which ironically (on one reading at least) has thus far served the interests of the trade unions in the field of industrial relations marginally better than those of management. This has arisen from the inherently contested nature of the change process. It will be possible to see how this has occurred by taking a close look at the substantive terms of reference forming part of the 'V6' agreement. However, before it is possible to describe and evaluate both the 'V6' and its key outcomes in relation to the basic issues of changes to the workplace, we need to draw attention to the industrial relations background at EP. Following this, a general assessment will be drawn (in the limited terms in which it is possible to do so from one plant) of the extent and character of the new production arrangements in the context of our general question, 'whither the new production model?'. The outcomes that concern us here are specifically those regarding teams, the production process and managerial change, particularly with respect to front-line supervision and employee involvement.

Industrial relations

Given the preceding account, the outcome of the process of change has to be seen as reflecting the peculiarities of GM's adaptation to both the host environment and the realities of the history of industrial and employee relations on Merseyside and Liverpool, including the EP plant itself. This historically derived set of contingencies has allowed for the development of the pre-existing arrangements for the operation of industrial relations institutions, allowing management to introduce what we might call 'novel socio-technical changes' (both innovatory around new forms of social organisation, namely Teams, JIT, reduction of buffers) and to develop what are normally viewed as 'traditional technical changes'. It is worth recalling that, more often than not, trade unions in the UK have been historically predisposed to the latter and certainly more committed than is popularly imagined (Daniel, 1987). In the automotive sector this general principle has been reflected in the unions' willingness to accept technological innovation after negotiation. Where technological innovation has impacted upon work organisation, unions have shown a preparedness to engage with management on the boundaries between managerial and employee concerns – the terms and conditions of employment. This has meant that contemporary changes have either been addressed in the traditional fashion (as technical changes considered under the usual guidelines affecting terms and conditions of employment) or in novel ways, where technical change has led to – or raised the possibility of – the fragmentation of the existing pattern of industrial relations. The nature of the new management initiatives in the automotive sector is now forcing unions to address an agenda which is historically beyond the institutions of British collective bargaining for both management and unions.

Of course, for management, this *cordon sanitaire* between an industrial relations focus upon the terms and conditions of employment, and its own prerogative to institute change in work organisation, is what is supposed to underwrite the guarantees of plant harmony and union subordination in the new company philosophy. Although this might be said to constitute the formal logic of the GM's 'Quality Network' formula, the substantive rationality is, as described below, somewhat more commensurate with the realities of the institutions of joint regulation. Yet this is what is being challenged by management's very own attempts to bring about change. This is not the same as saying that the introduction of technical and organisational change will fail – quite the contrary – but the point is that management is not to be the sole actor in the process. In effect, the new forms of work organisation and technical innovation are being articulated (in some areas) as much by the trade unions as by management, and it is this which is creating a very interesting agenda for the trade unions at plant level (Stewart, 1994). One hypothesis here is that this has had the impact of pushing the leading union in the plant into addressing issues of the labour process at a level of engagement hitherto unknown among UK unions in the automotive sector. By turning to the agreement itself we can obtain some sense of how this has come to pass. Both the nature of the agreement and its outcomes have allowed the unions to adopt a formally optimistic view of the impact of changes in new management practices at GM.

The contested nature of the management of change

It is surely a misnomer with regard to the automotive industry to view change as simply a process of discontinuity. Indeed, by considering the case of sub-assembly, engine and trim operations at Ellesmere Port, it is possible to assess the existing aspects of manufacturing and industrial relations as reconfigurations of previous practices as well as departures from past practices in management–union relations. In this sense, changes in the form of management initiatives and industrial relations can be understood as uneven, pointing both forward and backward at the same time (this unevenness applies to both management and unions). In other words, while management has been the driving force behind new forms of workplace involvement, it has been the trade unions which in practice have pursued the consequences of this agenda, essentially by subtly redefining aspects of the role of the shop steward. We shall examine the consequences of this below with respect to the trajectory of the 'V6' Agreement.

The 'V6' Agreement – 1989

The 'V6 Agreement' is axiomatic to the introduction of GM's European corporate plan for the introduction of new management and industrial relations initiatives. The central dynamic of 'V6' is to introduce a raft of new workplace institutions with respect to teamwork and Just-in-Time operations. In this respect the 'V6' is understood by the plant management to constitute cultural change and is complementary to the 1988 GM Europe initiative known as Quality Network Production System (QNPS). This links together the prescribed technical change at plant level with new forms of work organisation (teamwork) which the company hopes will be underwritten by new provisions in plant-based bargaining. The four signatory unions are: Transport and General Workers' Union (TGWU); Managerial Scientific and Financial Union (MSF); Amalgamated Engineering Union (AEU); and Electrical, Electronic, Telecommunications and Plumbing Union (EETPU). The TGWU represents unskilled employees in all assembly operations while the AEU and the EEPTU cover skilled grades on the shopfloor. The AEU and the EEPTU merged in 1992 to create the AEEU. The MSF pursues the interests of white-collar staff. The TGWU represents the overwhelming majority of employees in the plant [2].

A statement early in the 'V6' notes that: 'Local agreements outside ['V6'] continue to exist unless they are in conflict with [the] main agreement, in which case they may be amended, substituted or eliminated". In addition, all means must be taken to ensure that: "a harmonious and dispute free environment [is] in accordance with the needs of the customer in terms of quality, quantity and cost. . . ." This philosophy is pursued under the auspices of a set of so-called 'General Principles' (contained in *Your Guide to the Agreement* (Vauxhall, 1989)) which can be summed up thus:

- New working practices, including the 'elimination of undesirable demarcation problems and restrictive practices' will be pursued 'at a pace that all involved can sustain'
- 'Continuous improvement'
- 'Flexibility and Mobility'
- 'Involvement of People'
- Retention of multi-union environment
- Pursuit of 'highest levels of Quality and Productivity'
- Commitment to desist from 'confrontation'
- 'Highest standards of Health and Safety'
- 'Highest Standards of Conduct and Attendance'
- Commitment to technical change
- 'Respect of the full worth and dignity of all employees'
- 'Develop the spirit of care, unity, teamwork, mutual trust and co-operation'

Teamwork as the central tenet in the new agreement in sub-assembly, engine and trim

According to 'V6', teamwork: 'is a critical part of the new manufacturing system and the big ingredient in the concept is that Employees have an opportunity to impact the success of the business through their own decision making, pride in their work and co-operative efforts among each other'. It is recognised that this will take some time to introduce and that a degree of 'training' will be essential to ensure it is successful.

The (unremarkable and expected) aim of teamwork is to ensure the development of, and correspondence between, individual and corporate objectives which, we should not be surprised to find, conforms reasonably well with the goals of GM's competitors for institutions such as teamwork. However, what may be distinctive in the Vauxhall case (and for GM in general) is the *de facto* recognition that it is possible to achieve these objectives within a framework of union–management joint regulation. This is despite (or, perhaps ironically it is part of?) the new and managerial driven corporatist ideology that is being created. It should be pointed out however (see below) that this situation is best interpreted as having arisen more from the unions' negotiating stance rather than as a climb-down or failure on the part of management to achieve their objectives.

Therefore, while the aims of teamwork have been directed to promoting flexibility (via job rotation) and continuous improvement in 'cost quality and waste elimination', the important question is the extent to which these also lead towards the development of a 'new' workplace. Presumably the latter would be delineated by attitudinal changes among the workforce, patterns of work organisation and employee involvement which constitute a break from the past and, perhaps most significantly, by the absence of what might be termed 'traditional workplace' attitudes among the unions. Before considering this issue further in the closing remarks to the chapter, the section will assess the extent of team working, using a section in 'final trim' as an exemplar of the way in which this dimension of change is taking place.

The entire EP facility is engaged in teamwork, with the appointment of over 400 team leaders within the first year of the agreement. There are between 3 and 4 teams per section in sub-assembly, engine and trim, with varying numbers of personnel. Thus, Section one (concerned with electrical installations) *Team A*, on 'hood' = 9 operatives: *Team B*, 'harnesses' = 14 operatives: *Team C*, 'auxiliary harness' = 10 operatives: *Team D*, 'tail lights' = 10 operatives. Total for Section 1 = 41. The objective is to run this section with 40 personnel. The reduction will be achieved via kaizen. As is clear from the repertoire of tasks for all the teams in each section, employees are required to undertake all the tasks in their section, these tasks all being within the same cognitive framework. The benefit of this is that it allows for the maximising of task experiences which is seen to promote the psychological and technical conditions for job rotation. The latter in turn is believed to be indispensable for reducing boredom and task dependency. It is important to remember that task rotation is not peculiar to new forms of work organisation but rather rotation in the contemporary auto assembly workplace is possible only (in most instances but not air) under the sanction of the team leader in negotiation with the shop steward. Previously, under the regime of the 'gang system', employees defined and allocated 'task and time' among themselves under guidance from the shop steward in negotiation with the front-line supervisor. On Merseyside where EP is located, this was known in local parlance as 'welt working' (a term taken from a working practice among local dockers to describe the custom whereby employees covered for one another during absence [3]) and as such represented the terms of reference of employee and union job controls. What we might in our context term 'welt working' thus described employee-deliberated working practices and was considered by the unions to be one of the main institutions targeted by management in the 'V6'.

Although the 'V6' Agreement successfully allows for the reassertion of the principle of interdiction by front-line supervision in the newly constituted teams, the dominant role of the steward in terms of controlling communication between management and employees remains. In this respect, the negotiating framework for job allocation is bounded by the principles of joint regulation. Indeed, the 'V6' Agreement specifically signals the centrality of the shop steward in the regulatory framework:

All aspects of how teams and team leader concepts work are of interest to the Trade Unions and all representational procedures will apply where appropriate ('V6' Agreement, p. 16)

It is for this reason that we can argue that some of the forms of regulation from the previous regime have been retained and this was established during negotiations for the engine plant in 1988–89.

The pattern of the numerical distribution of personnel is similar throughout sub-assembly, engine and trim sections, but the key industrial relations feature is that while employees are allocated work in team units, their primary unit of association is the 'section'. It is at the level of the section that decisions on job mobility and job loading are taken in negotiation between the shop steward and the supervisor. This is another significant element in the 'V6' agreement from the unions' standpoint and it has allowed them to cope with the impact of a reduction in shop steward density. This reduction was inevitable given GM's corporate interpretation of new management practices. As a result of this, the identification of employees with their section rather than their team has created the interesting development whereby despite the displacement of the gang system ('welt working') by teamwork, the continuity of the shop steward as the key actor in the workplace has been retained, albeit in an altered state.

This distribution is reproduced throughout sub-assembly, engine and trim, with the goal (in addition to those already stated with regard to, for example, quality) of taking labour out of production. However, here again, the part played by the shop steward is crucial. The centrality of the steward is again underlined by the role played by the senior stewards in the company's recruitment process (the senior union lay officials in the plant *can in practice* veto a percentage of applicants and are allowed to conduct their own interviews with potential 'new starts'). This typifies what has happened since 1989 in that the trade unions have remained hegemonic in the communications process, exemplified by the requirement that all information from the company to employees regarding the substantive elements of 'V6' must first be disclosed to the trade unions. As a result of this, the steward is also the focal point in the communication process with teams.

Analysis of data from previous research at the plant and discussions with the plant convenor and senior stewards suggest that employees have a more positive attitude to new forms of management when their union is centrally involved in the change as was (*and still is*) the case in GM in general and at Ellesmere Port in particular. However, there is no *majority* predisposition among employees at the plant in favour of new management practices.

Team leaders and the internal functioning of teams

It has taken some time but it is now the case that all production personnel are now in teams but, as pointed out above, the crucial thing to note is the joint regulatory framework within which teams operate. Management is effectively committed, as part of the 'V6' to building the team around existing trade groups and the erosion of the principle of demarcation is limited to functional boundaries within each craft domain. (This observation is broadly supportive of the findings of Jürgens *et al.*, 1993, for UK final assembly). Moreover, the functional boundaries *inside* the team are team leader managed. The implications of this for team governance and the restriction on the extent of polyvalence are that at present there is little interchangeability between teams. Even where this occurs it is between cognate tasks, e.g. within the paintshop or the bodyshop areas.

Polyvalence within the functional boundary of the section is, as pointed out above, high though contingent, as is multi-tasking within teams. The team leader is appointed by management and the successful incumbents obtain a small additional payment to their normal salary. (At Rover UK, there is a mediated electoral process (see Chapter 11); for Rover's Longbridge and Cowley plants, see Stewart and Garrahan, 1995.) Team leader benefits are not defined as a percentage of pay. It is agreed that although team leaders should be completely flexible, this needs to be limited to allow them to perform administrative tasks relevant to team stability. The fact that at present the team leader is appointed and is therefore seen to be part of management perpetuates the hierarchical division between team leader and team members, because of the (public) assumption garnered by the QNPS agenda whereby teamwork is designed to break down social boundaries. It could of course have been predicted that the consequences for General Motor's QNPS of the non-elected status of team leaders on employee perceptions would be significant, perhaps even negative, although this has not been demonstrated *per se*. The issue of elections, while important, is not in itself crucial as a determinant of employee commitment to the change process. Indeed, the issue, in so far as we are concerned with it here, is not even about commitment – more realistically is it to do with employee perceptions and the various forces determining these. As research into the change process at other final assembly plants in the UK demonstrates, the crucial intervening variable on employee perceptions of new management techniques is the trade unions (Stewart and Garrahan, 1995). It is they who have highlighted the way in which new management nostrums can be taken on board by the different actors in a variety of ways. The interesting aspect of this is the extent to which trade union practice(s) can be seen to be not simply contradictory but in many unintended respects, complementary to the discourse of GM's corporate philosophy for employee involvement. In other words, and it is important that the point be made somewhat cautiously, it is the unions as much as management that are making QNPS work. This dependence upon union sponsorship is hardly new, but it is important to stress the fact as an important corrective to the assumptions of the lean production school, who would argue against an Anglo Saxon approach to industrial relations.

Conclusion

The key characteristic of the process of managerial renewal at EP is the central role played by the trade unions. Certainly, trade unions were reluctant participants in the introduction of the new management practices as elaborated in the terms of reference of the 'V6' Agreement. In addition, even when their participation was guaranteed (in different ways and with varying consequences for each of the union participants,) they had little if any substantial impact upon the kinds of institutions defining change at the *technical level* (namely, teamwork, JIT, lower inventories and team leaders). However, what can be argued with certainty is that trade unions have had a considerable impact upon the character and direction of these new workplace institutions in social terms, and that employees tend to regard these institutions more favourably when their trade unions are centrally engaged in the change process (Stewart and Garrahan, 1995).

For employees at this plant, the trade unions have been able to oversee the allocation of tasks and work time and, although this has not allowed for the continuation of all previous workplace practices, specifically 'welt work', managerial determination of these has been considerably tempered. In effect, the unions have been able to retain significant institutional elements of joint regulation from the previous workplace regime. Nevertheless, one of the central points of 'welt working' has undoubtedly been eroded – employee driven autonomy defined, in the first instance, as the ability to control time. In other words, while the unions have been largely successful in mediating both the formal institutional mechanisms of the new management practices (team working, for example) and some of the consequences of these upon employees (health and safety matters, for example), their success in retaining the scope of employee job discretion has been somewhat more circumscribed. However, it is still plausible to describe this situation, in general terms, as positive for collective bargaining since it has arisen because the unions, and the TGWU in particular, have been able to reconstitute relations with their respective memberships both during and after the introduction of the 'V6' Agreement in 1989. The ability of the unions to insist upon the retention of many of the previous terms and conditions of employment, including joint decisions on, *inter alia*, staffing levels, job loading and rotation, 'stand-down' (i.e. lay-off) benefit and aspects of company recruitment procedures, points to the perpetuation and consolidation of these close shopfloor links between employees and their union representatives.

The key factor in all of this has been union, specifically the shop stewards, hegemony of the communication processes. In part this is linked to the historical and national character of joint regulation in the UK automotive sector, but what gives this significance today, in the light of retrenchment by many unions in the UK more generally, is the commitment by GM to the continuance of the company's localisation strategy with respect to employee relations. Where union shop committees are powerful – as is the case at EP – this has – unintentionally – reinforced their existing rights, *and power*. This is obviously related to, while at the same time reinforcing, the hold that the trade unions have on the communications process(es) – direct and first-line dialogue with the shopfloor. Why this is so derives from the primary role of the unions in managing the social relations of power on the shopfloor – labour utility, staffing, and the terms and conditions of employment in general. Specifically, stewards at the point of production were in the past, and from recent research clearly remain, identified as the protector of employee rights at work. This acts as a powerful constraint on employer actions in many aspects of the employment relationship at EP, from personnel strategies to teamwork organisation. For the trade unions, significant elements of their pre-existing strength have continued into the new era of the 'V6' Agreement. (Indeed, one could interpret the success of the unions during the 1995–96 dispute as adding further weight to this assessment.) Finally, this is of further significance in that it serves as a powerful reminder of the reality of the sociology of change in the workplace – management, in other words, can never be the all-powerful player as so often conceived in management panaceas.

Giving primary consideration to these issues is vital in our deliberations over the definition of change in the automobile sector, since it reminds us of the extent of continuity in any new system of social and technical organisation. Understanding the role of the distinctive actors, including their own relative autonomy in the innovation process, is at the centre of these deliberations. The emphasis here is necessarily on unions because they are often ignored in the lean production debate. As emphasised above, in describing teamwork, researchers are often tempted to define collective endeavour in the work group as if it had never previously existed. Memories can be short where social relations are being transformed! Whatever is read into new forms of workplace practice in respect of schema for putative industrial models, these need to be viewed in terms of the necessary contestation over social power at work.

It is important that we avoid the methodological temptation to generalise from one plant in one company, although the view presented here is informed by research in progress in GM more generally (Stewart and Martinez Lucio, 1998; Stewart and Wass, 1998). On the other hand, we do have a range of views within GERPISA regarding the question of change, including the broader questions of firm trajectory and general models of production and regulation. Case studies are fundamentally fruitful in helping to assess many of the claims posed by determinate models of change, with their often broad-brush approach to historical processes. However, what we can begin to build up from focus upon the particular is a series of case studies that highlight the problematic assumption implied by the conception of the new productive model. That a model, or indeed models, are in the process of undermining and transforming a Fordist frame of reference is a highly tendentious, not to say premature, conclusion for (at least) two reasons. The first objection has been persuasively made by Clarke (1992) who has emphasised the problematical claims of post-Fordists concerning the overall co-ceptualisation of Fordism. Secondly, the case of GM suggests that a more helpful approach is to assess the scope for firm specific forms of development that allow for a better account of change at the micro-level. This is because the political economy of the

auto sector has to be understood in terms of concrete developments which means that we have to begin at the level of the (in
this instance transnational) firm and the national–political environment, as opposed to an abstract account of global ideal types. This
will allow us to avoid the trap of falling into the One Best Way
imperative of the lean production school while at the same time
describing tendencies which highlight specific trends in management as they are articulated by actual companies. In addition, we
will then be better placed to locate change in more realistic terms,
not as transformation (or simply continuity) but rather as a contested social process. By paying closer attention to the social relations of change-as-contested-social-process, we will develop a more
suitable account of firm trajectories since we can see these as contradictory and uncertain.

End-notes

[1] In addition to the V6 engine facility, the company invested in an
automated press shop, body shop and new paint shop facilities.

[2] The TGWU has developed a very interesting agenda of engagement
with the new management practices, combining scepticism towards
some aspects of the new techniques with an attitude which is described by the union locally as one of 'Engage and Change', which is
a variant of the national position. As the leading union actor in the
plant, the TGWU has thus far led the way in terms of attempting to
develop a specific trade union portfolio of alternatives, via negotiations, for plant-level stewards. The AEEU, despite (at national and
regional level) its professed commitment for various forms taken by
new management practices, is sometimes less than enthusiastic at
plant level. However, despite the sympathies of some AEEU stewards for TGWU practice, the former generally has accepted the ethos
behind new management practices and this is commensurate with its
prosecution of the so-called 'new realist' (accommodationist) position of the 1980s. The organisational (and some might argue political) strength of the TGWU is seen to derive from the more central
role given to the stewards and senior stewards in deliberations with
front-line supervision. The MSF union is much more constrained,
both in terms of constituency and its relative numerical weakness
throughout the sector, but it adopts a position rather more close to
that of the TGWU than the AEEU.

[3]   *Welt work.* Thanks are entirely due to John Bohanna of Ford Halewood
      (UK) for the following account. Traditionally, when dock workers
      on Merseyside needed time off for shoe repair, they were able to
      utilise management-sanctioned relief time. This was one means by
      which dockers could creatively use the porosity in the working day
      for individual and collective breaks. The term 'welt work' has been
      incorporated into local parlance to describe the practice of 'saving'
      time for short relief periods during work.

References

Clarke S. (1992) What in the F...'s name is Fordism? In Gilbert N.,
Burrows R. and Pollert A. (eds.), *Fordism and Flexibility: Divisions and
Change*. London: Macmillan.

Daniel W.W. (1987) *Workplace Industrial Relations and Technical Change*.
London: Policy Studies Institute.

Jones D. (1992) 'Lean Production (an update)', paper presented to the
Conference on Lean Production and European Trade Union Co-operation,
TGWU Centre, 6–11 December 1992.

Jürgens U., Malsch T. and Dohse K. (1993) *Breaking from Taylorism:
Changing Forms of Work in the Automobile Industry*. Cambridge University
Press.

Kelly J. (1996) Union militancy and social partnership. In Ackers P., Smith
C. and Smith P. (eds.), *The New Work Place and Trade Unionism*. London: Routledge.

Marsden *et al.* (1985) *The Car Industry. Labour Relations and Industrial
Adjustment*. London: Tavistock.

Starkey and McKinley (1989) Beyond Fordism? Strategic choice and
labour relations in Ford UK. *Industrial Relations Journal*, Vol. 20, No. 2,
93–100.

Stewart P. (1994) A new politics for production? Trade union networks
in the European automotive industry. In Totsuka *et al.* (eds.), *International Trade Unionism at the Current Stage of Economic Globalisation
and Regionalisation*. Tokyo: Friedrich Ebert Stiftung.

Stewart P. and Garrahan P. (1995) Employee responses to new management techniques in the auto industry. *Work, Employment and Society*,
Vol. 9, No. 3, 517–536.

Stewart P. and Martinez Lucio M. (1998) Renewal and tradition in the new politics of production. In Thompson P. and Warhurst C. (eds.), *Workplaces of the Future*. Basingstoke: Macmillan.

Stewart P. and Wass V. (1998) From 'embrace and change' to 'engage and change', *New Technology, Work and Employment*, Vol. 13, No. 2, September.

Storey J. and Bacon N. (1993) The 'new agenda' and human resource management: a round table discussion with John Edmunds. *Human Resource Management Journal*, Vol. 4, No. 1, 63–70.

Vauxhall Motors (1989) *Your Guide to the V6 Agreement*.

CHAPTER 11
The Introduction of Teamwork at Rover Group's Stamping Plant

Andrew Mair

Introduction [1]

The Rover Group's factory at Swindon, in southern England, is the company's main site for the stamping of major steel body parts and the welding of body sub-assemblies from smaller stampings. The factory was originally built by the Pressed Steel Company in 1958. In 1965 Pressed Steel was purchased by the British Motor Corporation (BMC: formed from the 1952 merger of the main domestic mass car producers, Austin and Morris). Ultimately, the wave of mergers and acquisitions culminated in the formation of the conglomerate British Leyland Motor Corporation (BLMC) in 1968.

During the 1960s, the Swindon factory employed mostly unskilled workers on its lines of stamping machines, who loaded and un-loaded machines manually. The factory also employed semi-skilled workers in welding areas. There were separate groups of skilled maintenance and die changing workers, and skilled craftsmen who manufactured stamping dies at a significant tool-making facility. Both the maintenance/die changing and tool making workers had to serve long apprenticeships before being qualified for their work.

As BLMC and the successor companies evolved through its crises during the 1970s and early 1980s (Mair, 1998), the amount of activity at Swindon declined commensurately. Sub-assembly welding work was stopped in the early 1980s. Employment declined in steps from a peak of 6,600 in 1965 to 2,800 in 1993. Between 1986 and 1988, the company, by now known as Rover Group, sold many of the BLMC components-making companies it had inherited, and the Swindon factory appeared to be threatened too.

In 1985, however, the Honda Motor Co., Rover Group's infor-mal partner in product technology transfer, product design and joint manufacturing since 1979, selected Swindon as the site of its own automobile factories in Europe. The Japanese company opened an engine manufacturing plant in Swindon in 1989, and a car assembly plant in 1992. Honda agreed to purchase the major body stampings needed for its own cars from Rover Group starting in 1992, contingent upon the purchase of two Japanese Hitachi–Zosen Tri-axis presses. Rover Group also secured welding sub-assembly work at the factory for the first car to be made by Honda at Swindon, the 'Synchro' (the Honda Accord/Rover 600), the first such work at the factory since 1985. The Swindon factory became the largest site of 'Rover Body and Pressings' (RBP) when the company was reorganised into separate business units in 1990–91.

The lowest level of employment was reached in 1992, and almost 1,000 permanent new employees were hired between 1993 and 1995 as welding and stamping work expanded.

The evolution of work organisation at the Swindon site

The technical organisation of body parts stamping and sub-assembly welding at Pressed Steel's Swindon factory had been well suited to the piecework system of the traditional British industrial model (Mair, 1998; Tolliday, 1995; Tolliday and Zeitlin, 1987; Whipp and Clark, 1986; Whisler, 1995; Wood, 1988). Until the 1970s, work, although nominally in the control of factory managers, was in practice largely organised by small autonomous working groups led by a shop steward. This trade union official negotiated piecework rates with management on behalf of his workers. The work groups or-ganised their own work, and so detailed Taylorist time and motion studies were not undertaken by managers or industrial engineers. Thus, besides 'rate fixing' (i.e. determining pay-per-piece), man-agement focused on ensuring that the working groups received adequate raw materials and supplies. When work groups had fin-ished their daily quotas, they could stop working. Since over time the work groups were able to reorganise their own work to be-come more efficient, without necessarily sharing the results of these productivity increases with the company, they often simply went home well before the end of the nominal working day.

The work groups formed trade unions which defined themselves according to their particular tasks, or crafts, of which there might be twenty or more in each of the larger factories. The trade unions for some crafts helped to organise the apprenticeship systems which restricted the entry of qualified 'skilled' workers, hence increasing the bargaining power of the shop stewards in their piecework negotiations. It was nevertheless in the interest of the shop stewards to ensure that production was organised smoothly, in order to protect the financial interests of their workers. On the other hand, they were frequently able to disrupt production elsewhere by getting their particular group to strike or work slowly if necessary, in order to buttress their bargaining positions.

Under this overall system, on the Swindon press lines, gangs of workers, working either in pairs or individually, manually fed the first press in a line with sheets of cut metal, unloaded the first press and manually passed the stamped sheet into the next press for further stamping, until the dies in a line of between three and six presses had sequentially stamped the sheet into its final shape. The gangs could work at their own pace. In the welding areas, workers could work individually with their hand-held welding tools, to build up sub-assemblies, also at their own pace, until their quotas too were reached. Sizeable inventories of work in progress between production areas permitted overall production to advance smoothly despite the diverse paces of individual production areas.

The management of BLMC had introduced the system of Measured Day Work (MDW) during the early 1970s to replace piecework. Under this system, the focus of managerial bargaining with the unions shifted from money-per-units to units-per-day (or 'standard work'). This was designed to give management greater control over work organisation and productivity. Yet MDW failed to result in increased productivity. Management had virtually no experience or competency in work study, and there were few managers or engineers who understood the details of production. While foremen ought now to have played a pivotal role in ensuring continued and smooth production, there were very few experienced foremen able to command and gain respect from shop stewards and work groups. Moreover, the trade unions were able to negotiate formal 'mutuality' agreements under which management had to obtain union approval for any changes it wanted to make to the organisation of work (Pontusson, 1990; Wood, 1988). Even when 'mutuality' was unilaterally ended when management reasserted its 'right to manage' during the early 1980s, the company appeared unable to substantially reform work organisation, except in cases where radical new technologies were introduced (Scarborough, 1984, 1986; Williams *et al.*, 1987).

Even after two decades of MDW, at the start of the 1990s, work tasks on the sixteen lines of presses at RBP, like the equipment itself, had scarcely changed from the piecework system. The majority of workers were unskilled and received virtually no training. Their work still involved passing sheets of steel between presses, loading and stacking. Even by 1993, only on one of these traditional lines had handling between the presses been automated. The workers still worked in mobile gangs, which shifted from line to line either when a job was completed (the quota had been achieved) or there was a mechanical breakdown or quality problem on the presses. The guiding philosophy behind manufacturing management was squarely focused on achieving high utilisation of direct labour. The presses themselves were used at only 30% of their potential capacity, whereas RBP management now believed that a 'world class' utilisation rate would be 70%.

Skilled work also involved gangs of workers who undertook their specialised tasks, either maintenance or die changing, on a line of presses, and then departed. Prior to 1979 seven separate crafts, or trades, were needed to change a die, and each did its work in succession. Under this system, it might take 36 hours to change the dies on a line and set them up for production. Given the lengthy die changes, a gang of workers might then spend several days or even weeks making the same parts, building up stockpiles, before the dies were changed again. In 1979, however, at the end of a prolonged phase of industrial relations restructuring under the now state-owned British Leyland (BL) (Scarborough, 1984, 1986; Willman, 1984, 1987), at Swindon the seven trades were amalgamated into one, the setter. Setters became members of the AEU (the skilled mechanical workers union), even though they were in fact only classified as semi-skilled. Existing fitters, one of the main old trades, either took voluntary redundancy (were paid to leave the company) or became unskilled operators.

Further reforms to skilled work at Swindon took place during the early 1980s, when an electrical–mechanical apprenticeship programme was launched to begin the amalgamation of the still separate electrical and mechanical maintenance trades and thus create a cadre of multi-skilled workers. This programme was halted in the mid 1980s, however, when plans for new capital investments, to which the new training was linked, were abandoned.

Attempts by local management in the late 1980s unilaterally to introduce a 'cell management' system (see Smith, 1988) were successfully resisted by uniformly hostile trade unions at Swindon. In part, resistance was based on the principle that the new ideas would reduce the authority of the trade unions. It was also argued strongly that the imposition of inappropriate centralised and standardised ideas for restructuring working practices on the Swindon factory in the past, without flexibly taking local circumstances into account, had been partly responsible for poor performance. United trade union resistance to the teamwork ideas associated with cell management at the factory was successful.

New initiatives at company level

Starting in the late 1980s, senior management of Rover Group signalled a significant shift in the company's approach to the reform of work organisation. A series of five major linked initiatives were launched across Rover Group between 1987 and 1992. Within a new overall organisational context, a new managerial strategy to introduce teamwork throughout Rover Group was launched.

The first initiative was a Total Quality Improvement (TQI) programme. TQI was cascaded down the managerial hierarchy to teach concepts of quality, process control and measurement, problem-solving techniques, and the importance of teamworking as a principle. By 1989–91, lower-level managers were teaching TQI techniques, such as how to reduce scrap and other wastage in production, to the mass of production workers, in short courses lasting several days.

The related Total Quality Leadership (TQL) initiative posed the question 'what is the Rover manager of the 1990s to be like?' The TQL answer was that the manager must become a 'leader' rather than a 'manager'. The leader role, it was emphasised, would involve coaching and counselling rather than the top-down control that the company had been attempting to impose since the introduction of MDW twenty years previously.

A third initiative was the 1990 establishment of a 'company within a company', Rover Learning Business (RLB), as a parallel human resource development activity. The goal of RLB was to 'ensure learning opportunities for all'. Its establishment was seen as a means to promote both a willingness to be flexible among employees as well as to 'send a message' to employees that the company did indeed want to encourage their personal and career development.

Fourth, in 1991 a series of groups of lower-level employees (training staff, supervisory staff, some production workers) were sent to the United States to spend extended periods at Honda of America Manufacturing (HAM) factories, in order to observe first-hand how Honda managed a Western workforce and organised the work process. This was the first such organised learning effort since Rover and Honda had started to collaborate in 1979.

Fifth and finally, in 1992 a new agreement was signed by Rover Group with its trade unions, the T&GWU for unskilled workers, the EEPTU and the AEU (since merged into the AEEU) for skilled workers, and the MSF for managerial and technical employees. The 'Rover Tomorrow/New Deal' package included a number of important features: single status clothing and restaurants, no clocking-in when arriving at work; no compulsory redundancies (very close to an explicit job-for-life); employees to be willing to be completely flexible in task allocation; a phased eradication of all trade demarcations; and acceptance of teamworking in principle (though without detailed specification of how teams would be organised).

In the context of these five initiatives, Rover Group began to implement a teamwork form of work organisation and work supervision across the company. Each business unit (essentially, each factory) was expected to move at its own pace. Senior management did not attempt to impose a precise model of teamwork in the sense of specifying how the teams would function, how many members they should have, what should be the precise roles of team leaders, the extent to which teams could reorganise their own work, and other details of production. Factory managers were expected to negotiate locally appropriate practices, and in particular to negotiate local trade union support.

Preparing for teamwork at RBP, 1990–92

It was therefore from about 1990 that the pace of change in reforming work organisation at the Swindon factory began to accelerate. A new management team changed the atmosphere for local negotiations with a number of positive actions. On every issue management now approached the factory's trade union representatives directly to discuss the best ways to implement change. The new management team soon gained a reputation for giving full and adequate information and explanation for changes rather than shielding knowledge from employees.

The cascading of the TQI programme in 1990 and 1991 also played a role in 'lubricating' management–union relationships at Swindon. In part this was because it set a clear agenda for the future improvement of manufacturing operations. Quality, lead-time reduction, and better materials utilisation (it was estimated that RBP wasted 50% of the steel it used, compared with 30% at Toyota) became goals behind which all parties could unite. The previous managerial focus on headcount reduction had been difficult for most employees to accept willingly. Importantly, TQI also permitted participation and feedback from workers for the first time.

In 1993 the factory started an employee development review process inspired by RLB, in which line managers held individual discussions with every employee on their qualifications and aspirations. Line managers were expected to find ways for employees to learn other jobs which already existed in the factory, as a means to encourage flexibility and personal development simultaneously. At the same time, and only indirectly influenced by RLB, senior management at the factory decided to construct their own 'learning centre'. The centre opened in 1995, and included trade union representatives on the governing board appointed to oversee it.

By 1991 local managers were openly discussing the introduction of teamwork, describing the proposed changes as 'common sense', and emphasising that they would bring far more job interest for unskilled workers. Leaders of all the unions recognised the potential attractions of the type of teamwork that was being discussed for production employees. It was being proposed to make people and tasks 'captive' for each line of presses. Instead of roving gangs of unskilled and skilled workers, teams would be assigned to their own line. All workers would be more flexible in future, with a focus on 'all mucking in' (a British phrase meaning everyone willingly working to get things done together). The whole team would work together to change dies between production runs, adding variety to their work. Instead of the separate categories of setters and operators, there would be a single category of 'operator–setters'.

Despite these attractions, there were still widespread suspicions among elements of the workforce and union leaders. In particular, there was concern over the future role of trade unions in the new organisational structure. RBP began to lag behind the other Rover Group plants in making progress towards implementing teamwork. Yet, as management had described it, teamwork was viewed positively by press line operators. The T&GWU leadership was now under growing pressure from its own members, who increasingly viewed the old system as illogical. The senior T&GWU shop steward, who had been strongly opposed to teamwork, retired in 1991. From that point on the T&GWU began to favour teamwork. The union's case in part rested on expected improvements for individual workers. Not only would teamwork upgrade the skills of unskilled members, but it would also improve their status and possibly their wages, and it would open up possibilities for promotion for all workers (previously blocked for unskilled workers).

While the factory's senior managers appeared to play a positive role, a continuing sense of external pressure also formed part of the context for the shift towards teamwork. Management cited Honda's apparent unhappiness about the lack of teamwork at Swindon, whereas the Cowley factory (30 miles away) had accepted change. By 1992, as the Rover Tomorrow/New Deal agreements were being concluded, RBP appeared to be the last site of resistance to teamwork at Rover Group.

The AEU leaders, who represented the setters, the maintenance workers and the toolmakers, were still opposing teamwork. Yet they knew that they were caught in a dilemma. On the one hand, they represented the setters, whose jobs would disappear. On the other hand, they were now being squeezed by pressures from both management and the mass of unskilled workers. Despite misgivings about the long-term future of trade unions under a teamwork system, during 1992 the AEU carefully changed its position to support teamwork.

Union leaders recognised that management had taken care not to explicitly play the two unions off against each other. Indeed discussions now revolved around how to raise the skill levels of the AEU skilled workers further to prevent their positions simply being taken over by the mass of rising unskilled workers. The unions believed that the local management strategy was constructive, with its arguments that teamwork would improve the lot of production workers, and that it represented 'progress'. The structural difficulty for the trade unions on the site had been how to move towards what many believed could well be a better system of jobs and work for employees, while reducing the risk that the unions themselves would lose all authority and power to ensure that the system that eventually evolved would indeed benefit the workers. As it was to emerge, the unions had perhaps under-estimated their importance to management.

Under the Rover Tomorrow/New Deal agreements, each business unit negotiated its own local settlements regarding work organisation. The Small and Medium Cars business unit at Longbridge, for instance, negotiated detailed written understandings about flexibility and the future roles of team members. It is significant that management and unions at RBP decided not to draw up such a detailed document but to proceed with less formal, more flexible, mutual understandings as frameworks for the transition to teamwork. A number of joint management–union working groups were established, to deal with matters such as the introduction of 'single status' employment, to plan the learning centre, and to consider new forms of training for union shop stewards. These were important indicators of a growing trust between senior management and trade union leaders at the Swindon site.

The formal introduction of teamwork, 1992–93

Once agreed in 1992, the formal introduction of teamwork at the Swindon factory proceeded, at first developing unevenly across the plant during 1992 and 1993 as management selected particular work areas on which to focus the change effort. It is instructive to examine the progress that was made towards teamwork, and the particular forms teamwork appeared to be taking, in different work areas during the first year of its introduction: a new sub-assembly welding area, the traditional press lines, the new Tri-axis press area, and the tool room.

New sub-assembly welding area

Teamwork was first introduced in the new manufacturing area established for the welding of body parts sub-assemblies for the 'Synchro'. Production started in 1992. As the first welding work to be located at the factory for several years, this was to all intents and purposes a completely new process for most RBP workers at Swindon. The new area was therefore deliberately conceived as a 'greenfield site within a brownfield factory' which could form a 'beacon' for other work areas to observe as far as new forms of work organisation were concerned. However, the fact that this was not a true greenfield site but drew its employees from among existing RBP press shop workers formed an important context for planning the new form of work organisation. In particular, the transferred employees could directly compare the new processes with the traditional methods they had experienced themselves.

Planning for manufacturing had started in late 1991. The manufacturing manager for the area was an outsider to Swindon who nevertheless had long experience at other Rover sites. Three key objectives were established in designing work organisation: shifting previous demarcation barriers related to maintenance skills so that skilled maintenance workers did not need to be called in so frequently; meeting Honda's high quality standards; and introducing a capability to deliver sub-assemblies two–four hours after ordering if necessary, based on a Just-in-Time system.

To create the launch team, the managers outlined the characteristics of the people it would need, and interviewed workers from within RBP. There were 85 applications for the initial five positions, and eventually nine workers (aged between 23 and 57 years old, only two of them with previous welding experience) were in fact chosen. The launch team was told that its aim was to match Japanese companies in quality and productivity. These factory workers, who were also prospective team leaders, drew up and agreed the appropriate quality specifications themselves, so that they fully understood and supported them. The 'Team Aim' portrayed the work area as a semi-independent 'internal supplier' which had to satisfy its 'customer'. The workers were under further pressure since this type of sub-assembly welding work was a prime candidate for outsourcing to supplier companies. The knowledge that Honda, with its well-known high-quality standards, was indeed their direct customer, also added a certain urgency to the atmosphere.

Demarcation of skills was to be reduced as far as possible. Manufacturing operators were to understand tasks around the periphery of their job. Moreover, skilled workers would have to undertake other tasks if necessary; electricians would weld bolts if required. Upgrading of skills would be limited only by people's abilities (and not by the socio-political barriers of demarcations as in the past).

Management sought to establish team ownership and empowerment, so that workers would be able to make their own decisions, because they would know the team's objectives. For example, with skills upgrading, removal of demarcations and ownership, production workers would for the first time at Rover Group change copper welding heads when necessary. Jobs were thus to be enlarged and enriched in what was portrayed as a more 'common-sense' process.

Quality control was also introduced to production. During training, workers compared their own work with a model, until they learned exactly what the finished part should look like and could make it 'right first time'. At the same time, sequential spot-weld checking was introduced, with the next person on the line marking errors with a pen and handing them back to the responsible worker. Hence the workers internalised the specifications and became 'experts' on the specifications; traditionally, only separate quality control staff would have had this knowledge.

The launch team generated its own skills and training matrix (see Figure 1 for an example). Task teams were formed to look at all aspects. Thus these production workers (who were candidate team leaders) were deeply involved in planning the facility and work process, rather than having the procedures handed to them by industrial engineers. While there is no doubt that they were also closely guided and directed, they did have their own balanced input from the start. For instance, launch team members spent days visiting other companies as part of a benchmarking and learning process to help them generate their own teamwork methods.

Workers were to be permitted to learn the new tasks in the skills matrices at their own pace, as a function of their interest and desire to make their work more challenging. This was viewed by the workers as an indicator of a regime of 'fairness', and was explicitly compared with the situation prevalent in other parts of the factory where workers were said to be pressed into doing tasks they did not want to. A voluntary system, guided by a team leader, was to replace the atmosphere of 'bullying' and pressure that was said to persist in other work areas. Leaders organised training for their team members, where team members trained each other in skills they had acquired. In parallel, the tasks of skilled workers were also viewed differently. Skilled workers were now expected to focus on active planning, not the reactive 'firefighting' which had been their implicit philosophy traditionally.

Legend:
- ● Training complete; individual is competent
- ○ Training ongoing

SKILL	P. STRANGE 202605	C. BOWLER 201477	I. WATTS 202249	T. PHIPPS 202486	M. OSBORNE 200392	C. RICH 201375	E. CURTIS 201414	J. TYRELL 201394	J. WHEELER 202655	B. COONEY 201130
BASIC SPOTWELDING	●	●	●	●	●	●	●	●	●	●
MIG WELDING	●	●	●	●	●	●	●	●	●	●
GAS WELDING	●	●	●	●	●	●	●	●	●	●
STUD WELDING				●	●					
REWORK, DEBURRING, GRINDING		○	●	○	○	●	●	●		○
TIP DRESSING	●	●	●	●	●	●	●	●	●	●
TIP CHANGING	●	●	●	●	●	●	●	●	●	●
WATER, AIR, PIPES	○	○	○	○	○	○	○	○	○	○
COUPON TESTING	○	○	○	○	●	●	●	●	○	○
CHISEL TESTING	○	○	○	○	○	●	●	●	○	○
WELD DESTRUCT										
SEALER APPLICATORS										
AIR PRESSURE										
DRUM CHANGING										
SAFETY	○	○	○	○	○	○	○	○	○	○
FIRST AID						○				
PART NUMBERING										
LOT CONTROL										
MANUFACTURING OPERATION PROCESS	○	○	○	○	○	○	○	○	○	○
MATERIAL CONTROL										
PROCESS QUALITY CONTROL SHEET	○	○	○	○	○	○	○	○	○	○
DIEMENSIONAL INSPECTION		○	○		○					
COMPUTER SKILLS					○		○		○	○
TOTAL QUALITY IMPROVEMENT	○	○	○	○	○	○	○	○	○	○
TOTAL PRODUCTIVE MAINTENANCE	○	○	○	○	○	○	○	○	○	○
INDUSTRIAL ENGINEERING										
COST CONTROL										
COMMUNICATION SKILLS	○	○	○	○	○	○	○	○	○	○
MANAGEMENT TECHNIQUES		○	○	○	○	○	○	○	○	○
PRESENTATION SKILLS	○	○	○		○					
PROBLEM-SOLVING										
'DRIVING' LICENCE HOLDER		●		●				●		

Figure 1   *Synchro training matrix.*

A teamwork organisational style was viewed as central, and within this the team leaders became the key players. Those who were selected as team leaders were promoted on Rover Group's skills ladder (from Grade 3 to Grade 1: equivalent to skilled workers). Candidate team leaders clearly saw possibilities for further advancement, which had always been denied to unskilled workers traditionally. Several of the new team leaders were young, with four–five years' experience previously working on the press lines, where they had been frustrated to find people 'set in their ways' and unwilling to change. Some now saw themselves as part of a new 'elite'. They were aware that the task of the team leader would be much harder on the traditional press lines with their old equipment, older workers and fixed attitudes, and they recognised that they were fortunate in being able to start their new form of work organisation at a slower work pace as the new product was launched.

Team leaders organised shift-start meetings for their own teams. They also began to take turns to run the weekly meetings for the whole shift, traditionally the job of a production manager. From the perspective of the team leaders, there was a certain absence of management support to start with, since management itself – so they believed – was not sure quite what to do. This impression may have been more deliberate than some team leaders realised. However, it was true that the future division of labour between production co-ordinators (one step up from team leaders) and lower-level managers remained unclear. In any case, both managers and team leaders viewed themselves as pioneers. Visitors came from other parts of Rover Group, including company directors, and from outside companies (e.g. British Steel). Team leaders showed the visitors around.

Lastly, there were deliberate attempts to create a sense of social unity in the Synchro work area. The launch team was sent to the mountains for a course in outdoor survival to help them bond as a team. Once a larger number of employees had been drawn in, dances were organised with spouses invited. Members of work teams went bowling together. A sense of obligation to participate in these events was created when target attendances were set for social events.

Traditional press lines

While some of the workers in the Synchro welding area held negative views of work in 'C Building', which housed the 16 traditional lines of presses, progress was nonetheless being made. Until 1993 it was still possible to observe the traditional system of work organisation in some parts of C Building, with its transitory labour gangs moving from line to line to carry out their tasks as needed. However, by 1993 one part of C Building had already begun to adopt a teamwork model of work organisation. This was an area where three lines produced smaller stampings for the Synchro, in part to feed the Synchro welding area described above.

Here too RBP management had selected a work area associated with the introduction of a new product for an important client in which to attempt dramatic changes in work organisation. Moreover, since the pace of production was relatively slow as the product was launched, a core team of workers could be thoroughly prepared before new workers were added and output targets increased.

Manufacturing managers in C Building viewed the introduction of teamwork and a new form of work organisation as an integral part of the recently signed 'Rover Tomorrow/New Deal' programme. The Rover Tomorrow ideas were seen by some managers as a milestone which marked strong support for teamwork principles from the trade unions. Now, the T&GWU at RBP was pressing managers hard to obtain more skilled work for its members, which some managers in C Building believed was entirely consistent with their own vision of teamwork.

In the C Building Synchro stamping area, there were now captive teams for each production line. Several advantages were expected to flow from this new arrangement. Most importantly, there would be 'ownership of equipment', and a better sense of responsibility, since breakdowns would affect the workers directly. Second, with a fixed set of 15 jobs for each worker to learn (a total of 45 tool sets, capable of making 71 different parts, for the Synchro area, divided into the three lines), workers would become specialised. They would be able to learn much more about their equipment and the car parts they produced, in terms of which were the most critical parts of the job, the most critical parameters, what could be modified and how, and what could not. With more practice on each job, efficiency would also be raised. This model was also anticipated to increase job satisfaction, since under the previous random rotation between lines, skilled workers and managers had retained a monopoly over problem-solving. Third, the team would train together and get to know each other personally, which would help them work together.

To make the new system work, changes had to be made to 'indirect' work as well. Die changes had traditionally required separate gangs of skilled workers. Moreover, in the past, the press lines had broken down frequently, a further rationale for the system of mobile gangs, since mobility kept direct labour utilised while the skilled maintenance workers were brought in to make the repairs. Now, however, in the Synchro press area, when tools had to be changed, or when there were tooling problems, managers no longer had the *luxury* of releasing people to work elsewhere. The workers might stand idle, and obviously so, until the problems were resolved. To solve this problem, management was therefore dividing up the tasks of the skilled workers, assigning several of the tasks which did not in fact require much training to the operators.

Hence the operators were becoming 'operator–setters', capable of changing dies themselves, as a team. Similarly, routine maintenance tasks, such as oiling and checking equipment, could be assigned to the operators after little training. Skilled maintenance teams were now 'resident' in the Synchro area, ready to resolve major problems quickly. Moreover, management was pressing for 'multi-skilling' among the skilled workers, to create joint electrical–mechanical maintenance teams.

Two further factors were viewed by manufacturing managers as working in their favour. First, new, younger employees, were now being hired, with 'new attitudes', not 'hardened by past experience', and some of these were assigned to the Synchro area. Second, Honda's indirect and direct influence provided a useful pressure for change. For instance, Honda required detailed documentation, in terms of quality specifications for instance, and Rover now used the same documentation.

New Tri-axis press area

Two Hitachi–Zosen Tri-axis automatic transfer presses were purchased by Rover Group to stamp large body parts, initially for Synchro production starting in 1992. Several production operators who worked in this new area were sent to Honda of America Manufacturing's Marysville, Ohio, operation in the United States to observe similar machines in operation and study how a teamwork system might function in conjunction with this technology.

By 1993, production operators in the Tri-axis area were already left very much to their own devices in terms of how they would fulfil fixed quotas of body parts during their shift. Workers who were transferred to Tri-axis from C Building strongly believed that the key difference, and advantage, in the new facility was the absence of direct supervision by lower-level managers. Much of the rest of the Swindon factory, they argued, remained 'top down'. By contrast, in the Tri-axis area workers were able to undertake their tasks 'undisturbed', without what they perceived as the constant and claustrophobic supervision associated with traditional work organisation.

Compared with the traditional press work in C Building, there was already job rotation on the Tri-axis presses, and rotation involved a far broader set of basic tasks. Job enlargement started with quality inspection, and new tasks were viewed positively, as making the work more attractive. Consequently, work was said to be much less boring than in C Building, where boredom was said to set in soon after work started.

Workers in Tri-axis were told by their managers that there was no limit to what they could learn. 'Skills matrix' boards indicated what jobs had been learned. When there were technical problems, even when they lasted all day, the production workers themselves tried hard to resolve them rather than follow the traditional model in which maintenance workers would have been brought in while production workers were sent elsewhere.

Simultaneously, the separate maintenance team was upgrading its own skills, with electricians and mechanics learning each others' work. Maintenance workers too had their own skills matrix. They were now recording and graphing their own data, such as problems encountered and resultant down-time. From the viewpoint of the production workers, this indicated that skilled workers had nothing to fear from teamwork; the new system would allow skilled workers to do more skilled tasks, and so everyone could improve their competencies.

At least some of the production workers in Tri-axis clearly felt sufficiently 'empowered' by the principles in Rover Tomorrow/New Deal and by the pronouncements of senior RBP managers to criticise some middle-level managers. These managers, it was argued, did not always communicate well among themselves. In one incident, the night shift was supposed to do press work but had no raw materials (steel) to press, the responsibility of a middle-level manager. Generally, they did not consider that their managers were very well organised, although, in Tri-axis, workers who were 'anti-management' in principle (a characteristic associated with many in C Building) were quickly criticised by their peers. One manager was singled out for praise, but other managers were said still to 'descend' from their offices to shout at the workers, or still to operate according to paper plans and never ask workers how processes could be improved. Factory area meetings with these managers were frequently very brief, for production targets to be communicated, and were seen by workers as having no real value.

The workers clearly recognised that these behaviours contravened the principles of Rover Tomorrow/New Deal. However, in the new context, it was at least possible for production workers to argue openly with their managers. Senior RBP managers did indeed support the 'empowerment' of production operators, as a means to add further pressure (beyond the authority of senior managers themselves), on to middle- and lower-level manufacturing managers in an attempt to persuade the latter to change their practices: pressure that might well be more effective than top-down authority in effecting change.

Hence by 1993 the press work areas were at different stages of development towards teamwork. Most of C Building was now at what was described by production managers as 'level 1', in which in principle operators had agreed to become setter–operators and learn how to change their own dies, and teams had been formed which had been assigned to their own press lines. The Synchro press area was at 'level 2', in which production workers were now taking on setting and some maintenance tasks, while the Tri-axis area had reached 'level 3', the most advanced stage. This analysis was shared by workers in Tri-axis and senior managers. The workers, however, also noted that since the most enthusiastic workers had now been syphoned off to the Synchro welding, Synchro pressing and Tri-axis areas, the majority of C Building would be more difficult to change. Most worker resistance to change was now said to be concentrated in this area, where those who were supportive of management plans were frequently labelled 'trouble makers' and criticised by fellow workers.

Tool room

Progress towards the formal implementation of teamwork was also being made in the tool room, the area of the factory dominated by the crafting of stamping dies by skilled toolmakers. A transition towards multi-skilling and the dismantling of job demarcations was already well advanced by 1993. Possibly, however, different forms of teamwork would be appropriate for the tool room.

The skills of the toolmakers were becoming broader over time. Young apprentice toolmakers were now receiving more training than older workers had received even in the 1980s, such as competencies in drilling metal, which was formerly the task of a separate group of workers. There used to be separate trades for crane drivers and slingers (responsible for moving materials about), but now the toolmakers did most of this work themselves too. Older skilled workers were learning the new skills through special courses and on-the-job training. Moreover, some of the skilled toolmakers were now willing to learn what were previously considered very unskilled and low-status jobs, such as driving fork-lift trucks. Hence the long and complex process of dismantling traditional job demarcations was already advanced.

Yet some toolmakers still felt uneasy about undertaking 'lesser' tasks. For short breaks it might be positive to have a break in routine. Some had even worked in the press shop in C Building, previously, when there was a lack of toolmaking work. Sweeping the floors of their own work areas was not viewed as a problem. However, it was still strongly maintained that toolmakers 'did not work for four years as apprentices merely to sweep floors'. So long as their core job was still recognised by management there was a willingness to be flexible, but there were also limits.

While the concepts associated with 'Rover Tomorrow/New Deal' had not percolated into all parts of the tool room, the changes under way in formal forms of work organisation clearly fitted with it. In addition to multi-skilling and job flexibility, the new hierarchical structure, with its team leaders and production co-ordinators, had also been introduced formally.

However, roles and relationships at the bottom of the managerial hierarchy remained uncertain. The existing foremen had been promoted to become production co-ordinators. From the point of view of the skilled workers, this merely meant that there were now more 'unproductive' managers. The toolmakers believed that they were essentially doing the old foreman jobs themselves, and that their new team leaders were being paid far less for this work. There were therefore fewer workers with more responsibilities, while more managers had less work. Moreover, lines of communication were now uncertain. Traditionally, toolmakers could ask foremen questions directly and get problems resolved quickly. Now, some managers seemed to have 'withdrawn' to their offices, and it was taking longer to get answers to questions. These toolmakers felt more abandoned than empowered, and were still inclined to interpret the new model of work organisation with a degree of suspicion.

The evolution of teamwork by 1995

How had teamwork evolved at the Swindon factory by 1995? Some areas now had three years' experience with the new teamwork model of work organisation, which had progressed well beyond the experimental stage of 1993, and had diffused throughout the factory. It was now possible to identify some of the emerging characteristics of teamwork at RBP. Some of the remaining problems were also coming into sharper focus.

Organisation of teams and training

By 1995 all workers on the Swindon site were members of teams, and 200 team leaders had been appointed. Workers had been asked to form themselves into 'teams' when they were ready to do so. Most teams had been formed around 'natural working areas' such as a group of machines, or an area of the factory. The size of teams therefore varied as a function of the work area. There had been a degree of individual-level bargaining over precise team membership. Union leaders agreed that management had tried hard to accommodate 'associates' (the new word for all Rover Group employees, which, like the titles in the hierarchical structure, had also been borrowed directly from Honda of America Manufacturing) who wished to change teams.

Associates were now being encouraged to become polyvalent within their teams, by learning previously 'indirect' tasks such as quality control and primary maintenance. The overall management perspective remained that associates could learn as many tasks as they wished. In C Building, for instance, production workers were now able to learn not only quality control and primary maintenance, but also how the various machines worked and how to change dies (previously the 'setter' job). However, managers were not obliging all team members to learn all tasks. Older workers who did not wish to learn new skills were not being pressed (some might be functionally illiterate and therefore find some new tasks impossible). Management's goal was to obtain sufficient flexibility within teams that they could operate relatively autonomously.

Job rotation had become the norm. While teams were tied down to particular press lines or welding areas, individual workers rotated tasks, in patterns agreed within each team. The timespan varied, and could be daily, weekly or monthly depending upon the task. However, in C Building, where the majority of employees worked, tasks were often rotated hourly as a means to add variety to the 'pick and place' tasks that were still intrinsically tedious.

A significant innovation was the design, by RBP's management and trade unions, of an *Associate Development Review Process (ADRP)*, introduced in 1995. The ADRP marked an advance on the RLB-inspired training review process in which individuals held discussions with line managers. The ADRP was to encompass both company needs and team needs in the determination of training plans in the planning of the training process (see Figure 2). The ADRP partially removed the hierarchical character of the previous scheme, shifting the accent towards self-management of training by teams. While the trade unions had pushed hard for just such a team-centred approach to the planning of training, they did not object to management proposals that individuals were still permitted further training beyond what was agreed by their team. The emergence of ADRP, as a learning process that was built on teamwork in the context of the wider organisation, rather than on individual aspirations, was an important innovation created as a result of local discussions at RBP. It did not result from a central Rover Group initiative, but was precisely the type of initiative that some senior company managers had hoped would occur under the company's decentralised approach to change management.

Team leaders

Team leaders were directly elected by their team members. Volunteers first had to pass an elementary English and maths test before an election was organised by management in conjunction with the trade union shop steward from the team. The elected leader was then appointed by management. Each team had a single leader (the position did not rotate), although the appointment was not permanent. By 1995 some team leaders had already been de-selected

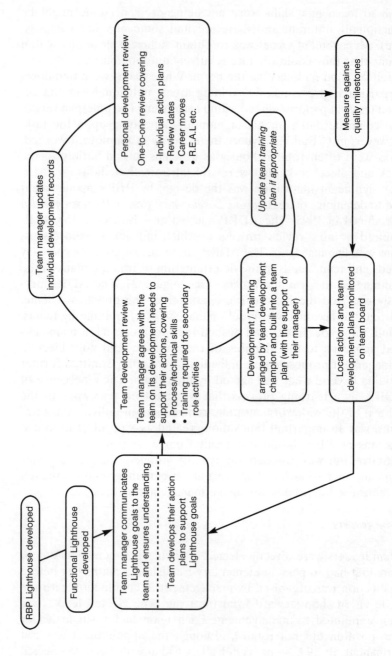

Figure 2 *RBP's Associate Development Review Process.*

because the team had become dissatisfied with them. Others had already resigned because they were uncomfortable with the actual functioning of the team system at RBP, in particular with the way some manufacturing managers were acting towards them (see below). In a few cases, where there had been no volunteers to become team leaders, managers had finally selected one. In new work areas (principally those created by the expansion of sub-assembly welding between 1992 and 1995) managers selected the initial team leaders, but the trade unions had insisted that the workers of the teams that were eventually formed in these areas held a new election; it appears that most teams ratified the existing team leaders. From the trade union perspective, this selection procedure was democratic and was widely supported. The possibility of de-selection placed limitations on the powers of team leaders over members.

While the team leader position did not rotate among team members, management had accepted a significant variant in the tool room, which again suggested that different forms of teamwork might be appropriate there. The skilled toolmakers in some teams had proposed a system in which the functions of 'team leader' were divided among team members with no one person nominated as official team leader.

What precisely were the roles of the team leaders in relation to the managerial hierarchy, on the one hand, and team members, on the other? There remained considerable ambiguities in practice. In principle, the team leader was a working member of the team. As far as communications were concerned, managers were supposed to communicate first to team leaders, who then communicated to their team (a cascade). Team leaders had no formal disciplinary powers, although in practice some team leaders had sometimes acted as if they did. Neither were team leaders the 'spokesperson' for their group, since that remained the role of the trade union shop steward, although again in practice some managers had acted as if team leaders were the official spokespersons of the team. Indeed there appeared to remain considerable issues to be decided in arriving at a workable model for the hierarchical line, particularly in cases where manufacturing managers had attempted to treat team leaders as front-line supervisors, expecting them to discipline their teams. While some team leaders had resigned rather than accept this pressure, others had adopted the role all-too-willingly. In either case, the functioning of the teams had been weakened.

Planning and doing production work

On the traditional press lines, the details of many basic production work tasks had changed little. Body parts, such as car roofs or doors, were still manually passed between presses approximately every 10 seconds (the cycle time of each press machine). However, there were important changes in the cycle times of production runs. Changes of tools to make different parts (the dies needed to make roofs or doors) could now take place about once during each eight-hour shift. The teams decided the precise timing of the tool changes themselves, as a function of their pace of work on a given work allocation. In general, these 'run cycles' (the length of each production run) were becoming shorter, as a function of dramatically quicker tool changes since the teams had learned to do this themselves.

In the welding areas, each team was given an allocation of work for its shift. The team then organised its own mini-production system, in which each worker undertook X of the Y functions (such as individual welds) before passing the work-in-progress to the next team member. The number X could be varied (the span of tasks enlarged or reduced) as could the number of workers assigned, in order to speed or slow the 'mini-production line' as necessary. Hence cycle times varied accordingly.

The determination of standard work (what could reasonably be expected of workers during an eight-hour shift) by manufacturing managers remained subject to trade union involvement and negotiation. Under the traditional system, industrial engineers had set 'parts-per-hour' targets in an attempt to force a high work pace: a pace which was rarely achieved over long periods because of machine breakdowns, quality problems and the like. Now, within a production zone (an area containing several teams), a weekly target was set, and the teams were allocated daily targets by manufacturing managers to ensure that the weekly output was attained. The manufacturing planning department within C Building could then ensure that the tools (dies) necessary to meet the weekly targets of each stamping line team were available when needed.

Hence manufacturing managers set overall targets for a shift which were achievable, with the team organising its own work pace on a consensual basis. Such was the new-found freedom of the production teams, that some managers were trying to stop workers, in control of their own work pace for the first time since MDW was introduced in the early 1970s, from working very fast for six of their eight hours, reaching their targets quickly, and resting for the remaining two hours. The managers were trying to persuade teams to spread out their work loads and take breaks every hour, which would improve quality, be better for the machines as well as the health of the workers, and reduce the temptation of senior management to raise targets. Nonetheless, some production managers now believed that teams should be given even greater freedoms to plan their own work schedules, by establishing weekly production targets and permitting the teams to organise how the targets were to be reached over the whole week.

The production teams had yet to begin systematic *kaizen* (continuous improvement) activities, although this was being planned. RBP management had formed an 'Involvement Strategy Working Party' with trade union representatives. Significantly, the goal of the working party was to encourage *team improvement projects* rather than individual-level improvement projects. Both senior managers and trade union representatives were seeking to develop a formalised team-oriented improvement process, and they were beginning to consider ways to measure team – as opposed to individual – achievements. The working party was not aiming to set targets for suggestions, but did want to be able to measure the level of suggestions. There did not appear to be any tendency to put pressure on individuals to make suggestions. Thus by 1995 a kaizen process was on the future agenda, and appeared to be developing a distinctive team focus, but it was not yet a subject for practical activity. There remained other basic priorities; in some work areas there were not yet places for workers to sit down and hold meetings.

'Indirect' tasks

All employees were now directly responsible for the quality of their own output. While the factory retained quality audit employees for specialist quality control work, there were very few of them in comparison with the 300 quality inspectors who once worked at Swindon under the traditional system. Quality standards were set by the factory's customers (the Rover Group assembly plants, the Honda assembly plant). If, for instance, Honda reported a quality problem, an RBP manufacturing manager would visit the nearby Honda assembly plant to examine the defective part, and then trace the problem back to its source. An RBP team, involving a cross-section of managers, production workers and quality specialists, would then be established to resolve the problem and report back to Honda.

While all demarcations within teams had been abandoned (except for some tasks reserved for team leaders), the separate category of maintenance workers had been retained. Maintenance workers formed their own teams, rather than being attached to each production team. Now, however, each maintenance team was made responsible for a particular zone of the factory, and undertook some routine maintenance work while awaiting any necessary emergency intervention. Maintenance workers had also taken on a completely new type of task, which would have been quite impossible under the traditional system. RBP had launched its own Total Productive Maintenance (TPM) programme, in which maintenance workers were directly teaching production workers how to do basic maintenance work on the presses, such as topping up oil, and checking that bolts were tight. In the welding sub-assembly areas, primary maintenance was also carried out by production workers (e.g. copper tips of welding guns) (see Figure 1), and workers now received training about how their spot-welding gun actually functioned. TPM activities were judged very successful by maintenance workers and production workers alike, according to their trade union leaders.

Production workers found that their range of tasks was now far more interesting. Maintenance workers were proud to show their expertise and confident that their own skills levels were also being raised, since they were encouraged to use their time to develop more strategic overviews of their responsibilities, thus retaining a clear differentiation between them and the production workers. Indeed most maintenance workers were now multi-skilled (electromechanical) and no longer interpreted the passing-on of their own low-skill tasks to production workers as a threat to their positions. This transition process was eased by the fact that many of these 'semi-skilled' jobs had been taken on by the skilled workers only in the mid 1980s, when management had sought to simplify classifications by eliminating semi-skilled classifications. These tasks had never, therefore, been associated with the apprenticeships which marked out the skilled workers.

First level of management hierarchy

The role of the team leaders, who were not formally part of the management hierarchy, was discussed above, as was the role of manufacturing managers in planning production. What role was played by the production co-ordinators, the first formal level of the management hierarchy?

Many production co-ordinators were former foremen and lower-level managers. However, for the first time a career route had opened up by which production workers could aspire to become managers. The first step on the rung would be to become a team leader. The second step would be promotion to a position as production co-ordinator. There was now discussion taking place over whether the production co-ordinator position should be a permanent or rotating role. RBP management had made it a permanent role, but this was preventing team leaders from learning new skills since the existing layer of production co-ordinators formed a blocking layer above them. Some team leaders were now arguing that the production co-ordinator role should be occupied by team leaders in a rotating pattern.

In principle, production co-ordinators were expected to assist the teams, helping them resolve technical problems. Co-ordinators were to be trouble-shooters, but were also to help plan the week's production and the correct scheduling of delivery of tools such as stamping dies with the planning department.

Co-ordinators did have a role to play in any disciplinary actions against workers. For instance, in cases of repeated absence from work, it was the co-ordinator who actually 'cautioned' the habitual absentee or late-comer. However, co-ordinators did not have any formal supervisory powers of their own. And since there was no individual employee-appraisal scheme at RBP, it was not possible for co-ordinators to exert control here either.

These formal characteristics of the production co-ordinator role fitted closely with the 'inverted triangle' model of managerial hierarchy that had been publicised within Rover Group as part of Rover Tomorrow/New Deal, in which management's tasks were portrayed as helping production workers achieve their goals, rather than the reverse. Yet the practical implementation of this organisational form was made more difficult by the fact that most production co-ordinators were still former foremen, and many still saw themselves as supervisors and/or as production experts with authority to tell the production teams what they must do. Some still intervened in what had now been defined as team responsibilities to resolve problems, finding it difficult to relinquish their traditional 'fire-fighting' role. This reflected a wider problem that was emerging as characteristic of middle–lower-level manufacturing managers at RBP.

Worker involvement and participation

Why did many production workers appear to be keen to participate much more fully and actively in their work, taking on new tasks and responsibilities? The causes did not seem to lie in direct labour market pressure, such as fear of losing their jobs. Unemployment in the Swindon area was relatively low on a national basis. Very few employees were ever dismissed by RBP (for discipline problems, for instance). There was no threat of closure or redundancy currently, although the uncertainties of the 1980s may still have weighed on some. Indeed between 1993 and 1995 RBP had expanded its workforce, taking on nearly 1,000 new employees to reach a total about 3,500 by early 1995.

At company level, Rover Group certainly raised the spectre of Japanese competition and its potential impacts on European automobile makers during negotiations over Rover Tomorrow/New Deal in 1991–92. This was designed to create what the company called a 'compelling need' for the workforce to accept change. At the same time the New Deal effectively offered workers a 'job-for-life', with the abolition of compulsory redundancy. Indeed a new set of employment problems was now being faced by Swindon management. There were now attractive early retirement programmes for employees in some areas of the Swindon factory that management wanted to slim down, such as administration, which were leading to resentment among older workers in other areas who did not receive the same offers.

Neither were the causes of involvement and participation to be found in the salary and promotion system. Overall salary levels were very competitive in the local economy (higher than at Honda, for instance). Unemployed workers hired by RBP were said to be pleasantly surprised to suddenly receive pay amounting to £350 per week (including the shift-work premium) plus six weeks of holidays per year. Indeed pay levels at RBP had consistently caused problems for other local businesses, whose best workers frequently left to join RBP.

The grading structure which classified employees by rank or grade had been negotiated between Rover Group and its trade unions at company level. The company was seeking to make the structure simpler, to merge the separate structures for administrative and production workers together, and to draw up consistent rules that would permit each employee to progress through the grades. The

Rover Tomorrow/New Deal agreement declared these as aims, the details of which would be negotiated in future years. It was thus recognised that appropriate career structure patterns had to be negotiated in parallel with other developments. In 1994, for instance, the company and trade unions agreed that all employees would fall into three bands, a simplification. Negotiations now involved the extent to which progress through the grading structure for each individual should be measured in terms of an externally validated measure such as the British government's new National Vocational Qualifications (NVQ) system (portable for workers who left the company), or some internal Rover Group measure of competency in which individuals could attain higher pay as their skills were built up, but for which training was purely company-focused with no external validation.

In principle, there had been a system of individual appraisals for staff members ('white collar') in the past, but in practice this had not taken place for four years. All employees shared in a profit-sharing scheme (relatively small, given Rover Group's low profits), which was dependent (pro-rata) upon their attendance level (absenteeism). While there was a complex scheme in which, if the factory's attendance level was higher than a certain level, all those with 100% attendance received a small bonus, there was no attendance bonus at the individual level.

In general, then, it seems clear that there was very little systematic connection between individual performance, evaluation of an individual's work, promotion or advancement, and payment, that might encourage workers to co-operate actively and participate in the teamwork form of work organisation. Neither was the local labour market a strong constraint. To the extent that workers were to become more involved and seek to participate, therefore, this appeared to depend on a desire to make work itself more interesting, to produce high-quality products, and to participate in a more rational and less psychologically draining system of everyday work.

The outcome, management and union agreed, was that by 1995 roughly half of employees actively desired to be more involved in their work, while the remainder still refused to participate actively, even if they accepted the new system passively. Among those who were active participants, many believed strongly in the company and its products and were now proud to work for Rover Group. Among a significant group of workers, then, morale was high. In particular, many workers now appeared to have a strong commitment to produce high-quality parts, and they did indeed halt the production lines, as they were supposed to, when they encountered problems. In general, there was said to be a particularly high level of involvement in quality control.

And yet, by 1995 active participation appeared to have reached a delicate stage. As has been mentioned, there were continuing difficulties related to the roles of the production co-ordinators and lower-level manufacturing managers. If these could not be overcome, they threatened to reduce the willingness of production workers to actively participate in implementing the new work organisation system, a system which relied for its potential efficacy precisely on that involvement.

Conclusions

By 1995 there had been widespread progress towards the adoption of teamwork at Swindon. Support for the new concept among the workforce appeared to be relatively strong, despite the absence of several possible incentive mechanisms. Moreover, a number of significant organisational innovations had been developed at Swindon as an outcome of Rover Group's decentralised strategy for implementing teamwork: including the learning centre jointly governed by management and unions, the 'Associate Development Review Process' which focused decisions over training needs firmly within the production team, and the training courses run for shop stewards.

Nonetheless, there remained important issues to resolve regarding the roles being played by some production co-ordinators and lower–middle-level manufacturing managers. As a result, the model that would be adopted for relationships between the teams and the hierarchical line remained unclear. By 1995 the evolution of teamwork at RBP therefore appeared to have reached a delicate phase, one whose outcome might influence the precise pattern that teamwork at Swindon would eventually take. On the one hand, it remained possible that the difficulties associated with a lack of middle–lower-level management support would stifle initiative and create a downwards and defensive spiral back towards the moribund structures and routines of the 1970s and 1980s. On the other hand, it was possible that teamwork would continue to evolve in the direction of increased autonomy for the production teams in domains going beyond the planning of detailed work processes. These might encompass the setting of quality standards, the planning of weekly production schedules, the establishment and implementation of training plans for team members and, potentially, the creation of a team-oriented kaizen process, all of which had already been openly discussed at RBP. It might also encompass direct contact with upstream and downstream teams, planning overtime and managing costs, bottom-up appraisal of managers, and the recruitment, interview and induction of new team members (Figure 3 indicates the framework being used at Swindon to guide these discussions).

Several tendencies suggested that a further transition towards increasingly autonomous self-managed work groups was a distinct possibility at RBP. First, the technical organisation of the work processes involved in stamping and welding, none of which was controlled by moving assembly lines, lent itself to the possibility of greater autonomy (the pace of some work was certainly controlled by the speed of machines, but only within a separate set of processes: around one line of presses, for instance). Second, the revelation that management competencies at middle–lower management levels remained weak, despite the TQL initiative, suggested that some managers at least would continue to find it difficult to play the difficult roles that would be demanded of them in the different, more 'top-down', forms of teamwork towards which RBP might have evolved had the factory's managerial competencies been different. In other words, RBP might move towards more autonomous, highly competent teams of production workers precisely because certain 'managerial' tasks could not be carried out by 'managers'. Third, the significant strategic role being played by the trade unions in the management of change towards teamwork appeared to be giving the unions a certain level of influence over the precise form teamwork should take, and the union leaders wanted to maximise the decentralisation of decision-making. Fourth, a large measure of worker self-management had in fact been the traditional pattern of work organisation in the British automobile industry under the piecework system (admittedly with a very different general management approach). A strong sense remained among the Swindon workforce that they were indeed capable of managing their own work better than their managers could do it for them. All these factors suggested that the strong tendency to significantly increase the competencies, autonomy and decision-making powers of the

284

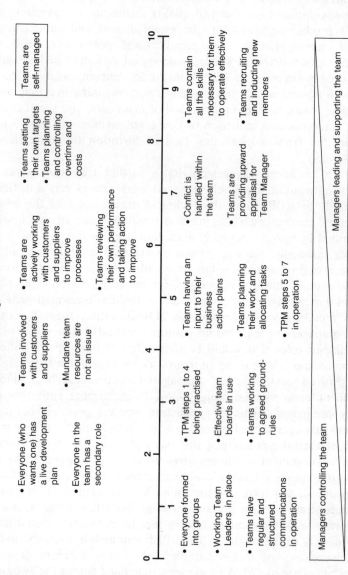

Component manufacturing – teamwork measures

0	1	2	3	4	5	6	7	8	9	10

Teams are self-managed

• Everyone (who wants one) has a live development plan

• Everyone in the team has a secondary role

• Teams involved with customers and suppliers

• Mundane team resources are not an issue

• Teams are actively working with customers and suppliers to improve processes

• Teams reviewing their own performance and taking action to improve

• Teams setting their own targets

• Teams planning and controlling overtime and costs

• Everyone formed into groups

• Working Team Leaders in place

• Teams have regular and structured communications in operation

• TPM steps 1 to 4 being practised

• Effective team boards in use

• Teams working to agreed ground-rules

• Teams having an input to their business action plans

• Teams planning their work and allocating tasks

• TPM steps 5 to 7 in operation

• Conflict is handled within the team

• Teams are providing upward appraisal for Team Manager

• Teams contain all the skills necessary for them to operate effectively

• Teams recruiting and inducting new members

Managers controlling the team

Managers leading and supporting the team

Figure 3 *Measuring the extent of teamwork at RBP (March 1995).*

production workers which had characterised the introduction of teamwork at Rover Group's Swindon factory during the first half of the 1990s had not yet run its course.

End-note

[1]   This chapter is largely based on in-depth interviews undertaken at the Swindon factory between 1991 and 1995. These interviews included manufacturing managers (4), team leaders (2), production workers, 'unskilled' (2), production workers, 'skilled' (3), human resources/training managers (4) and trade union representatives (3). In total, 22 in-depth interviews were undertaken with the 18 interviewees. In addition, shorter conversations were held with 8 further employees. Research at Swindon took place in the context of a wider programme of research interviews undertaken by the author at Rover Group, including over 50 further in-depth interviews with employees working outside Swindon during the 1991–95 period (covering manufacturing engineering, logistics, product development, marketing/sales and corporate strategy as well as work organisation and human resource management).

References

Mair A. (1998) From British Leyland Motor Corporation to Rover Group: the search for a viable British model. In Freyssenet M., Mair A., Shimizu K. and Volpato G. (eds.), *One Best Way? Trajectories and Industrial Models of the World's Automobile Producers, 1970–1995*. Oxford University Press.

Pontusson J. (1990) The politics of new technology and job redesign: a comparison of Volvo and British Leyland. *Economic and Industrial Democracy*, Vol. 11, 311–336.

Scarborough H. (1984) Maintenance workers and new technology: the case of Longbridge. *Industrial Relations Journal*, Vol. 15, No. 4, 9–16.

Scarborough H. (1986) The politics of technological change at British Leyland. In Jacobi O., Jessop B., Kastendiek H. and Regini M. (eds.), *Technological Change, Rationalisation and Industrial Relations*, pp. 95–115. London: Croom Helm.

Smith D. (1988) The Japanese example in south west Birmingham. *Industrial Relations Journal*, Vol. 19, 41–50.

Tolliday S. (1995) 'Transferring Fordism: the first phase of the overseas diffusion and adaptation of Ford methods'. Communication to the *Third International Conference of GERPISA*, Paris, June 1995.

Tolliday S. and Zeitlin J. (1987) Shop-floor bargaining, contract unionism and job-control: an Anglo-American comparison. In Tolliday S. and Zeitlin J. (eds.), *The Automobile Industry and its Workers*, pp. 99–120. Cambridge: Polity Press.

Whipp R. and Clark P. (1986) *Innovation and the Auto Industry: Product, Process and Work Organization*. London: Frances Pinter.

Whisler T.R. (1995) Design, manufacture, and quality control of niche products: the British and Japanese experience. In Shiomi H. and Wada K. (eds.), *Fordism Transformed: The Development of Production Methods in the Automobile Industry*, pp. 87–106. Oxford: Oxford University Press.

Williams K., Williams J. and Haslam C. (1987) *The Breakdown of Austin Rover*. Leamington Spa: Berg.

Willman P. (1984) The reform of collective bargaining and strike activity in BL Cars. *Industrial Relations Journal*, Vol. 15, No. 2, 6–17.

Willman P. (1987) Labour-relations strategy at BL Cars. In Tolliday S. and Zeitlin J. (eds.), *The Automobile Industry and its Workers*, pp. 305–327. Cambridge: Polity Press.

Wood J. (1988) *Wheels of Misfortune: The Rise and Fall of the British Motor Industry*. London: Sidgwick and Jackson.

CHAPTER 12
Manufacturing the Organisation of Work of the Future: A Factory Leader in Engine Production – FASA– Renault, Spain

Juan José Castillo
(Translated by Justin Byrne)

Introduction: an exceptional case of organisational transfer [1]

Academic debate and literature on technological transfers, or transplants, has tended to focus on what are considered normal or standard instances of this. That is, attention has centred on the export of new forms of work, nearly always from countries labelled central or dominant, to others somewhat imprecisely and ironically described as 'semi-', or even completely, peripheral. Discussion of lean production, in turn, has revolved around the question of whether, and to what extent, new forms of productive organisation now being developed conform to the model in the core companies, regions or countries. Significantly, these models are often imaginary, or what might more kindly be described as ideal types [2]. In this context, it would appear exceptional for a multinational corporation to select one of its 'semi-peripheral' centres to play a leading role in the experimental introduction of a series of technological and organisational innovations in its strategy to, in their own words, 'catch up with the Japanese'. It would also appear exceptional for the mother company to turn one of these centres of work and production into a laboratory for the new organisation in the search for the model of production for the 21st century – and for the company to invest its image and sufficient financial and human resources to enable the factory to meet a challenge of this scale. Exceptional but not unheard of, since this paper focuses on just such a case: Renault's FASA plant in Spain.

A factory (which must be) leader

Renault established its 'Acceleration of Progress' policy (known as the PAP in company jargon, for the Spanish Plan de Aceleración del Progreso) in 1988. The basic objective of this was to enable the company to 'match the performance levels of Japanese factories'. Although this target was to be achieved as quickly as possible, the absolute deadline was set for 1998, by which time the liberalisation of the European internal market was expected to be completed.

To implement this strategy, senior management in Paris selected one plant from each area of production (assembly and *mécanique*) to serve as 'laboratories which will enable us to generalise the progress made to other factories' in the Renault Group. This entailed the intensification in the chosen plants of a number of innovations already being introduced (Just-in-Time, Acceleration of Progress Plan, Elemental Work Units, Production Groups, Quality Circles, TPM, employee participation). These plants would also receive the resources necessary for them to 'outstrip the Japanese' in lean production, and attain at least comparable levels of productivity. The two factories chosen for this experiment were Douai in France, selected from the Group's thirteen assembly plants, and Valladolid in Spain, one of Renault's seven *mécanique* factories [3].

Conceived as a *'usine cible'*, the operation eventually got under way in the Valladolid engine manufacturing plant in January 1992. Originally known as the *hare factory*, the project was definitively rechristened the *leader factory* a few months later. Both within the company as a whole and in the Motores plant itself, the operation is seen as comprising two distinct but interrelated dimensions of the transfer. The factory must be capable of copying all the good elements of its counterparts, testing them, evaluating them, etc., so that, as a result of this, all these advances may be copied, that is, so that the other Renault factories can benefit from the experience. The FASA–Renault Human Resources Manager clearly explained the thinking behind the project in a round table on competitiveness: "The best innovation is that which copies the good things and then improves on them [. . .]. We start by copying. This maxim is now being taken as Renault's strategy. To copy the good things is to win. [. . .] We established two factories as models and they are given great freedom to do whatever is needed for them to be the best in their field. And this will generate experiences and processes which can be copied by other people so that we can all advance together" [4].

The creation phase of the project lasted from 1993 to 1995. This took place in the context of the preparations for the production of the new E-1600 engine, a project in which it is expected to invest a total of 546 million dollars in the five years before 1998 [5]. The significance of the Motores experiment is enhanced by the fact that it is also the 'testing ground' for the preparation (regardless of where production will finally take place) of Renault's next major operation: Engine D. It is this which allows us to affirm that we are dealing with the 'manufacturing' of the systems of work and production with which the company will enter the new millennium. Given the importance of the company, of the sector and of all that is at stake, the Motores project constitutes an emblematic case of the future direction of the best experiments in the organisation of work and production in Spain [6]. As the company itself declared; "our 'Leader Project' is defining the model of organisation which our factory should aspire to and which should serve as the paradigm for the rest of the Renault Group. Shaped and determined by the company's own culture and structure, this model constitutes an experience which may culminate in the year 2,000" [7].

The questions

In this context, the principal problem raised in our research, and which is at the heart of the series of questions posed in this chapter, is 'Why was FASA and Valladolid selected as a laboratory for this experiment?'. Evidently, we can only aspire to make a modest contribution towards resolving this problem in the explanation presented here. One answer put forward by those involved is that the decision was taken as a consequence of the 'local productive character' of the region. Thus, one engineering manager emphasised the 'advantages in terms of labour' which Valladolid has over other Renault factories. Workers are more willing to work on Saturdays, to work more intensively, to accept flexible hours and tasks, or to put in the hours on training outside the normal working day. One of our main concerns, therefore, is to examine this line of argument. 'The carrot and the stick' is how senior Motores managers summed up the effect of competition between factories in the same company. This suggests a second type of explanatory factor. When a production plant, in this case FASA, achieves its objectives, the benefits gained must be transferred (or copied in company terminology). In other words, the progress made by one factory must be matched by all those in the group. This is how many managers and workers see the process from the inside. They accept commitments, challenges, obligations, redundancies and anything else considered necessary to prevent production being transferred elsewhere with the consequent threat of factory closure [8].

We have already noted that a specific and multi-faceted approach is required in order to analyse the way in which tomorrow's organisation of work is being created. This must enable us to relate the study of organisational transformations, in a particular and well-defined social and productive context, to the ways in which these are transferred to other engine manufacturing plants in the group. That is, it must allow us to capture and analyse the globalisation of these changes. This dimension of the research is explored through an analysis of two other Renault plants: the Cacia factory in Aveiro (Portugal), and Rimex in Gómez Palacio (Durango, Mexico). As will be seen later, the 'Efficiency' and 'Ideal Plant' projects, now being implemented in these two plants respectively, share many of the characteristics and objectives of the Leader factory experiment in Valladolid [9]. In the conclusions to this chapter we offer some initial hypotheses regarding the impact of intra-company competition. How far, it might be asked, can one expect experiences to be transferred to competitors?

An engine factory

The Motores engine plant is located in Valladolid, the capital of the Spanish Autonomous Community of Castilla-Leon and the centre of the region's car industry, two hundred kilometres north-west of Madrid. The project, or more accurately the projects, for the development of the plant have been supported by the regional government within the framework of its Regional Development Plan, created as part of its policy of anchoring the productive fabric of the region [10]. In October 1994, the Regional government decided to seek the Ministry of Finance's permission to concede a major subsidy to the project. This envisaged the provision of 166 million dollars of the total planned investment of 546 million dollars up to 1998 [11]. At the same time as the current process of reorganisation began in 1992, the factory, which in 1989 had employed almost three thousand workers, also began to implement its 'Planned Management of Human Resources' policy. It was intended that by 1994 a similar output to that of 1992 would be achieved, while reducing the workforce during the same period from 2,475 to 1,530 workers [12].

In this respect, planning and reality have gone hand in hand. As one senior manager put it: 'we are doing the same work but with ever fewer people'. Of the almost 2,500 jobs in the plant when the transformation of the 'leader factory' began in February 1992, only 1,211, that is, fewer than half, still existed two years later [13]. During the same period, there was a slight increase in output: 354,000 engines in 1994 compared with 347,000 in 1992. According to one senior manager, these accounted for 21% of all the engines made by Renault.

The current situation: between discourse and reality

The project *leader-mécanique* was agreed at the end of 1991, at a time when, in common with other pioneering companies in the reorganisation of production in Europe, Renault introduced a policy of unifying previously diverse productive strategies [14]. The first practical steps were taken the following year. These included changes (and continuities) in the management of the factory and its functional structure. This phase of changes included forms of Planned Human Resources Management: the implantation and diffusion (once again) of a strategy for employee participation, the creation or re-creation of production groups, and most importantly of all, the generalisation of the UET, *Unidades Elementales de Trabajo* – 'Elemental Work Units' (EWUs), an innovation which senior management in Paris had decided to implement throughout the company. One of the priorities for our research is a detailed analysis of the way the EWUs were actually developed on the ground. By Spring 1994, more than 60 of these 'Units' were in operation. Usually consisting of groups of not more than 20 workers, they were introduced in processes in which it is possible to identify the product of a particular work group and to establish client–supplier relations between different units [15]. At the time of writing, the entire Motores

plant is officially organised into EWUs. Yet, even those responsible for 'EWUifying' the company admit that, as we shall see below, the "implantation of these is far from complete" [16].

The Leader factory project has already passed through two clearly
differentiated phases. The first coincided in time with another organisational innovation: the creation, in consultation with workers,
of 'production groups' and the introduction of bonuses for those
agreeing to work in these. This strategy was rooted in a whole series of earlier experiences and organisational developments [17].
This first phase paved the way for a new stage in the making of
the future organisation of work. This second phase of the operation, labelled 'Leader II', was launched in April 1994 and coincided with the arrival of a new Managing Director of the Motores
plant. According to the original timetable, an initial assessment of
the results of this phase of the operation should have been possible in Spring 1995 when it was intended to begin normal production of the new E-1600 engine [18]. As one manager put it in April
1994: "Leader II is the team's conceptual discovery of the best
direction for improvement in this factory [...]; we are still in the
phase of constructing even the idea itself" [19].

A year later, in February 1995, the various different stages in
the design and introduction of the EWUs had been executed throughout the entire plant [20]. However, there seems to be almost unani-
mous agreement among those responsible for introducing the EWUs
that these have been rushed. They consider that, because of failure to fully analyse the labour processes in which the new organisation must be rooted, there is a need to start afresh. The mesh
which constitutes the very foundations of the whole EWU system
should be redefined on the basis of improved knowledge and understanding of the existing work organisation. "The units have been
devised," one manager reported in 1995, "but not consolidated,
developed, or used". According to another manager: "our diagnosis is that the implementation [of the EWUs] was too mechanical
and that an organisational fabric based on deeply-rooted habits has
not been woven or created".

We need to examine the particular work environment in which
this new form of organisation is being established. A similar process is currently being carried out by the Motores plant itself, since
as one of those involved emphatically declares: "we established a
discourse, but not the reality". Or as another puts it: "we should
first have created the necessary conditions, but failed to do so".

Those responsible for defining the mesh of the EWUs "were not even given a course, at most a poor lecture, and that was all they started out with". The mesh was created "so as not to introduce changes; since the manager pushed for it from above . . .".

We believe that a particular type of theoretically orientated research is necessary in order to evaluate the current situation. Only in this way is it possible to carry out a realistic analysis, to get as close as possible to the real situation, to the difficulties and possibilities which now exist, and to the way in which the different social actors have experienced the changes introduced [21]. In discussions with company managers and supervisors, union representatives and workers, as well as with the 'EWU consultants', we have examined the available statistical data, the innovations already implemented, and the new problems these have created. In the light of this, and of the insights gained from *in situ* analysis, we have selected a number of work situations, usually corresponding to individual EWUs, which illustrate some of the factors which appear to explain the different tendencies identified, and the greater or lesser repercussions of the difficulties facing all the EWUs. In each case we have considered the following characteristics of the work: *previous* experience of new forms of organisation (semi-autonomous groups, quality circles, etc.); the age and type of machinery used; the *physical demands* of the work carried out; the inclusion of 'service work'; the strategic importance of the partial product or of the process under consideration; and, finally, the extent to which each EWU is affected by the company's mobility policy which, in particular from 1994, has forced the suspension of many changes already under way, so disrupting the work groups of each EWU and the policies of commitment and motivation. After extensive discussion, comparative analysis and reflection, we have chosen to focus on different EWUs which combine these variables in a number of different ways and have been the object of deeper analysis [22]:

(1) *Cylinder crankcase EWU* for the E model (1400), but which is now a place of training on the production of the new E7M with completely new machinery. This work, which is generally considered to be very hard and to involve a difficult product and demanding levels of performance, is carried out with very old machinery which was last updated in 1989.
(2) *Rear chassis assembly EWU*. This work has been performed by a number of very different forms of work group since the 1980s.

There are no problems of compulsory mobility of workers. We have studied two different groups, although both are managed by the same EWU head. One of these was created as a 'production group', with a monthly bonus (some 64 to 75 dollars), while the other is a 'simple EWU' [23].

Two cases of EWU

Cylinder crankcases

The *cylinder crankcase* EWU operates on an old *transfert* which has been in the factory for over twenty-five years and which was refurbished and modernised in 1989 for the launch of the 'E' engine. Until September 1994, the EWU consisted, on each shift, of 14 direct workers, a machinist, an electrician and a quality control worker. As a result of the weak demand for this product, only 8 people, in each of the two shifts, were working in this EWU in February 1995. Nevertheless, they still worked under the orders of an EWU head.

It was in *cylinder crankcases* that the EWUs were first introduced into the Leader factory in January 1992. The construction of the EWUs was thoroughly planned and prepared: "people did not believe in it much, since it was something new". As we noted above, this is a hard job which is performed by workers with extensive experience both in the company and in the specific posts they occupy. Here, workers only become completely versatile after a number of months in each post, some considering that this takes as long as six months to a year. As a result, it takes years to train a 'wild card' or 'line head', that is, a fully versatile worker on the *Transfert* [24].

The new organisation in EWUs has been crippled by the company's policies of internal mobility, which have been intensified in response to the reduction in factory output. As a result, the number of workers employed here has been reduced by almost 50%. The most immediate consequence of this has been a reduction in the number of EWUs. Previously there was one EWU working on each of the three shifts, while now there are only two. At first, personnel were retained ready for employment on the new line, since it was expected that full production of the E7M engine was imminent. However, in February 1995 it was eventually decided to reduce the number of workers. According to one manager: "everything has begun to break down, since people have become disheartened". A group of 'integrated' workers has been replaced by a very sceptical and more distrustful group. The question of the order in which workers are to leave the group is a source of tension among workers, and between these and their superiors, the EWU and Workshop heads. In accordance with the collective agreement, the least versatile (*polivalente*, now) are the first to go. However, additional problems arise in the case of trade workers who, in terms of the workshop are less skilled than the specialists with seven or eight years' experience of the job: "when it comes to working on the machine [the specialist worker] was much more professional", "much more versatile". This has created a situation in which "many have gone to Palencia, others are working on engine assembly here, others are in [car] assembly in Valladolid and, well, they have *disfigured* the EWUs" [emphasis added]. After "investing many hours in getting them used to the idea", "everything has begun to break down" [25].

The *EWU head* was previously employed as a foreman. He sees little difference between his old and new role as a supervisory worker, although he does consider that he has been given more responsibility and some training (nearly 300 hours). He was co-opted by the line or designated to the post: 'in reality, what they expect of us is that we will steer through everything introduced or still to come in the EWU'. Despite counting on the support of the 'Technical Assistance Cell' 'attached' to the EWU, he is required to fulfil a large number of tasks, all in a context of personnel reductions. "They tell me, 'go out and get ready, supervise this or that, and then you have to report, and then you have to go to meetings, and then you have to persuade people to do whatever has to be done'. But then, basically, most days I am putting in parts, taking them out or dealing with a mechanical breakdown, that is, I am not doing my job. Of course it has been better. It was much better when there were more men".

The EWU head, who uncritically accepts that "production targets must be met", is forced in these circumstances to act as a substitute worker or to carry out internal maintenance, "because with seven blokes I just can't cope". His co-operative attitude towards company objectives can mean that the unions accuse him of being a 'mule driver'. "Yes, everything is tightened up, although people aren't really pushed to the limit". The direct workers think that any improvement to the EWU always ends up meaning 'one less job'. This gives rise to a highly ambivalent and conflictual attitude:

in order to be competitive and maintain production in the factory, the workforce must be reduced. Despite this, the new EWUs have improved relations with the workers: "There is a difference between not speaking to people, or only speaking when absolutely necessary, to sitting down with them, meeting and talking all together", says a head of EWU. That is, "there are warmer relations between people". According to one EWU head: "one thing that seems clear is that people co-operate. If you can persuade them to do something, it gets done. The only thing I do is to put on a bit of extra pressure".

The direct workers still in the EWU have worked in the same workshop, and even in the same or similar jobs, for years, although they have been employed in a number of different categories, even when carrying out similar tasks. The emblematic job, the one with the best possible characteristics, is that of the line head, or 'wild card', the worker capable of performing all the tasks and who can actually do what all workers should be able to do: 'the worker who previously operated one *transfer* now runs three' simultaneously. All these workers have worked seven or eight years on engine *blocks*.

The meetings and development of the EWU are seen in a very positive light. They are considered to have reinforced the role of both the group and its individual members by encouraging closer relations between them. This is despite the fact that the work has not changed: "you do the same and work on the same machines, but it is essential to get on well with the blokes working beside you".

Given this fundamental idea, the mere possibility of mobility significantly weakens the group. "The work isn't the same if you are thinking that they are going to send you to Palencia, to assembly". A change of workmates, of habits, of 'environment' is experienced as a rupture which it is hard to overcome. On the other hand, personnel reductions limit the possibilities for co-operation and threaten the cohesion of the work group. When the EWU is complete, the role of the wild card workers is to help 'whoever is busiest', but 'if we are missing people, you can't help anybody out'. Moreover, this also means that the group has to work through breaks and that, even then, there is no time for dialogue between workers. On occasions, there is no time even to read the announcements on the EWU notice-board.

The conclusion is quite obvious: "you work more, firstly because you have more responsibility, and also because you are working on more machines. In other words, you work quite a bit harder". And despite this productivity, "always pushing the worker", appears inevitable. Now "one man on one machine, that's just impossible". "You have to work harder, you have to work more machines".

Rear chassis assembly

The Motores plant is divided into two Departments. Management wants to apply to both the organisational policies implanted in Motores-1, the Engine Department where the innovations of the Leader factory project are concentrated. However, in practice, the implementation process has been very uneven. As a result, the plant is still known as 'the two Spains'.

Almost 600 people, that is, nearly half Motores' total workforce in April 1995, work in Department II, the 'Mechanical Parts' department of the plant. This has a head, the Departmental Manager, who has three Workshop Heads under him. These in turn, are responsible for various EWUs. In total, including the Managing Director of Motores, Quintana, it is intended that no more than 5 hierarchical levels should exist within the factory, including the EWU Heads.

Originally, and perhaps for a year or more, the EWUs in this department "existed more in theory than in practice". As the same manager puts it, "it was all on paper, just on paper", "as if they were just forced on top of everything". The EWUs are more solidly established now, but they have always suffered from problems of definition and design. Moreover, in a number of cases there is confusion as to the roles of those involved. There are EWU heads responsible for not one but various Units, and Workshop heads performing tasks of co-ordination which originally corresponded to the 'Uhs' (as the EWU heads are known in the factory argot). There are also problems in giving autonomy to the Units if one is not the 'owner' of the 'little business' on the two (or three) shifts, except for a half or third of the day.

The main problem impeding the consolidation of the EWUs, and the whole organisational programme behind these, is that time (or its equivalent in staff) is needed to attend meetings, resolve problems, etc. "There is a kind of inertia which comes from output and quantity; in other words, to do this [meetings, training, etc.] you have to stop, If you want to take two people off the line to take part in a problem solving group, well then, in a mechanised line, which are highly automated lines, the line stops [. . .] and although you might say that it doesn't matter, that we still produce the same, there is no way it can be done [. . .]. That way of thinking has to change".

In the new organisational model, the EWUs are supported by Technical Assistance Cells, the TACs. These are directly linked to workshops, and within these, to a particular EWU, or more often a number of these. This is the case of the 'Quality of mechanical parts' EWU, situated close to the Units in the shopfloor, and previously existing as a service unit. This unit of eight members and a Unit Head who was previously the Quality Control supervisor is now an EWU in the new standardised terminology.

The success of this type of EWU will lead to their disappearance, since the role of these people should gradually be reduced to a minimum as 'the responsibility for quality is progressively transferred to manufacturing'. On this path to death by success, the 'quality men's' role as overseers should steadily decline, as they become co-workers or suppliers of a service within the shop.

Our interviews have focused on the case of an EWU Head with two 'loves', although both EWUs are responsible for rear chassis assembly. The comparative approach outlined above is reinforced by the distinct nature of these EWUs. While one is also a 'production group', in which workers are paid bonuses for performing certain tasks, quality standards, etc., the other is a 'simple EWU'.

The 'production group-EWU' is said to 'work quite well', 'almost autonomously'. It is made up of eight people, with 'total flexibility' to carry out all the operations required for the production of rear chassis. "The second EWU has a few more problems, due to the fact that it does not have group [payment], because [. . .] just like everything else, if you give something you can demand something in return". The EWU head believes that if further responsibility is given to this second EWU, in a short time both EWUs "should work in the same way". However he is not sure what incentives should be used to achieve this: upgrading workers, recognition of flexibility in pay packets, etc. One thing he is sure about is that "people have changed a lot, in every way, they are more willing to do almost anything".

The EWU head's workload 'is much greater now and involves more responsibility' for problems previously dealt with by other people. These EWUs are not affected by mobility and hence escape what can be considered the problem facing other EWUs in the plant. People can no longer be 'pushed harder' at work since, in recent years: 'things have been tightened up everywhere'. Direct workers clearly perceive the way in which work has been tightened up or overburdened, but they see it as inevitable if the factory is to remain open. "In the EWU, we have been changed by two things: they have made us responsible for what we have, that is, for our work. So, since I am in charge, they are automatically going to say that the mistake is mine", says a direct worker. "What the EWU has given us is individual responsibility for the work we do".

Conclusion: history as explanation or a learning experience

From what we now know, it is quite obvious that any explanation of this 'manufacturing of a new organisation' must be rooted in an understanding of Motores' history, and of the experiences of both the management and the intermediate supervisors and workers in the plant. The current process of change is being constructed on ground conditioned by the various organisational transformations and the different policies implemented in the plant over the last twenty years [26].

During the last three years, the construction of the structure based on EWUs appears to have been marked by improvisation and imposition from above. It also seems to have suffered from the failure to exploit the company's 'historical capital'. The concern for innovation at all cost has probably prevented those responsible for designing and implementing the new work organisation from taking advantage of the progress made in previous experiments in the plant.

Further research and analysis are required before we will be in a position to answer the basic question posed above, that is, to explain why Valladolid was chosen as the experimental centre. However, it is possible that the factory's assets in the form of experience, know-how, semi-autonomous groups and so forth, may have influenced this decision. One of the main objectives of our research is to produce a more conclusive answer to this key question.

Little analysis is required to identify one of the most obvious consequences of this process, that is, the drastic reduction in the company's workforce and intensification of work. Only with difficulty can this be squared with a whole series of problems in the implementation of the new organisation which are invariably attributed to 'staff shortages'. Despite this, we have found a surprising degree of consensus regarding the 'need to compete', in order to keep production in the region and 'guarantee the future' of the plant among workers and new middle managers. It also seems evident that the workload has increased relatively in inverse proportion to the reduction in personnel. It would certainly be interesting to study the way this has affected workers' lives.

We have begun to analyse the new work organisation in Cacia (Portugal) and Rimex (Mexico) in order to consider the nature and extent of the organisational transfer to other centres [27]. In both cases, it is clear that the 'Efficiency' and 'Ideal Plant' projects now being developed, respectively, in these two countries, are based on the same strategy and principles as those put into practice in Valladolid. The Portuguese project began almost at the same time as the Spanish one, while the Mexican project was initiated in 1993. In the Mexican case, the drastic reduction in the workforce appears to have been an indispensable pre-condition for the realisation of the 'Ideal Plant' project. In 1992, 1,270 people produced 1,100 engines a day; in 1994, a workforce of 830 produced 1,250 engines a day. Judging from the employees' attitudes and response to this project, and the level of participation in the change programmes, Rimex 'seems to be obtaining considerable worker commitment to the company's objectives' [28].

On the other hand, as suggested above, competition rather than imitation appears to be the principal factor encouraging organisational exchanges. The most immediate 'result' of Cacia's uncertain future (production of the C36 engine is expected to end there in 1996) is the very high level of 'productive competitiveness', quality and commitment shown by the entire workforce. This is explained by the desire to ensure that the plant will not be overlooked when senior management in Paris decide where to locate production in the future. The very different ways in which the company's maxim, 'to copy is to win', functions requires further analysis.

The situation for the unions is now more difficult in Valladolid, even as far as numbers are concerned. Work centres (engines, assembly, coachwork) have been regrouped in response to the reduction in FASA's workforce. Although the unions are continually searching for new areas of negotiation, union publications and noticeboards rarely suggest the existence of concrete proposals or alternatives relating to the organisational changes currently under way.

The unions' room for manoeuvre in relation to the new realities of production is defined by the choice between a defensive option, which would maintain their objectives within traditional boundaries, or, alternatively, redefining their strategies in order to enable the unions to take the initiative and actively participate in 'the design of work and workers': "It is as necessary to reject attempts to introduce socially retrogressive measures as it is to defend the workers' interests by putting forward proposals and alternatives to technological changes and to the flexibility of the market. It would be suicidal for the unions to refuse to take into account the new conditions of production and so fail to secure the necessary social guarantees. That is, our objective cannot be to correct an unstoppable process in the industrial dynamic now under way in our country and in Europe as a whole. Rather, we must struggle to incorporate corporate social and labour demands into this, anticipating the process of innovation itself, its design and development" [29].

However, whatever the reasons, in practice there is no formal negotiation with the unions, nor any concrete proposals from them regarding the content of this great organisational reform.

End-notes

[1] The author acknowledges the research assistance of Javier Méndez, Centro de Estudios de Gestión, Madrid, and the valuable observations of Jean-Pierre Durand.

[2] See Womack *et al.* (1990); Boyer and Freyssenet (1994); Castillo (1994).

[3] An internal company memorandum explains that the terms '*Mécanique* and assembly [. . .] distinguish between the elements connected to propulsion (engine, gear box, transmission, steering, suspension, brakes . . .) and those connected to coachwork (the coachwork itself, doors, bonnets, seats, headlights . . .)'. (Document *Factoría Motores fábrica líder*, April 1993).

[4] Coello (1993) – quoted from an interview with the Human Resources Manager of FASA–Renault.

[5] In this chapter we obviously focus on the first phase of this operation during the period 1992–95. Different sources suggest that this will account for some 29% of the total final investment. However, the company's plans, and hence ours too, were subsequently modified. Normal production of the new E7M, 1600 cc engine was originally intended to begin in Spring 1995 but has now been delayed.

This has forced significant organisational readjustments which illustrate, above all, the difficulties and limitations inherent in any complex process of productive reorganisation. (The rate of exchange applied is 1 dollar = 125 pesetas.)

[6] This research began in March 1992 and continued with field research during Spring 1993, throughout 1994 and in further visits to the plant in February and October 1995. Apart from these visits to Valladolid and carrying out extensive documentary research, we have conducted a number of workshop studies and semi-structured interviews with management, with those responsible for participation, training, progress systems and personnel, with workshop heads, heads of department and of UET (Unidad Elemental de Trabajo), EWUs (Elementary Working Unit), as well with direct workers. We also interviewed the psychology students who formed the team of 'Consultores UET' working in the factory in February 1995. All quotes in the text are taken from transcriptions of these recorded interviews.

[7] *Memoria Técnica. Factoría de Motores. FASA–Renault*, September 1994, p. 1 [Primer Premio a la Calidad, Consejería de Economía, Castilla y León].

[8] This factor was mentioned on various occasions in relation to the production of the 'Laguna' in Palencia. It was also said to account for the organisational and productive vitality of the Cacia factory in Portugal, given that production of the Twingo engine there ended in 1996. Echoes of this 'democratic' *disciplinary* effect, as Burawoy would call it, can be found in numerous documents, interviews and statements: keep jobs in the region; keep the company going; be competitive if you want to survive, etc. (Burawoy, 1985, p. 150).

[9] Cacia employed 850 workers in 1993, while in 1992 Rimex had 1,084 workers.

[10] The policy of support for the project has been reinforced through the creation of a Regional Development Agency (December 1994), an initiative included in the Industrial Pact signed by unions, employers and the regional government in April 1993. In this respect we should also note the creation of the Boecillo Science Park with the participation of FASA–Renault. For a history of the Motores plant and of the organisation of work and attitudes of workers and managers, see our 'Diseño del trabajo' (Castillo, 1991).

[11] The press reported that "to compensate for the disadvantages of investing in Castilla-León", the European Community has authorised a public subsidy of 8.9% of the total investment, that is, 49 million dollars. "The project, which should be completely finalised in 1999, envisages the modernisation of existing installations and

the creation of new production lines for the eight and sixteen valve models of a new four cylinder engine". "The project", the report continues, "should guarantee a total of 1,009 jobs until the end of the century, including 161 new permanent posts". *El Mundo*, Madrid, 27 October 1994.

[12] *"Empleos 'clave' en una factoría para 1993"*, DAS, FASA–Renault (no date). This includes the same plan for the Cacia engine factory. It should be pointed out that this policy would also be applied in Rimex as a mandatory pre-condition for the development of the 'Ideal Plant'. See also *'Plan de formación 1994'*, FASA–Renault, April 1994.

[13] It should be noted that we were told in interviews that more than 200 workers who have been transferred to other plants, because of reduction in demand, expect to be recalled to Motores when full production of the E7M, 1600 cc engine begins. However, it is important to note that this drastic reduction in the number of employees, but not production, has even modified the form and shape of union elections: leading to a considerable reduction in the number of representatives. The figures in the text have been calculated from the data published in FASA's *Annual Reports* relating to the redundancy payments made under the 1989–93 *Plan Social*. This was introduced to encourage voluntary redundancy for 6,849 workers. The 4,968 employees who left the firm between 1990 and 1993 alone cost nearly the same amount (546 million dollars) as the total investment in the engine plant. We are informed that the company paid 60% of this redundancy sum since the rest was financed by State welfare agencies.

[14] Camuffo and Micelli (1998).

[15] In a press statement, the Managing Director of FASA–Renault, J. Antonio Moral, declared that "in recent years, FASA–Renault has undergone a series of organisational changes intended to improve management. These have included reducing the number of the hierarchical levels in the organisational structure of the EWU, developing the instruments of Total Quality Management, Process Control, Application of Self-control, Application of TPM (Total Productive Maintenance), cutting costs to the minimum, and developing Human Resources". *El Mundo*, 'Business' special, 28 October 1993, p. XIV.

[16] According to management, only in 20% of cases did it prove difficult to identify the different 'productive fragments' which form the base or *mesh* of the EWUs.

[17] For an outline of the earlier evolution of the factory and the situation prior to the current reorganisation of the Motores plant, see

Castillo (1991). We have been able to consult detailed internal company reports on the introduction of the EWUs, as well as to gather the changing opinions, impressions and experiences of those responsible for and affected by these changes. See FASA–Renault – Factoría de Motores: *Dossier Motor E. Fábrica Cible*, Valladolid, 6 November 1991; Brangier B. and Couvreur E., Développement des Unités Élémentaires de Travail en fabrication, RENAULT–DPAS, January 1992; Situación de los grupos de producción-Factoría Motores-1 and 2, February 1992; Las Unidades Elementales de Trabajo y la mejora continua en la Dirección Industrial, Editorial in *Comunicación Mandos*, No. 30, February 1992.

[18]　As already noted, and will be seen again below, this was delayed and disrupted by the fall in demand and the need to 'lose' people through redeployment within the company in the Valladolid-Palencia area. Between September 1994 and February 1995, more than 200 workers left the Motores factory if, in theory, only temporarily.

[19]　The company distinguished between EWUs and ESUs or 'Elemental Service Units' up to December 1993. These were then merged into one, a step definitively confirmed in March 1994. In the words of the new Managing Director of Motores, Carlos Quintana: "Our Elementary Work Units follow the same model wherever they are [...]. Our message is one of simplicity and unity through the creation of a single organisational model which it has been decided will be the basic and only one for the entire Renault Group", Editorial and interview in *UET*, No. 6, March 1994.

[20]　These stages are: (1) identification of the 'mesh' ('*mallaje*' in the company's French-influenced jargon); (2) definition of clients–suppliers; (3) processes of improvement and indicators; (4) progress plan; (5) cost analysis; (6) activation plan.

[21]　Boyer and Freyssenet (1994).

[22]　The complete research includes also: (1) *Crankshaft EWU for the new E7M (1600) engine* – full production should have begun in April 1995, but because of lack of demand, this is still in the experimental phase. (2) *Quality of mechanical parts EWU* – this service unit serves all the units in this half of the Factory, Motores-2; it is supposed to disappear when the EWUs definitively assume this function. (3) *Engine Assembly EWU* – we have analysed an EWU from the existing assembly line, because of the delay in the implementation of the new one. The new assembly line, along with shafts, cylinder blocks and heads, is one of the main technical innovation designs.

[23]　An average net salary of around 1,000–1,200 dollars per month may be taken as representative for comparative purposes.

[24] In Spanish, a *comodin* or *cabecera de línea*, is a worker able to work in any of the machines of the *transfert*. At this time the term *polivalente* was not so much in use.

[25] The issue of mobility was at the centre of negotiations over the 1995 collective agreement. The latest offer from the company, made on 21 April 1995, consisted of the equivalent of 17,600 dollars compensation for those definitively transferred from Valladolid to Palencia. The company also offered a 'transport supplement' of 120 dollars a month for redeployed workers. The unions are asking for 128 dollars (16,000 pesetas) [Internal *Hoja informativa*, FASA, No. 17, April 1995]. This proposal was reproduced in *El País* (Madrid), 4 May 1995, which adds that 1,200 workers have to travel to Palencia at an average cost for the enterprise of 200 dollars (25,000 pesetas). See also *El Norte de Castilla* (Valladolid), 9 March 1995.

[26] See, in particular, Charron (1993) and Castillo (1991).

[27] The research in Mexico is being undertaken in conjunction with Patricia García Gutiérrez and Fernando Herrera Lima, the authors of the notes on which the following comments are largely based. The research in Portugal is being carried out in collaboration with Antonio Brandao Moniz, Ilona Kovacs, Manuel Secca Ruivo and Paula de Oliveira. See these entries in the Bibliography and also Santos (1993).

[28] The company enjoys the unconditional support of the 'single' Mexican union. We are not yet in a position to carry out a full comparative analysis of the attitudes of the Spanish and Portuguese unions. However, it is surely significant that the average age of the Mexican workers in the Rimex factory is 28, compared with an average of 47 in FASA–Valladolid (García Gutiérrez and Herrera, 1995), See *Rimex. Planta Ideal*, Renault, Gómez Palacio (Mexico), 1994.

[29] CC.OO., *Boletín de CC.OO. Renault–España*, No. 8, Valladolid, October 1993; *UGT. Sin fronteras*, No. 1, October 1994.

Bibliography and references

Azofra Palenzuela V. (ed.) (1992) *Influencia y repercusiones de la industria del automóvil y componentes en Valladolid y en la Comunidad de Castilla y León*. Valladolid: Ayuntamiento de Valladolid ed.

Boyer, R. and Freyssenet M. (1994) Émergence de nouveaux modèles industriels. Problématique et prémiers résultats. *Meeting of the International Steering Committee of the GERPISA Network*, 3 December.

Brandao Moniz A., Oliveira P. and Secca Ruivo M. (1995) *Fábrica líder em Aveiro? A propósito de un conceito de organizaçao do trabalho na fábrica de Cacia da Renault*. Monte da Caparica-Aveiro. [Preliminary report for the 'Manufacturing the organisation of work of the future' project].

Burawoy M. (1985) *The Politics of Production*. London: Verso.

Camara Oficial de Comercio e Industria de Valladolid (no date) *La economía de Valladolid en 1992, Informe de Coyuntura (Avance 1993)*, photocopy.

Camuffo A. and Micelli S. (1998) Teamwork and New Forms of Work Organisation in Fiat's 'Integrated Factory'. Chapter 9 in this book.

Castillo J.J. (1991) Diseño del trabajo y cualificación de los trabajadores. En una Fábrica de motores. In Castillo J.J. (ed.), *La automación y el futuro del trabajo*, 2nd edn, pp. 261–336. Madrid: Ministerio de Trabajo.

Castillo J.J. (1994) De qué postfordismo me hablas?. Más sobre reorganización productiva y organización del trabajo. *Sociología del Trabajo*, new series, No. 21, 49–78.

Castillo J.J., Jiménez M.V. and Santos M. (1991) Nuevas formas de organización del trabajo y de implicación directa en España. *Revista Española de Investigaciones Sociológicas*, No. 56, October–December, 115–141.

Charron E. (1993) *Fasa–Renault: un cas d'hybridation. First International Meeting, GERPISA: 'Trajectories of Automobile Firms'*, Paris, 17–19 June.

Coello F. y otros (1993) Formación, innovación y competitividad. Mesa redonda. *Alfoz* (Madrid), No. 100–101, pp. 83–96. [Coello is the Head of Industrial Relations for the Fasa–Renault Company.

CC.OO. (1993) *Boletín informativo de CC.OO. Renault España*, No. 8 (October) and No. 9 (December). Valladolid: Sección Sindical Intercentros CC.OO.

Durand J.-P. (1998) Introduction to this book.

Freyssenet M. (1998) Transformations in the Teamwork at Renault. Chapter 8 in this book.

García Gutiérrez P. and Herrera Lima F. (1995) *Reporte sobre Rimex*. Preliminary Report for the 'Manufacturing the organisation of work of the future' project, Mexico, D.F.

García Gutiérrez P. and Herrera Lima F. (1995) 'Organización del trabajo, capacitación y relaciones laborales en una empresa productora de motores para la exportación', paper presented at the *Conference on the Automobile Industry in Mexico*.

Jacou P. and Lucas F. (1992) *Au coeur du changement. Une autre démarche de management: la qualité totale*. Paris: Dunod–Institut Renault de la Qualité.

Ridruejo Z. (1994) Mercado de trabajo y actividad productiva sectorial. *Papeles de Economía Española. Economía de las Comunidades Autónomas*, No. 14, 148–166.

Santos Jorge M.A. (1993) *Acerca de Circulos de Qualidade*, December. Lisbon: Universidade Nova de Lisboa.

UGT (1994) Los nuevos sistemas de organización. *Sin Fronteras. Portavoz de las Secciones Sindicales de Fasa–Renault*, New Series, No. 1 (October), 10–11.

Womack J., Jones D. and Roos D. (1990) *The Machine that Changed the World*. New York: Rawson.

CHAPTER 13
Volvo–Ghent: A Third Way?

Rik Huys and Geert Van Hootegem

Introduction

Although Belgium is by far the largest automobile assembler per capita in the world, the five car assembly plants [1] located in Belgium enjoy scant attention within international literature on the organisation of work. Volvo's major assembly plant of the 850-model in Ghent is probably the one most often referred to, because of the widespread interest in Volvo's production concepts. In such references, the Ghent plant is described as a traditional Fordist plant. One of its features is that "the assembly line regime was never questioned at Volvo's car factory in Ghent", as Berggren (1992, p. 14) correctly states.

Equally the plant is well known for its outstanding performance in productivity compared with the other Volvo plants. This, in combination with its perceived traditional stance on work organisation, is considered as a contributing factor to the demise of Volvo's 'alternatives to lean production'. While Berggren formerly argued that "although Uddevalla was still far behind in productivity, reaching the goal of Ghent did not seem to be an impossible task given sufficient time" (Berggren, 1992, p. 165), as soon as closure was announced, the productivity gap between this 'traditional' plant and that aimed for by the Swedish assembly plant was singled out as one of the underlying reasons for the decision (Sandberg, 1995, p. 92).

There is however a lack of substantive information to these qualifications on how Volvo's assembly plant in Ghent operates. Even so, there is an obsession in trying to equalise assembly line production to that of the short-cycled and mechanically paced work produced by the Fordist production concept. Advocates of Volvo's radical shift in production lay-out emphasise the need to change the technology that chains workers to the assembly line when re-organising work. In the end, they argue, repetitive and restricted work can only be overcome by parallelisation and complete assembly.

Certainly, the short-cycled, repetitive and mechanically paced work entailed by the assembly line severely constrains options in work organisation. Equally, it is correct to say that Volvo–Ghent strictly adheres to line-assembly throughout its production process, and as such its classification as a 'Volvo' factory seems inappropriate when referring to the plant. However, as we attempt to point out, this sole characteristic of the production process is insufficient to qualify the plant as Fordist, and cannot help us to understand plant management's efforts to alter work organisation and the job content of production workers.

How Volvo–Ghent developed

Starting as a low-volume final assembly plant, Volvo–Ghent acquired an increasingly important role within the company, actually emerging as Volvo's biggest production facility outside Sweden. The decision to erect the plant in Ghent was taken in 1963 in the wake of the creation of the EEC. Since imported cars were taxed by the (then) six members of the EEC at 22%, it was important for Volvo to establish a foothold in this important market that could operate under similar circumstances to its European competitors. Because the number of vehicles grew rapidly and transportation and repair costs, because of the transfer of painted bodies from Sweden, soared, the plant was equipped in 1972 with a body and paint shop. In subsequent years, the fate of the plant was not without its problems. In the mid 1970s, output fell dramatically and the just installed two-shift production process had to be switched back to one-shift production. More recently, in 1990 output dropped steeply again. In an effort to limit stocks of unsold cars in a slack market, production was halted for 24 days and the speed of the line was reduced.

However, the simultaneous phasing out of the 740 and 950 models and the phasing in of the new 850 model in that year would prove to be a turning point. On the one hand, output increased steeply, involving the plant in a continuous struggle to meet the huge demand for the 850 model. As it was assigned, for the first time in its history, the exclusive production of a new model, the plant benefited fully from these increases in demand. Built at a capacity of 90,000 units, the plant finally realised an output of over 150,000 units in 1994, by moving to three-shift production in the body and paint shop and by steady increases of the line-speed in the final assembly. On the other hand, an ambitious plan was implemented to introduce teamwork on the production floor. To meet increased demand, a considerable number of new workers were recruited, which in its turn facilitated the transformation towards a new work organisation.

Workers were grouped into smaller VEC teams (Volvo Europe Car) of around 10 members in the body and paint shop and 15 members in final assembly under the supervision of an appointed team leader. Within the teams a flexible allocation of workers was reached through extensive and systematic rotation. More importantly, however, was the long-term plan to establish an increasing involvement of the teams through subsequent steps in maintenance and quality assurance in their area, at the same time as restructuring the formal organisation in order to achieve closer support from staff departments to the production teams. Usually, such additional responsibilities for teams are assigned to a specific function within the team or for the teamleader, while the job content of the other team members remains unaltered. At Volvo–Ghent, however, additional responsibilities for the team must be interpreted as allocated to all team members. Moreover, the VEC team plan was not restricted to a certain area, but would involve all production workers throughout the plant. Yet, no consideration was given to parallelisation or dock assembly, as the VEC team implementation had to be compatible with the line assembly, even with an intensification of mechanically paced work on one single production line.

Only in 1994 did the pressure to increase production weaken, as production of the 850 model started in Torslanda (Sweden), though Ghent remains its main producer. In addition, the newly built water-based paint shop, with a capacity of 200,000 units, opened in 1994. Similar investments in body shop and final assembly should raise the plant's capacity to 200,000 units by the year 2000, putting it on a par with Volvo's main production facility at Gothenburg.

Features of the production process

Automation is high in all three production units even surpassing levels of automation at the four other car assembly plants in Belgium, despite Volvo–Ghent's comparatively small production output. The production process has quite a number of distinctive features: several additional production steps which are absent at other car assembly plants; a specific build-up of the car in the body shop and final assembly; and some area's of automation unique to Belgian car assembly. Yet, in view of the debate on line production, we pay special attention to another specific feature of the plant: its use of carriers rather than a mechanically driven belt.

Because of these carriers, of which there are different types [2], the production line has a distinctive outlook in comparison with other car assembly plants. In fact, so distinctive that it would be tempting to argue about a break with the traditional belt-driven assembly line. The carriers were pioneered at Volvo's plant at Kalmar in 1973, and are extensively described and praised in Gyllenhammar's (1977) book *People at Work*. In the book, the link is continuously stressed between this technical innovation and the innovations in work organisation. However, in view of the Ghent plant's implementation of carrier transfer two observations should be made:

(1) Introduced in 1984 with the introduction of the 700 series, the use of the carriers is still limited. In the body shop, as well as in the transfer of body to paint shop, the carriers serve merely as a means of transfer of bodies from one production step to another, and no workers operate on these carriers. To put it differently, all workers [3] in the body and paint shop operate on a traditional machine-paced driven belt. Even in final assembly, less than half of the production workers operate on these carriers, as only the first stages of the production process are equipped in this fashion.

Equally, within the numerous sub-assemblies to the main final assembly line, the use of Automated Guided Vehicles (to be considered as small carriers) is restricted to a minor part of the motor dressing sub-assembly. While an eye-catching feature of the plant, in the end only a minority of the production workers experiences working on carriers.

(2) While facilitating alternative work organisation, much, if not all, depends on the way the carriers are utilised. As Berggren vividly describes, in the Kalmar case the use of carriers became increasingly restricted. While at first a parallelised assembly system existed that enabled a team to perform its entire assembly task at a single station in so-called dock assembly, sequential operations were increasingly introduced, as the

incorporation of parallel assembly into the main flow proved to be a difficult marriage. After ten years – the time when carriers were introduced at Volvo–Ghent – the last docks were removed. Equally, buffers between the area's which at first gave workers some possibility to change work speed were gradually reduced. In the end, workers experienced similar machine-pacing as on a conventionally belt driven operation. Instead of abandoning the idea, this experience was rather a starting point for Uddevalla's radical break with sequential production – to use the full potential of the carriers in a extremely parallised dock assembly. However, this is certainly not the way the carriers are implemented at Volvo–Ghent.

At the plant, no parallelisation whatsoever has been introduced. The carriers follow one another sequentially in a single line. Nor is it the aim to take bodies out of the production line, e.g. for inspection or repair, as the well-thought-out sequence in which the bodies enter final assembly must be maintained throughout the unit. Moreover, neither are the carriers used as a flexible buffer between production steps, in order to provide workers with a limited temporal autonomy, such as provided by the buffered mini-line concept of Toyota's new production facilities. The number of carriers in a given area is almost equal to the number of workstations, and therefore there is no possibility of stocking in-process bodies between adjacent production steps. This reality is a far cry from Gyllenhammar's (1977, p. 59) vision whereby 'the system is so flexible that there is nothing to stop a work group from getting on a carrier and going down the road for a picnic'.

Equally, at the described motor-dressing sub-assembly, the AGVs follow each other sequentially on a single line without storage capacity between workstations. The AGV gives a warning when the pre-determined work cycle has passed, and moves further automatically, *not* at the instruction of the worker when the job has been finished. Once again, the implementation of the AGVs is extremely conservative, and differs from the effective use of the AGVs potential, as we found in modules at sub-assemblies in other Belgian final assembly units (see Figure 1). Production work in Volvo–Ghent's implementation of this innovation is to such an extent similar to traditional mechanical transfer lines, that one wonders at the reasons for its introduction, other than the involvement of some Volvo subsidiaries in carrier production.

313

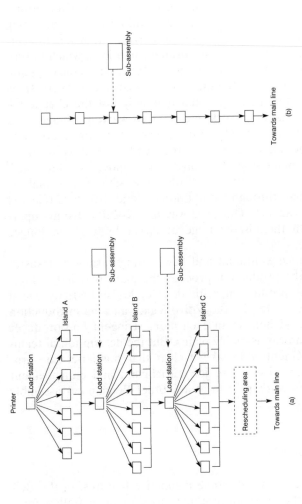

Figure 1 (a) *AGVs in a sub-assembly at GM-Antwerp:* The sub-assemblies enter at random each of the three subsequent boxes, depending on the one that is emptied first. Workers enjoy some temporal autonomy (because of the buffers between the islands), longer work cycles (5–10 minutes, as a result of parallelisation) and standing work. A rescheduling buffer is required at the end of the module to restore the pre-established sequences before transfer to the main assembly line. (b) *AGVs in a sub-assembly at Volvo-Ghent:* The AGVs follow one another on a single line. There is no parallelisation, and therefore no temporal autonomy. The AGVs have no buffers between subsequent boxes, and therefore no temporal autonomy. The carriers merely allow for standing work, as the AGVs have a stop-and-go transfer. A flashing light warns operators that the AGV is about to move.

Obviously, the carriers offer a much improved lay-out flexibility. The induction tracks can easily be redrawn if need arises after rebalancing, or the introduction of additional options. Even after a complete model change, the carriers can still be used by adjusting the fixtures. In line with many other of Volvo's initiatives, the carriers offer enhanced ergonomical working conditions, which in turn allow for improved productivity and quality. However, as the crosswise pallets at the final assembly unit of GM's plant at Antwerp show [4], carriers are not the only – and definitely not the cheapest – way to allow for standing work and reduced walking distances.

Apart from its considerable initial investment, an overlooked restriction in the use of carriers is the need for battery recharge time during the night stop. As Volvo–Ghent moved to three shift production to increase output, this was impossible at the final assembly unit, except through an additional – and therefore rejected – investment in carriers. This gave way to a 2-shifts, 3-shifts operating plant, with the disadvantage of larger buffers and longer throughput times.

Despite the unconventional and bewildering variety of transfer mechanisms in the production process, the plant is strictly adhering to single-line production, with short cycles and strictly paced work for operators. Despite the Volvo legacy and the introduction of carriers, Volvo–Ghent is an even more stringent line producer than other Belgian car assembly plants. But the description of teamwork at Volvo–Ghent will make it clear that this strict line producer nevertheless gives more job enrichment and enhancement for its production workers than at any other Belgian car assembly plant.

Teamwork Volvo-style

We now shift focus towards some distinctive features, in the Belgian context, of the team concept at Volvo–Ghent that allow for a modified job content for production workers, as aimed at in the VEC team plan. Considering a fixed cycle time of around 100 seconds in the body and paint shop and 83 seconds in final assembly (longer than at other Belgian car assembly plants), there seems to be few possibilities for production workers to do anything else but simply repetitively execute a carefully balanced workload of predetermined operations. However, one should not take this assumption for granted. Indeed, a whole range of options is available to assign workers additional responsibilities in conjunction with the belt-driven assembly line, some of which are elaborated at Volvo–Ghent as a means of gradually implementing the VEC team plan.

Rotation

Rotation between work places allows the workers' job content to be enhanced. Rotation at the Volvo–Ghent plant is *systematic*. This means that all production workers are involved in rotation schemes within their team, with only a few exceptions for medical or social reasons. The rotation scheme implies a frequent rotation for production workers, often on a daily basis in the body and paint shop, and every two hours in final assembly. Rotation is also *extensive*, as usually full rotation is established within the teams of the body and paint shop, containing about 10 workstations. In final assembly, workers rotate within two or three separate cells in the team, a cell consisting of on average five workstations. At the other Belgian car assembly plants, we found rotation to be much more limited and incidental. Workers have some polyvalence in order to fill in for unforeseen absentees, or to absorb a redistribution of operations after rebalancing, but the degree of polyvalence never achieves such high levels for all workers. The frequency of rotation is also rather incidental, with workers able to chose if and how they would like to rotate.

But most importantly, the rotation schemes at Volvo–Ghent are extensive, owing to the integration of a large number of different and indirect jobs within the teams. Therefore this rotation implies more than just 'doing more of the same'. For example, the part feeder in the body shop not only shifts to other part-feeding workstations, but equally to spot welding, an off-line repair workstation, a quality inspection deck and (to a limited extent) the job of the machine operator.

On the one hand, this is made possible by the plant's restructured organisation, whereby former staff functions are not just integrated within the production department, but also assigned to lower levels of the production hierarchy. The teams therefore contain not just executive operations, but are more heterogeneous, allowing for job enrichment through simple rotation between team members.

On the other hand, such rotation is made possible by the plant's radical abolition of job classifications. While most Belgian car assembly plants have four or five job classifications, production workers at Volvo–Ghent, apart from a few exceptions for specialised inspection and repair functions at the end of the paint shop and final assembly, all have the same job classification. As job classifications are coupled to wages, this is a sensitive area for the unions. Together with a substantial influx of new workers, thereby creating a partly 'greenfield'-situation facilitating changes in work rules, the management at Volvo–Ghent was able however to foster a willingness to co-operate from the unions on this matter.

Working off-line, freed from the mechanically determined pace

Notwithstanding all that has been said, rotation at the assembly line does not reduce the mechanical pace that must be maintained while performing the different operations. The question therefore remains: how can team members be assigned additional responsibilities in regard to maintenance or quality assurance? The solution elaborated through the VEC team plan is to periodically unlock the operator from the assembly line by means of a stand-in who relieves the operator from work on the line. Every team is provided with an extra VEC team member who, like an ordinary relief operator in any other car assembly plant, daily relieves all workers so as to enable them to take individual breaks. What is specific here is his additional relief by daily rotation to a single worker in order to allow him to support other members of the team (see Figure 2).

As the first step of implementation this relief from the line is short, merely keeping the area tidy. Yet, through several steps the relief time is extended, currently around 2 to 2.5 hours in the fourth of the five stages, entailing an impressive shift of tasks from staff departments to the production floor. What these steps mean in general is illustrated by two pillars which are of primary importance for production workers, namely autonomous maintenance and autonomous quality (Figure 3).

The plan is characterised by its gradual implementation. Team members receive off-the-job training to enable them to jump to a subsequent stage and take on additional responsibilities. However, the time provided to reach a next step is only loosely defined, allowing for individual differences between teams. In fact the team evaluates each step on a weekly basis, which consists of answering a number of questions. When a team feels confident in mastering

Using rotation, production workers perform several production jobs. By means of additional relief from the VEC team member, they thus perform the team task

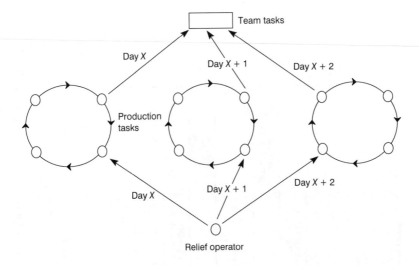

The relief operator provides relief to all production workers at individual breaks. He provides additional relief to allow workers to support other members of the team on the assembly line

Figure 2 *Additional relief allows team members to support other members of the team on the assembly line.*

the additional responsibilities, a screening committee is invited to repeat the evaluation. If approved, the team is awarded a green circle on its VEC team board, and may move on to a subsequent step.

Further implementation of these steps can be delayed, in case of more urgent priorities in a given area. The gradual nature equally avoids collisions between production and staff departments, as these are not suddenly deprived of a substantial number of responsibilities but are able to accustom themselves to their new relationship to the production teams. And finally, the plan has a large growth potential, as the time during which workers are removed from the assembly line can easily be extended.

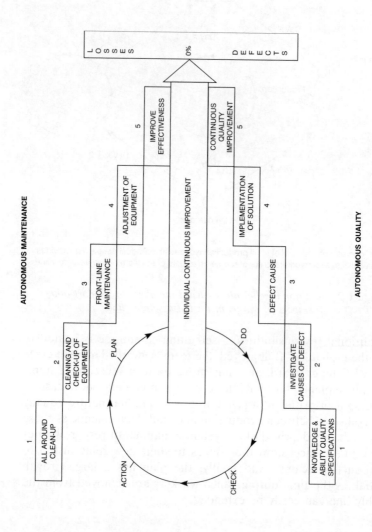

Figure 3 Steps of implementation of autonomous maintenance and autonomous quality [5].

A third way?

Results are ambiguous and difficult to interpret. The technical pre-conditions for an alternative production organisation, such as carriers, are available. Yet, the plant does not take advantage of this potential. Production lay-out is almost exclusively single line, thereby restricting the options for new work organisation. Socio-technical design theory points out that a line structure can be designed alternatively. Parallelisation and segmentation are the main parameters in this innovation (de Sitter, 1994, p. 275). But at Volvo–Ghent, we look in vain for parallelised and segmented production lines. This production structure results in short-cycled work, getting even shorter as line speed is increased. Are comments justified that describe Volvo–Ghent as a traditional Fordist plant?

The answer must bear in mind the implemented team concept, supported by intensive rotation-schemes. This rotation includes an unusually broad range of heterogeneous jobs. Most importantly, rotation is extended to a supporting job mainly containing maintenance and quality assurance tasks. This integration of different jobs within production functions was made possible through an impressive shift from staff departments towards lower levels of the production hierarchy. Finally, the teams' ability to determine the speed of their own trajectory must be stressed.

These characteristics of the VEC team model cannot be labelled as Fordist. But how then can one interpret the – seemingly divergent – developments at the plant? This question is often addressed by positioning a plant against ideal-type models, usually a triad of Fordism, lean production and Volvoism. As the Fordist model is considered old-fashioned, a choice between the two other models is currently at stake. The lean production model is typified by the Toyota Production System. Although Berggren doubts the existence of 'Volvoism', the label is understood as referring to alternative work organisation as implemented at Kalmar and Uddevalla.

But identifying the ideal models against which a given plant can be positioned, the answer remains dependent on the factor one considers as most discriminatory. By associating the models with the production jobs they generate, Fordism is characterised by short cycles and merely executive production work. 'Volvoism', in contrast, is characterised by long work cycles accompanied by enriched jobs. Because the lean production model is equally linked to short-cycle work, one does not share the enthusiasm of its initiators

(Womack *et al.*, 1990). It is rather referred to as 'neo-Fordism', because the Toyota system merely adds elementary tasks to the short work cycles, such as keeping the work area tidy and participation in kaizen activities.

In positioning Volvo–Ghent by means of this characteristic, the plant is indeed Fordist, as production jobs contain mainly short-cycle tasks. But this evaluation falls short, when considering the implemented team concept. As a consequence of the allocation mechanism, workers perform a multitude of short-cycle jobs as well as supporting jobs. The same conclusion is valid with regard to the production structure. Deviations from the assembly line are considered a necessary, if not sufficient, pre-condition in characterising a car assembly plant. While the belt-driven assembly line is an essential part of Fordism, Volvoism radically breaks with mechanically paced work. Once again, the Toyota system is close to Fordism, and Volvo–Ghent is again in line with this Fordist principle. But an unease remains, as the decentralisation of staff departments is not evaluated in these categorisations.

The above characteristics are indeed inadequate to position Volvo–Ghent. This can only be resolved in considering the structure of the division of labour as a whole, and the inclusion of the allocation policy in the analysis. These two features allow for a more precise positioning. The implemented relationship between production and staff departments at Volvo–Ghent clearly breaks with Fordist principles. Support and preparation on the one hand, and execution on the other hand, are brought closely together. By reducing this kind of division of labour, supporting tasks can be performed in the immediate proximity of the line.

While the assembly line inhibits the integration of such tasks in the assembly jobs, the extensive and systematic allocation policy offers a solution. If those jobs cannot be altered, then the way in which jobs are allocated to the workers can be reconsidered. Here, the Fordist adage of 'the right man in the right place' is abandoned. As a result, a disconnection emerges between jobs as characteristics of a structure of the division of labour, and functions as characteristics of a broader allocation policy. While jobs at Volvo–Ghent retain their Fordist features, the functions become heterogeneous and consist not just of assembly jobs.

Both the break-down of the staff departments and their integration within the production department, as well as the systematic and extensive rotation of workers, are a clear shift from Fordist principles. True, the elimination of barriers between departments as well as between production workers in order to allow a flexible allocation of the workforce are features of a lean production approach. But the Volvo–Ghent plant goes beyond this stage. The rotation is not merely aimed at operating the plant with a minimal number of employees. In addition, it is a prerequisite to involve workers in the support of their team. It is obviously impossible to deliver support to other workers within the team if one is not acquainted with their operations. Simple rotation, though it might be considered as 'doing more of the same', is therefore a pre-condition to shift a substantial amount of supporting tasks to production workers.

This attempt by Volvo–Ghent to mobilise all production workers in off-line support to their teams goes beyond lean production practices. At the same time, the approach is far from the innovations of the Kalmar or Uddevalla type. The model chosen by Volvo–Ghent could therefore be considered as 'a third way', a way between the Japanese and the Swedish approach. While clearly not elaborating on the company's legacy of parallel assembly, Volvo–Ghent could be seen as another example of Volvo's heterogeneous production concept. As Berggren emphasises: 'there is no such thing as Volvoism, in the way one can speak of Toyotoism'. However, the plant's achievement, despite its traditional production lay-out, to assign production workers an amount of additional responsibilities that goes further than at any other Belgian car assembly plant, must be attributed to the company's legacy of alternative work organisation.

This conclusion is more straightforward than expressed in *Enriching Production*, a publication that offers perspectives with regard to Volvo–Uddevalla as an alternative to lean production. Berggren's above-mentioned assertion is shared in the book by many contributors. Sandberg states in his introduction: "Volvo plants are characterized by a diversity of both technical and organizational concepts. . . . Social conditions in different countries lead to different solutions" (Sandberg, 1994, p. 7). Thompson and Wallace support this view: "Volvo has no intrinsic interest in particular forms of work design. Rather, the repertoire and choices made reflect the company's strategic response to shifting market conditions" (Thompson and Wallace, 1994, p. 229). Even our own evaluation of teamwork at Volvo–Ghent went in the same direction: "As such, both Volvo–Ghent and Uddevalla may be proof of Volvo's ability to

adapt itself more swiftly and thoroughly to the changing environment" (Huys and Van Hootegem, 1994, p. 248).

This statement must be viewed with reference to the Uddevalla
model, rather than to the view that 'societal effects' are in any
straightforward sense dominant over company policy. A thorough
comparison of the structure of the division of labour and the allocation policy of the five car assembly plants in Belgium shows clearly
that Volvo–Ghent follows the most innovative path. This can be no
coincidence, especially bearing in mind that Belgian 'societal effects' – as research points out – have a conservative influence.

This conservative effect has several origins. Belgian social laws
favour high-volume production. Because of the small internal market, in combination with the absence of Belgian multinationals,
companies can only survive through excellent productivity and quality
results. This inhibits experimentation with innovations, which can
only prove their effectiveness in the long run. The strong but pragmatic unions, which are usually recognised in their role by management, equally contribute to the *status quo*. Volvo–Ghent's choice
of 'a third way' can only be understood once we recognise that
'societal effects' and 'company trajectories' are complementary explanatory factors.

The existence of a Volvo trajectory is supported by the attempts
of the Volvo–Mitsubishi plant at Born (The Netherlands) to copy
the model of Volvo–Ghent. For those who hope for a spread of
'Volvoism' as an Uddevallean model, it is disappointing that merely
a team concept within the constraints of the assembly line seems
to be viable. Indeed, Volvo–Ghent's third way is much closer to the
lean production model than the Uddevalla approach. Yet, this third
way, in contrast to the lean production model, offers hope for an
improved quality of working life.

Moreover, a number of features at the Volvo–Ghent plant should
facilitate a break with the assembly line. Through the reduction in
the number of job classifications, and the decentralisation of staff
departments, two important obstacles to an alternative production
concept are removed. Workers' ability to perform a variety of jobs
is a starting point to change the content of these production jobs.
Since workers have received a considerable amount of training, the
investment in human resources necessary to implement an alternative production concept has already been partly provided. In short,
the chosen model bears the seeds of a break with the assembly
line. Certainly the current management is not taking this option

into consideration. But developments in production design could decide otherwise. A labour shortage as a consequence of demographic evolution may equally contribute. Perhaps Uddevalla was too far ahead of its time, and a middle third road had to be chosen in the meantime as a viable solution.

End-notes

[1]   In addition to Volvo, V.W., Renault, G.M. and Ford have car assembly plants in Belgium. (This chapter was written prior to the controversial closure of Renault–Vilvoorde).

[2]   There are 'normal' carriers, 'liftcarriers' with adjustable heights depending on the operation or the individual worker, and 'high' carriers for overhead work. Kalmar's famous 'tilt'-carriers have been scrapped since, because of the specific body construction, almost no overhead work is needed in final assembly. Where necessary, a small number of 'high' carriers were introduced.

[3]   This excludes, of course, 'off-line' repair workers, a small number of sub-assembly workers who enjoy some temporal autonomy as a result of buffers between them and the main line, and machine operators whose job is unconnected with the pace of production.

[4]   This transfer mechanism was copied from GM's Saturn plant (USA).

[5]   Figure from Saey (1991), page 14.

References

Berggren C. (1992) *Alternatives to Lean Production. Work Organisation in the Swedish Auto Industry.* Ithaca NY: ILR Press.

de Sitter L.U. (1994) *Synergetisch produceren. Human Resources Mobilisation in de produktie: een inleiding in de structuurbouw.* Assen: Van Gorcum.

Gyllenhammar P.G. (1977) *People at Work.* New York: Addison-Wesley.

Huys R. and Van Hootegem G. (1994) Volvo–Ghent: A Japanese transplant in Belgium or beyond? In Sandberg A. (ed.), *Enriching Production. Perspectives on Volvo's Uddevalla Plant as an Alternative to Lean Production*, pp. 231–248. Aldershot: Avebury.

Saey E. (1991) *VEC–TEAM: a Volvo Lean Manufacturing System*. Volvo Cars Europe Industry.

Sandberg A. (1994) The Uddevalla experience in perspective. In Sandberg A. (ed.), *Enriching Production. Perspectives on Volvo's Uddevalla Plant as an Alternative to Lean Production*, pp. 1–33. Aldershot: Avebury.

Sandberg, T. (1995) Volvo Kalmar – twice a pioneer. In Sandberg A. (ed.), *Enriching Production. Perspectives on Volvo's Uddevalla Plant as an Alternative to Lean Production*, pp. 87–101. Aldershot: Avebury.

Thompson P. and Wallace T. (1994) Volvo truck and bus in the UK: the clash of the titans. In Sandberg A. (ed.), *Enriching Production. Perspectives on Volvo's Uddevalla Plant as an Alternative to Lean Production*, pp. 217–230. Aldershot: Avebury.

Womack J.P., Jones D.T. and Roos D. (1990) *The Machine that Changed the World. The Story of Lean Production. How Japan's Secret Weapon in the Global Auto Wars will Revolutionise Western Industry*. New York: Harper Perennial.

SECTION FOUR
EUROPE IN SEARCH OF AN ALTERNATIVE MODEL

CHAPTER 14
The Swedish Model of Lean Production: The Volvo and Saab Cases

Göran Brulin and Tommy Nilsson

Introduction

In 1991, management at Torslanda, in Gothenburg, launched a so-called KLE programme, the Swedish acronym for Quality, Precise Delivery and Economy (reduction of lead-time and assembly hours). One year earlier, Saab had introduced its corresponding QLE programme. Later an 'H' was added, for Human Resource Development. Here we will give an account of the changes of work organisation at Volvo Torslanda and at Saab in Trollhättan, the main assembly plants of the two Swedish car producers.

As to the manufacturing and final assembly of private cars, it is not possible to make sweeping statements about the organisation of work. A possible dividing line in this production area could hypothetically be the different characteristics of the cars and the segments in which the companies compete. If it is a matter of more or less luxury cars that are manufactured when ordered by the customers, as is the case of Volvo's 800 and 900-series and Saab's 900 and 9000 models, work development seems to be occurring, even in traditional line production systems. As regards small car production, e.g. Opel, Fiat and Renault, work development does not seem to be progressing very much. If there is any development, it is very limited.

The concept of work development catches the change from a solidaristic wages policy to a solidaristic work policy on behalf of the trade unions. Work development is a general instrument that the local bodies use to create a work organisation where repetitive jobs are abolished and where the employees are trained for better and more productive work tasks. The process towards work development will be supported by new pay systems that reward great and wide skills within a group work organisation. The Metalworkers' Union programme to modernise the Swedish 'model' and make it compatible with the demands of competitive and flexible production has served as a guide for the union movement (The Swedish Metalworkers Union, 1985). According to this, a compromise at the micro-level may revolve around a constantly learning work organisation built on semi-autonomous (quasi-supervisor-less) groups with authority to request better tools, machines and organisational design. These joint actions should be supported by a participative infrastructure that is flexible and less oriented towards bargaining.

The case of Volvo

Torslanda is where Volvo's 800- and 900-models are manufactured. The 800-model is also assembled in Gent, Belgium. At the manufacturing plants of Torslanda 4,500 blue and 600 white collar workers are employed. In 1994 the total production of the 800- and 900-models was 242,000 cars. At the Torslanda plant, the numbers of the 800-model and the 900-model were 17,000 and 77,000 respectively.

The change that has been taking place at Torslanda since 1991 relates to Volvo's efforts to create an integrated production system. The characteristics of such a system are an orientation towards customer orders and short delivery times, and an integration of the product development and production departments. The aim is to speed up model renewal as well as to rationalise capital and time investment (cf. the concept of lean enterprise in Womack and Jones, 1994; see also Clark and Fujimoto, 1991). Furthermore, as an obvious part of the assumption, the product must be of high quality with predictable delivery. According to management, Volvo's work group concept, the so-called KLE work groups, is an important instrument to achieve the integrative production system.

The labour-market situation in Sweden is worse than ever, seen from the industrial workers' point of view. Unemployment is more than 10% which is the highest figure since the crisis in the 1930s. These conditions make it fairly easy to recruit labour, despite the fact that the jobs are simple and monotonous. This obstructs the development tendency in work processes. Another circumstance that points in the same direction is the growing demand for Volvo cars during the last few years. It has resulted in the employment of personnel who do not get adequate training. In the late 1980s, when there was a shortage of labour, the demand for work development was a crucial argument in order to make industrial work more attractive. (The well-known work organisation of Uddevalla, the Volvo plant that is now reopened, was created as a result of the labour shortage.)

The new work organisation and employment relations

In introducing the KLE organisation, Volvo decided to produce saloon cars on the assembly line principle. The socio-technical experiments in Kalmar and Uddevalla for the serial production of saloon cars have been abandoned. (Berggren, 1996, gives an overview of these socio-technical approaches.) However, the ambition is to create the prerequisites for job development within the framework of an assembly line-based work organisation. Accordingly, in response to pressure from the Swedish Metalworkers' local union, the conditions were created for workers on the line to develop themselves in their job and improve their earnings (see below). According to the management of the assembly shop, if the prerequisites for genuine job development are to be created, the work groups on the line must be provided with increasingly difficult work tasks, and the short balance times must be abandoned. Long balances also create improvements from the ergonomic viewpoint and make a contribution to quality assurance.

Most of the operators we interviewed feel that the KLE organisation has improved production at Torslanda in a number of ways: better-structured work, fewer repetitive strain injuries, better job content etc. At the same time, many people think that greater demands are being made on the workforce and work has become more onerous. Work has become more intensive, not in the sense that the speed of every single work operation has been increased, but that rest time, caused by breaks on the line or other problems (which were solved by maintenance people or technicians), has decreased.

The Metalworkers' local union at Torslanda has accepted the phasing-out of the alternative production systems and the adoption of the line system, and the focus is now on creating the conditions for job development for the union's members within the framework of the line system. At present the greatest threat is, paradoxically enough, growing demand. But the promise of job development on the line can soon lead to frustration among employees who are well aware that assembly work is to be upgraded within the framework of the KLE organisation. In other words, this has led workers to have great expectations in terms of job development.

The KLE group work organisation has been agreed on both by management and the Metalworker's union. In fact, the draft of the document was made by some representatives of the local union body. Work groups have been introduced in assembly, the paint-shop and the body-shop. According to the document, the KLE work groups will be self-regulating, participate in change and development as well as making their own follow-ups on production outcomes. Self-regulation means that the work group, in addition to producing, maintains, solves everyday problems, plans its activities and keeps in touch with subcontractors. The work groups identify the necessary competencies needed to solve problems in everyday production. Furthermore, self-regulation means that the work groups are responsible for material supply, which affects the suborders from the subcontractors as well as the movement of stock internally. The participation in change and development work means that work-group members co-operate with other supportive teams that integrate several functions, for example, at the Pilot plant (Volvo's experimental department). This vision includes the possibility for work-group members to analyse problems, make propositions for solutions and participate in the realisation of those solutions. The KLE strategy also involves the fact that the work groups themselves are responsible for the results of their work. They can focus on ratios, not only such aspects as the number of flaws per body and the degree of scrap, but also on the number of working hours. The idea is to make the KLE work groups skilful both as 'customers' and 'suppliers' in the company's internal customer–supplier relations. The work groups, which are goal-oriented, will also handle the recruitment of new work-group members themselves.

The KLE group work concept means that the work groups become involved in assignments that used to be outside the current manufacturing environment. The objective is to break down the barriers between operators and officials close to production. The result may be the creation of a new profession, a kind of technical KLE-generalist, with certain basic specialities, who performs both manual and intellectual work. Every member of the work group is supposed to develop in a car-assembly station: to gradually become involved in more and more difficult assignments. According to the present view, operators should perform a total of some 10% of intellectual work with the rest given to traditional assembly activities. A future vision suggests the proportions of 20% and 80%. The development of technical generalists at the same time involves a redefinition of what can be called productive work. And that redefinition is already about to appear since the distinction between direct and indirect time (time for maintenance and official work) is being questioned. In the body-shop, they have started to use the ratio 'man-hours per body' where man-hours are defined as all employees' working hours.

A new wage model

There is a new wage model to go with the above work organisation, one that radically differs from the old contract system. In principle it looks like this: the basic idea is for a ladder of development which is set by the different assignments that an operator can actually execute; the more assignments a worker performs and the more difficult they are, the better the pay. On top of that, there is a group bonus which depends on the work quality performed by the group as a whole. That part can amount to a maximum of 10% in average basic wages. The third part of the ladder consists of an individual part and can also amount to a maximum of 10% of the average basic wages. This part is determined by the production leader and depends on the operator's level of activity at work, willingness to co-operate, to take initiative on changes etc. (At the very top of the system, there is a bonus which depends on Volvo's financial results. Everybody gets the same share.) This wage model is supposed to work as a signal to make the operators take on more assignments, i.e. widen their area of competence, and make them take initiatives that will lead to improvements in production and the preservation of high quality.

Group work organisation – KLE work groups in practice

The spreading of KLE work groups has been going on since 1991. The development varies. In some places they have come a long way, in others they are just at the beginning. The most advanced work groups (some work groups in the body, painting and final assembly) are responsible for quality, the production engineering (they do their own line balancing), the recruitment of new personnel (which is otherwise done by the production leaders) and training. Furthermore, they keep in touch with some subcontractors and take part in development work concerning the process and the working environment (ergonomics). The contact with the subcontractors means that if the work group discovers any defect in the components, some member of the team immediately gets in contact with the subcontractor. The team member then orders new material. A dialogue could also start between the two parties about the nature of the problem. In several KLE work groups there is someone in charge of the purchase of materials and safety equipment. This person also keeps a record of possible 'waste' of resources. In some work groups in final assembly there are no work group leaders. Instead they have introduced so-called resource persons. They are versatile and can work as instructors and troubleshooters in the work group.

Some of the most advanced work groups also have their own follow-up systems. Guided by overall goals that concern quality and output per unit of time, they do their own planning towards ratios such as number of flaws per body, degree of scrap, their own analysis of staff time, and material consumption.

In an increasing number of work groups, the members are starting to develop a quality consciousness, both towards the product and the process. The work-group members have become more interested in quality indexes such as that used by the American J.D. Powers. They are also starting to see production from a customer–supplier perspective. If there is a problem, for example that the quality from the preceding stage is not as good as it ought to be, the person in charge of quality will approach the work-group leader or the person in charge of quality in the preceding stage to make sure the problem is solved. Almost every work group has taken on responsibility for quality control and adjustment, which has resulted in a dramatic reduction of 80% in the inspectors and final adjusters.

Among the work changes we also find that the model sequences are now longer, as are the cycle times, particularly in final assembly. In former days, an assembly area was usually made up of several model sequences and each sequence never extended beyond two minutes. Today, long model sequences have been introduced.

In addition to the introduction of KLE teams, there have been substantial changes in technical equipment and production technology. Firstly, a high degree of automation has been achieved with the 800- and 900-models, not least in the body shop and the paint shop. In the final assembly shop, the assembly line has been modified, with more carriers and a substantial reduction in work 'from beneath'. Assembly work now involves less walking alongside the line. Instead, one rides with the car on the line. The amount of off-line assembly has largely remained constant. There has been a sharp increase in automation, particularly in the body shop, and this has resulted in an increase in the volume of process work, i.e. when operators are manning equipment. But this has meant that many of the residual jobs have become simpler and more monotonous. In the former less automated process, more skills were required in, for example, sheet metal working. Demand for this kind of skill is diminishing. It is expected that a continued process of automation will eliminate these residual tasks in the work groups.

New roles of production leaders and work-group leaders

The new group work organisation involves the exclusion of traditional supervisors. They are replaced by so-called production leaders. This is a new type of supervisor with a broader area of responsibility for the manufacture and handling of financial follow-ups (the presentation of resources) and the development of personnel competence. The former supervisors mainly gave orders, made detail decisions and solved everyday problems. In order to co-ordinate the group work, the function of work-group leader has been introduced. But he or she is supposed also to do ordinary work tasks in the work groups. Furthermore, it is intended that this assignment should rotate between at least two members of the work groups. At Volvo, the work-group leaders are assigned by the work groups after some discussion between the whole group and the production leader.

Worker participation

Thus far, KLE work (that is to say, non-manual work tasks) accounts for only a small part of the total working time. In some teams – the most developed ones – these tasks account for about 10% of the working time, while in many other teams this figure is not more than 5%, and the percentage is even lower for some individual operators. There are a number of reasons why development in the KLE teams is slow. Some reasons are to do with inertia in the social system; another reason is the scheduling of the work. An expression of social inertia is that maintenance staff are reluctant to become integrated into the work groups. Integrating maintenance work into the group organisation, and thus into the work flow, would probably be the most efficient solution. The KLE group representatives we have interviewed think this would give the groups greater flexibility. Another problem is that some production leaders and product workshop managers find it difficult to delegate responsibility and authority to the groups. They still seem to harbour a traditional Taylorist view of assembly work. For that reason, in some groups the group leaders rarely perform any other work than KLE work, and they act like traditional work supervisors. Some of the goals are related to developing the workforce, maintaining a high quality of production, maintaining lead-times and constantly improving the work process. At the same time, the goal is to reduce the man-hours in production, i.e. increase productivity. This means that some production leaders and group representatives give priority to a low level of manning. They consider that they have no time to 'experiment' on the work organisation along the line or to upgrade the qualification levels of the group members. There is a risk that the man-hours objective will become dominant, reducing the operators' motivation and having an adverse effect on quality, lead-times and the reliability of deliveries. There are also production leaders and other managers who have no faith whatsoever in the new ideas; they think the old order is better and that it is sufficient to have just a few employees improve their skills levels.

There appears to be a lesser problem in that some group members are reluctant to develop themselves in their work, although only a small minority of workers has this attitude. A large problem is the fact that many people, particularly in the final assembly shop, lack the training needed to take on KLE tasks. Another problem is that no new form of 'metalworker identity' has as yet emerged. If the people who work in the KLE group actually managed to be self-reliant, united in their demands for development and took on new work tasks – for which there is scope – they would make a traditional work management hierarchy superfluous. A related problem is that the status of work on assembly line manufacture has yet to be upgraded to a satisfactory level, even though this work has for some years been prioritised in terms of wages.

The Saab case

The Saab company in Sweden is the smallest producer of standard cars in the world. For a long time its engineers have been innovative in product design, pioneering dual brake circuits in the 1960s, and turbo-charged engines and direct ignition in the early and late 1980s respectively. During the time of acute labour shortage in the mid 1970s, Saab's main plant in Trollhättan launched an advanced form of semi-autonomous group work in its body shop, the so-called 'line-out system'. Ten years later this tradition was taken further by the construction of the new Malmö assembly plant in southern Sweden. In Malmö, the traditional assembly line was replaced by a system of several buffered parallel lines. This was a combination of 20-minute work cycles in parallel sections and 2-minute cycles in a line section (which constituted only 20% of the final assembly). Car bodies and major components were transported by a complex system of automatic guided vehicles. The approach was presented as a 'high-tech alternative' to Volvo Uddevalla, since Malmö's production lay-out facilitated the gradual introduction of automated sections, for example, automated glazing and engine docking ('marriage' of engine/sub-frame and body). The plant suffered from major technical problems during production ramp-up, but was very successful in achieving its quality goals. In early 1990, Malmö built the best Saab cars ever produced.

Saab has never been a profitable business and in the late 1970s the company was in deep crisis. A merger with Volvo was suggested and negotiated by its owners, but thwarted by the resistance of its engineers and managers. In 1988, Saab barely broke even; in 1989, the opening year of the Malmö plant, the company booked major losses. The owning family, Wallenberg, a major financial dynasty in Sweden, unsuccessfully negotiated with Mazda and FIAT but finally concluded an agreement with General Motors in late 1989. A new, 50/50-owned company, Saab Automobile, was formed. General Motors took management control, and appointed the new CEO. The reason for this involvement was the race between GM and Ford to acquire a European luxury producer. Ford took over Jaguar, and now GM was determined to make Saab a success. The new company faced imminent and serious problems. In 1988, Saab had produced 121,000 cars. Five years later, this figure was down to only 74,000. The new management decided to close the new plant in Malmö, to cease production of Saab cars in the Finnish subsidiary Saab–Valmet (Opel Calibra are now assembled here) and consolidate production to its main plant, where a new shift was added. Currently two lines are operating, the 9000-line and the new 900-line. In 1990–91, a tough rationalisation programme was launched in Trollhättan. From 1988 to 1993, employment in Trollhättan was cut from 9,800 to 5,300. Manning levels were reduced, work was intensified and services such as cleaning and catering were contracted out. In-house production of components such as seats and wire harnesses ceased. Saab now purchases seats from the American company Lear Seating, which has started operating in Sweden.

The new production management had a strict focus – to achieve high quality in the process, without subsequent adjustments and repairs, and to reduce assembly hours per car. At the end of the 1980s, Saab had on average one thousand cars waiting for final adjustment at the end of the assembly line. In 1992 this figure was almost eliminated. Man-hours per vehicle had been cut from more than 100 to less than 60. In 1993, when the new 900-model was introduced, the figure was further reduced to 45 hours per car and today, four years later, it is being reduced still further. The figures for labour turnover and absenteeism which were serious, about 30%, at the end of the 1980s, have now, as elsewhere in Sweden, gone down to about 5–7%.

History of change in work organisation and employee relations

The closure of the Malmö plant brought to an end Saab's trials of socio-technical production structuring along the lines of the Uddevalla model. Since that time, the assembly line principles have been applied, without necessarily meaning an acceptance of neo-Taylorist work organisation à la Toyota. Saab is hesitant on this matter, but GME has applied considerable pressure to introduce the type of work organisation used in Eisenach and NUMMI. At the same time there are several counter-forces at work. The trade unions are one such force, the employees another. Furthermore, some of the management (primarily those responsible for work organisation) is aware of the risks of forcibly impeding a Toyota-type system in the Swedish labour market. Neither are some managers convinced that this is the most effective model for a small automobile manufacturer producing a small number of sophisticated products in relatively short series.

Unlike the Metalworkers' local union at Volvo Torslanda, the majority of Saab Metalworkers' local union top representatives has not accepted that the alternative socio-technical model for organising automobile production has been abandoned. Several of the union representatives at the plant are more or less in favour of the 'alternative' approach. But there is now no alternative to the assembly line. Instead, in the face of severe resistance from the Metalworkers' local union, Saab management is attempting to eliminate the existing islands of off-line production. Production management wants all production to be carried out on the line. (This is one reason why union representatives set themselves up against the new concept.) The operators are to rotate a number of stations (five to seven) on short model-in-line sequences. The pace is between 2.5 and 3.5 minutes, depending upon capacity utilisation. As demand falls off, the pace is reduced. Every individual in the group works normally between two to four hours at one station, and then he or she moves to another. In some areas where the work is heavy, the workers only work 30 minutes at one station.

Work-group organisation

Following an agreement between the management and the union at the beginning of the 1990s, the QLEH organisation was introduced into assembly work, the sub-frame shop, and the paint and press shops (in the long term, it will also be introduced for white collar workers). The idea is that as well as assembly, the groups will be responsible for all work such as balancing, material supply in the shop, day-to-day work planning (who in the group should do what), quality, follow-up and daily improvement work. The groups were also to perform some administrative jobs such as reporting on the hours worked. There are at least two group representatives for each group. Not only do they work on co-ordination and some administrative work, they are also always involved in the assembly work. But this occurs to different degrees in different sections, depending on the individual production leader's view of the group representative's role and the skills level of the members of the group. In highly skilled groups, the group representative carries out a great deal of assembly work and the other work tasks are shared among the rest of the group.

Some members of company management want the QLEH organisation to be made similar to the work group organisation in Eisenach or NUMMI, but the group's development is more like the 'work group' organisation than a 'team organisation' (cf. the Toyota system). It was not until the last six months that the direction of development has become evident, owing to the very extensive programme of cutbacks that the company introduced in 1993 and 1994. The management was unwilling to have a discussion about work organisation experiments and was firm in its opinion that the groups should concentrate on pure assembly work. As the QLEH organisation has been accepted, management's attitude to work development within the framework of a concentration on line production has become less rigid.

There are three to four groups in a production leader's area of about 40 employees. (At Saab, the production leaders are still called supervisors.) A work group has 8–10 members. The group representative is appointed in consultation with the members and the production leader. But the production leader normally puts forward the suggestion and has a right of veto. The work representative has no authority over the group but has to work to make the group function well and able to perform their tasks. Thus, the group representative is not a new sort of work supervisor, but a member of the group. When the management of the gearbox plant in Gothenburg attempted independently to appoint group representatives in the work groups, which provoked protests from group members, the Saab management in Trollhättan intervened to ensure that these appointments would in future be made in co-operation with the employees. However, it was said that the group representatives in some production leader areas in Trollhättan were appointed by the production leader, so in these cases the consultation process did not work in practice.

Saab management argues in favour of having short rather than long model sequences on the assembly line, and a rotation system between all the manual work operations. But at the same time it attempts in various ways to break with the Taylorist heritage, i.e.

the classic division into planning work and performing work, detailed control and simple work tasks. The production leader gives the definition of the tasks and is supposed to delegate responsibility to the group representatives, in a broad sense. The group representatives work to ensure the planned and efficient co-ordination of the group's work on the assembly line and to ensure that the QLEH work is carried out. Q stands for quality. Here, the group itself follows up quality developments on a weekly basis with the help of a so-called 'Right First Time' formula. In the final assembly plant there used to be six control stations where a special controller inspected the work as an integral part of the line. These have now been removed. L stands for lead-time reduction, which means that the groups deal with flow interruptions. They also analyse the causes of interruptions. E stands for economic efficiency and means that the group itself balances the work to eliminate any unnecessary activities. The group representative has taken over this latter task from the production technology department. H – for human resource development – means that group members' skills are to be improved with a view to the group becoming more self-regulating.

The task of the group representative is to encourage group members to perform other work tasks than pure assembly work. The group has an extra resource person, normally one person in ten, who can be allocated to different work tasks or be brought in when an individual is off sick or away from work for some other reason. Each group also has a rotating reserve who is summoned when problems arise. With this employee resourcing, the group has to perform the following functions:

- carry out detailed balancing of model sequence and related issues according to the basic balancing done by production technicians;
- plan job rotation itself, who is to do what, on a day-to-day basis;
- administer time usage and absenteeism with the assistance of time cards and decide on group members' time off (up to 8 hours);
- carry out improvement work on detailed lay-out, tools and equipment;
- be responsible for keeping the group's work area clean and for good housekeeping when it comes to instruments and equipment, standardising tool positioning, for example;
- simplify problem solutions;
- simplify maintenance;
- order materials for the stations.

In the event of faults in incoming material, a properly functioning work group will itself make contact with the department for incoming material at an earlier stage in the flow. Either the reserve person or someone else from the group will make this contact.

The QLEH work was accompanied by more extensive training than has hitherto been carried out and most people are given a four-week basic course, focusing largely on how to build a car but also featuring aspects of production techniques, quality assurance and safety at work. There is also an extension course which covers, for example, production technology, quality techniques, economics and programming. The more advanced training courses are intended mainly for people who are to be appointed as group representatives and other people put forward by the production leaders.

The most experienced people from different groups take part in development work, where they work together with the production technicians and designers. They are taken off line work and can begin to work in the experimental workshops, where they work on test models and modifications. These experimental workshops also act as a training station for new employees and others. Almost everyone in the workforce has spent between two and three weeks in this workshop.

New roles for production leaders and work-group leaders

Work-group leaders are responsible for balancing the workstations within their area, but this work task is done in co-operation with other group members. Previously, this task was carried out by industrial engineers. Within each supervisory section, there are walls with charts displaying the workstations. The height of the columns indicates the time needed for each station. The columns consist of small paper cards, representing various sub-tasks and using different colours to indicate assembly activities on standard cars (green), assembly of options (yellow), operator movements (red – signalling that this time should be reduced) and extra time needed for components with technical problems (blue). To produce these charts, work-group leaders use operation sheets supplied by industrial engineers. They are supposed to find ways to reduce 'non-value-added time'. Since 1994, work-group leaders have been deployed in so-called 'focused continuous improvement' activities. The goal is to compress the time of each station, second by second. Many of the proposed improvements, which have been given great importance and higher priority, are to do with improvements in line balancing.

The Metalworkers' local union is critical about members taking part in the work of automating and rationalising the production process. It sees no point in having workers automating themselves out of jobs. That is the task of management. But other operators we met think that this job should be done by the workers themselves, partly because it would make the company more efficient. Improved efficiency will ensure the company's long-term survival. They also think that by balancing workstations themselves, they obtain some power over management. When they are familiar with the process and are responsible for introducing efficiency improvements themselves, they are in a much better position to argue with the production technicians when presented with automation proposals. Several groups have now made enough progress for the group to adjust the balance (according to the wall chart – see above) so that the production technologist, when faced with the facts, accepts these adjustments.

The introduction of the QLEH organisation meant that the old work supervisors, who were responsible for a single assembly section of between 10 and 12 men, disappeared. Their task was to control work in detail, solve problems in the flow, and fetch material and the requisite help in the event of interruptions and breakdowns. Their task was also to staff their manufacturing section. This was a delicate operation because there was often a lot of absenteeism. Over-employment sometimes meant that too many workers were available. The new role of production leader has a completely different content. Firstly, he has overall responsibility for planning and production flow (volume and quality), but in practice this is dealt with by the group itself (in most cases). When major problems occur it is usually the production leader who contacts the Logistics and Development Department. He is also responsible for the budget for his area. But perhaps the most important task on paper is developing the group members in the job, both so that they become efficient operators and also so that they take on more and more QLEH work tasks. Of course, the standard of production leaders varies. Some are good at delegating work to the group and allowing the group to run itself. A small group of leaders has definitely not progressed from a very traditional way of thinking, and would prefer to manage the groups in an orthodox fashion. These people find it less important to allocate QLEH tasks throughout the entire group and would prefer to see group representatives as a new kind of work supervisor.

Worker participation and the role of the unions

According to the Metalworkers' Union, the QLEH organisation did not turn out as planned. The union's view is that QLEH was a retrospective move, that it was about taking work organisation (with its line systems) back to the 1960s. Work becomes more strictly controlled because the group has fewer buffers and the assembly routines are more standardised. The work also becomes more stressful when the buffers are removed. The pace of work on the line has actually not speeded up, but there is less porosity in the working day because the flow is better (fewer stops).

The Metalworkers' local union feel it has been ignored in the matter of group representatives. There is less scope for the group members' QLEH work than the trade union thought. The union is also sceptical about the work of improvement and change which the groups are to undertake. In its view, it is nothing more than 'self-rationalisation'. It does not want its members to have to take responsibility, for example, for station balancing which results in a lower degree of staffing and a higher pace of work. Line balancing and similar so-called work improvement activities should be entirely the responsibility of the production technology department. Most of the union representatives are in favour of some sort of system along the lines of the Uddevalla model and, as we have mentioned, they would like to expand off-line assembly. They do not really believe it is possible to bring about a substantial work development on the basis of a line system.

In other words, the trade union is bitterly disappointed. The 1992 development agreement was recently terminated and in the union's view this agreement contained many good ideas, which management have been unwilling to live up to. In the union's view, a growing number of members feel stressed and disappointed, especially the people forced to work on the line when their fixed workstations were removed. There is also the fear that the ergonomic aspects will worsen and repetitive strain injuries will increase. Having argued this, however, the union recognises that ergonomic changes have led to improvements in some aspects of the production process. Thus, for example, the work 'from beneath' style of assembly has been substantially reduced by tilting the cars on the line. Similarly at Volvo, the line system allows the operators to travel on the line as they carry out their specific work tasks.

The payment system

The payment system is stepped: the idea is that the more work tasks you have, the higher your pay. Formerly there were six levels. In the union's view this is a rather ineffective system in terms of the signals it gives, because most group members, i.e. all the people who do not become group representatives, do not benefit very much. The group representatives are on level 6, while the majority of employees are on level 3 and it takes about two years to qualify for level six. There are also supplementary payments for the amount of time employees have worked in the company and a system related to the basic degree of difficulty of the work which gives different points for different work, a system which favours the craft workers in the body shop, some operators in the paint shop and the maintenance staff.

Conclusion

The interesting result of our empirical investigations at Volvo and Saab is that it is possible to create job development for operators on the line, at least in the upper market segment occupied by Volvo and Saab. At this level it appears to be more productive (productivity includes the quality aspect) to break away from the strict Taylorist heritage than to continue to divide work into planning and performing work. In other words, it appears that it is not only alternative socio-technical production systems (Volvo in Kalmar and Uddevalla, and Saab in Malmö) that can create developing, fulfilling jobs. Concurrently with this type of work development you can also find that work intensity has increased. The pace of the single work task is not necessarily speeded up, but the porosity of the working day has decreased.

When it comes to generating development on the line, Volvo has obviously been more innovative than Saab. Two examples of this are the efforts to create long balances and the efforts to channel work tasks to the groups on the line. But Saab is perhaps the

344 Teamwork in the Automobile Industry

more interesting case because, as a result of the very severe crisis and pressure from the new owner, GME, it decided to introduce an almost textbook group organisation. But when faced with reality, it seems that it may be inefficient to attempt to fully imitate Eisenach or NUMMI in such a small production unit. A pragmatic attitude among management makes the differences between Volvo and Saab appear to be not so large: even the work groups in Saab are given additional work tasks. However, they have retained short balances, even though there are also those in Saab who argue for long balances for quality assurance reasons. Although the production leaders have a formal right of veto when it comes to appointing group representatives, these representatives are now appointed in consultation with the group members.

Both Volvo and Saab experienced considerable problems at the end of the 1980s in terms of high workforce turnover and a high incidence of sick-leave. They found that substantial over-staffing was unavoidable, yet still had difficulties in achieving their quality goals, not to mention their productivity goals. Demands were made from several quarters for trials using alternative socio-technological production systems to deal with these problems. Unlike the union at Saab, the Metalworkers' local union at Volvo accepted that these trials had stopped, and are attempting to create conditions for job development for their members within the framework of the line system. However, it is worth remembering that none of the alternative production plants was closed because their quality or productivity was worse. Instead, it was the rapidly decreasing capacity utilisation caused by the crisis in the motor industry that forced these plants to close (Berggren *et al.*, 1991). At least at Torslanda, according to Volvo, they used the experience they had gained from the 'alternative' production system. Furthermore, in the early 1990s they opted to re-open one of them – the Uddevalla plant – together with a British partner, albeit for special production purposes.

References

Berggren C. (1996) 'A second come back and a final farewell? The Volvo trajectory 1970–1994'.

Berggren C. *et al.* (1991) *Alternatives to Lean Production. Work Organisation in the Swedish Auto Industry*. New York: ILR Press.

Clark, B. and Fujimoto T. (1991) *Product Development Performance. Strategy, Organisation and Management in the World Auto Industry*. Boston MA: Harvard Business School Press.

The Swedish Metalworkers Union (1985) *Rewarding Work. The Swedish Work Environment Fund*. Stockholm.

Womack J.P., and Jones D.T. (1994) 'From lean production to the lean enterprise. *Harvard Business Review*, March–April.

CHAPTER 15
Teamwork at Opel Antwerp
Michel Albertijn, Johan Van Buylen and Leen Baisier [1]

Introduction

Occasionally, a radio at Opel Antwerp [2] might play 'Something better change', a song released by The Stranglers in the 1980s. Managers at the plant might turn down the volume, as the punk band scream their message to the audience. Yet, those managers should be sympathetic to the theme of the song. As Opel Antwerp demonstrated, it was an enthusiastic pupil of the lean production prophets, advocating change and a new way of organising car assembly.

Opel Antwerp was one of Europe's pioneers in teamwork, starting with the implementation of teamwork in its paint shop back in 1986. By 1989, most employees at the plant were working in teams.

The plant seemed happy with its 'new approach'. It opted for an elaborate form of teamwork. Team members were obliged to learn at least 80 % of the jobs in their team. An extensive rotation system assured team members of a slightly broader job content. The teams met once a month and team members could appoint their team leader. An extensive union involvement safeguarded employee concerns.

From 1995 to 1996, the Opel plant in Antwerp was buzzing once again with the watchword 'change'. In June 1995, a proud chairman, Leo Valvekens, announced that a sweeping $370 million investment programme was to be implemented to prepare the plant for the next decade.

Since the second half of 1995, the plant has been undergoing considerable changes and the introduction of a press shop was finalised. Press production began in the summer of 1997 and employment was given to around 140 people. At the same time the production process has been transformed. Part of the plant's new design includes a remarkable division of its single assembly line in the Trim and Car Final into two separate lines. As the body leaves the paint shop, it is transferred to one of the two assembly lines. One line produces only the Opel Astra. The second line focuses on the assembly of Opel's Vectra. About 10 Opel Astra an hour pass on the Vectra line to keep the operators' knowledge up to date. The number of operators on this line is also much higher. The two-line system increases the volume flexibility of the plant, an asset since the markets for both models continue to fluctuate. On both assembly lines the different car model options (colours, seats, dash boards, accessories, etc.) are assembled one after the other. As the Astra and Vectra are built on different platforms, spreading the production of the models over two assembly lines reduces the option mix and increases the balancing of the workstations, the productivity of all operations, and the flexibility for producing non-standardised models on each line. The former single assembly line delivered 80 cars every hour. On the two new assembly lines 45 cars each hour are produced, or 90 in total. The cycle time has been increased from 47 seconds on the former single line to 80 seconds on each of the actual assembly lines [3]. On top of these innovations a model change was implemented with the assembly of the brand new Opel Vectra. In the meantime, investments for a new Opel Astra model were also initiated.

In addition, Opel Antwerp nurtured other ambitious plans, namely, to accompany the technical overhaul with radical organisational changes. It is firmly committed to 'andon', the organisational concept successfully pioneered by General Motors at NUMMI, the General Motors–Toyota partnership in the USA. Management proudly predicts that its combination of measures will allow Opel Antwerp to become the first Western European brownfield site to reach the productivity levels of greenfield assembly plants. Only time will tell whether Opel Antwerp can live up to its ambitions. But implementing the andon strategy also involved rethinking the organisation of teamwork, and this makes the plant worthy of closer assessment.

This chapter will first look into the andon system, being the driving force of the organisational revamping of Opel Antwerp. We then turn towards teamwork in the plant and outline the changes andon required in the teamwork approach. Special attention goes to the 'team representative', as his/her supporting job is crucial to the proper functioning of the andon system and the teamwork. Apart from this, personnel policy needed to be adapted. Finally, the co-operative approach of the trade unions is highlighted.

Opel Antwerp

Opel Antwerp has a long tradition in assembling the smaller cars from the Opel range. It was home to the Opel Kadett for over 20 years and then went on to assemble its successor, the Astra, as well as producing the Vectra. In 1994, Opel Antwerp assembled a total of 319,000 cars, consisting of 266,000 Vectras and 53,000 Astras. Halfway through 1995, the plant switched to the assembly of the brand new Vectra. Antwerp is building both the four-door and the five-door model. Bearing in mind that the Opel plant at Rüsselsheim assembles only the five-door version and Vauxhall Luton limits itself to the four-door model, the model mix at the Antwerp plant adds flexibility to the production of the European GM division.

In mid 1995 Opel Antwerp employed 7,200 people. As in most other car assembly plants, that number is substantially lower than the employment figures of, say, a decade ago. Since 1991, a restructuring has significantly reduced employment to 2,300 persons. Nevertheless, the plant survived the recent turmoil reasonably well and successfully avoided making any compulsory redundancies.

Why andon?

Plant management's objective is to fully implement the andon system. It considers this a logical next step, in line with the 'new approach' which changed the Antwerp factory considerably. The plant is well prepared, thanks to Doug Friesen, a former assistant general manager of the Toyota plant in Georgetown and new production manager at Opel Antwerp since 1993, but also through the experiences with andon at the greenfield plant in Eisenach, Germany. The andon system was put into use on the Astra assembly line on 1 January 1997 and was subsequently implemented on the Vectra/Astra line.

The andon system relies on the simple notion of stopping production immediately a problem arises. While this may sound like an obvious thing to do, it is far removed from the notion of mass production on car assembly lines.

When a worker notices an error or a difficulty, he 'pulls' an andon cord connecting the workstations on the line. His team representative immediately joins the worker to help solve the problem. Together, they might find a solution, opt to remove the car from the production line or stop production altogether. The root of the problem can lie almost anywhere: lack of components, a difficult or misfit operation, a necessary repair, and so forth.

Andon in practice

The car bodies, put on subsequent pallets reaching not higher than the actual floor, move along the line at a certain speed. The operator can easily step on the pallet to perform the necessary operations at his workstation for the specific car without having to walk along with the car. Components boxes and material handling equipment are put on fixed spots at each workstation.

Colour marks on the floor define each workstation reach. This system was pioneered at Opel Eisenach. Two white lines, about three metres from each other, represent the beginning and the ending of the tach time for each station. A green line, half a metre from the first white line, indicates when the operator can start performing the first operations on the car. A yellow line at 70% of the tach time indicates the moment at which the operator is supposed to finally pull the andon cord should a problem occur. When this happens a tune is heard. The number of the team involved is indicated on a sign board next to the line. A lamp lights at the relevant workstation and immediately shows the hot spot. When the car body pallet in the meantime reaches the next white line (the end of the relevant workstation and the beginning of the next workstation) and if the problem is not yet resolved, the whole line section containing between 22 and 33 car bodies (work operations for four teams of 7 to 8 operators) stops.

The team representative is supposed to help in maintaining the tach time. Starting from the yellow 70% line, he has 30% of the tach time for an intervention before the car body pallet stops at the fixed stop position. The team representative has to decide whether he will be able to finish the operation in the tach time or whether it will not interfere with the next workstation if he continues executing the operation. He must be mindful of the next tach time and his judgement must be on whether or not a faulty car should be removed from the line. Production management tries to spread the car operations in such a way

> over the workstations that they interfere as little as possible with one another.
>
> When the representative takes over, the operator can move to the first operation of his work cycle again. The tach time is also his broad job cycle time. If the line section stops, he has to assist in solving the problem. By pulling the andon cord once again the line is started.

Andon pulls are not rare incidents. If andon pulls occurred only occasionally, this would indicate that the production time was too generous and that no part of production was stretched to its limits. Andon pulls should therefore happen almost continuously, for they serve as an indication that the production system is being used optimally.

By continuously being balanced on a knife-edge, the andon system provides a deep insight into bottlenecks in production, enabling a company to address the relevant difficulties and end up with a smooth and ever-improving flow of production. Thus, the andon system induces companies to indulge in the ongoing improvement of their production. Moreover, it serves as a quality control. No car body should pass to the next workstation before the work on the former station has been finished properly. Yet, quality audit stations have been added on each line section again, even though quality inspection was initially abolished. It was felt that regular control was needed because the overall control by the operators was not entirely satisfactory. As a result of all quality measures, the repair section at Opel Antwerp was considerably reduced and offers nowadays only space for 10 cars to be repaired simultaneously.

Although it is continuously balanced on the verge of interrupting production, the andon system should not actually hinder production. Nobody really expects an andon system to keep on stopping the assembly line. The productivity consequences would be disastrous. Over one day the andon cord is pulled about 1000 times, but the actual andon stops represent on average 5% of the production schedule. When the andon cord is pulled, a quick response should be guaranteed. Therefore, the new assembly lines are divided into shorter line sections, with small buffers of around five cars in between. The process lay-out adds some flexibility. So should an andon pull actually halt production, these buffers allow a time-span of four minutes. During that period the buffers fill up (or empty), without any major hindrance to production. After that time, work will effectively stop in the surrounding sections.

Standardisation

Relying on an andon system places severe constraints on an organisation. A great deal can go wrong and the potential stakes are high. The answer lies in creating a predictable environment, where everyone knows exactly what to do, when events should occur, where to find help, how to react, etc. Obviously, this is the only way in which a complex organisation can present an adequate reaction within 80 seconds. That is why the urge to standardise has become a driving force at Opel Antwerp.

Standardised jobs are necessary in order to work in a time-span of 80 seconds with the andon system, the colour marks and the fixed stop position. Operation times are accurately calculated so as to balance operations over workstations in the best way and to use the cycle time at each workstation to its full stretch. The average use of the cycle time has been optimised from 80% up to 90%.

It should be noted that it is rather ironic that a car assembly factory should concentrate more on standardisation. For decades, car assembly has been synonymous with straightforward work routines and highly standardised jobs. The andon system aims to go one step further along that road, notwithstanding the increased complexity in the assembly process due to increased car options and the consequent difficulties to balancing the car mix. Because of this latter problem, the work sheet with work instructions for each car and each workstation, put on the car body, has been simplified and standardised. At the same time Opel Antwerp is focusing increasingly on poka yoke systems, to prevent production errors by eliminating the ways in which workers can make them. It plans to use computer systems and to put light signals next to component racks in order to indicate what a component operator has to pick when a certain car reaches his workstation, or to use material racks that open automatically when the car passes.

Ergonomics

Another strong point is ergonomics. Opel believes that the improved design of the workplace can markedly improve working speed and substantially reduce errors. This concern for ergonomics is being shown in different ways. One (not entirely) new approach involves a team of experts (dubbed 'VVP', a Flemish abbreviation which translates as 'Improving for better productivity') which analyses each workplace and then suggests improvements. Both the unions and the management admit that a workstation reaches nearly 100% effectiveness after being scrutinised by the VVP.

By paying such attention to ergonomics, the plant also hopes to reduce the negative effect of its policy of standardisation. Indeed, the combination of a short cycle time and enhanced standardised work implies that workers are more vulnerable than ever to being subjected to excessive stress. Consequently, the operator is not allowed to start the first operations at the car before the car body pallet reaches the green line. This prevents any working-up or working-ahead. According to the company, the andon system can only function when operators respect their own recuperation time.

A general concern is also a strict organisation of tools and machinery. By standardising the place and position of each tool at its optimal position, the company hopes to reduce fatigue. As in Opel Eisenach, Opel Antwerp plans to move material kits at assembly along with the workers, instead of forcing the workers to walk back every time for their material. Every item now has its specific place, visually indicated by a drawing of its contours on work benches.

Do integrated or outsourced pre-assemblies facilitate lean production and andon?

The whole shift towards andon on two assembly lines is facilitated because pre-assembly is integrated again at the assembly lines, in contrast to the former situation where pre-assemblies were executed on docks and transferred to the main assembly line on automated guided vehicles.

The question is whether the decision to create a Supply-In-Line-Sequence centre (SILS) in a joint venture with Katoen Natie on the factory premises for outsourced pre-assemblies, played a role in this matter. The unions' approval of this centre – despite their reluctant standpoint concerning outsourcing and especially insourcing – was certainly linked to the investments in the assembly line. In the SILS centre, production material, delivered by several suppliers, is handled and modules are pre-assembled. At the moment, only pre-assembly of bumpers and cooling installations takes place by workers other than Opel workers, who deliver the modules directly to the assembly line. The company states that it has no intention of going further than supplying directly to the assembly lines – installation of the modules will remain a task for Opel workers. It is of course the intention to reduce logistic costs per car produced and to raise the quality of the supplied parts. In a first phase, 50 people will be employed in the centre but the intention is that this will rise rapidly to around 100.

Teamwork revisited: an early adoption of teamwork

By European standards, Opel Antwerp was early in its adoption of teamwork. The first teams were set up in 1986, in parallel with the installation of a new paint shop. By 1989, teamwork had become widespread in the 'underbody' department and 'paint shop'. The 'body shop', 'final assembly' section and supporting services followed in 1990–91. One noteworthy aspect is that even supporting departments such as 'catering' or 'industrial relations' have been organised in teams. Moreover, they followed the 'industrial' teamwork concept as closely as possible.

The original view on teamwork resembled the model pioneered by SATURN. Both companies belonged to the same group and at the time the American greenfield plant was regarded as *the* showcase for General Motors' new ideas.

By following in the footsteps of SATURN, Opel Antwerp opted for an all-encompassing form of teamwork that was closer to the German model of 'Gruppenarbeit' than to teamwork as developed by Toyota. Teamwork at Opel Antwerp included monthly meetings of all the team's members, with extensive union involvement, but comparatively little attention paid to the improvement of quality and kaizen.

Most teams consisted of 16 employees [4]. A team representative co-ordinated activities, dealing with issues such as quality control, production targets and communication outside the team. He or she spent part of the working time participating in regular production work. Interestingly, the team representative was also in charge of training. New employees joined a one-week training programme, before starting work under the close supervision of the team representative.

For the employees, teamwork primarily meant job rotation. Opel Antwerp valued versatility and required team members to learn several tasks performed by their team as well as the surrounding teams. The plant's managers estimated that it took an employee two years to become 'fully productive', i.e. to become expert in a sufficient number of different jobs. The 'sufficient' number of jobs differed from the total number of tasks within the team. A 'regular' employee and team member was supposed to be able to fulfil at least 80% of the team tasks. Since 50% of these tasks were a result of integration of indirect jobs (such as preventive maintenance and quality control), this meant a team member had to know at least 5 jobs. One relief person in each team had to ensure continuous production and cover for employees during breaks.

Teamwork, version 2

The switch toward andon made it impossible to maintain the existing teamwork set-up. A major stumbling block was the large size of the teams, for there was no way in which the team representatives could guarantee swift assistance to 16 team members in the event of andon pulls. The walking distance to be covered might simply be too great to reach the andon spot in time. Another incompatibility was the production activities of the team representative. While he was producing, it was impossible to provide the necessary assistance to solve problems. Finally, supervision (in the sense of more control on quality) simply had to be increased. The company felt the quality of the cars had to improve.

It is with a view to answering such problems that Opel Antwerp reshaped its teamwork. The plant's management clearly saw teamwork as a means to an end, rather than an end in itself. It believed that teamwork had to facilitate the operation of the andon system. And this meant that the form of teamwork had to change. Since

Opel Antwerp looked to the NUMMI plant for inspiration on andon pulls, its 'new' form of teamwork now closely resembles team organisation at NUMMI.

The most influential change is the decrease in team size to 7–8 members (or even to 4–6 members in the future), a huge reduction from the 16 team members that most teams used to have. Teams still have a representative, but no relief person, as the plant has switched to collective breaks.

The reason for this decrease is straightforward. Andon requires team representatives to respond quickly. Only by having small teams is Opel sure that its team representatives get to the heart of the problem quickly enough. Line sections have also become smaller, being limited to 4 or 5 teams. The team leader and the section head provide two levels of help within the andon system.

For experienced workers this change involved a reduction of job rotation. Since teams are reduced to 4–6 jobs, less rotation is possible. The plant hopes to counterbalance this by rotating whole teams, e.g. having the team working on the left side of the car swap jobs with the team working on the right side.

Team meetings

Team meetings have always been a weak point of teamwork at Opel Antwerp. Although the concept originally included monthly meetings, most teams only gave the idea a lukewarm reception. Moreover, the meetings did not succeed in generating suggestions for improvements. So Opel Antwerp was forced to establish separate 'kaizen workshops'.

Consequently, the feelings about team meetings are mixed. For instance, during 1995, hardly any team meetings took place. However, the plant did not abandon the idea. Indeed, now two short meetings during each shift are taking place: a 5-minute meeting before the first collective break, and another 5-minute meeting before the second collective break. Throughout the production areas, a few corners are equipped with chairs and tables, allowing the team members to meet together. The first meeting focuses on safety issues, job rotation and maintenance. The second is held together with the other teams of the line section and deals with company information. It is meant to increase workers' awareness of company costs. Workers are free to formulate any questions, apart from social matters, discussed by the company works council or the occupational health and safety committee, where the unions are represented.

The company and the unions are not completely satisfied with these team meetings. They are considered to be too short to have any great impact, but the plant still looks for a solution for team meetings to be held without stopping production or paying costly overtime rates.

Kaizen workshops

As mentioned above, teamwork did not result in enhanced quality or improved working methods. In response to these weaknesses, Opel Antwerp initiated kaizen workshops. After undergoing introductory training, in special meetings the team leaders, section leaders and some older, well-trained employees focus on the improvement of a particular production issue. Any group proposing an improvement that turns out to be successful can expect some financial reward. Two union representatives attend all meetings, keeping a watchful eye on the subjects and procedures discussed.

The company proudly claims that, up until 1992, its 96 kaizen workshops generated improvements that were equivalent to 170 jobs. So it is hardly surprising that the system was continued and expanded during 1993–94. During the introduction of the new Vectra model and the andon system, the kaizen workshops were temporarily halted. Obviously, when the entire production process is changed, not much kaizen can take place. Employees first have to acquaint themselves with the machinery before they can improve on it.

Besides the kaizen workshops, an individual suggestions scheme for continuous improvement (in production and working conditions) was installed. In 1996 operators made approximately 5,000 suggestions. By the end of 1997 the number of suggestions had increased further. As is the case with so many other car companies, team results featuring such items as down-time, polyvalence of team members, production results and targets, andon pulls, quality, absenteeism rate, suggestions for improvement and so on, are represented in graphics in team areas on the shopfloor. The team representative continuously updates these results.

The team representative

The team leader has always been an interesting figure within Opel Antwerp. At first, the job of team leaders resembled the task of the previous first-line managers. This was hardly surprising since after the widespread introduction of teamwork, most of the former first-line managers took on the job of team leader. After the first few years, the former first-line managers relinquished their team leader jobs because the internal dynamic of the teams required a whole new way of thinking and working. Now most of the team leaders come from within the teams themselves. The plant's new teamwork structure has various consequences where team leaders are concerned. First of all, Opel Antwerp needed a lot more team leaders. Decreasing the size of its teams from 16 to 7–8 production operators constituted a major change and virtually doubled the number of team leaders required. The move towards having smaller teams involved a considerable organisational change.

The decision to reduce the span of control of a team representative from 16 to 7–8 employees sounds as if it would enlarge the task of internal supervision, representing a move away from the broad ideas of lean production, which aims to reduce the number of 'non-productive' supporting staff. But Opel representatives deny that the supervision of teams increased, claiming that the change was merely necessary to facilitate the switch to the andon system and create a larger span of support by the team leader.

Given the constant 'threat' of blockages, to prevent the assembly line from actually stopping after an andon pull the team representative has to be very fast in order to assist the worker who is in difficulty. This is only feasible with small teams, where the team representative has to cover only a few metres to reach the problem area. In a short time-span, help has to arrive (provided by one or more of the team representatives), the problem has to be diagnosed and the necessary corrective action must be taken.

First among equals

Team representatives do not control the team members. The team representatives are not managers. They do not feel like managers and such an attitude would not be accepted by their fellow workers. They do not even have any disciplinary responsibilities. Opel has discovered something far superior to supervision, namely social control, whereby team members now implicitly control their fellow workers. A team routinely knows its job. This ensures the smooth flow of work and guarantees that each team has a precise insight into the work to be done, which – in turn – allows self-control and social control to flourish, since each member of the team knows what is expected from both himself and his fellow workers. Union representatives confirm this, although they admit that they are sometimes confused by the lack of management on the shopfloor.

Taking decisions remains the responsibility of the team leader. This means that the whole andon system stands or falls with the team leader. After an andon has been pulled, he has to choose between four different options:

(1) solving the problem immediately;
(2) solving the problem at the next workstation;
(3) deciding to remove the car from the production line – this solution should be opted for in the event of a lack of spare parts;
(4) halting the assembly line.

Opel Antwerp aims to establish links between the various teams. Team members should therefore be familiar with the work done by other teams. A leader of one team might assist a second team during an andon break, for instance when the regular team leader is working on production to replace a sick colleague. Management was opposed to the unions' propositions to introduce polyvalent pool-teams to cover these problems.

Team leaders chosen by their fellow workers

Opel Antwerp's employees have a say in the appointment of team leaders. All able employees can apply for the post of team leader following very specific procedures. When a new round of recruitment was launched in 1995 when the switch to smaller teams called for more team representatives, the company went looking for candidates. All applications were evaluated and the successful candidates were given the necessary training. Good candidates were picked on the basis of an assessment. All the would-be team leaders who passed the assessment stage were then presented to the team members who took a vote to appoint their new team leader. There were several possible outcomes to this secret ballot. If within the team only one employee applied for the job, then the team members simply took a vote on that single candidate. However, it might very well have been that several employees aspired to the position of new team leader, in which case the employees' vote had to decide who their new leader was to be. Opel Antwerp offered the rejected candidates a post as team leader of another team, but once again this was subjected to a team vote. People who qualified as potential team leaders, but failed to find a team, ended up in a pool which the company used to fill any vacancies for team representatives arising over the coming years.

Once a team leader was approved by the team members, he was not automatically installed for life. Only after a 4-year period were team leaders to be definitely assigned to the job. Part of the assessment procedure included an evaluation by the other team members. Dissatisfied employees could always ask for a new vote on their team leader. Originally, Opel Antwerp planned regular elections, but this idea failed to deliver from the company's standpoint, since some team leaders began to use the lead-time for the vote almost as an election campaign. Once approved, a team leader is now kept in position, unless the members explicitly show their disapproval.

Working conditions

Similar to other plants working in teams, Opel Antwerp reduced its job classification system considerably. Coming from 13 wage categories and 2 levels of wage per category (more or less than 5 years' seniority), nowadays all production workers fall into just three categories: trained production worker, specialised production worker and maintenance worker. Regular production line assembly workers are all trained production workers. Workers only become 'specialised' for jobs where extensive training is required, e.g. for work in the paint shop or driving a fork lift truck.

This classification system dates back several years and Opel Antwerp plans to fully maintain it. Obviously, it is hard to imagine how the system could be reduced even further, and any extensive reclassification would appear to be incompatible with the idea of teamwork. Team representatives are classified as belonging to one of the three regular categories outlined above. Nevertheless, they receive a bonus for assuming additional responsibilities. Most team representatives receive something like an extra 30 Belgian francs on top of their regular salary, a figure which in turn translates into a wage increase of between 3% and 5%.

Linked to the classification system is a new flexibility dimension, ensuring that polyvalence is rewarded. Within the two wage categories, there are four steps according to the level of polyvalence:

- entering the company;
- after 6 months – when hired definitely;
- after another 6 months – total polyvalence within the team;
- after another 6 months – polyvalence within the section over several teams.

It takes a new employee two years to reach the full wage for a versatile employee. This reflects the time required to become expert not only in the various tasks performed by the team, but also some of the jobs performed by surrounding teams. Only then can the employee be truly labelled 'versatile', i.e. capable of functioning in different teams. Although it is decreasing the size of its teams, Opel Antwerp wants its team members to maintain a high level of versatility. Simple arithmetic leads one to conclude that smaller teams means less possibilities for job rotation and thus a lower degree of versatility. However, the plant management firmly believes in versatility. Workers have to learn the different jobs in their team and also some of the jobs undertaken by the surrounding teams. For instance, workers must be able to switch from assembling the left side of a car to performing similar tasks on the vehicle's right side.

What changed regarding versatility was the way in which job rotation takes place. The teams used to possess a fair amount of freedom in the organisation of job rotation, with some teams rotating every hour, others daily, or on an *ad hoc* basis, but the important point is that this decision was left to each team. The new style of teamwork shows a stricter job rotation system, with once again the aim of work standardisation as much as possible and the reduction in the risk of faults. Polyvalence is not necessarily aimed at facilitating job rotation but covering for absent team members. To ensure production continuity, job rotation only occurs during periods of collective team breaks.

What is striking is that the company is willing to pay for the extra knowledge which workers gain and the extra input that operators offer. This is by no means the dominant point of view in the car industry. For example, the plant is also considering special individual or team bonuses for valued suggestions for improvement. The monthly wage of team members would consist of a fixed wage plus some additional percentage payment.

The plant's management is convinced that its employees are highly motivated in their work because of the high scores achieved in an internal survey measuring attitudes towards work. These compared favourably with a survey carried out just after the introduction of 'the new approach'. According to the trade unions, workers also feel more committed to their job because of the alarming economic situation in Belgium. People are overwhelmed by the endlessly repeated media reports on high Belgian labour costs. The workers at Opel Antwerp know that their wages are higher than in most other European car assembly factories, and they know that the labour market provides few alternatives for ex-car assembly workers [5].

Unions and teamwork

The first experiences with teamwork resulted in the introduction of teamwork throughout the entire plant in 1989. Teamwork became part of a new vision ('our new approach'), aiming for optimal customer satisfaction and enhanced mutual trust between the employees and management. In the framework of lean production and andon it is meant to increase productivity, flexibility and quality [6].

The plant prides itself on its 'European' consensus approach to car assembly work, referring to intensive union–management consultation and the election of team leaders as an illustration of its more consensus-oriented attitude, compared with a stricter orientation geared towards lean production in the more rigid sense of the term.

Opel Antwerp opted for intensive union involvement during the introduction of teamwork. Shop stewards and external union representatives participated in meetings discussing teamwork, even though the actual concept was developed before this co-operation started. As a result, teamwork was introduced with union support. This co-operative approach was fostered and subsequently became a feature of daily industrial relations at plant level.

A parallel representation structure on the side of the unions has existed since the end of the 1980s. The unions are organised through the plant and at all levels (body-shop, paint-shop, assembly) with shopfloor representatives. But a hierarchically organised and union centred structure also channels information, prevents misunderstandings, and is a strong means of communication and consultation for both unions and management. In particular, the overall representation facilitates the scrutiny of teamwork from the unions' standpoint.

Conclusion

Over ten years ago, in 1986, Opel Antwerp began experimenting with teamwork. After a long process of continual change, the plant decided in 1993 to take a definite turn towards lean production and the introduction of andon as a means of bringing the plant's productivity, flexibility and quality up to a comparable efficiency level with the American and Japanese high-performing car factories. The concept of teamwork was adapted to fit this new framework. Operations and the division of operations on the assembly line were even more standardised. Accurately calculated operations are supposed to be properly executed for the first time within a standardised cycle time of 80 seconds. Operators guard the quality of their operations and can even stop the line if a problem occurs and needs to be solved. In order not to hinder production, the assembly line is divided into short buffered line sections. Teams are quite small (and will become even smaller), so that the team representative can give full support when a team member signals a problem and needs to solve it. Both quality and the constant support of the team representative to his team are high priorities. The polyvalence of operators is enhanced so that they can fill in for temporarily absent members, yet job rotation is nevertheless limited because of the possible negative impact upon quality unless team members decide otherwise. However, even then, job rotation only occurs at specific moments when teams take their formal breaks.

There was considerable consultation and participation in the development of the andon and teamwork systems at their inception, and this is still continuing today. Indeed, workers at Opel Antwerp are experiencing increasingly stressful work because of the optimised use of job cycle times, and attendant problems of model mix and the knock-on effect of this on line balancing: a constant worry for all car factories. The unions constantly monitor the daily situation and workload and are especially concerned about the impact of these on older workers. Notwithstanding the close union–management collaboration, the unions' power and control is still considered to be very important. According to the unions, teamwork and andon were initially proposed by the management and subsequently approved by the former.

A difficult point remains the involvement of team members in the company's continuous improvement of production and working conditions. Team members have some say over changes proposed by kaizen workshops, but team meetings are limited to a couple of five-minute sessions per day, which generate very little in the way of individual suggestions. It seems to be quite difficult to create space for mutual team members' consultation, without interrupting production on a regular basis with the consequent necessity of having to pay for overtime.

Together with the introduction of teamwork, a new personnel policy simplified the functional boundaries and classification system to three operator categories. Encouraging improvements and stimulating polyvalence by paying for them are also strong issues for Opel Antwerp's management. Nevertheless, the company considers that further changes in personnel policy instruments are necessary, in order to support the existing teamwork, the proper use of the andon system and, finally, the increase in productivity, flexibility and quality.

It is clear that the plant's management has focused on the introduction of lean production and andon to reach its goals of productivity, flexibility and quality. This priority determines the concept of teamwork and the accompanying personnel policy.

End-notes

[1] Michel Albertijn established the independent research bureau Tempera. Johan Van Buylen is an expert from the Socialist Metal Workers Trade Union – ABVV. Leen Baisier works for the Social Economic Council of Flanders/Flemish Foundation for Technology Assessment. The authors have been researching the Belgian car industry for several years.

[2] General Motors Continental started in 1924 in Antwerp. The plant changed its name in 1994 to Opel Belgium.

[3]   The trade unions argue that the company first envisaged a shorter cycle time. Management finally agreed to the present cycle time on the demand of the unions, who were concerned about the possible workload for the operators.

[4]   Opel Antwerp always held a rather flexible attitude towards its teamwork. Since its debut in 1986, the management did not hesitate to reshape the teams. The number of team members was changed several times. In 1986, the number depended on the team's task and department. Afterwards, the plant opted for a fixed membership of 11 persons (8 operators, 1 team representative, 1 absentee replacer and 1 relief person). In 1993, that number was expanded to 16 members. This move originated from a concern to improve productivity, by decreasing the number of team leaders and relief personnel.

[5]   It has to be remembered that this is before one even considers the impact of Renault's Vilvoorde plant.

[6]   With regard to the productivity matter, the national trade unions nowadays wonder whether it makes sense to have enlarged the plant's production time up to 110 hours a week and, when the market goes down, switch to temporary technical unemployment of the workers who then fall back on social security.

Bibliography

Trade unions interviews: Walter Mertens, ABVV Socialist Metal Union Representative (2 November 1995); Frans Troch, ABVV Socialist Metal Union Representative (30 and 31 January 1997); Flor Hansen, ACV Christian Metal Union Representative (10 February 1997); Walter Goormans, ACLVB Liberal Union Representative (13 February 1997).

Management interviews and company visits: Dany Van den Bossche, Personnel Department (September 1995) Doug Friesen, Manufacturing Director; Maurice Vrijsen, People Systems Development Manager; Bob Schelfaut, HRM Manager; Tom Van Cleemput, Manager Assembly; Frank Nuyts, Team Representative Astra assembly (17 February 1997).

Albertijn, M., Van Buylen J. and Baisier, L. (1994) *Teamwork in the Belgian Car Assembly Plants*, Paper for GERPISA.

Baisier, L. and Albertijn M. (1995) *Met teamwerk in turbo-drive. Onderzoek naar teamwerk in de Europese auto-industrie*. Brussels: Stichting Technologie Vlaanderen/Flemish Foundation for Technology Assessment.

Baisier, L. (1996) *Kampioenen in flexibiliteit en kwaliteit. Trends bij toeleveranciers aan de Vlaamse auto-industrie.* Brussels: Stichting Technologie Vlaanderen/Flemish Foundation for Technology Assessment.

Baisier, L. (1997) *Teamwerk in de Belgische auto-industrie* (working title). Brussels: Stichting Technologie Vlaanderen/Flemish Foundation for Technology Assessment.

Centrale der Metaalindustrie van België (1993) Altijd al in team. *CMB-Inform*, No. 134, July/August/September.

Centrale der Metaalindustrie van België (1996) Toelevering. De buitenspelval omzeilen. *CMB-Inform*, 1996, 112.

Huys, R. (1995) *Teamwerk in de Belgische auto-assemblage.* Nota na een rondgang in de vijf Belgische autofabrieken (voorjaar '94) t.b.v. de informatienamiddag STV, 2 maart 1995. K.U. Leuven, Departement Sociologie van Arbeid & Bedrijf.

CHAPTER 16
Group Work in the German Automobile Industry – The Case of Mercedes-Benz

Detlef Gerst, Thomas Hardwig, Martin
Kuhlmann and Michael Schumann

Introduction

Starting in the mid-1980s, attempts to depart from Taylorist and Fordist structures of production and work organisation, and efforts to establish a new politics of the workplace could be observed in the German automobile industry. These developments coincided with a ten-year span of expansion in which the German auto industry, in particular, was very successful and in which employment increased – in contrast with most of its European and American competitors. Over the 1980s, the production concepts of the German auto industry [1], were considered successful on an international scale (Dertouzos et al., 1989; Streeck, 1988). More recent empirical studies, though, show that real changes of the structures on the shopfloor were only hesitantly implemented before the early 1990s (Jürgens et al., 1989; Schumann et al., 1994). While the present attempts to implement team concepts or group work are influenced by the reception of management concepts such as lean production, the course and pattern of reorganisation cannot be understood without their history of slowly moving reorganisation of work structures in the 1980s and attempts to introduce group work within the framework of government programmes such as HdA (*Humanisierung der Arbeitswelt* – a QWL programme funded by the government), started in the 1970s.

The 1980s, thus, can be characterised as an era of transition lacking the explicit discussion of 'group work' on the shopfloor that the 1970s had seen, but in fact experiencing a set of changes without which the present renaissance of group work concepts cannot be explained. Even if it was not always reflected in discussions within the companies, automation efforts in practice resulted in a slow diffusion of important elements and principles of new forms of work organisation and their growing acceptance by management (Kern and Schumann, 1984).

The transitory character of the 1980s is also evident in that the metalworkers union (*IG Metall*) and some works councils advocated new forms of work organisation and job redesign, but – based on ambivalent experiences [2] and a lack of competence – did not (yet) support them in a broad sense or very eagerly. Still, many companies followed a policy of higher-skilled production labour and greater worker autonomy, fostered by external consulting and active job redesigning, and the socio-technical HdA concepts of the 1970s – by now labelled the Scandinavian or Swedish way (Roth and Kohl 1988) – offered important points of reference. At this time, not only were there positive experiences from concrete shopfloor projects that changed the internal discussion, but also a growing know-how with regard to the organisation of work. In contrast to the fear of the 1970s, that group work would be a threat to the existing structures of workers' interest representation, the prevailing view is that elected group speakers are not a menace but – on the contrary – an extension of and a broader base for democratic principles, opportunities for co-determination, and the development of collective bargaining and employee participation.

A study of the German automobile industry concluded, for the 1980s (Schumann *et al.*, 1994), that once group work is conceived not as a complete and fully implemented grand design but rather as a combination of individual elements, there have indeed been no sweeping changes on a broad scale in terms of concepts and structures of work organisation. But, on the other hand, the climate changed and work organisation was in a process of change: in automated production areas, there was at times an exhaustive programme of upskilling, based on a greater acknowledgement of the necessity of skilled production labour. In addition, a policy of integration of tasks and functions was begun in the 1980s. An institutionalised form of self-organisation (such as delegation of supervisory functions) has not yet evolved and aspects of group development (group meetings, social skills, empowerment) were not explicitly considered in the formation of task-integrating production teams. But in automated production areas within a number of plants, skilled and autonomously operating production teams have evolved. Changes remained largely informal, though they were dependent on the initiative of individual departments and persons, and did not find their way into the general policy of the company or a reorganisation of its structure. In the areas of manual work, there were – very reluctant – initial attempts at integration of tasks and functions, also aiming to increase flexibility in the use of work and to better balance the line. However, all these were not group work concepts or even their early forms by today's standards.

While changes on the shopfloor had only been implemented in a very controlled and restricted manner until the early 1990s and had at times failed because of internal resistance, since then there have been increased efforts to reorganise the shopfloor and to introduce new forms of work at all German auto makers. The publication of the MIT's International Motor Vehicles Program study (Womack *et al.*, 1991) and the crisis in auto sales that hit the industry shortly after eventually led to a much broader discussion of organisational concepts and an unusually fast diffusion on the shopfloor. The industrial community, too, quickly focused its debate on team concepts and group work, respectively, as a core principle of modern plant organisation. Because of its tradition of HdA and the strong advocacy of the metalworkers union and some works councils (Hans-Böckler-Stiftung/IG Metall, 1992), the issue of 'group work' was pushed strongly in the German discussion [3].

Currently, the shopfloor reality in the German automobile industry is characterised by a large array of forms of group or teamwork. Yet in the present discussion, two divergent concepts are beginning to take shape, which we will contrast as two poles of shopfloor organisation in the next two sections.

Taylorised group work – the structurally conservative model

As Taylorised group work, we classify the model of group work inspired by Japanese transplants because it adheres to Taylorist organisational principles in critical dimensions. Yet even this model of group work – more or less programmatically – departs from the Taylorist–Fordist factory regime in several aspects:

(1) It is characterised by a factory culture based on partnership in which a new type of lower-level 'manager' plays a key role. These 'team leaders', usually appointed by the management and

specifically trained and prepared, are tied into the team's work process which distinguishes them from otherwise common foremen. In contrast to traditional supervisors, their relationship to production workers contains moments of mutual commitment and is characterised by a greater degree of social proximity.

(2) Also, there is a marked expansion of plant-internal communication and information that explicitly includes regular production workers. To that end, group meetings hosted by the team leaders are established. These meetings also serve to solve problems in production and to optimise the processes. It is crucial that the increased communication and information do not operate in a top-down fashion. Group meetings and the new role of the team leader are to improve bottom-up communication also.

(3) In addition, these team concepts increase the flexibility within the workforce and rely on more multi-skilled workers, although this usually remains limited to a lower-skill level.

(4) Another novel feature is the efforts to permanently optimise the process and increase performance which – other than in the Taylorist model – is to be achieved by mobilising the employees themselves. This system which critics have labelled 'management by stress' (Parker and Slaughter, 1988) is based on the principle of tight manning. This kind of permanent, potentially boundless increase of performance and the tight manning would however be hard to implement in the German system of industrial relations, which guarantees the works councils legally codified rights of co-determination, as it would include the departure from fixed and verifiable standards of performance that have been institutionalised in the course of Taylorist rationalisation processes.

If looked upon from a labour process perspective though, these forms of group work – often referred to as team concepts – in critical dimensions remain caught in the traditional Taylorist structures of work organisation and factory regime:

(5) The tasks of production workers overwhelmingly maintain their repetitive nature. Standardisation and routinisation of job execution are still a central concern. Much as in the Taylorist–Fordist factory, this leaves little room for autonomy and discretion on the part of workers. Strongly routinised job designs are still seen as the best way to achieve high efficiencies, and more integration of indirect tasks (parts procurement, maintenance,

quality control, etc.) is seen as interference, as a flow production coupled tightly to the line pace gives management a high degree of transparency.

(6) Because of this, skill requirements and process-regulation competencies of the workers are confined, although they are usually above those in traditional plants.

(7) The institutionalised opportunities for participation and the level of self-organisation of production groups are limited by a set of time and material constraints. Those resources that make self-organisation feasible in the first place are particularly tight [4]. Organisational and planning responsibilities are primarily taken on by the appointed team leader, so that the scope of the group's self-organisation strongly depends on the team leader's demeanour and on general conditions within the plant. The say in the use of labour as well as control and evaluation of work performance largely remain in the hands of supervisors.

(8) Changes in the relationship between production groups and technical experts are also relatively minor. Depending on the plant culture, the relations may be closer or less confrontational, but a strong separation, different status, and separate responsibilities for conception and execution are essentially being upheld. The structurally conservative nature of this concept, which we term Taylorised group work, is also displayed by the fact that production workers are not given sufficient time margins, skills and competencies to form a new relationship towards the technical experts. The decentralisation of the company organisation and the dilution of the line between production and experts, so typical of traditional Taylorist structures, are accomplished primarily through the team leaders. This is particularly evident with regard to the transfer of responsibilities for optimisation: in contrast to Adler's (1992) assessment for NUMMI, a transfer of such responsibilities into the production groups rarely occurs in the German context. Kaizen essentially remains the responsibility of special teams of experts. These teams, on the other hand, often do include team leaders as well as foremen [5].

So far, there are few cases of group work designs rigorously patterned after Japanese models in the German automobile industry. Distinctive traditions and institutionalised rules have proven too strong. One example, though, of the growing importance of this variant of group work in Germany is the development at Opel: while the concept that was agreed upon with the works council and operated at the Bochum plant in the early 1990s was patterned after the model of self-organised group work (Minssen *et al.*, 1991), the new 'Opel Eisenach GmbH' subsidiary and plant are an attempt to implement Japanese-inspired concepts which have been tested in the North American transplants at a German facility (Enderle, 1994). Production technology, work organisation, and company culture in Eisenach largely match the solutions chosen at NUMMI and CAMI. Eisenach's management too was partly recruited from there, and the exceptional situation in East Germany offers some specific advantages, given its circumstances. By now, the transfer of the 'Eisenach production system' (Opel) to the other plants as a best practice is on the agenda – despite the resistance of the company works council (*Manager Magazin*, 12/1994). The recent (summer 1994) 'Betriebsvereinbarung' [6] on the extension of group work into other areas of the Bochum plant (particularly assembly), for example, provides a modified role for group speakers: in future, they will participate in assessment centres and, increasingly, they are to take over supervisory duties (Jennen and Vorberg, 1994).

The post-Taylorist concept: self-organised group work

The other pole of contemporary group work development – which we call self-organised group work – in contrast to that described earlier, picks up from German experiences with HdA. Here, the evolution of a decentralised, task-integrated work organisation is connected to socio-technical principles, such as autonomous groups, in order to fundamentally depart from previous Taylorist structures. Based on this combination, more profound changes have been possible since the early 1990s than were realised over the 1980s. The key elements of this explicitly non-Taylorist, structurally innovative model of group work can be depicted as follows:

(1) Job designs as well as a range of discretion and decision-making by the groups are extended. Indirect and conceptional functions are explicitly included as they are particularly apt to increase the degree of freedom on the job and to launch effects of upskilling. A combination of tasks that follow the pace of the line and those that do not is generally pursued, even though

the scope differs because of diverse production technologies.

(2) Groups are formed and developed around the goal of self-organisation and empowerment of the groups. They are given an extended responsibility for the organisation of their work area and opportunities to influence events on the shopfloor. To that end, they are provided with the appropriate resources: group speakers are elected, remain a part of the group and act as speakers and co-ordinators. Self-organised group meetings serve to foster mutual co-ordination and to solve operational as well as social problems. Finally, resources for self-organisation include supporting the groups' social development in the direction of democratic principles.

(3) The concept of self-organised group work seeks a new role for lower management on the shopfloor, in particular the foremen. They are to delegate responsibility and indirect tasks to the groups. In so doing, they are to gain time for new, more sophisticated tasks, such as assisting the groups with the solution of organisational and job-related problems, training, and interdepartmental co-ordination and organisation. The foreman is to represent the group's interest vis-à-vis other units. Yet while this new role perception is currently a feature of the concept, it describes shopfloor reality only in a few areas. The limited occurrence of this ideal type in practice is rooted in the foremen's problems in accepting the new role as an alternative to their function in Taylorist production.

(4) Another element of this concept is the more distinct decentralisation of commercial and technical management functions. In contrast to the structurally conservative variant, however, this coincides with the formation and extension of co-operative and communicative structures in which the groups themselves take on additional responsibilities. For example, the groups have the power to invite technical experts to their meetings and have a greater capacity to influence the completion of assignments. Ultimately, the changing of superiors' responsibilities as well as the reorganisation of co-operative relationships between production groups and experts aim at a de-hierarchisation of structures and manners.

(5) The concept of self-organised group work also takes seriously the attempt to include the production groups themselves into the optimisation of events on the shopfloor and not leave these responsibilities exclusively to technical experts. This pre-

supposes that – in a departure from traditional time and motion studies (MTM or REFA in the German context) – new forms of bargaining about performance standards develop which also in this regard emphasise the direct involvement of the production groups. In contrast to the team concepts in the transplants, the notion of fixed performance standards is maintained. But self-organised group work is structurally innovative in comparison with the traditional mode of bargaining over performance standards, in which the influence of employees was limited to grievance rights of the works councils. Now, bargaining over work rates includes the groups themselves. Also, it entails developing the entire production process and includes both optimising operations and creating improved work conditions for the employees.

The case of Mercedes-Benz

Even though the concept we refer to as self-organised group work rests on German institutional traits like skilled production labour, co-determination on the shopfloor, and a union policy aimed at more advanced group work, it is only found in a minority of plants owing to inevitable ongoing structural adjustments. Not only the concept as such, but also the social process of organisational change necessary for its implementation, demand particular policies on the part of the actors involved. At Mercedes-Benz AG and within the plants we studied, the concrete form of individual group work projects is still disparate, even though the broad direction set by top management and the now-ratified *Betriebsvereinbarung*, which covers all plants, is clearly geared towards self-organised group work (Tropitzsch, 1994; Springer, 1993). The most important regulations of this agreement in this concept are the following:

(1) The purpose of group work is defined as increasing productivity and improving the work environment, as well as creating chances for development and job training for the individual.
(2) Holistic job designs for the groups are to be crafted. An attempt is made to integrate direct, indirect and planning responsibilities.
(3) Opportunities for training and sufficient time margins for additional responsibilities are granted.

(4) The present workforce will be taken over, i.e. there will not be any selection or predisposition.
(5) Training for managers will be established, focusing on their new responsibilities and a new, participatory perception of their role.
(6) The group speaker is elected, remains integrated into the group's work process and has no supervisory functions whatsoever. The group speaker is a moderator, speaker and person to turn to for management; he organises the group meetings and receives an extra wage compensation.
(7) A time of about thirty minutes per week is guaranteed for group meetings. The meetings are organised by the groups themselves and are to channel information, to solve operational and social problems, and to further group development. Managers or experts can be invited to participate in the meetings.
(8) In order to co-ordinate and further develop group work, plant-level steering committees made up from representatives of top management and works council will be established. In addition, the individual projects are 'escorted' by project teams in which managers and works council members co-operate. The steering committee has been assigned the duty to support the top management and to establish broad guidelines and standards.

Despite this agreement, which is valid for all Mercedes-Benz plants, we assume that in future there will continue to be different variants of group work in various plants and production areas. This is not merely rooted in the – at many points – fairly vague language of the general agreement. Rather, most of the changes on the shopfloor will continue to depend on the respective actors' policies, for example the involvement of works councils and the social process of its implementation. Even individual provisions of the general agreement can be modified if there is a consensus among the players in the plant [7].

Having sketched out the key elements of the contemporary discussion of group work and the concepts pursued in it, we will now describe their effects on the work situation and its evaluation by workers on the basis of our own empirical research on group work at Mercedes-Benz. In doing so, we will employ some examples to analyse the process of implementing group work in greater detail. Our central concern is with the characteristics and conditions that determine the impact of group work on workers.

Our assessment is rooted in findings from an ongoing research project in which we evaluate concepts of group work with regard to their impact on employees. For this chapter, we chose four projects from three individual plants that differ not only in their group work design but also in production technology. Investigating each case over several weeks, we combined qualitative interviews with individual employees and the various other actors and a standardised questionnaire survey of all group members. Over the same time, we conducted workplace and group observations which provided us with a view into actual work situations. In summary, our results indicate that the experiences and evaluations of employees differ markedly along the lines of different organisational arrangements: the more elements of self-organised group work are employed, the more positive the reaction of the workers. Using four case studies, we illustrate potential constellations of group work and will speculate on their effects.

Self-organised group work: the case of machine operation with enhanced job design (case TM1)

This case provides the strongest and most broad-ranging positive evaluation of group work that we found. The concept pursued in this plant most clearly illustrates the pole of self-organised, structurally innovative group work. TM1 is a group work project in a relatively small (less than 3,000 employees) plant for engine parts and sub-systems which functions as a parts supplier to other plants and thus is under particular competitive pressure. Meanwhile, the plant has been chosen as the company's second facility for the final assembly of engines, which strengthens the plant's position within the corporation.

The plant has some experience with reorganisation projects following the model of skilled production work from the 1980s, and it became involved in the introduction of group work relatively early and rather systematically – long before there was an agreement for the entire company. The social process of implementing group work is characterised by a mature concept of introduction and a project organisation both strong and active ('steering committee' – 'Steuerkreis') which fully incorporates representatives from the individual production units and departments, independent coaches ('Gruppenbetreuer') and the works council.

Within the TM1 group work project, a limited number of product variants (exhaust pipes) are made in short cycle times and mostly in large batches (Table 1). The introduction of group work coincided with the creation of a new production area. Before group work was introduced, production jobs had been limited to operating individual machines only, so that the workers' jobs were basically confined to machine tending and handling parts under an individual piecework system. The job was strongly repetitive, and the employees were furthermore exposed to significant physical strain because of the exhaust pipes' heavy weight. Skilled work in machine set-up, adjustment and problem-solving was done by separate machine setters. All in all, the general conditions for the implementation of an advanced form of group work seemed rather adverse which is why, in the steering committee, the works council, in particular, initially voted against starting a pilot project in this area. Yet as the steering committee, the local planning team and the works council, based on lively debates and greater experience, agreed on the structurally innovative goals and conceptual traits of group work, there was an accord to integrate indirect responsibilities that had been detached from the machine workers into the groups as far as possible. This was to achieve more co-operation and a visible upgrading of work in terms of skills and discretionary freedom. Only where an appropriate conceptual arrangement was achieved did the works council go along. The broad integration of indirect and related tasks – there were no machine setters anymore – eventually lead to the creation of additional jobs. These non-repetitive jobs are rotated routinely among group members and therefore increase the flexibility of the whole group significantly.

Besides the relatively far-reaching functional integration, the TM1 group work concept is also characterised by a rather broad integration of tasks. Within the entire work unit, there is routine rotation which gives everyone the opportunity to learn each task. Interestingly, the employees were trained for their new jobs by means of specific programmes. As a result, there are enhanced, uniform and strongly overlapping job profiles that allow for a high flexibility in the use of work and mutual substitution. The implementation of group work was organised so that groups were not confronted with a detailed design. Rather, group members were involved in the design of their work area from the very beginning. Whether it was job enrichment or work procedures, technical arrangements or performance standards, most regulations were discussed with the

Table 1 *Synoptical view of group work projects – machine shops.*

Case TM1 (plant A)	Case TS1 (plant B)
• Machine shops: machine tending, mostly at separate machines; short running times, serial production	• Machine shops: systems regulation at CNC transfer lines
• Highly integrated tasks and functions (e.g. quality control, simple maintenance, machine set-up, production planning)	• Highly integrated task, but low level of integration of functions (e.g. quality control, machine set-up); specialists ('systems commander') for particularly elaborate tasks (complex set-ups, optimising NC programs)
• High degree of flexibility at work	• High degree of flexibility at work
• Intensive coaching of project development	• Little coaching of project development
• Group speaker: elected; fully integrated into the group and its work; very few additional external responsibilities; no extra wage compensation; 'speaker of the group'	• Group speaker: elected; fully integrated into the group and its work; very few additional external responsibilities; extra wage compensation; 'speaker of the group'
• Group meetings: 30 minutes per week; longer if necessary	• Group meetings: 30 minutes per week, not fully exhaustive
• Wages corresponding to scope of tasks performed; promotion to highest wage category possible for everyone in group	• Wages corresponding to scope of tasks performed; promotion to highest wage category (systems commander) limited

group and agreed upon jointly. This process was facilitated by the decentralisation of the functions of technical experts (industrial engineering, technical planning, quality control, production clerks, etc.) that had already set in, but more so by the fact that these departments and individuals were actively involved in the design of group work, resulting in a more co-operative relationship with the production groups.

Another decisive factor in the social process of introducing group work in the TM1 case was the existence and active role of plant-level coaching: the group development (towards a culture of co-operation, meetings and conflict resolution within the group and with neighbouring areas) was systematically supported on the basis of a coaching scheme. Also, the groups were assisted in generating and developing self-organisation up to the point where they could handle it themselves.

The close intertwining of reorganisation, coaching and training, as well as the active role of members from the implementation teams and steering committee, ensured that even conflicts (over manning, quality and output problems) did not lead to a lasting setback or standstill of project development.

Even though the work day after the introduction of group work continues to be characterised by a rather short-cycle production of large batches, task and functional integration nevertheless resulted in a distinct upgrading of the job in terms of skills and discretionary leeway. At the same time, improved opportunities to cope with strain were created by assuming indirect tasks and by job rotation. This can be seen from the overwhelmingly positive to very positive evaluations of the effects of group work (Table 5(g)). In contrast with most other cases, the positive evaluation here explicitly includes the aspect of strain. While the workers in TM1 also maintain that the level of performance required has increased in parallel with the introduction of group work, overall, i.e. with regard to the evaluation of strain over the long run, the majority gives a positive assessment (Table 5(e)).

Coinciding with the changes in task distribution, in this case there was also a particularly far-reaching realisation of the principle of self-organisation. The groups were granted a broad freedom for the design and organisation of their work process, and significant steps towards real empowerment were reached. The daily tasks of the groups include organising the manning of machines, the production programme and the sequence of orders to be fulfilled, on top of its production responsibilities. Some of this is accomplished in co-ordination with the foreman, who seeks to hand over new responsibilities to the groups step by step and to intervene actively only in case of bigger or long-term problems. A higher level of self-organisation and extended responsibilities for planning for the groups also result from the more intensive co-operation with the largely decentralised technical departments.

"The foreman's role is principally changed. He now isn't dealing with individuals any longer but with an entire group, so eventually he has to change his way of thinking. Now he's showing up with a list saying what to deliver and when, and he puts it into one of our hands. We're taking care of the rest ourselves. Then we co-ordinate things within our group if a machine needs retooling or if we leave the production plan as it is on that given day. It's none of the foreman's business anymore, it's all left to the group. The foreman is just some kind of partner, something like a 'friend', I would say. Delivery registers and orders still involve the foreman. He's something like a manager outside the group." (Worker, TM1)

The high level of self-organisation in the TM1 case was reached through elected group speakers who are integrated into the group and the work process, and whose role can be described as co-ordinator, moderator and speaker for the group. The group speakers hardly assume more related or additional responsibilities than their colleagues. Besides their production tasks, their only responsibility is in preparing and managing group meetings as well as in being a mouthpiece for their colleagues. Decisions are made by the entire group and not by the group speakers. Once a week, the groups are given discussion time which the group uses according to the numbers of problems to be solved.

The TM1 case stands as an example of what can be achieved for the employees by a practical implementation of self-organised group work. While TM1 is among the most successful group work projects in the plant, its thoroughly positive evaluations by the employees are not exceptional. One reason for this is the joint conviction of management and the works council that participatory and skilled job designs yield not only improvements on the job but also in terms of productivity. Another reason is to be found in the successful project organisation, i.e. its conception, implementation and coaching of the group work areas. In the TM1 case, employees have actively been involved in a process of continuously increasing productivity. Because the group members see improvement and cost reduction to be in their own interest, and also because of the high degree of self-organisation, arguments over performance standards with superiors do not necessarily lead to permanent or unsolvable conflicts. Rather, productivity matters are characterised by joint solution efforts and rational bargaining for compromises.

Systems regulation in a transfer line (case TS1)

The TS1 case is also located in a machine shop, but in a much larger main plant for the production of engines, transmissions and axles (over 10,000 employees). The tasks of the production workers include monitoring and running a highly automated CNC transfer

380 Teamwork in the Automobile Industry

line. It is not machine tending as in TM1 but systems regulation (Schumann *et al.*, 1994). Differences prevail not only in the kind of work but also in the skills required. While the skill requirements at TM1 are on a level of semi-skilled work, TS1 is a case of skilled work. The products made are brake disks in varying batch sizes. With regard to their job contents, the employees at TS1 are very satisfied in their work.

Even greater are the differences between the two cases once the social process of reorganisation is taken into account. As a result of the policy of integrating and upskilling of the 1980s, the job classifications were already relatively broad when group work was introduced. The classical division of labour between (low skill) machine operators and (high skill) machine setters was partly lifted when the new CNC production lines went into operation in the late 1980s, and machine operators were given the opportunity to qualify for jobs as machine commanders ('Maschinenführer'), whose skill profile and tasks came close to former machine setters. The latter were increasingly given responsibilities for optimising CNC programmes and production before they were promoted to a newly created systems commander classification. At a later point, the quality inspectors were also given additional training, and transferred from the quality control department into the groups. Before group work was introduced, there had already been job rotation – albeit not systematically or consistently – and the work group was jointly responsible for the entire transfer line and its performance. At the time of our research, only the very complex tasks of machine setting (major changes in the CNC programme) were completed exclusively by the technical specialists (systems commanders).

The introduction of group work at TS1 took a markedly different course from that at TM1, which has also to do with the plant's shorter experience with group work and the generally minor importance that this concept of reorganisation enjoyed there at that time. Actors involved in the implementation of group work were almost exclusively local management and the foremen, and the necessary measures of cost reduction were – in contrast to TM1 – largely achieved without involvement of the work groups. There was no assistance or issue-oriented discussion of the plans by a central steering committee, let alone a systematic process of introduction based on additional coaching such as that in plant A (TM1). All in all, the introduction was much less participatory, and indirect or neighbouring production areas as well as the works council were much less engaged in the reorganisation process. In contrast with plant A, the conceptual discussions about the goals and configuration of group work had been controversial within management and between management and works councils. The critical issues were the definition and status of the group speaker vis-à-vis the systems commander. While parts of management sought to retain the position of the systems commander and some longed to make them group speakers, the works council insisted on the free election of group speakers and sought to strengthen their position vis-à-vis the systems commander. In the end a solution emerged in which the group speakers have no additional tasks in the production process, so the group is multi-skilled and fully flexible, as in TM1. However, the former machine setters were promoted to the newly created 'systems commander' classification. Besides normal monitoring, they still perform more advanced set-up, programming and planning tasks, although in practice there are no formal demarcations between the skilled regular production workers and the systems commander. In some cases, this dual structure of group speakers and systems commanders both trying to organise the daily work schedule has led to tensions or conflict, in particular where the systems commander acts like a subforeman.

Eventually, the job and task design of individual employees as well as the group has changed little through the introduction of group work. Yet, with regard to skill requirements one can speak of a skilled variant of group work, although the integration of indirect and planning responsibilities was much more limited than in the TM1 case. The level of self-organisation is lower compared to the TM1 case. The group's responsibility hardly stretches into planning tasks. The employees do have the opportunity to organise their work schedules and patterns but the group does not have any control over the sequence of production jobs, batch sizes or times for tool changes. On top of that, it is not tied into the decision-making process of indirect departments like maintenance, planning, and industrial engineering. Self-organisation is almost limited to organising work arrangements within the group, the election of group speakers, and the conduct of group meetings – as the situation is, the groups comes together for meetings less often than allowed by management. With regard to the frequency and character of the group meetings, in particular, the lack of coaching in group development is highly visible. The group meetings have not yet become the place to discuss and solve problems of the group, operation or the production area.

Table 2 *Overall: how satisfied are you with your job?*

In per cent	TM1 n = 30	TS1 n = 29	M1 n = 29	M2 n = 58
Satified	66	52	60	17
Undecided	17	33	36	32
Unsatisfied	17	15	4	51

Despite the much more limited scope of reorganisation and the less systematic implementation of group work, TS1 nevertheless is a case of group work that can be counted among the structurally innovative variants of self-organised group work in a number of elements (Table 1). Among the TS1 employees, too, positive evaluations of group work prevail (Tables 2 and 5(g)). It is due to the persistent deviations from the model of self-organised group work that the overall assessment and evaluation in almost all dimensions are less positive than in the TM1 case (Table 5). The scope of innovations in the TS1 case is limited, particularly with regard to decentralisation and de-hierarchisation of shopfloor structures, but also by a less-pronounced focus on participation in bargaining processes and planning. There has not been a sweeping change in the social relations of production groups and the supervisors or the technical experts.

Group work on the assembly line: plant C

Based on two cases from final assembly on the line, we can further analyse the consequences of structurally conservative solutions and the internal relevance of the different dimensions in the design of group work. To anticipate an important finding: in the assembly line areas we observed that group work concepts were much more restrictive on every dimension. This is rooted in the much more confined tasks and job classifications in assembly. Yet in the dimension of self-organisation we did find an example of enhanced group work even on the assembly line.

The group work projects M1 and M2 are typical areas of assembly line work in the final assembly of the Mercedes-Benz main plant (with over 30,000 employees). This plant, too, lacks an active steering committee that would support the diverse actors involved, although the issue of group work is discussed more widely in the entire plant (i.e. from plant manager to works council, etc.) and more actively than in plant B (TS1). The implementation of group work is within the responsibility of individual production units, and the degree to which concepts have been realised is accordingly very disparate. As in plant B, there is no coherent, procedurally organised system of implementing group work. The concrete shape and practice of introduction were left to the local managers.

Line assembly with enhanced self-organisation (case M1)

The M1 case includes assembly line operations and related sub-assemblies in the marriage point area where body and drive train are merged (Table 3). The introduction process was characterised by the experience management had already made with a pilot group work project in a nearby section that was seen as a positive model, and thus it was prepared for potential obstacles in introducing the group work. Even if the process of conception and implementing group work is not compatible with the exceptionally participatory procedure in the TM1 case and the job classifications in the group hardly changed except for job rotation, the M1 case is one in which the rearrangement of the environment for work and performance was discussed with the group, and solutions were reached jointly. The distribution of tasks within the group and the rotation plan were left for the group to administer. The group was – in contrast with the TM1 case – not monitored and tracked by a coach nor counselled in its development. Yet that was compensated for by foremen committing themselves to the group's concerns and by a shop steward (who was also one of the group speakers) advocating group development, a co-operative milieu and lively group discussions, drawing on experiences from other areas of group work. By a consistent training effort, all group members were enabled to accomplish the various tasks, by now resulting in a rather high degree of work flexibility and chances for mutual assistance.

The degree of self-organisation is lower than in the TM1 case, but still high when compared with traditional assembly line work or more conservative concepts of Taylorised group work. The group decides on work arrangements and job rotation, and it is given a lot of leeway by its foremen. For example, the group can regulate the line speed itself (although within tight limits) to cut down deviation in preceding or succeeding buffers.

Table 3 *Synoptical view of group work projects – final assembly.*

Case M1 (plant C)	Case M2 (plant C)
• Assembly line operations in the 'marriage point' area (merging of body and drive train)	• Assembly line operations in the interior trim area (roof panel, headlights, engine compartment wiring jobs)
• Short assembly cycles (2 to 5 minutes); little functional integration (quality control only)	• Short assembly cycles (2 to 12 minutes); little functional integration (quality control only)
• High flexibility in the use of work (full rotation)	• Moderate flexibility in the use of work (limited rotation)
• No group coaches, but assistance by supervisors and shop steward	• No coaching of project development
• Group speaker: elected, but special status because of additional responsibilities; extra wage compensation; perceived as 'speaker of the group'	• Group speaker: elected, but special status because of additional responsibilities; extra wage compensation; perceived as 'quasi-subforeman'
• Group meetings: 30 minutes per week	• Group meetings: 30 minutes per week
• Wages corresponding to scope of tasks performed	• Wages corresponding to highest rated task

Much like the two cases of automated production, there are elected group speakers in the M1 case. Yet they are much less integrated into the group's work process. Related responsibilities such as parts procurement, providing tools, rework or replacing colleagues, are within the responsibility of the group speaker alone. In the M1 case, they nevertheless act as co-ordinators, speakers and partner for the group – despite their special role. All groups in the final assembly area are given thirty minutes a week for group meetings – to that end, the line is stopped. In the M1 case, the groups use this time for an active co-ordination of activities, mutual information and solution of problems. When needed, this time is extended a little by using up a small succeeding buffer and break time.

In terms of production technology and in some aspects of work organisation, the M1 project remains in the area of structurally conservative solutions (high degree of coupling to short work cycles, little functional integration, accumulation of indirect responsibilities with the group speaker), yet the group organisation strongly points in the direction of the structurally innovative model. It is of particular importance that the group speakers' role perception, in addition to the co-ordination of managers, group speakers and the groups, is focused on strengthening the groups' self-organisation. In the evaluation by employees, the more restricted job design in the assembly line areas is evident (Table 4). But the more important finding is that in the M1 case the remaining organisational dimensions are modelled after the principle of self-organisation and thus lead to a significantly more positive assessment of group work (Table 5). It is particularly revealing that the level of positive evaluations in many dimensions reaches that of the TS1 case. Yet while in TS1 it was primarily the skill level of the job itself (task integration, job enrichment, upskilling), in the M1 case it was the aspects of self-organisation and empowerment of the groups (group speaker as moderator and speaker, self-organised group meetings for problem solving, and a new role perception of supervisors) that were realised.

"The group is being handed over responsibilities. That's why we don't rely on the foreman alone. In the old days, the foreman did it, now it's the group speaker or the whole group. Changes are now discussed in the group, like the distribution of work, for example. That forces you to be more active. The foreman doesn't interfere in the work process anymore. He says: You gotta know how to do it best. The numbers and quality must be O.K. I'm approaching the foreman more often now. Maybe it's a good thing he's been freed and can take better care of workers' problems. He's not part of the group, but he's somehow involved. He does take group interests seriously. If there is something coming down from the group, he'll stand up for it." (Worker, M1)

By comparing the two projects in assembly, it can be shown that even under very unfavourable conditions with regard to the socio-technical arrangements, positive effects can be achieved if management is willing to strengthen the groups' capacity for self-organisation. Except for the role of supervisors and the state of the groups' self-organisation, the two assembly projects hardly differ (Table 3).

Line assembly with limited self-organisation (case M2)

In the second assembly case (M2), the management concept, which at its core aims at self-organisation, failed to gain ground against

Table 4 *Evaluation of work: challenge in terms of skills?*

In per cent	TM1 n = 30	TS1 n = 29	M1 n = 29	M2 n = 58
Positive	64	58	28	15
Undecided	23	31	48	47
Negative	13	10	24	38

Table 5 *Changes brought about by group work.*

In per cent	TM1 n = 30	TS1 n = 29	M1 n = 29	M2 n = 58
(a) How interesting is the job?				
More	97	61	59	14
About the same	3	18	38	50
Less	0	21	3	36
(b) How autonomous are you in your work?				
More	80	48	61	28
About the same	13	38	36	69
Less	7	13	4	4
(c) How do you rate co-operation with colleagues?				
Better	90	48	62	26
About the same	7	45	21	49
Worse	3	7	17	25
(d) How much strain, stress, etc. are you experiencing?				
Less	12	7	21	2
About the same	28	21	24	14
More	60	73	55	84
(e) How do you rate your chances of coping with strain in the long term?				
Better	52	13	23	3
About the same	31	42	35	31
Worse	17	45	42	66
(f) How do you rate co-operation with the foreman?				
Better	47	17	41	16
About the same	47	59	52	67
Worse	6	24	7	18
(g) All in all, has the overall work situation changed through group work?				
Improved	73	48	49	17
Partly yes, partly no	10	28	28	35
Worsened	17	24	23	48

the existing Taylorist structures on the shopfloor. In practice, there has evolved a model which in many respects resembles the variant of Taylorised group work we characterised as structurally conservative. The case we studied belongs to the interior trim area and includes the assembly of headlights, roof panels, glove compartments and wiring (engine compartment, cockpit area). The conception and introduction process in this case were particularly unsystematic, and the lack of support by a coaching concept was – in contrast to M1 – not made up for by special experiences or involvement of managers or works council. In terms of the work process, the introduction of group work was basically limited to merge various tasks into a longer work cycle. In contrast with M1, job rotation is still very restricted: most of the group members can accomplish only a few jobs because of the lack of training opportunities. Accordingly, work flexibility and chances for mutual assistance among colleagues are low.

In the M2 case, the group work concept was largely fashioned without the involvement of the group members. Group work in this case has not even resulted in making the employees actors in organising arrangements on the shopfloor, as M1 did. Nor has there been a more intensified co-operation of the group and its related departments such as planning and industrial engineering. Employees were informed about upcoming changes, at best. The small scope in the reorganisation of shopfloor structures (decentralisation, functional integration) is typical of all forms of group work in assembly that we have studied so far – there is no difference between M1 and M2 in that respect. Yet in contrast to M1, there are no discernible changes in the way supervisors perceive their role or in the behaviour of local management and the foremen (Table 6).

In contrast with the cases of automated production (TM1 and TS1), the group speakers in the M2 case are also in a special position. Yet unlike those in the M1 project, they are not (yet) 'spokespersons' who represent the group externally and assume a moderating role internally. They are almost exclusively specialists with specific responsibilities such as rework, job assignment, or parts procurement.

While the group leaders are elected, the foremen view them as replacements of the old subforemen, hold them personally responsible for the group, and pressure them to accomplish management goals. On the other hand, individual group members burden the group speakers with responsibilities, as the latter receive an extra wage compensation. In contrast with the other projects, the group

Table 6   *Experiences with the foremen.*

In per cent	M1 n = 29	M2 n = 58
(a) Are they less of a superior than before?		
Yes	29	14
Partly so	46	32
No	25	54
(b) Do they make arrangements with the group?		
Yes	55	32
Partly so	35	44
No	10	24

speakers find themselves in an exceptional role, are burdened with additional tasks and accordingly resemble 'quasi-subforemen' (Table 7). The overall level of self-organisation and empowerment of the group in the M2 case are lower. In that, it is a good example of how dependent on prerequisites structural innovations on the shopfloor are within an environment still organised along Taylorist lines. The major importance of the group speakers' position notwithstanding, to merely have them elected without changing other environmental conditions for the groups (in terms of tasks, skills and hierarchy) will not suffice for the development of self-organised group work.

In stark contrast with the M2 case, the group speakers in the M1 project see themselves as representatives and backers of the group: they co-ordinate, involve colleagues in decision-making and are accepted in this role by management. In project M2, on the contrary, colleagues – and also some group leaders themselves – distrust the latters' role and often explicitly reject it.

"In many departments, these guys are called foremen-speaker, not group-speaker. We're all aware high output has priority here, yet in some instances, the group speaker should be showing more staunchness against management. But most of them are afraid to. [. . .] We're doing group work here now, that's a totally new thing. And he is the old subforeman, he's also substituting for the foreman – that just doesn't make sense. Then he's standing around and yells at people when he's supposed to join in with us. But he's trying to look good in front of the foreman rather than in front of the group." (Worker, M2)

Table 7   *Experiences with the group speakers.*

In per cent	M1 n = 29	M2 n = 58
(a) Are they different from the old subforemen?		
Yes	44	28
Partly so	30	41
No	26	31
(b) Do they make arrangements with the group?		
Yes	74	53
Partly so	26	33
No	0	14

In the evaluation of work, it shows negatively when the nature of group work is strongly characterised by enduring Taylorist structures (Table 5). The extent of criticism and its explanation in this case somewhat resemble the reactions of employees as documented in research on the transplants in North America (Babson, 1993; Robertson *et al.*, 1993).

Concluding remarks

(1) With its version of group work, Mercedes-Benz AG seeks to develop a concept of its own that takes into account and picks up from its traditions and competitive conditions, and which departs from the Japanese-inspired team concepts in the North American transplants in several respects. It centres around the creation of skilled job designs and an extension of self-organisation on the shopfloor oriented to socio-technical principles. This concept, specified in a collective bargaining agreement at company level, does not however translate into the various plants along the same lines.

(2) Because of the more or less favourable external conditions (manual work vs. automated production) in the various areas of production and plants, and major differences in the social process of the introduction of group work, there is a large array of solutions in its implementation which depart from existing Taylorist structures more or less strongly. The structurally innovative concept of self-organised group work is more often

implemented in high-tech than in manual work areas. The process varies between departments and plants as a result of the more or less professionally administered processes of implementation. Attempts to modify social relations and structures at the point of production show mixed results.

(3) Between the two poles of group work we defined, significant differences with regard to the effect on the work situations of employees and the evaluation of group work can be discerned. We found particularly positive effects where several aspects of group work had been combined: (a) task-integrated, cross-functional work systems; (b) self-organising work groups and empowerment of shopfloor workers; (c) a redefinition of the tasks and roles of supervisors and first-level management in the direction of coaching; (d) a process of decentralisation and less hierarchy in the organisational structure; and (e) an integrative process of implementation which relies on direct participation of the work groups and the works council (Gerst *et al.*, 1994).

(4) With regard to production technology, the areas of manual work at Mercedes-Benz AG remain characterised largely by assembly line structures and a more perfect production flow. Uddevalla is not a model for Mercedes-Benz either. The picture is different with regard to the social structures: our findings show that a consistent implementation of self-organisation has positive effects even under otherwise unchanged work structures. These effects are more constrained however, and it might be that they are particularly unstable, as Berggren's research on Volvo suggests (Berggren, 1991). The case of Mercedes-Benz shows that, even under restrictive technical conditions such as line production, it is possible to transform Taylorist forms of work into self-organised group work characterised by greater participation, upgraded jobs in terms of skills, and improved workplace conditions in general. Yet this is a difficult process of transformation for social relations and social structures in which solutions have to be found for the many legacies of Taylorist work organisation. Those areas in which the foremen were unwilling to accept the loss of conceptional responsibilities, decision-making competencies and control over their realm have posed some problems. The foremen have tried to preserve old work structures by tolerating little in terms of self-organisation, by making the group speaker a substitute for the old subforeman or

by ignoring the speaker of the group altogether. This behaviour cannot be explained by the personal characteristics of the foremen alone however, since these areas were mostly distinguished by management's inability to show an acceptable and plausible alternative to their previous role in the production process. A further hurdle in the implementation of group work was those employees in special functions, such as the former subforemen or systems commanders in the TS 1 case. Management often lacked the willingness and sometimes the vision to either transfer these employees into other areas or to integrate them into the groups as equally entitled members. Where subforemen or systems commanders remained in the groups with their job design almost unchanged, conflicts and frictions over competencies often arose.

(5) Taken together, the processes of reorganisation that we investigated show that the implementation of the non-Taylorist concept of group work is a procedure of reforming social structures on the shopfloor, which is highly dependent on a set of premises. Without management policies on various hierarchical levels consistently aimed at that goal and without an active co-management by labour representatives (works council and unions), the critical mass for the necessary organisational change cannot be achieved. An efficiency analysis conducted by management paralleling our research concludes that significant productivity gains can be achieved with the concept of self-organised group work, but this does not mean that the direction of change is already clear. Because of the scope of necessary social change, social prerequisites and political pressure will be important for the process of reorganisation on the shopfloor. This is true not only for Mercedes-Benz. The future of group work in the German automobile industry is therefore still open.

End-notes

[1]   Elements of this concept usually include a diversified quality production, flexible use of re-skilled production labour, and co-operative modes of conflict regulation on the basis of powerful interest representation.

[2]   In the 1970s, union and works council scepticism was rooted in the fear that there would be an intensification of work without proper wage compensation, and that elected group speakers would be taken over by management and thus become a counteracting force to the existing system of employee representation.

[3]   See Turner (1991) for a good historical account of IG Metall's concept of the group work. Muster (1990) considers only the concept promoted by the unions as 'group work' and refers to the work designs promoted by parts of management which in particular take the North American transplants as a model of 'team work'.

[4]   Resources for self-organisation can be: discretionary leeway, opportunities for skill-enhancement, time for group meetings and co-ordination processes, in addition to institutional regulations such as the election of group speakers or the promotion of democratic group processes.

[5]   By foremen, we refer to *Meisters*. In the industrial system of Germany, *Meisters* are first-level supervisors typically with a blue-collar background, acting as a link between middle management and the workforce.

[6]   A *Betriebsvereinbarung* is a collective bargaining agreement between management and the works council on plant or company level that is provided for under German labour law regulations.

[7]   In one of the plants we investigated, group speakers categorically do not receive any additional financial compensation. The idea behind this practice is to emphasise the responsiblity of the group in its entirety and the denial of an elevated role for the group speaker. This policy is supported collectively by all actors involved: management, works council and the group speakers themselves.

References

Adler P.S. (1992) The 'learning bureaucracy': New United Motor Manufacturing, Inc. In Staw B.M. and Cummings L.L. (eds.), *Research in Organizational Behavior*. Greenwich CT: JAI Press.

Babson S. (1993) *Lean oder Mean? Die schlanke Produktion bei Mazda*. In Lüthje B. and Scherrer C. (eds.), *Jenseits des Sozialpakts*. Münster: Verlag westfälisches Dampfboot.

Berggren C. (1991) *Von Ford zu Volvo: Automobilherstellung in Schweden*. Berlin: Springer.

Dertouzos M.L., Lester R.K. and Solow R.M. (1989) *Made in America – Regaining the Productive Edge*. Cambridge MA.: MIT Press.

Enderle P. (1994) Das Opel-Produktionssystem im Werk Eisenach. In *Lean Production II. Erfahrungen und Erfolge in der M + E-Industrie. Schriftenreihe des Institus für angewandte Arbeitswissenschaft*, Band 29. Köln: Wirtschaftsverlag Bachem.

Gerst D., Hardwig T., Kuhlmann M. and Schumann M. (1994) Gruppenarbeit in der betrieblichen Erprobung – ein 'Modell' kristallisiert sich heraus. In *Angewandte Arbeitswissenschaften*, Heft 142.

Hans-Böckler-Stiftung/IG Metall (eds.) (1992) *Lean Production. Kern einer neuen Unternehmenskultur und einer innovativen und sozialen Arbeitsorganisation?* Baden-Baden: Nomos Verlagsgesellschaft.

Jennen O. and Vorberg U. (1994) Gruppe oder Team? Neue Formen der Arbeitsorganisation am Beispiel Opel. In *Sozialismus*, Heft 4.

Jürgens U., Malsch T. and Dohse K. (1989) *Moderne Zeiten in der Automobilfabrik. Strategien der Produktionsmodernisierung im Länder- und Konzernvergleich*. Berlin: Springer.

Kern H. and Schumann M. (1984) *Das Ende der Arbeitsteilung? Rationalisierung in der industriellen Produktion*. München: Beck-Verlag.

Minssen H., Howaldt J. and Kopp R. (1991) Gruppenarbeit in der Automobilindustrie – Das Beispiel Opel Bochum. In *WSI-Mitteilungen*, Heft 7.

Muster M. (1990) Team oder Gruppe? – Zum Stand der Sprachverwirrung über die 'Gruppenarbeit'. In Muster M. and Richter U. (eds.), *Mit Vollgas in den Stau*. Hamburg: VSA-Verlag.

Parker M. and Slaughter J. (1988) *Choosing Sides. Unions and the Team Concept*. Boston MA: South End Press.

Robertson D., Rinehart J., Huxley C., Wareham J., Rosenfeld H., McGough A. and Benedict S. (1993) *The CAMI-Report: Lean Production in a Unionized Auto Plant*. Ontario: CAW Research Dept.

Roth S. and Kohl H. (eds.) (1988) *Perspektive: Gruppenarbeit*. Köln: Bund Verlag.

Schumann M., Baethge-Kinsky V., Kuhlmann M., Kurz C. and Neumann U. (1994) *Trendreport Rationalisierung: Automobilindustrie, Werkzeugmaschinenbau, Chemische Industrie*. Berlin: Ed. Sigma.

Springer R. (1993) Neue Formen der Arbeitsorganisation – Ursachen, Ziele und aktueller Stand in der Mercedes-Benz AG. In *Angewandte Arbeitswissenschaft*, Heft 137.

Streeck W. (1988) *Successful Adjustment to Turbulent Markets: The Automobile Industry*. FS I 88-1, Wissenschaftzentrum Berlin.

Tropitzsch H. (1994) Effizienzsteigerung durch mehr Partizipation – die neue Arbeitspolitik bei Mercedes-Benz zeigt Erfolge. In *Angewandte Arbeitswissenschaften*, Heft 142.

Turner L. (1991) *Democracy at Work*. Ithaca NY: Cornell University Press.

Womack J.P., Jones D.T. and Roos D. (1991) *Die zweite Revolution in der Autoindustrie*. Frankfurt/M.: Campus Verlag.

CHAPTER 17
Group Working at Volkswagen: An Issue for Negotiation between Trade Unions and Management

Anne Labit
(Translated by Teresa Hayter)

Translator's note: In the British motor industry the terms 'supervisor' and 'foreman' are used interchangeably. In this text the French word *maitrise* and the German *Meister* have been translated, variously, as 'supervision', 'supervisory staff' and 'supervisors'.

In order to examine the recent transformations of employee relations at Volkswagen, it seemed important for us to look at one of its essential dimensions: the development of group working. At VW, much more than elsewhere, group working is an issue for permanent negotiation, at all levels of the company, between members of management and representatives of the employees organised in the very powerful confederation of trade unions, IG Metall [1]. Two conceptions of group working confront one another at VW and, as the balance of power between the two partners evolves, these conceptions profoundly influence the concrete forms taken by work reorganisation projects in each factory.

We shall be concerned here with the case of the Hanover factory and in particular with its body plant, where we have had the opportunity to carry out our most intensive fieldwork. This case is exemplary, in the sense that it allows us to present two typical forms of organisation, one in production cells (*Fertigungszellen*), the other in work groups (*Arbeitsgruppen*). The first of these projects is promoted by management, the second by the trade union. After the initial definition of each of the two projects, we shall concentrate on the ways in which their implementation is negotiated by the two partners, as well as the evolution over time of these negotiations.

Since we wanted to gain an understanding both of the richness of each organisational project and of the direction in which it was developing over time, we chose a method of qualitative investigation over a long period. A first phase of exploratory research, concerning the Gruppenarbeit project promoted by the IG Metall trade union at the Hanover factory, was carried out in the first six months of 1992. A second phase, in the first three months of 1993, consisted of in-depth research in the body plant, and was concerned with all of the work reorganisation projects and in particular the role of supervision. During the years 1994 and 1995, we were able to carry out interviews to update the information collected earlier, with some selected interviewees, representatives both of the trade unions and of management, again at the Hanover factory [2].

Our discussion will be in three parts. The first emphasises the differences which separate the two main reorganisation projects experienced in the Hanover body plant, the project of Fertigungszellen (production cells) and the project of Gruppenarbeit (group working). In a second part, these differences are interpreted in the light of a re-examination of the conditions in which the two forms of organisation emerged and developed. The third part of the chapter suggests a widening of perspective, linking these two forms of work organisation to the two other dimensions of the employee relationship, as it has been defined by Jean-Pierre Durand in the Introduction to this book: the roles of supervision and the nature of employees' involvement (or commitment). At this stage – and thus on the basis of this Hanover case study – several hypotheses will be advanced on the nature of the employee relationship operating at Volkswagen. The future of this relationship and the questions it raises on the emergence of one, or several, new industrial model(s), will be considered in our conclusion.

Recent evolution of work organisation in the body plant

The VW factory at Hanover has recently become famous in Germany as a result of the particular difficulties which have been experienced there in applying the agreement known as 'the four-day week' (Thoemmes and Labit, 1995). This agreement, based on the principle of a reduction in working time, was met with great incomprehension by the employees, faced with a strong increase in the demand for the main product they make: the utility vehicle Fourth Generation Transporter (T4). Nevertheless the question of surplus labour, even though it is less crucial than at the company's other sites, remains also an issue at Hanover, which currently employs around 14,000 people.

The body plant at Hanover itself employs just under 2,000 people. Assembly of the T4 is highly automated (the figure of 90% is claimed by management). Only the final sector of body manufacture (the final finishing lines, including bolt-ons and metal finishing) is unaffected by this automation. From the organisational point of view, this final sector has however been the scene of important innovations. In 1991, part of the line was eliminated in order to make room for a 'box' form of organisation. This involves the assembly of small parts which are specific to the shells for particular vehicles for the first time in the production cycle. The cycle times in the 'boxes' can vary from 6 minutes to 2 hours (Post Office vehicles or ambulances, for example).

Like many other body plants, that of the Hanover factory has gone through several stages of evolution. At the end of the 1980s this traditional sector of the production process, which is highly dependent on the factory's management and other services, acquired the status of autonomous 'cost-centre', responsible for its revenues as well as its expenditures. New functions were allocated to it, in particular management of the important sector of machines maintenance. Other services were also decentralised and then integrated into the body plant: quality management, part of the engineering services, etc. In parallel, a continuous process of eliminating hiercharchical levels began: first that of Hauptabteilungsleiter (senior department head) at the end of the 1980s, then Vize-Meister (first level of supervision) in 1990, then Gruppenführer (group leaders, equivalent to setters) in 1991, then Unterabteilungsleiter (deputy department head) in 1993 [3].

Among these changes, the development of collective work practices has some of the most momentous consequences. This heading, however, covers several types of projects for the 'modernisation' of work organisation. An initial distinction must be made between those which are added on to the existing organisation of work without changing its basic structures, and those which fundamentally alter these structures.

The first category includes projects which are inspired by 'participatory management' techniques, such as the practices of Kaizen or quality circles. At Volkswagen, among these concepts the one which is currently most prominent is KVP (Kontinuierlicher-Verbesserungs-Prozess, or Continuous Improvement Process). Within this framework, time is regularly set aside for workers' meetings, overseen by supervisory or technical staff, which aim to resolve the production problems raised by the workers, who are in turn expected to keep a kind of permanent watch over their workplace. Other practices of the same nature are grafted on to KVP at the body plant at Hanover, such as that of Qualitäts-Regel-Kreis (Quality Rules Circle).

The principles on which these concepts are based are, on the one hand, the analysis and monitoring of activity with the help of various indicators and, on the other, the joint resolution of problems thanks to clearly delineated methodologies [4]. The activities which are based on these concepts are added to the daily tasks carried out by the workers and are linked to the holding of a production job. Depending on the particular circumstances, they take up varying amounts of time. It is certainly the case that not all of the factory's sections devote equivalent amounts of time to these activities, which they are all nevertheless officially bound to undertake. The degree of impetus provided by middle management is, in this case, the determining factor.

The other two reorganisation projects, which are of more interest to us here, are designed to bring about a fundamental change in the traditional structures of workers' activity. It is only in respect of these that it is really possible to speak of group working. For the sectors or parts of them which are not affected by one or other of these projects, it seems preferable to continue to speak of team working in the Fordist sense used by Jean-Pierre Durand in the Introduction to this book, even if these areas experience the participatory management practices described above.

It should first be noted that group working in the Hanover body plant is only of relative importance, considering that no more than 450 people, or a quarter of the total numbers employed in production in the body plant, work in one or other of the projects. Among these, around 200 are allocated to 16 production cells (Fertigungs-zellen), while around 250 are in 24 work groups (Arbeitsgruppen). This means that on average a production cell or a work group contains about ten people. Production cells and work groups however differ in a large number of ways.

The production cells are established in the most automated sectors of the body plant. Their aim is to enable the machines to be run continuously. To achieve this there is a complete range of skills within a cell, including generally one section leader (Anlagenführer), two skilled workers (Facharbeiter) of different specialisations (mechanical and electrical) and six or seven workers with more limited skills relating only to production (Mitarbeiter). It is certainly true that there is specialisation of each person within the cell (machine functioning, maintenance, loading, etc.), but rotation between jobs appears to be frequent; in particular there is no system of reserve workers to cover any absences of the cell's members. Thus the employees working in a production cell are expected to organise themselves in matters of holidays and to train themselves as far as possible to be multi-skilled. No member of the cell plays the role of external spokesperson. According to all the managers interviewed, the system of cells has now proved its effectiveness. The goal which had been set for them, the successful management of 80% of cases of equipment breakdowns, has been achieved almost everywhere.

The work groups, on the other hand, are established in the manual sectors of the body plant, in particular in the 'boxes' of final finishing described above. Their goal is an improvement in production quality and in the productivity of work (measured here in the traditional manner, that is to say in terms of the number of cars produced in a certain time period). A group includes workers of equivalent status (Mitarbeiter), but whose skills obviously vary. A principle of rotation between jobs, left to the initiative of the group, is expected eventually to bring about an increase in the skills of all members of the group. The group elects a spokesperson, responsible for relations with management (Gruppensprecher), and it is expected to hold regular group meetings (Gruppengesprächer) in order to decide on its organisation and to resolve the various problems that might arise.

At the time when I undertook my research, the whole of the body plant staff – from supervisors to the department head – expressed doubts on the efficacy of the Gruppenarbeit form of organisation and said that they much preferred that of the Fertigungszellen. Beyond these projects' ability to fulfil the objectives which were set for them, it is important to take into account the conditions in which the two forms of organisation emerged and developed. This means considering them as political objects, that is as tools in the strategies of each of the two partners concerned – on the one hand, the majority IG Metall union, which is very much involved in work reorganisation, and on the other hand, management.

Production cells versus work groups?

From its origins, and up to now, the concept of Gruppenarbeit has been and remains an instrument of IG Metall, designed to promote the re-skilling of work and the strengthening of workers' autonomy. Although the development of the concept at the level of the company as a whole was only envisaged at VW at the beginning of the 1990s, it should be remembered that the first experimental project of this type of organisation dates from 1975. In the framework of the government programme 'humanisation of work' (Humanisierung der Arbeit), a work group strongly inspired by Swedish experiences of semi-autonomous groups functioned for two years in the engine factory at Salzgitter.

Subsequently, in the framework of the growing automatisation of the 1980s, this same Salzgitter factory, and then the factory at Kassel, became the sites of experiments in work groups in newly automated sectors (Buhmann and Mihr, 1988). These experiences are interesting to consider today for what they reveal of the conceptions of IG Metall in the matter of workers' jobs around automated equipment. The concern of IG Metall at the time was to avoid the risk of a polarisation of skills between a highly qualified elite, managing the new systems, and a reserve of unqualified labour, servicing the sytems, and likely to disappear. IG Metall's solution, which could only partly be put into practice, was based on the setting up of work groups which were to take charge of all of the tasks necessary for the running of the machines through the internal rotation of its members, who would all be qualified to the level of section leader(Anlagenführer).

From the mid-1980s, under the influence of the ideas coming from Japan in particular, management began to become seriously interested in the concept of work groups, as a means of increasing productivity. It was then necessary for IG Metall to defend its own conception of work groups, based on earlier thinking than that of management and around the idea of the democratisation of work, in an economic context that was more and more difficult.

The Fertigungszellen project, now functioning at Hanover, can clearly be considered to be the result of management interest in new organisational ideas. Its goal is undoubtedly an increase in productivity which depends, in the automated sector, on an increase in the availability of the machines. IG Metall, through the medium of its representatives on the Betriebsrat (plant council), was admittedly present at all the stages of the slow process which led to the development of Fertigungszellen in the body plant. The project was considered for the first time in 1986, then pursued from 1988 through a pilot phase which lasted for more than two years, and led finally in 1991 to the setting up on a genuinely large scale of the production cells. The fact that negotiations did take place during the lengthy process of their establishment cannot, however, disguise the reality that the production cells are above all a tool of management, rather than of IG Metall. The hierarchical structure of skills within the cell, described in the first part of this chapter, is far from being the egalitarian structure, in which everybody would be a section leader, of which IG Metall dreamt in the mid-1980s.

The same gap between the aspirations of the trade union and the reality of the facts can be observed in the absence of any increase in the workers' ability to carry out interventions, including maintenance, on the automated systems. Far from being reversed, the tendency for the analysis of breakdowns to become the responsibility of increasingly skilled personnel outside the cell has been reinforced. The cell is now only responsible for assuring the smooth functioning of the machinery in normal conditions and for dealing with the simplest breakdowns. 'Optimisation teams' (Optimierungsteam) made up of technicians and responsible for the reliability of the machines, working as closely as possible to the shopfloor, have thus recently been created in the body plant.

The current Gruppenarbeit project therefore now remains the only real tool of IG Metall in the sphere of work reorganisation. This project is as much the inheritor of past experiences as it is the result of adaptation to new constraints. It is the inheritor of past experiences in the sense that, although it has evolved, it reproduces the essential characteristics hoped for by its first promoters: equality of status and wages within the group, including for the spokesperson; the enrichment and enlargement of tasks; the possibility of regular meetings; the fact that it is run by a joint management–trade union committee; etc. [5]. But the current project is also the result of new constraints, in the sense that the recent difficulties experienced by the Volkswagen company have obliged the union to accept adjustments to the initial concept, and also to give up hope of establishing it on the large scale originally foreseen.

In 1990 a framework agreement was signed between VW management and the general company council (Gesamtbetriebsrat) on the implementation of pilot projects entitled Gruppenarbeit in different factories, of which Hanover was one. This agreement, which was merely a minimum basis of understanding and which already revealed several areas of disagreement on the content of the project between management and the trade union, was in the end not followed by any other agreement at this general level. In the factories, on the other hand, the pilot phases took place and were followed in many cases by extensions of the project. The public revelations on the financial difficulties of the company and its takeover by a new leadership team (*Der Spiegel*, 1993) seem to have marked a turning point in the development of the Gruppenarbeit project, even though it had not officially been affected by the change of leadership. The case of Hanover will again serve as an example.

The first work groups started to function in the framework of a pilot phase in the paint department in the middle of 1991, after six months of preparation. They were then extended to other departments, including the body plant in the first six months of 1992, on a scale which was however limited in each case. Thus in the body plant only the finishing 'boxes' were affected. The planned extension to the rest of the final finishing lines in the end did not take place. In particular, the transformation of the production cells into work groups, envisaged at one time, has now become a very unlikely prospect.

In other departments, the same stagnation of the project compared with the original plans can be observed. No extension took place in the paint shop. The project remained a dead letter in assembly. The cable assembly sector, where the project was most actively pursued and above all conformed most with the trade union's ideas, is a rather peculiar sector, since it was expected to disappear as a result of the policy of sub-contracting. In this case the union was able to base its action on the strong motivation of the female employees, resolved to try and save their jobs, and the relative freedom of action conceded by the factory management.

By the end of 1995 it was clear that the IG Metall union had given up the attempt to negotiate an overall agreement with VW management to generalise the experiments conducted under the heading of Gruppenarbeit. This concept, unlike for example the managerial concept of KVP which we mentioned earlier, has thus not achieved similar recognition, either within or outside the company. But the concept of Gruppenarbeit continues to stimulate interest in trade union and research environments, and is often presented as the only credible alternative to the concept of lean production. Above all, in a number of companies and especially at VW it continues to produce concrete, though limited, results. New projects are currently appearing, notably at Hanover, where the whole of the production of a secondary product at the factory (the second generation LT) is supposed to be organised on the principles of Gruppenarbeit. If this occurs, a further 1,400 wage-earners at the factory will be affected by the reorganisation.

Management and the trade union both, curiously, advance the same argument against the possibility that the Gruppenarbeit concept can in practice be wholly effective: the inability of employees to change their old working habits. Management and trade unionists therefore agree on the idea that they will implement new projects only when a model is changed or renewed (this is the case with the LT2 at Hanover). In addition to this general, and rather dubious, argument against group working, it is clear that the establishment of new forms of organisation, whether cells or groups, gives rise to numerous conflicts between management and employees' representatives on several crucial points. These have a considerable effect on the other two aspects of employee relations defined by Jean-Pierre Durand: the roles of supervision and the nature of employees' involvement. The analysis of these points of conflict is of more interest to us than the supposed 'resistance to change' of VW personnel. They seem to us particularly revealing of the ideas held by the two partners on the organisation of work and therefore of the state of employee relations in the company.

New roles of supervision and the nature of employee involvement

The two reorganisation projects described above give rise to numerous potential conflicts between management and employees. It is, first, interesting to note that the conflicts have been dealt with in very different ways in the two cases. In the case of the production cells, the impression is that management has definitely given itself the means of neutralising sources of conflict. In the second case, management seems to have demonstrated much less goodwill, and has indeed at times retreated behind the notion of the difficulties of setting up work groups in order to justify its decision not to extend them. This phenomenon of course accords with the fact that the Fertigungszellen are a tool of management, whereas the Gruppenarbeit project is above all a tool of IG Metall.

The main conflict between management and the trade union concerns the question of whether or not the work groups are to be allowed to hold meetings. In the view of IG Metall, only regular and official meetings, during working time, can genuinely allow the groups to organise themselves, to settle their problems and conflicts internally, and thus to be fully effective in the tasks that are assigned to them. For management, these IG Metall requirements appear too expensive in terms of productivity. It has been impossible to reach agreement between the two partners at the overall company level, or even at factory level. At Hanover the situation therefore varies from one section to another. In the body plant, in the finishing boxes where work groups function, it has been possible to allocate time for meetings at times when the flow is interrupted (as a result of breakdowns in the automated sections upstream). The fact that this type of interruption does not occur on the other finishing lines is now an argument used by management to avoid the extension of groups in this section. As far as the other production sections at Hanover are concerned, the same management attitude is discernible. In the paint shop, since no 'natural' interruption of production allows the holding of meetings, the trade union obtained an agreement on officially planned, deliberate interruptions, which was subsequently challenged by management. In the cable assembly sector, since the technical situation allows meetings to be held without deliberate interruptions of the production process, meetings have regularly taken place.

The organisational tool of Fertigungszellen, which implies no constraint in terms of meetings, for this reason seems more appropriate to management. In the same way, KVP is in this respect very much a managerial tool. The meetings take place as needs arise, without making calls on production time, and without involving the whole of a production group (but only the few members competent on the subject). Beyond the 'technical' arguments used by one or other of the parties on the issue of workers' meetings, it is clear that two visions of what ought to constitute the modernisation of the work process are in this case opposed to each other. For IG Metall, the aim is not merely to increase the productivity of work, through mobilising the resources of employees' knowledge, 'tricks' or ideas which were previously not exploited, but very much to allow them to reappropriate their own autonomy in organising and taking decisions, of which the Taylorian division of labour had dispossesed them.

The second big source of conflict between management and the union, in relation to the work groups, concerns the method of choosing and the status of their leaders. This conflict has its roots, again, in two very distinct visions of what the nature of hierarchical organisation and employees' involvement should be. In the opinion of IG Metall, the 'leader' should be a spokesperson appointed by peers, who should not have a higher position in the hierarchy or receive a higher wage. On the contrary, management, arguing that it is more and more difficult to find employees who wish to be spokespeople, proposes paying a supplementary wage and giving hierarchical prerogatives, which would come back to reconstituting the post of Gruppenführer.

In the mind of trade unionists, the move from the title Gruppenführer (group leader) to that of Gruppensprecher (group spokesperson) is more than a mere question of vocabulary. The real point of the change is to break the old hierarchical structure, so as to promote a collective taking over of responsibilities by the workforce. To avoid this danger, management has maintained the substance of the manager's role within the group, through technical advisers (Fachberater), established as what was said to be a temporary measure in the sections which were reorganised along the principles of Gruppenarbeit, and responsible for the technical monitoring of the groups. At first intended to permit the redeployment of the Gruppenführer, these jobs are now being given to young skilled workers likely to achieve promotion within supervision, and they seem to be far from disappearing.

Analysis of the new role of supervision in the framework of reorganised work, based on the group principle, also makes it possible to evaluate precisely the differences of opinion between management and the union. According to IG Metall, supervisors should accept the loss of part of their traditional power over workers and confine themselves to a role of co-ordination between the groups. Management's position, at various levels, is opposed to such diminution in the powers of supervisors. On the one hand, shopfloor management has shown itself very tolerant towards the supervisors (Meister) who have continued to play a directive role. And, in addition, a recent project for reorganising the role of supervisors in production turns a future Meister into a Produktionsstätten-Manager (PSM), that is a manager of a unit of production. By thus increasing the responsibilities of the Meister for workers' productive performance, management in effect authorises the former to set limits on the transfer of its traditional tasks (administration, supervision) to the group in the framework of the Gruppenarbeit project.

It should be emphasised that in terms of qualifications, the PSM project implies a profound change in those required of the supervisors. From now on recruitment to the post of Meister will require prior possession of the diploma awarded by the chambers of commerce and industry (up to now only around 40% of the Meister at VW hold this diploma); this basic qualification will, in addition, be constantly re-evaluated and reinforced during the employee's career. This is far from the dream nurtured by certain IG Metall leaders of a supervisory staff elected by the workers, as the group spokesperson now is.

Finally, the issue of employee involvement, or commitment, itself merits much further discussion. This issue can be examined through a consideration of the three main aspects of working conditions for which employees' involvement (now considered by company executives so necessary for productive efficiency) can be exchanged: wages, the possibilities for gaining skills and promotion within the company, and job security.

As far as wages are concerned, certain parts of management continue to see this as the one real tool for motivating workers. They therefore propose linking part of the wage payment to individual performance within the group. But, in contrast, wage equality within the group remains for IG Metall an inviolable principle. On the other hand, the possibility of increasing skill levels and autonomy at work is, according to the union, the essential element against which productivity efforts agreed to by production personnel can be exchanged. This possibility is strongly present in the concept of Gruppenarbeit, through job rotation within the group, development of continuous training and self-organisation, and enrichment of production tasks (quality monitoring, first levels of maintenance, etc.).

As for job security, it has been recognised by VW senior management as essential for obtaining the willing commitment of employees to their work. The December 1993 agreement on a reduction in working time for all employees, which protected 30,000 jobs (the agreement known as the '4-day week'), therefore put an end to a period of severe uncertainty in the company. On the occasion of the signing of this agreement, the KVP programme was reinforced (it is now referred to as 'KVP to the power of 2'). According to Peter Hartz, labour director and promoter of the 4-day week, nothing should now prevent the workers from devoting themselves to the search for productivity gains, since they are from now on assured of keeping their jobs (Hartz, 1994). But the validity of this thesis is nevertheless questionable, considering the limited duration of the agreement – until the end of 1996 – even though it was re-newed in September 1995 for a further two-year period. However the VW solution did undeniably demonstrate the will of the com-pany's senior management to find original solutions to the crisis of productive over-capacity which it is going through.

The implementation of the Fertigungszellen project also demon-strates the importance of these matters of employee involvement from the point of view of maintenance staff. The potential con-flicts in this area were, in this case, dealt with from the outset by the body plant management. The main source of conflict arose from the transfer of maintenance staff into production. The fears of skilled workers (Facharbeiter) employed in maintenance, faced with inte-gration into a cell under the authority of a production supervisor, were classic: loss of status or advantages linked to belonging to the maintenance sector, fear of loss of technical skills, and technical illegitimacy of their new position in the hierarchy. These problems, while they were not totally resolved, were largely attenuated thanks to a certain number of measures. The Facharbeiter selected to join the cells were among the youngest in age and they had the least seniority in the maintenance sector. They were able to keep their status in spite of the transfer. Career possibilities were opened for them within production.

The observation of a particular case – that of the development in the Hanover site's body plant of two types of organisation, both of course connected with the notion of group working, but one of them promoted by the trade union and the other by management – has enabled us to appreciate the state of employee relations at Volkswagen in these middle years of the 1990s. We shall attempt in conclusion to indicate the ways in which the current debates around work organisation, the roles of supervision and questions of employee involvement are part of a more general evolution. Do the current transformations of employee relations at Volkswagen represent a break with previous forms of evolution, or are they an extension of them? Is there permanence or continuity at Volkswagen? Is it a question of adjustments to the Fordist employee relationship, or a new type of relationship?

Permanence and transformation in employee relations at Volkswagen

Because of the very specific ways in which decisions are made within the Volkswagen company, the company's development over time provides proof of the great stability of the initial industrial model (Jürgens, 1995 [6]). What characterises above all the Volkswagen company is undoubtedly the permanent state of negotiation between the various partners concerned, at all levels and in numerous areas. How, in this case, can one speak of rupture? Is rupture even possible? Jürgens prefers to speak of periods of uncertainty or internal struggles, and even of crises, which, at least until now, the company has always in the end succeeded in overcoming.

As far as employee relations are concerned (the specific element of the industrial model which interests us here), the evolutions which are currently taking place should be seen as part of a continuity, rather than rupture. Here again, negotiations between the different parties are permanent, preventing over-sudden changes of direction which could much more easily have taken place in the framework of a system in which decision-making was unilateral. The imbalance of forces at VW has never been such that one of the partners could wholly impose its strategy on the other.

In addition, we have up to now placed too much emphasis on the homogeneity of the strategies of the two partners: IG Metall and management. But within each 'camp' numerous disagreements should in fact be noted:

- on the side of the employees' representatives, between the higher levels of the trade union, giving thought to new conceptions of work, and the members of factory councils, confronted with the realities of day-to-day negotiations;
- on the side of the company's representatives, differences between central management and local management.

This first strategic differentiation, present within both the union and the management camps depending on the positions held within the hierarchy, should be supplemented by others, including for example those derived from location in different factories or different sectors of activity. According to a trade unionist responsible for the development of the Gruppenarbeit concept, what most determines different attitudes towards the new organisations is certainly not only membership of the trade union or management. Within IG Metall there are opponents of the Gruppenarbeit concept, who see in the increase in workers' autonomy which it implies a risk for their own prerogatives; and within management there are some who actively support this type of concept.

The analysis which we have presented here, though simplistic, has nevertheless the merit of clarifying some of the issues at stake: on the one hand a genuine increase in the autonomy of workers' jobs, essentially supported by IG Metall, and on the other an increase in their productivity, desired by management. Whatever the trade union leadership may say, the current crisis being experienced by the company, which has had a great deal of publicity, has undoubtedly given management a greater ability to win acceptance for its point of view. It has above all led IG Metall to revise its own conception of group working and to take into account the imperative of productivity.

For all of these reasons, we shall conclude by saying that today it is management's conception of group working, rather than that of the trade union, that is in the ascendant at VW. It is difficult to determine whether the latter, supposing it had been applied to the letter, would necessarily have led to a complete break with Fordist methods of work organisation. Some of the characteristics of group working as proposed by IG Metall, which we have referred to here, could have implied this possibility. A less doubtful proposition is that management's conception of group working, at least as far as can be seen from the case study carried out at Hanover, has more limited ambitions from this point of view. The concepts of Fertigungszellen (production cells) or indeed of KVP (continous improvement process) presented here, by revealing their relationship with the Japanese concepts of TPM (total productive maintenance) or Kaizen, also provide clear evidence of their objectives: to increase the availability of machines and the flexibility of labour, and to promote among workers an attitude of avoiding waste and taking responsibility for quality. While the achievement of these objectives certainly necessitates the correction of some of the most perverse effects of Taylorian organisation, nothing indicates that its foundations themselves must accordingly be called into question.

Appendix: Hanover factory organisational chart.

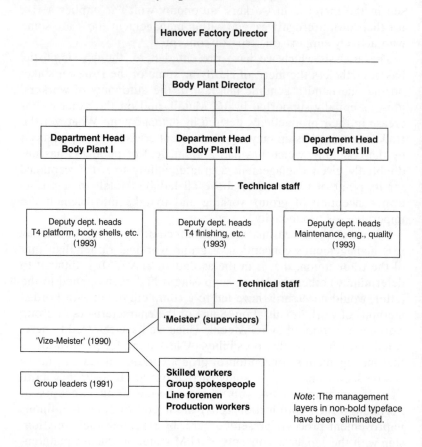

Note: The management layers in non-bold typeface have been eliminated.

End-notes

[1] 96% of VW employees belong to the IG Metall trade union, which thus holds a virtual monopoly of all of the seats on the plant council in each factory (Betriebsrat) as well as on the general company council (Gesamtbetriebsrat).

[2]   This research as a whole was carried out in the framework of a doc-
toral thesis, whose subject is a Franco-German comparison of the
roles of supervision based on the case of the automobile industry.

[3]   See the Hanover body plant organisational chart in the Appendix to
this chapter.

[4]   The methodology includes in general the following five stages: the
choice and location of the problem, the search for causes and then
for solutions, implementation, the monitoring of results, and standardisation. At the various stages of this process, numerous tools
are used: 'brainstorming', graphics and Pareto diagrams, tree diagrams
of causes, etc.

[5]   See the 12-point description of the project by Turner (English version) (1991) or by Muster (German version) (1998).

[6]   On this topic we invite the reader to consult the GERPISA book,
covering the development of automobile companies, in which the earlier
version of the work of Jürgens which we cite here is brought up to
date: Jürgens U., The development of Volkswagen's industrial model,
1967–1995, in Freyssenet, M. *et al.* (eds.), *One Best Way?* Oxford
University Press, 1998.

References

Buhmann H. and Mihr K.H. (1988) Erfahrungen mit Gruppenarbeit bei
Volkswagen. In Roth S. and Kohl H. (eds.), *Perspektive: Gruppenarbeit.*
Cologne: Bund Verlag.

Der Spiegel (1993) VW: Man kann nur betten. No. 49.

Hartz P. (1994) *Jeder Arbeitsplatz hat ein Gesicht. Die Volkswagen Lösung.*
Frankfurt/M.: Campus Verlag.

Jürgens U. (1995) 'Volkswagen's Trajectory into the 1990s', paper prepared to the GERPISA International Workshop on 'Firm Trajectories',
Berlin, 2/4 March.

Muster M. (1998) Zum Stand der Gruppenarbeit in der Automobilindustrie
in der Bundesrepublik. In Roth S. and Kohl H. (eds.), *Perspektive
Gruppenarbeit*. Cologne: Bund Verlag.

Thoemmes J. and Labit A. (1995) La semaine de 4 jours chez Volkswagen:
un scènario original de sortie de crise? *Travail et Emploi*, No. 64, 3.

Turner L. (1991) *Democracy at Work*. Ithaca NY: Cornell University Press.

CONCLUSION
The Transformation of Employee Relations in the Automobile Industry?

Jean-Pierre Durand, Paul Stewart and
Juan José Castillo
(*Translated by Teresa Hayter*)

In the Introduction, Durand identified the general configuration of work organisation in the sector (Table 2 – 'The four canonical models of work organisation'). He then distinguished three corresponding ideal typical forms of employee relations (Fordist, Japanese-lean production, Kalmarian), arguing that they are models in the double sense of the terms. Firstly, their systemic coherence allows us to make sense of particular situations at a particular moment. Secondly, they can be copied, imitated and reproduced by various actors who see in them the answer or answers to their problems.

On the basis of Table 1 (The state of employee relations at different automobile manufacturers), whose purpose is to bring our collective research together, we have isolated eight items which seem to us to be decisive, and which enable us to construct three figures representing the three canonical models. There is of course no absolute value attached to the form or the surface area of Figures 1, 2 and 3 relating to the three models: in particular, we could have inverted the numerical values accorded to the situations, and have had a figure of the Fordist model with a very large surface, and figures of the Kalmarian and Japanese models with smaller surfaces. It was to increase the legibility of the figures representing situations which go beyond the Fordist employee relationship that we chose a small surface for Fordism and an expanded surface for the Kalmarian and Japanese models.

Table 1 presents the rankings on the eight items under consideration for the three canonical models and the workplaces that

Table 1 The state of employee relations at different automobile manufacturers

	Traditional Ford model	Japanese type ideal	Kalmarian model	Toyota-Tahara	Toyota-Kyusha	Nissan Kyusha	Ford Dearborn (1996 actual)	Ford Dearborn (agreement of Autumn 1995)	GM Brazil	NUMMI	NUMMI (protest areas)	Saturn (GM)	Peugeot-Sochaux	Citroën-Aulnay	Renault-Flins	Renault-FASA (engines)	Fiat Melfi	Vauxhall (GM) Ellesmere Port	Rover Swindon (stamping)	Opel-Antwerpen	Volvo-Ghent	VW Hanover (body shop)	Mercedes (engine parts)	Mercedes (assembly line – marriage point)	Mercedes (assembly line – trim area)	Saab-Trollhätten	Volvo-Torslanda
Degree of implementation of teamwork	0	10	10	10	10	10	0	10	8	10	10	10	0	0	8	9	10	9	9	10	10	2	8	8	8	8	8
Degree of polyvalency	1	10	8	8	7	7	1	3	3	10	7	7	4	0	4	5	5	8	6	9	4	8	8	7	2	6	6
Negotiated decisions with hierarchy	0	2	9	4	4	2	2	3	2	7	3	3	1	2	4	3	5	9	3	7	0	10	8	4	2	2	3
Autonomy and responsibility of foremen	2	4	5	4	4	4	3	2	3	5	5	4	2	3	4	2	5	4	5	7	4	3	5	5	5	5	5
Salaries according to objective appraisal	1	5	8	5	6	4	0	0	4	5	5	1	2	1	4	3	7	1	2	3	1	3	8	8	2	6	4
Individual involvement of operators	1	8	8	7	7	6	2	7	5	7	4	5	6	3	5	5	5	2	3	8	7	7	5	4	2	6	6
Union support for organisational changes	0	8	10	10	10	8	0	10	2	7	4	4	3	3	4	4	5	10	3	8	1	8	8	5	5	2	6
Elected leader	0	0	10	1	1	0	0	8	2	4	1	10	0	0	0	1	0	0	6	4	0	0	10	10	10	1	10

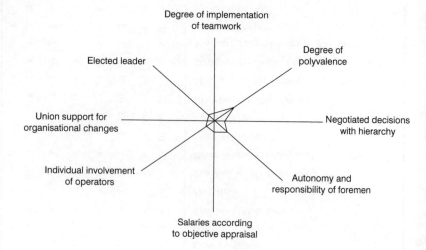

Figure 1   *Traditional Ford model.*

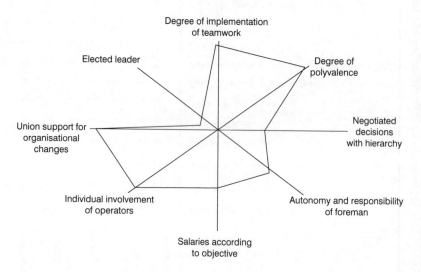

Figure 2   *Japanese type model.*

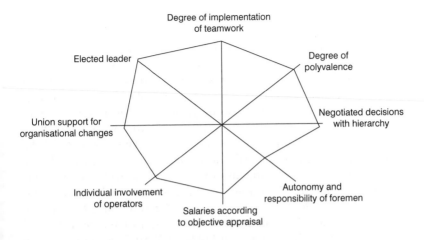

Figure 3 *Kalmarian model.*

were studied. As can be seen from the figures, the Fordist and Kalmarian models are imperfect models since the first is not a circle around the base point 0, while the second does not receive 10 for each item. In fact for us these canonical models cannot be 'perfect' models. The figures represent them as they have been conceptualised in the results of the different researchers. The same is true of the Japanese model which, in this case, is more of an ideal type constructed from the existing literature and research. Of course, the Japanese canonical model has therefore never existed actually because there are a multiplicity of plants representing the 'Japanese' way. The Japanese model, with its crescent shape, is a specific model which possesses its own internal coherence in a particular context (high educational level of the operators, company unions, meritocracy). It cannot therefore be considered a transitional or intermediate model between the Fordist model and the Kalmarian model.

The employee relations analysed in more than twenty workplaces which are the subject of the seventeen chapters in this book can be assembled in groups on the basis of the similarity of their essential characteristics. We shall group the various employee relations with similar characteristics into five types of employee relationships (see Figure 28).

Neo-Fordist type

The neo-Fordist type includes the Ford Dearborn factory (up to 1996–97), Peugeot–Sochaux and Volvo–Ghent, in spite of their diversity. As its name indicates, this type of employee relationship is the one that has been least influenced in reality by the principles of lean production or by those of group working (Kalmar). This however does not mean that these neo-Fordist workplaces have not experienced change for several decades. The demands of the market (lowering of costs and improvement in quality) have driven managements to new rationalisations of work which they have carried out within the traditions of the company and/or the social environment of the factory in question. The adherence to tradition derives for example from trade union refusal of the principles of lean production (the case of the UAW at Ford Dearborn) or from the fact that the grafting on of teamwork did not occur because too many other changes were taking place at the same time in the factory (Peugeot–Sochaux). Alternatively, excessively radical changes were not justified where productivity and quality levels were close to international standards (Volvo–Ghent and Citroën–Aulnay). At the same time, workplaces of the neo-Fordist type were preparing for some upheavals. The UAW has accepted teamwork, which will eventually effect its position, even though the form of teamwork, compared with the canonical model, will be considerably modified (for example, the election of the team leader and the retention of 65 classifications of assembly workers).

Among the several examples of the neo-Fordist type, Ford Dearborn, in its present state (see Figures 4 and 5 for projected transformations), is the most Fordist case [1], which is hardly surprising since the canonical model originated there. The most characteristic feature of the US system is the ability of local sections of the UAW to block the implementation of reforms which have been accepted by their national or international leadership, but which the workers consider to be contrary to their interests. Teamwork and more generally lean production are among the principles which are unacceptable to the trade union base. Thus, in spite of the impressions created by management speeches, a number of Ford factories have only recently begun to implement teamwork. This is even more the case for General Motors, whose older factories produce the great majority of the vehicles under its name and remain very traditional in their employee relations. In addition,

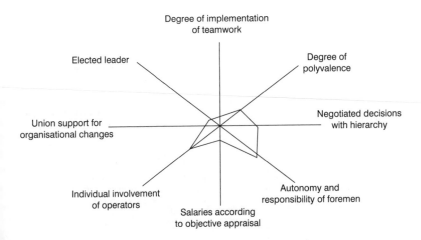

Figure 4   *Ford Dearborn (1996 actual).*

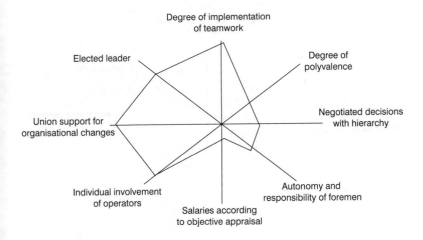

Figure 5   *Ford Dearborn (agreement of Autumn 1995).*

GM in what is known in the USA as 'whipsawing', sets its factories (and the UAW union sections) in competition with one another over the allocation of production capacity.

Peugeot–Sochaux (Figure 6) belongs to the neo-Fordist type, with paternalism as a dominant feature. This paternalism, even if it is

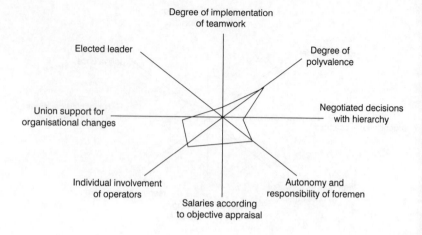

Figure 6   *Peugeot–Sochaux.*

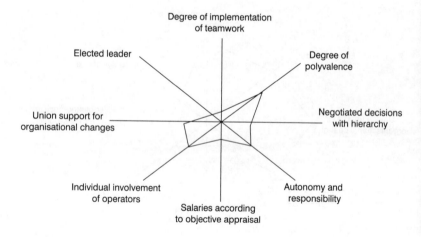

Figure 7   *Citroën–Aulnay.*

not what it used to be outside the factory and in domestic life, nevertheless retains some of its attributes, in the style of local management for example. The workers have a substantial degree of attachment to the company and involvement in their work, and a minority in the trade union's support management. The factory's other characteristics are fairly Fordist, with a high degree of poorly

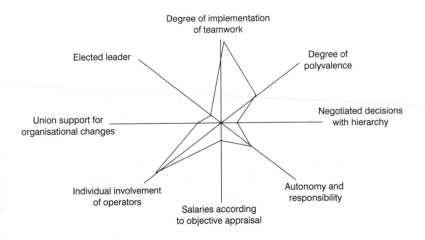

Figure 8 *Volvo–Ghent.*

rewarded multi-skilled activities. The whole system remains relatively effective from the point of view both of quality and productivity. At Citroën–Aulnay (Figure 7), which we added to enrich the neo-Fordist type, worker involvement is much less strong. This is partly because of the history of the factory, but especially because the Parisian labour market within which it is located offers many alternative employment opportunities; labour turnover is higher and workers do not commit themselves for life as at Sochaux. This lesser worker involvement is compensated for by a greater multi-skilling of the assembly workers.

In the factories described above, teamwork has not yet made an appearance. But at Volvo–Ghent (Figure 8), the whole factory is organised into teams with leaders appointed by management. This teamwork system, with tight supervision of the workers, both technical and disciplinary, compensates for the relatively low level of multi-skilling, trade union opposition and wages set according to the job, all of which are profoundly Fordist characteristics. The result is a factory whose performance is recognised as the best at Volvo and above the European average.

Mixture of neo-Fordism and lean production

This type characterises quite traditional Fordist factories which have borrowed the tool or technique of teamwork, but have not adopted its accompanying measures (meritocracy or great worker multi-skilling for example) or have encountered strong trade union resistance. This can lead to a lack of worker commitment, or at least to weak worker involvement. This is a type of employee relations which is no longer that of the Fordist model or even the neo-Fordist model described above, but which is not that of the Japanese canonical model either. It is a truncated Japanese model, making use of items which remain largely Fordist as Figures 9 to 13, representing employee relations at Renault–Flins, Renault–FASA, Fiat–Melfi, Saab–Trollhättan or GM Brazil show.

We propose to call this neo-Fordist type, which has taken up teamwork on a minimal basis, FFJ. This label underlines how much this type of employee relationship remains Fordist, with for example wages still paid according to the job (Renault–FASA or Renault–Flins), difficult negotiations with management (Saab–Trollhättan, Renault–FASA, GM–Brazil) and limited multi-skilling. The two Fs of this Fordist nature of the employee relationship are supplemented by a J to show the borrowings from, and the slow evolution towards, Japanese employee relations (individual evaluation based mainly on behaviour, team leaders appointed by management, weakening of the trade unions who do not really take an oppositional stance – except at Saab). The result is a qualified form of individual involvement.

This FFJ type is perfectly coherent, in particular if one considers that the Japanese employee relationship, tightly linked to Just-in-Time, constitutes a deepening and radicalisation of the Fordist system of struggle against the porosity of workers' time (Boyer and Durand, 1997). Thus the principle of Ohno and of Just-in-Time is to make the mistakes and errors of each employee immediately visible, so that they can be immediately corrected. This is supposed to mobilise the efforts of employees, themselves employed in ever-diminishing numbers, and to keep them occupied full time (cf. the famous Ohno notion, that: 'Three fractions of men do not make a man', by which Ohno means that two men occupied full time are worth more than three men under-employed).

While there is certainly continuity between the two models on the question of the porosity of workers' time, there is also rupture

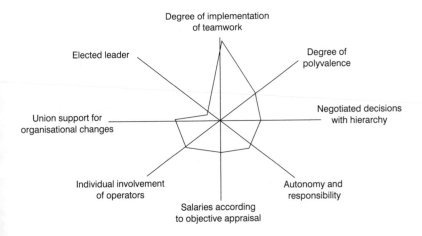

Figures 9 *Renault–Flins.*

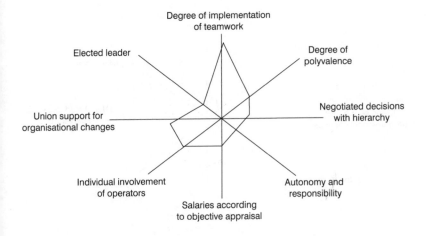

Figure 10 *Renault–FASA (engines).*

on the question of the mobilisation of worker subjectivity, which is to a large extent successful in the Japanese employee relationship. And this is where the FFJ type of employee relations fails. Because it is in transition and has no clear affirmation of its principles, or because conditions are not yet ripe for it (militant trade unionism is still in existence and educational levels are inadequate),

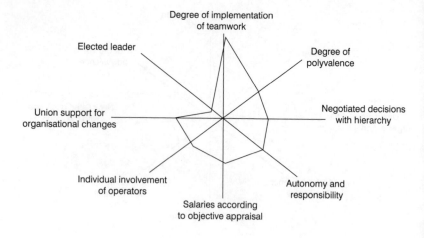

Figure 11   *Fiat Melfi.*

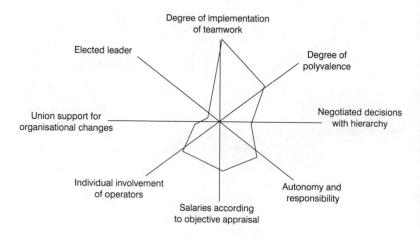

Figure 12   *Saab–Trollhättan.*

it does not achieve the worker involvement obtained by the canonical models.

This FFJ type possesses perhaps a quality which may seem paradoxical – that of a sort of 'industrial democracy', which may have been won through trade union influence (Renault–Flins [Figure 9], even Renault–FASA [Figure 10]) or desired by management (Fiat–

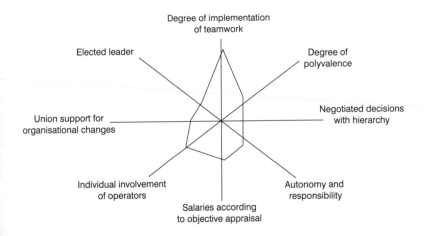

Degree of implementation
of teamwork

Elected leader

Degree of
polyvalence

Union support for
organisational changes

Negotiated decisions
with hierarchy

Individual involvement
of operators

Autonomy and
responsibility

Salaries according
to objective appraisal

Figure 13 *GM Brazil.*

Melfi [Figure 11]). This 'industrial democracy' assigns an important role to supervisors, who have a certain autonomy and accept
dialogue and negotiation with the workers (except at Saab–Trollhättan
(Figure 12 and GM Brazil [Figure 13]). In our view, this pivotal role
for supervisors consolidates and reinforces the coherence of the
FFJ type and partly compensates for the limitations described above.

In the FFJ type of employee relationship, we include two sites
which are completely heterodox: Vauxhall Ellesmere Port (GM)
(Figure 14) and Rover Swindon (Figure 15). These two plants have
at least one point in common, which is that they are British and
had an 'incomplete Fordism' (if this is the proper designation of
the truncated implementation of Fordism in Britain). In both cases,
teamwork is the organisational rule, with a fairly satisfactory level
of multi-skilling and wages based entirely on the job.

In both factories, the trade union supports the organisational
changes, but relationships with management differ completely in
the two cases. Where team leaders are elected, with validation by
management, as is the case at Rover Swindon, the trade union is
close to the positions of senior management, but relations are difficult
with local shopfloor management which sees its prerogatives under-
mined by the team leaders and by the co-operative stance of the
workers' trade union. At Vauxhall, where team leaders are not elected
but are appointed by management, the trade union has a much

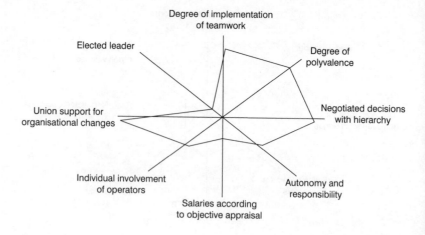

Figure 14   *Vauxhall (GM) Ellesmere Port.*

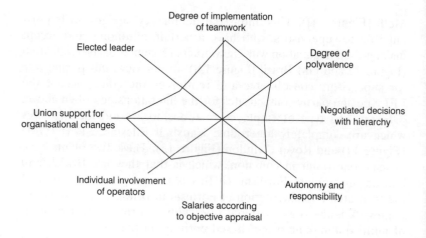

Figure 15   *Rover Swindon (stamping).*

more pro-active attitude and seeks to retain some control over the changes imposed by management. In particular, the trade union is wary of the 'models' of NUMMI and Eisenach admired by management. Relations with management can be stressful, up to the point of industrial action, as in 1995–96. The strength of the trade unions permits continuous direct negotiation with management and increases worker autonomy.

Finally – reflecting the durability of a 'British model' of strong trade unionism – the workers feel very little involvement in the objectives of the company. This is very clear for Vauxhall and somewhat less so at Rover Swindon, where part of the workforce follows the trade union in its co-operative stance while most workers do not want such commitment, or do not know what to do in the new situation.

The diversity of realities within the FFJ type demonstrates the ambiguities of the situation in Europe. For while a United Europe is certainly being built, national histories (especially the histories of trade unions, labour markets and employment law as they have been constituted) and the trajectories of firms conjoin to construct different and complex types in the same country and even between the same company's plants in different countries. This is true for Volvo and even more so for GM. As has been seen, British companies can be classified separately in the FFJ type, which is currently the dominant type in Europe. But in Europe the neo-Fordist type also exists and is more or less dominant in France (Peugeot, Citroën) and in Belgium (Volvo–Ghent). In this regard it will be particularly interesting to track the characteristics and impact of Toyota's putative assembly facility in northern France over the next period.

In all the continental European plants representing the FFJ type, the Fordist model continues to be the substratum which, little by little, is being transformed by the principles of lean production and teamwork in particular, with responses and resistance specific to each concrete situation. This is equally true in Northern Europe but with a particular feature which needs to be taken into account: the strength and role of workers' trade unions, when it makes itself heard (which is not currently the case at Saab–Trollhättan, hence its classification as FFJ).

The North European employee relations type, or type FKJ

The Northern European companies, especially Volvo, Volkswagen and Mercedes, have all been profoundly Fordist, in spite of the sometimes different images they may have had as a result of the implementation of innovative projects. Volvo and especially Uddevalla have been able to mask the profoundly Fordist nature of the company in general and of its biggest factory (at Torslanda near Göteborg).

These Fordist factories have had to accept the principles of lean production imposed by senior management, after long negotiations with the workers' trade unions, which finally accepted the principles emanating from Japan. IG Metall (Germany) and Metal (Sweden) accepted these principles both under the pressure of the threat of relocation, and with the desire or the hope that they could use the principles of teamwork to develop workers' autonomy and participation in some of the decisions arising in the workplace. It should be said that at the beginning of the 1990s NUMMI served as a 'positive model', boasting of liberty, democracy, skills development and worker creativity.

In some respects the proposals, rhetoric and promises of teamwork were perfectly in line with the concerns of group work advocated by workers' trade unions and certain managements or states ('the new factory' in Sweden and 'the humanisation of work' in Germany). The result was the possibility of acceptance by workers' unions, and above all a confusion in vocabulary sustained by senior management and sometimes repeated by researchers themselves, in spite of the divergent logic underpinning the two ideas.

This ambivalence is clear at Mercedes in its two assembly plants. Not only is local trade union support for change limited, negotiated on each occasion and conditional on the maintenance of certain guarantees, but workers' involvement remains less than that expected by management. As Chapter 16 shows, management commitment varies from one line to another and the results are substantially different. In the team we studied on the section operating body/chassis assembly (Figure 16), multi-skilling is much greater than in the team for body/trim assembly (Figure 17) (as a result of the past history of labour and the non-rotation of posts in the latter), negotiations with supervisory staff take place under better conditions and above all wages are no longer calculated according to the job, but according to an evaluation of the work provided (but not the behaviour and the subjectivity of employees). The omnipresence of the trade union to a great extent explains this situation, but in particular – and unlike in type FFJ – team leaders are elected, and are known as spokespeople. Since they are elected, they have worker and trade union legitimacy and moreover they also transmit the professional hopes and desires of their peers.

In our view, this type of employee relationship is characterised,

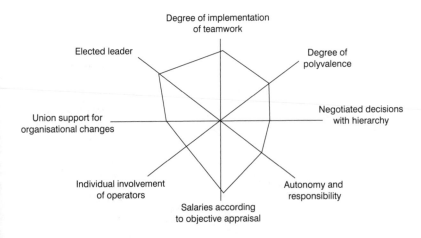

Figure 16 *Mercedes (assembly line – marriage point).*

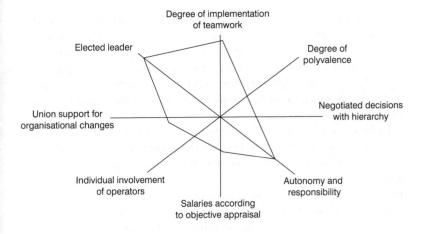

Figure 17 *Mercedes (assembly line – trim area).*

unlike the preceding one, by strong trade union representation (90 to 100% of the workers belong to a single workers' trade union) which has been able, in the past, to make its demands converge with management's projects (improvement in the conditions of working life through the concept of group working, with the aim of increasing workers' involvement) [2]. Hence the designation FKJ

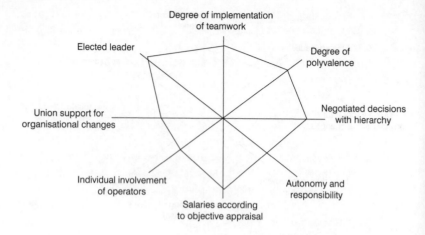

Figure 18   *Mercedes (engine parts).*

of the employee relationship which melds together the Fordist heritage, the influence of group working (characteristic of Kalmar) and the adoption of the Japanese principles of lean production. We do not, for the time being, have a better designation; since type FKJ extends beyond Germany to include some of the Swedish factories, this employee relations model cannot be called the 'German' or 'Rhine' model.

In Sweden, the Volvo–Torslanda factory belongs to the same type: FKJ. Although it remained Fordist for a long time, the factory has changed rapidly since 1993–94, which was also when the Uddevalla and Kalmar factories were closed and the agreement to fuse with Renault broke down. Volvo management has modernised Torslanda and introduced the principles of lean production in the shell of group working, while taking account of trade union strength. The trade union, whose support is not total (a fraction of the union is dragging its heels over the implementation of the reform), nevertheless supports the election of team leaders (also called spokespeople) and the rotation of workers between jobs, which rapidly increases their multi-skilling. The results of the research represented by Figure 18 show mainly how the factory is likely to remain in the medium term. While most of the factory is organised into teams, a number of these are based on practical divisions corresponding to the old Fordist teams, while effective multi-skilling is merely in the process of being developed. The resistance of local management to negotiation with the teams is one of the major features inherited from the Fordist system, and the relative weakness of worker involvement testifies to the ambivalence experienced by the operators on the line.

Type FKJ clearly has more chance of being achieved where the work is more skilled, since the concept of group working (the K) depends on the development of the workforce. That this is so can be seen in the section for machining engine parts at Mercedes (Figure 18) where monitoring work is required (this is very similar to the situation for Torslanda, see Figure 19). It is perhaps surprising that there is so little commitment among workers, who have considerable doubts whether the social transformations meet their expectations.

In the same way, the Volkswagen body shop (Figure 20) corresponds clearly with the FKJ model, with a workforce which is multi-skilled through job rotation. There the experiment was conducted on the initiative of IG–Metall (and partly abandoned after our research had been completed). The IG-Metall involvement explains the weak implementation of teamwork, the strong trade union support in exchange for the election of team leaders, the strong multi-skilling already mentioned and the existence of possibilities for negotiation with local management on the daily life of the plant. At the same time the low level of autonomy of supervisors in relation to senior management and the fact that wages are paid according to jobs testify to the continuing influence of the Fordist heritage.

Japanese–American type (or type FJJ)

As we have previously said, the great majority of US vehicles are produced by the Big Three [3] which have remained profoundly Fordist and which have only recently begun to borrow on any scale from the Japanese canonical model. The Japanese–American type, presented here, plays the role of a model for management in traditional plants. But the problem is that the interpretation of this Japanese–American type of employee relations is highly controversial, within the UAW itself and among researchers. The UAW is divided on whether it is a satisfactory solution to the concerns of employees (saving jobs, quality of life at work and high wages) and to those of management (competitivity and maintenance of adequate profits).

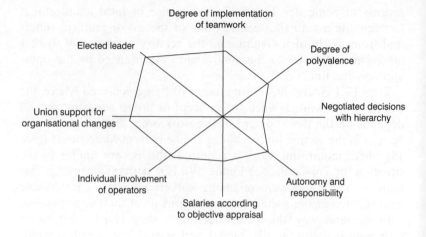

Figure 19   *Volvo–Torslanda.*

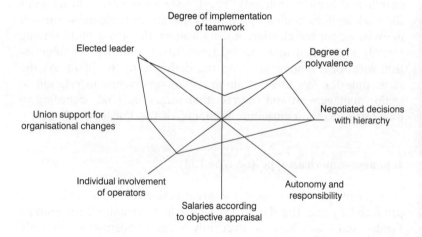

Figure 20   *VW Hanover (body shop).*

This Japanese–American type of employee relations has been implemented essentially by GM in two plants, intended to be replicated as models: in a GM–Toyota joint venture (under Japanese management), reopened in 1986–87 on a former GM site in Fremont, California (see Chapter 5) and in a pilot plant created from scratch

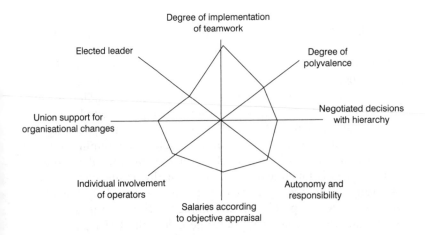

Figure 21 *NUMMI (GM/Toyota).*

near Nashville, Tennessee to demonstrate that 'a competitive vehicle, of world class quality could be built in the United States by
a unionised workforce' [4].

As a result of internal UAW differences and even conflicts [5]
on whether or not it is desirable or necessary to implement the
Japanese–American type, the current reality of this type is, to say
the least, uncertain and ambiguous. The presence and strength of
the union (all the workers are unionised, which is a condition of
their recruitment), as well as the divisions in the NUMMI union,
explain the limited support of the trade union for the changes, and
the equally limited involvement of the workers. Moreover multi-
skilling is not the same as it is in the Japanese canonical model.
While on the one hand the number of job classifications has fallen
from 65 to 2, on the other hand management balks at the rotation
of jobs and the workers' educational level is far lower than it is in
Japan.

At NUMMI (Figure 21), as in the Japanese canonical model,
the whole plant is organised into teams of five workers. But union
pressure has ensured that the appointment of the leader is not
merely a prerogative of management; team leaders are appointed
by a joint committee containing representatives of management and
the union, which choses from a list of candidates who have received
training and meet criteria fixed by management (multi-skilling, tech-

nical competence, leadership qualities). In the same way, the union's strength explains why some of the decisions on life in the workplace are negotiated with management (see Chapter 5).

But in a number of sections where the trade union co-ordinators (the designation of union representatives at NUMMI) do not accept or do not welcome teamwork and the working conditions which are linked to it, the Japanese–American type of employee relations is substantially different (Figure 22). Generally speaking, not only are union support and worker involvement diminished, but the role of the UAW and workers in the method of appointing team leaders is much less substantial. Finally, management asserts its strength and prerogatives rather more in the daily life of the workplace. More precisely, this implemention of the Japanese–American type – which could also be called the FJJ type – resembles the European type of a mixture of Fordism and lean production (FFJ), such as we have encountered, for example, at Fiat–Melfi or Renault. This is explained by their common (Fordist) heritage, by the trade union presence (even if its forms differ) and by the implementation of new principles common to all of them (lean production and teamwork).

The situation at Saturn (Figure 23) also expresses the ambiguity of the Japanese–American type, or perhaps the fact that it has not stabilised. The fact that the UAW promoted the project together with management, with the same will to innovate (in commitment to, for example, team working) together with an equally shared Fordist culture, produces a rather specific type which is, perhaps, how the Japanese–American type will eventually develop:

- generalised work teams;
- elected leaders;
- a degree of multi-skilling with the ending of job classifications and continuing difficulties with job rotation;
- reasonable relationships with management which are increasingly neutral and less based on grievance and dispute procedures;
- high wages, equal for all, according to seniority as opposed to individual evaluation;
- partial union support, declared in official agreements, but with relatively little significance on the shopfloor itself;
- a moderate degree of worker involvement which is based more upon high wages and a desire to remain in a large company rather than the superiority of management methods *per se*.

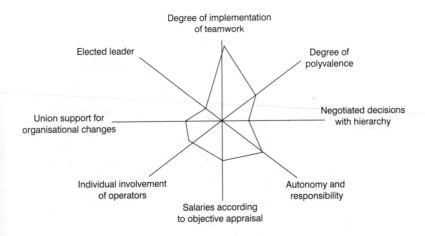

Figure 22 *NUMMI (protest areas).*

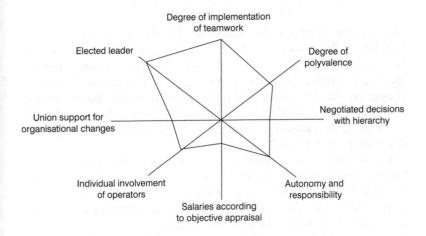

Figure 23 *Saturn (GM).*

It is probable that the Japanese–American type (FJJ) can be replicated outside North America. The employee relationship at Opel–Antwerp (Figure 24) – which is of course representative of General Motors – was remodelled according to the principles implemented at NUMMI, with a Fordist heritage and a powerful trade

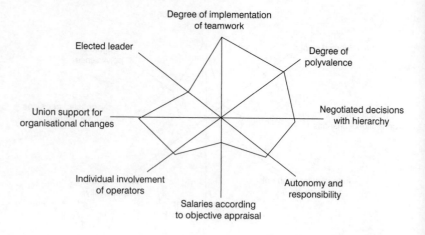

Figure 24   *Opel–Antwerpen.*

union which accepted the new order (unlike the union at Saab–Trollhätan, for example). The Fordist heritage can be seen in the fact that payment is based on the job. The trade union supports the organisational changes up to a certain point, but it also expresses its dissatisfaction in the face of increasingly harsh working conditions; for example, the union opposed the reduction of cycle times to 45 seconds. The union's strength enables it to negotiate day-to-day matters in the workplace.

The degree of multi-skilling is much higher than in the United States since it includes the functions of quality control and preventive maintenance; a permanent worker can only obtain multi-skilled status after two years of employment. The team leaders (called team representatives, showing the influence of the German and Swedish models) carry out the functions defined by the Japanese canonical model: relief, training of new workers and development of multi-skilling, co-ordination and leadership. Up to now they have not been elected, but are the former leaders of the Fordist teams who are only nominated by management once they have the agreement and support of the members of the team. This has certain similarities with the situation at NUMMI, with its lengthy process of negotiation for the appointment of leaders.

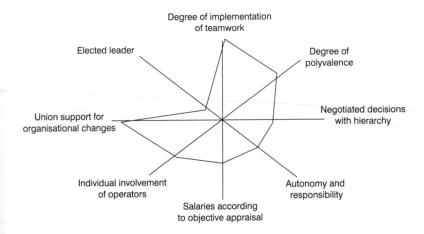

Figure 25 *Toyota–Tahara.*

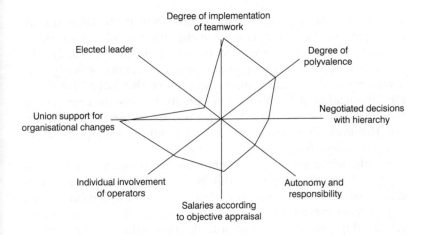

Figure 26 *Toyota–Kyushu.*

Japanese type of employee relationship

This last type of employee relationship is in reality close to the canonical model. However, unsurprisingly there are similarities with certain European and American factories. On the one hand, the

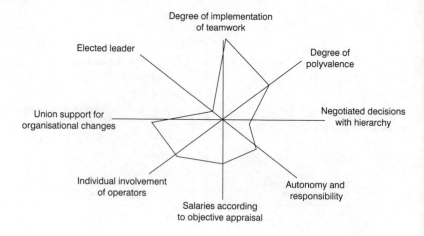

Figure 27   *Nissan–Kyushu.*

leaders must be accepted by the teams, even if the latter do not participate in their designation; on the other hand, certain informal negotiations, not recognised as such, 'humanise' the daily relationships between management and the teams. Finally, the involvement of workers remains well below that hoped for under the canonical model. This does not greatly surprise us even though the plants are among those in which worker involvement is strongest. However, involvement in general is not as widespread as its eulogists might have hoped.

Finally, while we do not differentiate between the situations in the two Japanese companies, this in no sense denies their specific trajectories, histories and productive organisation. Nissan (Figure 27) appears merely to be more traditionalist in its management relationships, with in addition a trade union which is experiencing internal conflicts which reduce its support for the management line. This could be refined by showing that there are clearer differences between various plants within the same company than there are between companies. The fact that the suggestions system has disappeared at Toyota–Kyushu (Figure 26), or that wages there are calculated less on seniority than on merit, has modified the employee relationship, sometimes bringing it even closer to the canonical model.

Conclusion

At the beginning of this book, Durand delineated the employee relationship in terms of four essential components (work organisation, hierarchical relationships, payments systems, the nature of trade unions), organised by management, so far as is possible, to increase worker involvement and work efficiency. In this Conclusion, we have subsequently outlined three canonical models: the Fordist model, the Kalmarian model and the Japanese model known as lean production. The latter has spread into a number of automobile companies. From this model, companies have borrowed teamwork, as the form of work organisation which best meets the technical and social requirements of Just-in-Time, which itself is tending to become standard practice and to replace the Fordist principle of an assembly line with buffer-stocks.

The adoption of elements of what has been described as lean production in the world automobile industry, which is not complete but is nevertheless dominant, must necessarily lead to diversity in its implementation and in the situations in different companies and production sites. On the one hand, some companies reject the principles of lean production and, on the other hand, those that do adopt them may do so in a selective fashion, in accordance with their history and the pre-existing nature of employee relations. Moreover, each company or workplace management imitates and adopts one or other of the principles in accordance with local possibilities. That is to say, it attempts to establish, maintain and develop coherence between the components of the employee relationship in order to increase work efficiency. In other words, the scope for innovation is framed by the necessary *social* constraints within which the different actors interpret the implementation (and the consequent outcomes) of elements of what has become known as lean production.

These diverse situations can be assembled into five types of employee relationships, from which we can draw up a map (Figure 28) constructed on the basis of the three poles of attraction constituted by the three canonical models F (Fordist), K (Kalmarian) and J (Japanese).

A refinement of the map would make it possible to situate each plant in the type under consideration and would show a relative continuity between the types of employee relationship. This classification therefore has no more than a representative value, making

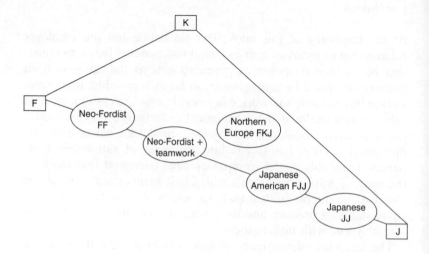

Figure 28 *Map of types of employee relations.*

it possible to locate groups according to clearly defined characteristics. At the same time, this classification does not rank one type
of employee relationship higher than another, since each type possesses its own coherence and produces a certain method of achieving worker involvement. Thus, although forced involvement is tending
to spread, it is not completely general and above all it is produced
through different methods and different forms of coherence.

The axis between the Fordist and Japanese canonical models is
the most densely populated. This is to be explained first by the
fact that there is no reason for the Kalmarian canonical model to
be current in this period since, in the face of chronic underemployment, no company management is seeking to improve the
conditions of life at work in order to attract workers. Second, this
density on the FJ axis illustrates the coherence between the two
canonical models, which is another way of agreeing with Wood (1991),
who demonstrates that Just-in-Time represents a deepening of Fordist
principles of work organisation.

There is clearly a very strong resemblance between the shapes
and figures representing the Japanese–American (FJJ) and North
European (FKJ) types. The question is then whether this resemblance is linked to the chosen comparative method or whether it is
more basic. In the first case, it can be shown that these similar

shapes hide essential basic differences. From work content to the nature of trade unions, from the method of selecting leaders to skills, nothing is the same. In the second case, it can be shown that the resemblance is more than formal. Because the Kalmarian model no longer has – for the time being? – any justification and because the trade unions have accepted – under coercion – the principles of lean production, therefore work organisation, the role of management and the functions of trade unions tend to converge.

We began this book by emphasising the prerequisites necessary for an assessment of the claims that a new industrial model is being created. Specifically, we argued that an understanding of the changing nature of employee relations is fundamental in comprehending the nature of change at the firm level. Our aim was to determine whether a new model of employee relations in the automotive sector was being established, or alternatively, whether we were witnessing modifications to the existing Fordist paradigm of employee relations. A third possibility was that not one but several models are beginning to emerge. Then again, perhaps the very notion of a model, as a normative guide, was itself unhelpful since it can suggest a static perspective in which aspects of the organisation or system which do not 'fit in' will be excluded from consideration. This is despite the truism that from a more open perspective they might be deemed central to our understanding of the processes of change. In addition, this static approach tends to view all ('positive') processes as somehow conflict free. Indeed, it is axiomatic to the lean production school that conflict avoidance be at the heart of all human relations strategies (Womack *et al.*, 1990). Yet, if we focus upon employee relations in this sector, it is also possible to illustrate the very conditional nature of managerial and employee perspectives in which conflict, dispute and collaboration are central to innovation. Specifically, one of the findings to be drawn from a number of chapters in this book is that the very idea of a model is problematical where it assumes, among other things, that conflict and difference cannot be central to what is a continual process of organisational and social renewal. The dominant model of change in this sector has been developed by protagonists of lean production who, like the Taylorists of a previous era, held to a view of organisational change in the auto sector in functionalist terms. Accordingly, aspects of the organisation not tending towards equilibrium are seen either as unwanted vestiges of the past, or negative influences on healthy organisational development. Moreover, since the whole enterprise depends upon a teleological assumption about change, this type of model leads to and reinforces a highly prescriptive narrative of sector developments.

Nevertheless, to address this problem of the model of the 'one best way' is not simple and our conclusions are, as ever in a project of this nature, both more straightforward and complex than any of the above possibilities allow. As Clarke (1992) has pointed out, one of the problems with the question of industrial development or transformation, notably from Fordism (to non- or possibly post-Fordism), is that it assumes some settled notion concerning the what, when and how of Fordism. Clearly, this can be a crushing burden for any invocation of an industrial model that might become a universal paradigm despite differences in national context. If we can question the efficacy of the concept of Fordism, except in the very limited sense of its significance as a model for industrial organisation, how much more problematical is the notion of 'non-Fordism' or post-Fordism? (Clarke, 1992). The short, but least satisfying, answer to the question of developments in employee relations since the 1970s is that these are both more uneven than might have been imagined while nevertheless highlighting crucial similarities and even some elements of convergence between companies. It is important that we avoid what Castillo derides as "thinking by opposites", which in turn leads to "thinking in terms of ruptures" (Castillo, 1994, p. 8). In short, in assessing the criteria for change we must recognise three interlocking dimensions which sometimes allow for novel developments to occur, even where these might be rooted in very different social and organisational environments; specifically the social effects, including national specificity of labour–management regulation; peculiarities of each firm and its unique labour–management culture; finally, the response by the latter to global changes in the industry.

Notwithstanding the dominance of the lean production paradigm and the model of change which is intrinsic to it, in the UK and North America this particular conception of the way to characterise the forces of development in the auto sector is rapidly being superseded. While the object of critique in the automotive sector has largely focused upon the weaknesses of the lean production school (Milkman, 1991; Babson, 1995; Robertson, 1992; Lewchuk and Robertson, 1996; Rinehart *et al.*, 1997), its precursor, the traditional account of prospects for manufacturing renewal, summed up by the epithet Japanisation, has increasingly been cast into doubt

(Elger and Smith, 1994; Smith and Meiksens, 1995; Ackers and Wilkinson, 1995; Stewart, 1996) after an early but damaging assessment in the *Industrial Relations Journal* (1988).

Of course, models for the sector do not have to contrive change in a one-dimensional fashion and within the GERPISA project, the potential for explaining contemporary developments in terms of a model is seen to be more successful where we can allow for dynamism, innovation and contradictions (Freyssenet and Lung, 1996). While the particular notion of models of change as conceived by GERPISA derives in the first instance from the concerns of the regulation debate in French economics and industrial sociology (Boyer and Durand, 1997), the results from the team of researchers covering the changing nature of employee relations suggests that all attempts at modelling need to be wary of prescriptive conclusions. This danger is implicit in any model which proffers one best way for change. Contrary to the agenda for understanding manufacturing and managerial processes advocated by the lean production school, as the work carried out under the auspices of the GERPISA network makes clear, there is essentially no one best way. However, it is certain that there are firm-specific and firm-inspired patterns and ways of working. Recognition and due care are required therefore in our pursuit of models which seek to allow for the degree of variation within each firm in any one country, let alone the range of alternative strategies for organisational development within any one firm across national boundaries. In particular, Chapter 13 and 14 on Volvo highlighted the profound variations both within Volvo Sweden and within the Volvo corporation across national frontiers. The same conclusion is also patently true of GM, although of country-specific import, and when focusing upon intra-company variation, of Mercedes. In short, the possibility of delineating the one best model for the sector holds out little prospect of success. Does this suggest we abandon models entirely? We argue that, while we need to be aware of the usefulness of 'models', the work of the 'Employee Relations' group suggests that the traditional view of a model of sector development must be sensitive to the uncertain nature of change. In short, where our analysis is also contingent upon an understanding of relations between management and employees, whether or not they are organised into trade unions, any temptation towards modelling will be aware of the role of social agency in developing a dynamic account of managerial innovation and organisational development.

Given what we have argued about the pitfalls of the lean production paradigm, the important question is, which type of models will help us make sense of contemporary forms of employee relations in the sector? Can models provide any efficacy in developing an understanding of the latter? Our answer offers support for such a project, provided there is sufficient plurality and complexity to allow for a recognition of the contradictions as well as the continuities in the change process.

The theme of this Conclusion has been our emphasis, case by case, upon the direction of change with respect to employee relations. While accepting the need for caution when using this methodological approach (see, for example, Morris and Wood, 1991 for an account of the strengths and weaknesses of the case study approach), it allows us to gain unique insights into the efficacy of the broad sweep proffered by models at what is arguably the most important level, the assembly plant. In addition, the emphasis upon company and plant-level processes affords the crucial reminder that the regulatory process, while constituted at the level of the social formation as a whole, is also played out in the micro-social politics of the employment relationship at the work place. Moreover, emphasis on this sector suggests that other research on the automotive industry should be mindful of the local, not to say national, political economy in which companies, plants, management and labour unions operate. However, the cases reported here do allow us to suggest ways in which an analysis of the developments in employee relations in the sector can best be taken forward. There is in particular one theme that should bear closer scrutiny in future research on the international character of the sector; specifically – *the nature of the relationship between the state, industrial relations and the role of the trade unions, including their impact upon employees.* What are the configurations between state, company and trade union strategies? In what respects have unions played an intervening role in the development of new production arrangements in the sector and what are the different forms of industrial relations which facilitate positive and pro-active trade union strategies in this regard? In what ways are state strategies interlinked with a weakening of labour and trade union controls of the bargaining and labour processes in the sector, as was the case in Britain after 1979. How does this impact upon the micro-politics of the shopfloor? Moreover, does some combination of neo-liberalism with continued state dirigiste strategies, however limiting, allow labour to retain some degree of extended bargaining over the industrial relations and labour processes, which one might argue is still the case, as exemplified in southern Europe? However weakened labour might be, the model of strong regulatory strategies still persists in many European countries, with its consequent benefits for labour. One significant issue here is the important question of the impact of new forms of working on employees' health and safety at plant level and on their social lives outside the assembly plants. Little has been written on this from an international perspective, although the work of the Canadian Auto Workers suggests that additional research is desirable.

It is crucial that we develop our understanding of these critical questions further, because the themes of continuity and transformation/revolution (permanent revolution in organisational learning?) are dependent upon a wider understanding of employee (and industrial) relations and conceptions of workplace hierarchy. The current state of the sector and the consequent character of employee bargaining over the terms and conditions of the workplace and the labour process are themes upon which future GERPISA research must focus.

End-notes

[1] Which did not prevent it from obtaining a high productivity ranking in the Harbor Report.

[2] The extent of unionisation should not be confused with trade union power. The latter has been reduced over the last decade through a decline in the trade union's combativity in its activities. If the high level of unionisation gives the organisations financial capabilities unknown in the Latin countries (with more full-time officials, trade union institutionalisation and the ability to support long strikes), management pressures considerably limit their actions – in particular in the matter of strikes. Under the permanent threat of relocation (which is actually being carried out in the cases of Mercedes and Volkswagen), the trade unions accept job losses, increases in the pace of work, stagnant wages, the end of centralised negotiations, individualisation of wages, etc. These are signs of a weakening of trade unionism which takes different forms from those in Southern Europe.

[3] As for the Japanese transplants in the United States, they constitute yet another model which has not been presented here, such is the

extent to which it has been studied elsewhere. It is characterised in the first place by the absence of a trade union in the factories (apart from a few exceptions), in a sector in which the UAW is omnipresent. The type of employee relationship in the transplants is thus quite close to the Japanese canonical model. The high wages paid encourage the operators to devote themselves to the company, in spite of the prevailing rigid discipline. The high level of unemployment characteristic of the Mid West where these factories have been established favours this involvement. In spite of the training policies of the Japanese producers in the United States, the levels of skills and multi-skilling remain below those of the canonical model.

[4]   Preamble to the Memorandum of Agreement of the Saturn Corp. (p. 1), Don Elphin, former Vice-President of the UAW, described to us in exactly the same terms the position adopted by the UAW, which he led at the time, in respect of the Saturn project.

[5]   There are, for example, conflicts between the UAW International leadership in Detroit and the President of the local UAW section at Saturn. The union majority at Saturn and at NUMMI win by only a narrow margin. The President of the UAW–NUMMI was elected in 1991 on the minority (People's Caucus) platform and subsequently joined the majority. Finally, the elected representative on the negotiating committee at NUMMI is a member of the People's Caucus.

References

Ackers P. and Wilkinson A. (1995) When two cultures meet: new industrial relations at Japanco. *International Journal of Human Resource Management*, Vol. 6, No. 4 (Dec.), 849–871.

Babson S. (ed.) (1995) *Lean Work: Power and Exploitation in the Global Automobile Industry*. Detroit MI: Wayne State University Press.

Boyer R. and Durand J.-P. (1997) *After Fordism*. London: Macmillan.

Castillo J.-J. (1994) *Which Way Forward for the Sociology of Work?* Charles Babbage Research Seminar, Working Papers Series 101, Department of Sociology University of Madrid.

Clarke S. (1992) What in the F . . .'s name is Fordism?. In Gibert N., Burrows R. and Pollert A. (eds.), *Fordism and Flexibility: Division and Change*. London: Macmillan.

Elger T. and Smith C. (eds.) (1994) *Global Japanization? The Transnational Transformation of the Labour Process*. London: Routledge.

Freyssenet M. and Lung Y. (1996) Entre mondialisation et régionalisation: Quelles voies possibles pour l'internationalisation de l'industrie automobile? In *Mondialisation ou Regionalisation*, Actes du Gerpisa No. 18, November.

Industrial Relations Journal (1988) Special issue 'Japanization', Vol. 19.

Lewchuk W. and Robertson D. (1996) Working conditions under lean production: a worker bench marking study. In Stewart P. (ed.), *Beyond Japanese Management. The End of Modern Times?* London: Frank Cass.

Milkman R. (1991) *Japan's California Factories – Labour Relations and Economic Globalisation*. Los Angeles CA: Institute of Industrial Relations, University of California.

Morris T. and Wood S. (1991) Testing the survey method: continuity and change in British industrial relations. *Work, Employment and Society*, Vol. 5, No. 2, 259–282.

Rinehart J., Huxley C. and Robertson D. (1997) *Just Another Car Factory? Lean Production and its Discontents*. Ithaca NY: Cornell University Press.

Robertson D. (1992) 'Canadian trade union experiences of the new management techniques and the development of counter strategies', paper presented to the *TIE/VAUXHALL Shop Steward's Committee Conference on New Management Techniques*, Liverpool, January/February.

Smith C. and Meiksens P. (1995) System, society and dominance effects in cross-national organisational analysis. *Work, Employment and Society*, Vol. 9, No. 2 (June), 241–267.

Stewart P. (1996) *Beyond Japanese Management. The End of Modern Times?* London: Frank Cass.

Womack J., Jones D. and Roos D. (1990) *The Machine that Changed the World: The Story of Lean Production*. New York: Harper Collins.

Wood S. (1991) Japanisation and/or Toyotaism. *Work, Employment and Society*, Vol. 5, No. 4, 567–600.

Index

446